Color contrast. If the reader fixates the
color, the complement emerges in the gray.
See discussion in text, p. 68.

Perception

McGraw Hill Series
in Psychology

Consulting Editors

Norman Garmezy

Harry F. Harlow

Lyle V. Jones

Harold W. Stevenson

Hurlock   *Adolescent Development*
Hurlock   *Child Development*
Hurlock   *Developmental Psychology*
Jackson and Messick   *Problems in Human Assessment*
Karn and Gilmer   *Readings in Industrial and Business Psychology*
Krech, Crutchfield, and Ballachey   *Individual in Society*
Lazarus   *Adjustment and Personality*
Lazarus   *Psychological Stress and the Coping Process*
Lewin   *A Dynamic Theory of Personality*
Lewin   *Principles of Topological Psychology*
Maher   *Principles of Psychopathology*
Marx and Hillix   *Systems and Theories in Psychology*
Messick and Brayfield   *Decision and Choice: Contributions of Sidney Siegel*
Miller   *Language and Communication*
Morgan   *Physiological Psychology*
Nunnally   *Psychometric Theory*
Rethlingshafer   *Motivation as Related to Personality*
Robinson and Robinson   *The Mentally Retarded Child*
Scherer and Wertheimer   *A Psycholinguistic Experiments on Foreign Language Teaching*
Shaw and Wright   *Scales for the Measurement of Attitudes*
Sidowski   *Experimental Methods and Instrumentation in Psychology*
Siegel   *Nonparametric Statistics for the Behavioral Sciences*
Stagner   *Psychology of Personality*
Townsend   *Introduction to Experimental Methods for Psychology and the Social Sciences*
Vinacke   *The Psychology of Thinking*
Wallen   *Clinical Psychology: The Study of Persons*
Warren and Akert   *The Frontal Granular Cortex and Behavior*
Waters, Rethlingshafer, and Caldwell   *Principles of Comparative Psychology*
Winer   *Statistical Principles in Experimental Design*
Zubek and Solberg   *Human Development*

Perception

*The basic process
in cognitive development*

Ronald H. Forgus

*Professor and Chairman, Department of Psychology
Lake Forest College*

MCGRAW–HILL BOOK COMPANY

*New York   St. Louis   San Francisco
Toronto   London   Sydney*

FOR SILVIA, MICHAEL, AND SANDY

Preface

William James, one of the outstanding American pioneers of the early days of psychology at the turn of the twentieth century, once remarked: "Neither the whole truth nor the whole of good is revealed to any single observer although each observer gains a partial superiority of insight from the peculiar position in which he stands" (related by G. A. Miller, 1962, p. 78). I suppose that anyone who has tried to write a representative book on any subject would find that James's words ring true. They are especially true in a young science like psychology in which changes in outlook occur with the same sort of rapidity that is observed in the growth patterns of the preadolescent child.

Perhaps we are at present witnessing the growth of scientific psychology into its adolescent stage. If that is so, then psychology will soon be evolving a more definite identity or at least be seriously struggling to find one. I found myself developing this attitude while my thoughts on perception and thinking were evolving in connection with preparing the present volume. Consequently some procedural decisions had to be made.

First, I became convinced that the field of perception would make a greater contribution to the emerging identity of psychology if it were related to the broader context of the cognitive processes. This conviction is discussed in Chapter 1, where it is strongly held that a course or a book on perception should extend itself to complete the treatment of what seems to be a unified whole, namely, the developing integration of perception, learning, and thinking in the processing of information.

The decision about the kind of breadth having been made, the problem of coverage arose. I felt that it would be foolish to include every known area or publication which seemed relevant to this task. It has been my experience that such encyclopedic coverage usually tends to overtax the channel capacity of the student and results in unnecessary and inhibiting "cognitive strain." The present approach has therefore been to select a set of guiding principles which appear to be directing our understanding about the nature of information extraction and its contribution to general behavior. The approach is outlined in Chapters 1 and 2, and any data which seem tangential to the main concerns are not included. Since the choice is personal, I apologize to the many authors whose experiments and writings, however relevant, could not be included because of space limitations.

The style of presentation is intended to be instructive rather than argumentative. By this statement I do not mean to imply that instruction excludes arguing. On the contrary, sophisticated instruction necessitates a certain amount of critical debate. The main concern in the present volume, however, is to transmit a body of meaningful knowledge about perception and thinking without spending much time on controversial issues, the status of which seems unclear at present. This choice was based on the fact that this text is intended primarily for the undergraduate student, although I hope it will be of use to others interested in the area, such as students in the first two years of graduate school or psychologists interested in cognition and perception.

Having developed in Chapter 1 my basic thesis that perception is the superset of information extraction, with learning and thinking as subsets, I go on to discuss why I think, on both logical and experimental grounds, that an exclusively nativistic or empirical theory of perception is untenable. Rather, as shown in Chapter 2, perception is organized in an ordinal hierarchy, beginning with built-in programs and developing by increasing degrees to modified programs. Chapter 3 and 4 deal with some basic psychophysical functions and problems of methodology, and then the principles organized around each level of the hierarchy are analyzed, from brightness through form to social perception and conceptualization. Since the concept of information extraction was used to analyze and conceptualize the process of perception, this analysis is extended to the area of thinking in the last four chapters, although technical langauge is held to a minimum.

My interest in the cognitive area, while undoubtedly a product of my developmental history, was aroused at McGill University, especially by two of my teachers, D. O. Hebb and Abraham S. Luchins. Although they are two very different people, each was very instrumental in the way my intellectual interests developed. Of the first five years of my university training, all of which were spent at McGill, I remember with special affection the fifth year, 1950–1951, when I was working on my master's degree in the company of a delightful, highly talented group of students. The intellectual atmosphere was vigorous and rarely strained, and we liked being with each other. I feel especially warm and grateful about the many discussions I had during that year with my close friends Rusty Wendt and Ivan Scheier. My intellectual debt to the McGill group is apparent throughout this manuscript, and they will always have my gratitude and affection.

Having left McGill with an embryonic fusion of gestalt psychology and Hebb's developmental approach to perception, I spent two years until receiving the Ph.D. degree at Cornell University, where Robert B. MacLeod's phenomenology and James J. Gibson's psychophysics were blended into my developing schema concerning the nature of the perceptual world.

Beginning in 1953 I spent five years on the faculty of the University of Pennsylvania and have been at Lake Forest College since then. My students and colleagues at these institutions contributed to my groping attempts to clarify my thinking about the interaction between perception, learning, and thinking. Special recognition is due John Gaito, who worked on his Ph.D. dissertation with me and contributed to the development of this book; Kenneth Welton, who, as a student of mine at Lake Forest, showed me what an undergraduate could do with information theory; and Jack D. Rains, a colleague at Lake Forest, who presented the basic materials for Chapters 3 and 4 and helped with Chapter 14. A special word of thanks is due Dean William L. Dunn of Lake Forest College for his continued interest, encouragement, and provision of clerical help.

I extend my appreciation to Clifford Morgan and Harry F. Harlow, as well as to the psychologists who reviewed the manuscript. I must also record my special gratitude to the one person most responsible for typing the manuscript, Mrs. Ferris E. Hurd; I also appreciate the clerical help given by Miss Kay Kornberger, Miss Astrid Aagaard, Miss Peggy Atkin, Miss Judy Johnston, and the late Miss Judy Van Zwoll.

The permission granted by authors and publishers to quote from their works or reproduce their illustrations is appreciated. Individual recognition is given where their material appears in the text.

Finally, and most of all, I want to express my affectionate appreciation to Silvia for the many ways she helped with this book and to tell her and our children, Michael and Sandy, that our lives will be a little more even now that this task has been completed.

Ronald H. Forgus

Contents

1

The Nature of Perception as an Information-extraction Process

There are many ways that a book on perception can be organized. I have decided to place the process of perception within the context of man's general need to adapt to his environment if he is to cope effectively with the demands of life.

DEFINITION OF PERCEPTION. In this quest for adaptive behavior the way the individual gains knowledge about his environment is of prime importance. The gaining of such knowledge necessitates the extraction of information from the vast array of physical energy which stimulates the organism's senses. Only those stimuli which have cue value, i.e., which trigger some kind of reactive or adaptive action from the individual, should logically be called information. *For our purposes, perception will be defined as the process of information extraction.*

When we compare the higher mammals and especially man with the lower animals, we are tremendously impressed with the fact that the adaptive perceptual processes of the latter are largely completed through genetic evolution. That is to say, their perceptual programs are *built in, wired in,* or *prewired* at birth. These three descriptive terms, which can be used synonymously, simply mean that the programs by which information is coded in the lower animals are largely inherited and therefore remain relatively unmodified with experience.[1]

[1] See, for example, Lorenz (1958) and Tinbergen (1952), who discuss such phenomena as instincts, tropism, and imprinting. All references are listed at the back of the book.

LIGHT, MATHEMATICS, PEOPLE, AND ART. As we ascend the phylogenetic scale, perception becomes increasingly influenced by learning. In the human infant, for example, the perception of light is determined by built-in programs. This is necessary for adaptive behavior to begin, but *the programs become modified* with growth, development, and experience. Let us just think, for example, of the highly complex and abstract kinds of information which have to be extracted in such diverse tasks as the esthetic appreciation of a painting or a great musical composition, the solution of a mathematical problem, or the perception of another human being.

It is this universal involvement of the process of information extraction in man's adaptive behavior which led me to believe that we must relate perception to the general problem of cognitive development if we are to understand fully the nature of the reception, acquisition, assimilation, and utilization of knowledge. Looked at in this way, perception becomes the core process in the acquisition of cognition or knowledge. I thus conceive of *perception* as the *superset,* with *learning* and *thinking* as *subsets* subsumed under the perceptual process.

While we shall not deal with the formal dynamics of learning as such (they are available in a number of good standard books on learning principles and theory), we must, to support our position, go more deeply into the relationship between perception, learning, and thinking. Then we can outline the subtasks or stages involved in the complex task of perception. Our aim will be to show that the higher tasks or stages involve the extraction of progressively more information.

Relationship between Perception, Learning, and Thinking

Our thesis that perception is a superset which subsumes the subsets of learning and thinking in the total act of information extraction may seem too novel or strange for some individuals to accept. Let us, however, begin to explore the relationship between these three cognitive processes.

Perception, learning, and thinking have traditionally been referred to as the cognitive processes since they all deal, to some extent, with the problem of knowledge. Perception can generally be defined as the process by which an organism receives or extracts certain information about the environment. Learning is defined as the process by which this information is acquired through experience and becomes part of the organism's storage of facts. Thus, the results of learning facilitate the further extraction of information since the stored facts become models against which cues are judged. The most complex of these cognitive processes, namely, thinking, is an activity that is inferred to be going on when an organism is engaged in solving problems, which also involves the use of models.

Now, the solution of complex problems requires the use of mediating symbols like language, mathematics, or some other powerful tool. The difficulty of the problem can be determined by the relative ease with which the information required for its solution can be extracted. When an individual can extract the information almost immediately, he has no problem. The problem becomes more difficult as the "potential information" is less available or more abstract. The way we extract abstract or more "hidden" information is to learn to use concepts. The greater our conceptual abilities are, the better are our general problem-solving abilities.

A way of summarizing what we have said thus far in this section is to state that as the perceptual set is broadened and becomes more complex and richly patterned with experience, the individual becomes capable of extracting more information from the environment. The process starts with simple *reflexive* action at birth and grows through maturation and learning to produce more powerful *sets,* which are mediated by concepts; hence *thinking* becomes more expert.

Even though we have differentiated perception, learning, and thinking in the definitions given above, the three cognitive processes are closely interrelated and difficult to separate in practical situations. Thus other individuals may define these three terms in a slightly different manner. Because of this aspect it is possible to become entangled in theoretical controversy. To avoid argument for the sake of argument and to handle more easily the cognitive phenomena descriptively, we wish to emphasize the continuity of the cognitive process. At the beginning of this process, learning and thinking either are nonexistent or operate at a low level. (In contemporary computer terminology, we may say that the programming is of a built-in or wired-in nature.) Where information extraction requires more active effort on the part of the organism, learning and thinking play an increasingly important role. (The basic programming becomes more and more modified.) Thus we consider learning and thinking as events or processes which aid in the extraction of information.

Having defined perception as the process of information extraction, it seems clear why we made it the parent construct, for adaptative behavior originates in perception. For example, the discrimination of a mother's face, which requires learning in the infant, presupposes a built-in reaction to light, which is perception.

The relationship between learning and thinking in the perceptual process is diagramed in Figure 1-1. Stimuli possessing potential information are observed by the organism, which extracts some of the information present, aided by the process called learning. This learning modifies the organism so that perception of the same stimuli later also will be modified. For example, John Jones is introduced to Bill Smith, hears his name, and learns other things about him. The next time that John encounters Bill, he perceives him somewhat differently than he did on the first occasion. Now he may have positive or negative emotional reactions because of his previous experience with Bill.

In Figure 1-1 it is indicated also that learning may lead to thinking (a manipulation of previously learned aspects); this thinking modifies the organism through the involvement of new learning, which in turn modifies the perception of the stimulus situation. This event can be illustrated by the change in perception which occurs as we gain insight concerning the solution of a particular problem through continuing to think about possible approaches. When we find an appropriate solution, the problem is no longer a problem and all aspects are placed in proper perspective.

VARIATION FROM SENSATION TO PROBLEM SOLVING. In the past many authors separated the constructs sensation and perception, defining *sensation* as the process containing the physiological or sensory elements out of which the percepts were compounded. The problem of perception is extremely complex, however, and such a limited conceptualization is no longer tenable, especially when we remember that few, if any, pure sensory acts occur after an organism has had a little interaction with the environment. We believe it is more useful to consider perception as a continuing process that varies from events which are of a simple, elementary nature (and are given immediately because of a built-in coding mechanism) to those of greater complexity which require more active learning and thinking.

Now let us look more closely at the interrelationship of learning and thinking in the perceptual process. Some percepts are necessary before we can learn since we cannot acquire facts until we have first received them. Obviously a blind person cannot perceive or come to know the color of an object. And who would deny that the tools of thinking and learning depend to a large extent on what the individual has previously learned? Anyone who has reflected for only a little while on his education must be struck by the underlying interdependence of these two events within the information-extraction process. How could we solve mathematical problems if we had not learned the meaning of signs or symbols, which, in turn, would have

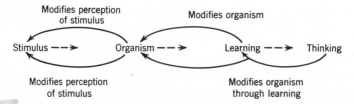

Figure 1-1

The relationship of learning and thinking in the complex process of perception. Stimuli possess information, which is extracted by the organism as learning. This learning modifies the organism so that later perception of the same stimuli will be different. The process of thinking (resulting from previous learning) also modifies the organism because new learning occurs; thus the perception of stimuli is modified.

been impossible if we had not been able to discriminate, i.e., perceive differences, between the patterns of stimuli which make up the symbols? The difference between an addition and a multiplication sign, for instance, involves only a slight rotation (the significance of which lower animals like rats are unable to comprehend without considerable training), and yet the difference in connotation is enormous. Or let us take an example from the English language: it requires extremely good visual acuity to discriminate between the words "bear" and "beer," and yet the distinction implied is rather significant.

As human adults we take this discriminatory process for granted, but such fine discriminations are not found in lower mammals like rats, unless they have received very special training; and their accuracy is questionable in young children. Hebb has suggested that the learning of young animals is of a slow, trial-and-error nature but that in mature animals quick, insightful learning frequently occurs; the insightful learning is possible because of the information which the organism has stored over the years. Similarly, Piaget and his colleagues have indicated that a child is unable to form certain concepts until he has learned to perceive certain relationships among stimuli.[2] Furthermore, Harlow has shown that monkeys, after receiving training in a long series of discrimination problems, are able to solve other problems, which involve totally different stimulus patterns, within a single practice trial (Harlow, 1949). The dependence of higher problem-solving ability on the level of conceptual ability attained is well established (Piaget and Inhelder, 1951). It is easy to think of many other examples from almost every aspect of human life, but these few instances from the areas of discrimination, concept formation, problem solving, language, and communication will suffice to emphasize the fact that important aspects of behavior, including social interaction, depend on the integrated action of the cognitive process.

It is known also that learning not only aids thinking ability but can also impede efficient problem-solving behavior. Everyone can recall instances in which the mechanized learning of a certain method or formula for solving a problem interfered with the solution of other problems because the individual found it difficult to change his mode of attacking the problem. This stereotypy of thinking, which is often caused by repetitive previous learning or training, has been called an *Einstellung* or set (Luchins, 1942). In the later chapters of this book we shall consider methods which might minimize the *Einstellung* effect.

INTERRELATIONSHIP OF THE PROCESSES. The relationship between the cognitive processes is by no means unidirectional. Thus far we have indicated only how some perception must precede learning and how previous percepts and learning affect thinking, but it is also known that the result of thinking modifies future learning and that learning in turn can influence

[2] See, for example, Forgus (1954); Hebb (1949); Piaget (1950).

the way we perceive our world. We have only to think of the stereotypes about certain social or ethnic groups or the nature of social attitudes to realize the extent to which learning determines the selectivity of perception. It is also established that learning improves perceptual discrimination and selection (Forgus, 1955a; 1955b; Eleanor J. Gibson, 1955; Hebb, 1949). Further, it has been suggested that efficient learning is improved by the way the individual organizes the problem task; i.e., learning is often dependent on thinking or directional sets. Thus it has been found that learning by principles facilitates retention and transfer (Forgus and Schwartz, 1957; Hilgard, Edgren, and Whipple, 1953; Katona, 1940). This has become particularly important in the field of modern education, in which scholars have stressed the importance of learning to develop the problem-solving attitude by directing learning through encouraging the child to express his intuitive hunches.

Stages in the Extraction of Information

Having conceived of perception as the guardian of the complex cognitive process, let us break it down into its component stages. Looked at in this way, the sequence of perception can be arranged into four stages.

I. *Physical energy (input).* Let us recall that perception guides man's task of adapting to his environment. It therefore follows that some set of events in the environment must place the process in motion. These stimulating conditions in the environment reside in physical energy; they provide the input for perception.

It is important to distinguish the aspect of physical energy which concerns the psychologist from that which is of more general interest to the physicist. When physical scientists or technologists think of physical energy, they conceive of a force which changes the physical structure of a machine or system in some permanent way, or at least for a relatively long period of time.

When the psychologist thinks of energy, he has in mind certain properties within the stimulus which affect the ongoing behavior of the system only while the energy is present or for short durations thereafter. That is, some characteristics of the energy are directly changing behavior. These characteristics are referred to as *informational aspects* of energy, and they carry messages to the organism. What is more, the informational aspects are limited: only units which fall within certain limits of the energy scale stimulate the senses informationally. For example, in the case of the visual perception of color, the eye is sensitive only to that portion of electromagnetic radiation (light energy) which falls between the wavelengths of approximately 400 and 800 mμ (the millimicron, mμ, is a physical measure of the length of light waves). The shorter wavelength is perceived as violet blue, and the longer wavelength as red, the other hues (colors) of the visible spectrum falling between these values. The eye is insensitive to the physical energy falling below 400 or above 800 mμ. Thus there are no informational messages outside these ranges.

Similarly, in the case of auditory perception of pitch, the average normal, not too old human ear is stimulated informationally only by physical energies of sound vibration which fall between approximately 10 and 20,000 cps (cycles per second). Human beings are deaf to basses lower than 10 cps and trebles higher than 20,000 cps.

Now, since the senses are differentially sensitive to specific kinds of informational dimensions in the vast array of energy, we must possess special kinds of sensory mechanisms which change the physical dimensions into message units that the nervous system can understand. This takes us to the second stage of the perceptual process.

II. *Sensory transduction.* The translation of physical information into informational messages that the nervous system can use is called the process of sensory transduction. In daily living we have to adapt to a variety of energy patterns. Most of these originate in the external environment, but some result from changes in the internal organs. The former are usually called *environmental stimuli,* while the latter are called *state stimuli* (in reference to the state of the organism).

The informational aspects of these stimuli impinge upon the various sense organs, which selectively transduce specific kinds of information. The specific sense organs and the kinds of informational energy they transduce are listed below.

   A. The exteroceptors, or distance senses
      1. Vision, which transduces light energy.
      2. Audition, which transduces sound energy.
   B. The proprioceptors, or near senses
      3. The *cutaneous* or *skin* senses, which transduce changes in touch (pressure), warm, cold, and pain energy.
      4. The chemical sense of *taste,* which transduces changes in the chemical composition of liquids stimulating the tongue.
      5. The chemical sense of *smell,* which transduces gases reaching the nose. Taste and smell are closely related. The sensation of different flavors within a specific taste (e.g., different flavors within the primary tastes of sweet, sour, salty, and bitter) requires the interaction of the taste and smell senses.
   C. The interoceptors, or deep senses
      6. The *kinesthetic* sense, which transduces changes in body position and the motion of the muscles, tendons, and joints.
      7. The *static* or *vestibular* sense, which transduces changes in bodily balance.
      8. The *organic* sense, which transduces changes related to maintaining the regulation of such organic functions as nourishment, water, and sex.

It is beyond the scope of this book to examine the anatomical, physiological, and electrochemical foundations of sensation, which are well documented in other excellent books.[3] A specific set of experiments aimed at determining the

[3] See, for example, Geldard (1953; 1962); Morgan (1951); Morgan and Stellar (1950).

way the Pacinian corpuscle transduces pressure stimuli into touch sensations is published in a *Scientific American* article which is easy to read and comprehend (Lowenstein, 1960).

The listing of the eight senses above should give the reader an idea of the scope of the contact between the organism and the environment. From these eight sources of energy the senses continually receive the stimulus information which the organism uses in its total adaptive behavior.

Once the stimulus information has been transduced or transformed into nerve impulses, the process of perception starts. While perception begins to be organized at the level of the senses (sensation), its organization continues to develop as the impulses or patterns of impulses ascend to the brain. To this intervening brain activity we now turn.

III. *Intervening brain activity.* When the nerve impulses or patterns of nerve impulses reach the brain, one of two things can happen. The brain can simply act as a relay and receiving station and pass on the information to the response system, thus completing the act of perception; or it can go further and select, reorganize, and modify the information before it passes it on to the response system. The brain does both things, and this becomes increasingly true as we ascend the animal kingdom (phylogenetic progression) or go from the infant to the experienced adult (ontogenetic progression).

Although this book will not deal specifically with anatomy and physiology, a brief statement of this third stage in perception seems in order. (More thorough bibliographic sources will be documented as we go along.) We said that the brain subserves two functions in perception, reception and selection. The reception and relay functions are organized by two anatomical-physiological systems, those of *arousal* and *projection.* Let us first recall that the brain consists of the cortex (gray matter) and the subcortex (white matter). While the cortex always has some ongoing activity, it needs to be excited beyond a minimal level before it can respond effectively to incoming information. For example, we do not perceive much when we are asleep. Somewhere above the state of sleep, the incoming stimulation sufficiently arouses the cortex so that it can use incoming sensory information. The arousal mechanism consists of ascending impulses which congregate at the brainstem and midbrain level of the subcortex and then diffusely bombard the cortex to "awaken" it and thus make it ready for specific incoming information.

For the details of how this arousal mechanism works and its specific anatomical locations, excellent sources can be consulted.[4] Again, there is an easy-to-read description of this arousal mechanism, which is also called the reticular activating system, in a *Scientific American* article (French, 1957). A related *Scientific American* report shows how important a varied sensory environment is for the integrated functioning of the brain and perception (Heron, 1957).

In addition to this arousing and maintaining of consciousness, the reticular activating system helps to select important sensory messages which will be relayed to the cortex. The more important relay centers, however, are located higher up in the subcortex. These relay or projection centers, as they are called,

---

[4] See, for example, Lindsley (1951); Moruzzi and Magoun (1949); Samuels (1959).

are so located anatomically that they direct the sensory impulses (informational messages) to the appropriate part of the cortex. The cortex has specific and different sensory areas which receive information coming from the different senses and then send it to the response or output side of the perceptual system.[5]

This statement needs modification. After experience, the cortex selects that information which it will receive and also integrates information from the various senses. A further word about this all-important cortical function of *selection, reorganization,* and *modification* in the perceptual process is called for. The parts of the cortex which do not serve a purely sensory function are referred to as the association areas. This mass makes up a large part of the cortex. In fact, as we ascend the phylogenetic scale, the A/S ratio (amount of association to sensory cortex) increases. Conceivably the association areas of the cortex become modified through learning and experience.

Since World War II there has been significant experimental and theoretical work on how the organizational relationships within the cortex and between the cortex and subcortex might change with learning and sensory experience. These developmental changes would correspond to the modified perceptual programs resulting from experience.

While we shall refer the reader to some excellent sources for original theorizing on the development of such brain mechanisms, we should like to state briefly now the kind of *brain model* we shall have in mind throughout this book. The brain model which will guide our thinking is stated simply in the following paragraphs. First, there is much evidence, which we shall discuss in detail later, to indicate that the infant must put his sensory mechanisms to use if perception, as we know it in the mature person, is to develop. The initial use of the senses follows from a reflexive or innate reaction to the simplest or gross informational content of stimulus energy. In the case of vision, the reaction is simply to light as light, without further differentiation; but this innate reaction to light stimulation during infancy gradually produces changes in the nervous system and the brain. With this change in the organization of the brain, its ability to extract more varied informational aspects from the stimulus pattern increases.

The emerging capacity of the brain to extract more and more information from the stimulus energy develops in stages. After reaction to light, the brain becomes capable of separating one light patch from another. The third stage, coming after more experience, brings the ability to see the patch as a vague figure. Finally, after trial and error and differential reinforcement, the brain develops the power to select patterns, forms, or identities which it can recognize and respond to within some meaningful context. This stage comes after much experience has been related in the association area of the cortex.

It follows from the last paragraph that, after maturation and learned experiences, the cortex does not merely receive information. The sensory contents of past experience have built up associational contexts or sets against which future sensory content is judged and coded. This attentional aspect of perception works as follows. After *testing* stimuli have been sent down from the cortex to let in selectively or *gate* incoming information, the sensory information

---

[5] For additional details on the anatomical and physiological relationship between the subcortex and the cortex, see Morgan and Stellar (1950), previously cited.

is organized in the cortex. As soon as this information has been *operated* upon, it is *tested* again against stored information before it *exits* in the perceptual response.

This test → operate → test → exit (TOTE) mechanism of mature perception follows the model of Pribram (1963) and Miller, Galanter, and Pribram (1960). The way the associational sets or contexts are developed could follow the neurological model of the building up of brain cell assemblies and hierarchical assemblies which are sequentially integrated, as suggested by Hebb; or the recent works on biochemistry which suggest that the chemical coding properties of the cell change with experience; or combinations of both approaches.[6]

If we were to summarize this brain model in behavioral terms, we could do so as follows. From birth on, the contents of perception produce the context for thinking and adaptive behavior. After the individual has learned from experience, thinking (which is directed by the brain models and sets) provides the context within which new perceptual contents are interpreted and identified. This model takes us from simple perception to the very complex perceptions, which involve active modification, selection, intervention, and even distortion and are evident in such acts as problem solving, esthetic judgment, and social perception.

IV. *Perceptual experience or response* (*output*). The last paragraph of the preceding section brought us to the fourth stage of the perceptual process. This last or output stage is simply a continuation of the third or intervening stage. While we study the output stage in terms of the verbalized or other objectified behavioral response, it is surely reasonable to suppose that the behavioral measure is an index of the intervening brain process or experience. It is therefore unnecessary to elaborate further on this stage, other than to say that we know that perception has taken place when the person tells us verbally or through some other behavioral indicator that he has perceived such properties as a gray patch, a red color, a short line, a long distance, an isosceles triangle, a receding surface, a familiar face, a moving musical composition, a problem solution, or a hostile act.

Informational Approach to Psychophysical Correspondence

We can integrate the four stages in the information-extraction process by using an approach which grew up outside the formal discipline of psychology. This approach, which came from communication engineering, in recent years has had a significant effect on psychology and related disciplines. The concepts underlying this approach are incorporated in what is called *information theory,* which deals with the coding of information. This theory is concerned with the encoding of a message at a source (input), the transmission of the message through a communication channel, and the decoding of the message at the destination (output). For example, a person in Chicago may wish to send a message to someone in New York. The message (consisting of linguistic units) is encoded in Morse code, trans-

---

[6] For further discussion, see Gaito (1961); Hebb (1949); Landauer (1964).

mitted through telegraph wires or similar physical means (the communication channel), and, in New York, translated back into linguistic units, or decoded (Miller, 1953).[7] Psychologists have used this approach in attacking a number of problems by considering the organism as the communication channel, stimuli or physical energy as input, and the responses as output. This conceptualization is illustrated in Figure 1-2. The organism is not, however, a static communication channel. Thus the dotted lines in the figure indicate that feedback occurs; i.e., the properties of the communication channel modify the apparent aspects of the stimuli, and the responses modify the properties of the channel. We discussed the first aspect of this feedback when we spoke of the intervening brain models or sets in the last section. The second loop of feedback is apparent when we realize that the way we extract information from successive stimuli is affected not only by what is in the stimulus and by which sets we process but also by the preceding perceptual response we had made.

From this diagram it is apparent that stimuli, responses, and the organism represent a complex interacting system in which variation in one portion of the system may effect variation in any other part. The organism extracts information not only from the stimulus situation (or message) but from within itself as well. This is especially true of the human being.

Where appropriate, in later chapters of this book, we shall discuss the way in which the formal methods of information theory have helped us solve certain perceptual problems for which the classical psychophysical approaches were inadequate. The reason for introducing the formal informational model here is to emphasize that the purpose of this book is to deal primarily with the *principles underlying* the correspondence between stage I and stage IV of the perceptual process, i.e., between *the informational aspects of the stimulus input and those of the response output.* This has traditionally been referred to as the problem of psychophysical correspondence.

The informational model depicted in Figure 1-2 helps us conceptualize the problem of measuring psychophysical correspondence more clearly. Since we can physically measure the encoded message (information in the

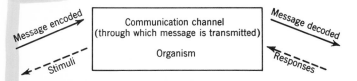

Figure 1-2
The information-theory approach in psychology. The dotted lines represent a slight modification to incorporate the notion of feedback.

[7] For additional details concerning this approach in the physical sciences, see Shannon and Weaver (1949) or N. Wiener (1948).

stimulus energy) and can also measure the decoded message (information in the perceptual response), the correspondence between these two stages will give us the amount of information transmitted through the communication channel (the perceptual process). Any deviation from perfect correspondence or transmission is contributed by two sources: (1) noise which is stimulus energy that blocks transmission and can come from either the input source or irrelevant sets in the organism and (2) relevant sets from the organism which modify the encoded message before decoding it. This second source of noncorrespondence deals, of course, with the question of individual differences in perception.

HISTORICAL CONTEXT. Anyone who thinks that the questions raised by the problems of investigating the nature of correspondence are relatively simple should peruse the rich philosophical and experimental history which is available in excellent sources.[8] A very interesting and novel approach to the analysis of psychophysical correspondence is seen in the creations of J. J. Gibson (1950), whose work we shall discuss in many parts of this volume.

Much progress has been made in our understanding of the nature of perception since the time of the theorizing of the early philosophers and scientists. Between the sixteenth century and the early part of the present century some individuals conceived of perception as nativistic while others conceived of it as wholly determined by learning. The former group usually stated that the entire stimulus pattern was capable of being perceived at birth, while the latter thought that it had to be built up gradually through experience. There were also many theorists who believed that the perception was an identical copy of the external stimulus pattern.

Today no such simple view of perception is held, and very few psychologists would dichotomize perception as an exclusively unlearned or exclusively learned process.[9] The consensus, rather, seems to be that we begin with unlearned, wired-in programs, which are reflexive and necessary to start the adaptive process going, and then progress to higher-order modified or learned programs. Thus it is easier to measure psychophysical correspondence in brightness and color perception than in the perception of such complex forms as a human face and music or in perceptual illusions. There is also more variation in the degree of correspondence found among people in the latter cases.

The modern theoretical advances made by such persons as Hebb, Gibson, Bruner, and information theorists in psychology like Attneave have brought us closer to a total, more integrated understanding of perception (Attneave, 1954a; Bruner, 1957; J. J. Gibson, 1950; Hebb, 1949). It will be the

---

[8] See, for example, Boring (1942; 1950); Murphy (1949).

[9] See, however, Francés (1962); Pratt (1963); J. G. Taylor (1962). The first reminds us of the debate, the second attempts an integration, while the third gives an extreme learning-theory interpretation.

purpose of this book to give the reader as authentic a flavor as we can of the cross section of perceptual studies, spanning the range from simple detection to complex identification.

Plan of the Book

Chapter 2 examines the evidence which suggests that the perceptual task consists of an ordinal sequence of subtasks. The level attained in the hierarchical process depends on the amount and kind of information extracted.

Before working out the details of the organization at each level of the perceptive hierarchy, we describe in Chapter 3 the methods which are appropriate to studying these phenomena.

In Chapter 4 we look at the first stages in the perceptual hierarchy. We deal essentially with the problem of perceptual detection and perceptual acuity. Some basic psychophysical functions are described.

Chapter 5 discusses why brightness constancy should also be considered as resulting primarily from built-in programs. Any contextual problems of brightness and color perception (e.g., seeing the color against backgrounds of different colors) seem to be accounted for by interactions in the stimulus conditions and their effects on the receptors and the brain.

By contrast, we see in Chapter 6 that size and shape constancy can be fully understood only if we consider the mediating influence of the cortex.

Chapter 7 begins an examination of how the perception of figure starts to develop and becomes organized. The determination of stable and unstable figures is investigated. The autokinetic effect as a special case of figural instability is discussed.

Chapter 8 starts the treatment of how pattern and form are recognized and identified, which includes a discussion of illusions. The value of applying the technique of information theory is highlighted in this chapter. We also discuss the facts which show that the images on the eye must change if the form is to persist. The adapting out of a steady stimulus is related to the fact that the effects of subsequent stimulation depend on the existing adaptation level of the perceptual system.

Chapter 9 deals more specifically with the rich data on how learning influences perceptual identification.

Chapter 10 carries on the discussion of pattern perception by considering the determination of the perception of space and distance. Included is a discussion of recent data from space flights.

Chapters 11 and 12 cover the broad scope of social perception, which includes the area of motives, personality, and the perception of persons.

In Chapters 13 to 16 we link the previous chapters to the rest of the cognitive processes. This is accomplished through sequential chapters on set, concept formation, problem solving, and creative thinking.

Because of the broad scope of this book and the data available, we have limited ourselves to the visual aspect of the superset perception.

Summary

This introductory chapter attempted to define the nature of the information-extraction process in man. A discussion and an illustration of the importance of considering the two-way interaction between perception, learning, and thinking in an understanding of this process were presented.

We then looked at the problem of information extraction, ending with our conviction that modern psychology subscribes to an approach to psychophysical correspondence which believes that perceptual patterns or organizations begin with an intrinsic structure based on built-in programs and that these become modified through the specific effects of learning and practice.

2

The Hierarchical Organization of Perceptual Segregation

In Chapter 1 we discussed the four stages involved in producing the final product of perception. These sequential stages were stimulation by energy; sensory transduction of this energy; brain reception, selection, and modification of this energy; and the perceptual response or experience.

In this chapter we shall show that detailed analysis of the perceptual process indicates that what we observe as the final stage, namely, the perceptual response or experience, is actually a complex task which can be broken down into subtasks. These subtasks can be ordered into an hierarchy from the simplest to the most complex task, in which *each successive progression up the hierarchy involves the extraction of progressively more information from the stimulus energy.*

We shall first state this *hierarchical order of perceptual segregations* and then go on to examine the evidence which suggests its existence and complex organizational properties. The order, listed from the simplest to the most complex task, conforms to the following sequence:

1. The *detection* of the stimulus *energy* (light) and a discrimination of change in stimulus energy.
2. The *discrimination* of a *unified brightness* or *figural unity* as separate from the background.
3. The *resolution* of finer details, which gives rise to a more *differentiated figure.*
4. The *identification* or recognition of a *form* or *pattern.*

5. The *manipulation* of the identified form; this happens, for example, in *problem solving* and *social perception.*

Emphasizing the fact that when we talk about energy, we are referring to its informational aspects, it is not hard to see how the progression from task 1 to task 5 involves the extraction of progressively more information. Concurrently, it is to be expected that the brain as an active, selective agent also becomes increasingly involved as we ascend the hierarchy.

Having simply stated the order in this hierarchy, let us examine the evidence which suggests its existence.

Studies on Threshold Determination for Light and Form

One way of finding out whether an hierarchy exists is to ask whether more energy is required for the perception of the higher segregations in the order as opposed to the perception of the lower segregations. An understanding of this problem necessitates a brief description of the concept of *threshold,* which will be analyzed more fully in Chapter 3.

We shall start with a subject sitting in a dark room until he becomes *dark-adapted,* that is, until the sensory receptors of the eye have become accustomed to the relative absence of light. The chemical changes occurring during dark adaptation have produced a stable change in the sensitivity of the receptors to light stimulation.

Now we begin to introduce into this dark room the smallest amount of light which the subject will probably not detect. We gradually increase the light energy until the subject reports that he can just notice or detect it. The energy level at which he just notices the light 50 per cent of the time is called the *absolute threshold* or *absolute limen* (AL). The problem involved in the determination of the AL and the methods used to study it are discussed in Chapter 3. That chapter also treats variations in the *difference limen* (DL), which is the smallest increase from an existing (and already perceived) energy level which the subject can just detect as being different, 50 per cent of the time.

We want, in this section, only to investigate the variations in AL connected with the emergence of the different segregations in the perceptual hierarchy. At the outset the reader might keep in mind that the energy level of light can be increased in three ways or in combinations of these ways. We can increase the intensity of the light, keeping its duration and spatial area constant; increase the duration of the light exposure, keeping its intensity and spatial area constant; or increase the spatial area of the light, keeping its intensity and duration constant. (The three laws relating intensity, time, and area in the production of energy levels are also discussed in Chapter 4.)

In most of the studies to be reported the analysis has been made in terms of the duration of light exposure, little attention being paid to the intensity and areal factors. We do not know, for example, whether the effects of short duration were due to lack of time or to lack of intensity. Since the data are not available, we can only guess that the increase in energy level coming from an increase in duration is contributed primarily by the temporal dimension. This uncertainty might be a criticism of the design of the experiments which we now report. For all the experiments conducted in a dark room it is assumed that the subject is dark-adapted.

EARLY STUDIES WHICH SUGGEST A GROSS HIERARCHY. One of the earliest experiments investigating the difference between threshold for light and form was conducted by Davies (1905) in a dark room by projecting a short flash of light on the shapes. The temporal durations of the light were varied from subliminal to supraliminal (above-threshold) values. The subjects always reported detecting the light at shorter durations before they could perceive the geometrical forms. The perception of forms required longer durations.

An experiment by Freeman (1929), which was also one of the earlier gross studies on the temporal effects of perception, demonstrated two additional dimensions of perceptual segregation. Inkblots and, in one case, eight silhouetted outlines of familiar forms were presented to subjects in a Whipple tachistoscope.[1] The duration of exposure was increased from very short intervals to longer ones, and the subjects were permitted to give a phenomenological description and commentary on the course of the development of the percept. As the exposure time increased, three well-defined levels of development were obtained with the inkblots, beginning with a "preperceptive" vague awareness and ending with a verbal naming of the object. The first stage consisted of a vague apprehension of general extent, which developed into a primary qualification of extent as either far or near, right or left, up or down. The second stage involved the generation of "thingness," during which there emerged the awareness of clearer contours and a figure was seen as having a "focus" and a "background." The development of this figure was from "something" to a "thing." Finally, there appeared a level of perceptive familiarity, during which the recognition (identification) and naming of an object occurred. Although the first two stages were often apprehended, they were highly telescopic, and it is the third stage which corresponds closely to the perception of familiar forms.

If we combine the results of these rather gross studies of Davies and Freeman, we get the suggestion of the first four subtasks in the order. The first level of Davies was the detection of light, which was differentiated in Freeman's study into discriminating a change in its orientation. The second stage of Freeman, namely, the development from something to a thing, corresponds to tasks 2 and 3 in our hierarchy. As the brightness patch,

---

[1] A tachistoscope is an instrument in which stimuli can be presented for controlled exposures from very short durations to longer ones.

Exper in light intens
demon. that d 5 steps followed
w/ increase in brightness.

18   *Perception*

which is really what constitutes the gross figure, develops *sharper contours,* the differentiated figure emerges. Finally, we get the identification of form, which corresponds to our task 4, in the last stage of both studies.

ELABORATING STUDIES, FROM BRIGHTNESS OR FIGURAL UNITY TO IDEN-TIFIED FORM. Other, more precise studies have, in general, obtained the same or a similar sequence of perceptual emergence. Thus Dickinson (1926), who presented tachistoscopically nine letters to seven subjects for 64 sec, found that as the subject continued to look at the letters, the perceptual process passed through three stages, which were not separate and distinct but gradually evolved from one to the next. The first, or "visual-pattern," stage, consisted of the mere awareness of thingness, a flat clearness which was clear in detail of illumination and contour but lacked logical meaning. During the second, or generic-object, stage, parts began to stand out slightly in relief and took on the properties of an object without definite or specific meaning. These two stages represent the transition from the unified brightness or figure (task 2) to the end of the differentiated-figure stage (task 3). During the third, or specific-object, level, the forms rose out toward the observer, the ground receded, and the figure became stable (task 4).

A comparable study was performed by Wever (1927), who also presented stimuli tachistoscopically but who went into greater detail about the transition from task 2 to task 3. He exposed 1,060 "nonsense figures" (irregularly formed fields) for durations of from less than 10 msec (milliseconds) to more than 2 min, using the method of constant stimuli.[2] In general, as the exposure time was increased, there unfolded four levels which were elaborations of the ones previously reported. First there existed a given degree of heterogeneity of the visual field in which two regions were discriminated, representing the perception of a brightness difference between them. This stage of simplest "figure-ground" was followed by a transition (good figure-ground) in which the features were more pronounced and in which the figural field presented a primitive type of localization, a protrusion in the visual field. Third, there emerged a contour which separated the two fields so that a primitive, poorly articulated form was perceived. Finally, there occurred an areal distribution of visual qualities so that the figure had a simple perceived shape. Throughout these stages depth localization or depth relief was least uniform and least subject to control, and *texture,* if present, *tended to appear at comparatively advanced stages.* We might add that texture, which depends on pattern, takes us to task 4. Wever summarized his results as follows: "A given figure-ground experience, then, is but one of many possible stages of the complex perceptual phenomenon, and its precise nature is a function of the various components of the situation in their entirety" (1927, p. 226).

Wever reported the following psychophysical relationships between the

[2] Psychophysical methods are discussed in Chapter 3.

perceptual structures and the temporal durations of exposure. There is no figural experience for durations of less than 10 msec; [3] simplest figure-ground occurs at 10 to 13 msec; good figure-ground, at 15 to 20 msec; and "perfect" figural experience, at 25 or more msec. The increase of durations from a few seconds to 2 min was not followed by any increase in the experience of "goodness" of figure. So the essential range for the development of these four stages within the experimental conditions used by Wever was between 10 and 25 msec. It is particularly important to note that these values of time duration were obtained with one fixed, constant level of intensity.

An experiment by Bridgen (1933) extended the threshold values upward until the perception of a patterned form was experienced. Using a Docheray tachistoscope, he found that gross figure-ground differentiation ended at 10 msec (task 2). This was followed by inaccurate discrimination of form between $\frac{1}{5}$ and 2 sec (task 3). The final stage ended in the finest differentiation of patterns between 4 and 13 sec (task 4). So it seems that the graduated segregation from a homogeneous field into unstable figure-ground, more differentiated figure, and finally pattern perception occurs at temporal durations of 10 msec to 13 sec. At least this is true under the conditions utilized, which, in general, consisted of exposing lights or forms of constant intensity to dark-adapted subjects.

The trend of the quantitative thresholds reported by Wever and Bridgen was generally supported by Helson and Fehrer (1932). They found that the recognition of form (task 4) required 25 times as much light as the just perceptible discrimination of light (task $1 \rightarrow 2$) and the perception of vague form (task $2 \rightarrow 3$) required a middle value of 15 times as much light.

All the studies reported thus far, with the exception of the one by Helson and Fehrer, varied only in duration, intensity remaining constant. Hence these absolute time durations cannot be accepted as correct. Douglas (1947), in establishing a similar order, found light detection at durations as low as 2.5 msec. According to other data, light may be detected at a duration as low as 0.001 msec, providing the intensity is high enough. What is necessary is simply that the absolute amount of light energy (Helson and Fehrer) is at threshold value to produce a receptor response. These studies, therefore, have to be evaluated against the Bunsen-Roscoe law, which states that $I \times T = K$, where I is the intensity of light, T the time duration, and K a constant energy level. The law holds for a time duration up to 0.1 sec.

More definitive values of the energy levels required for the AL of the various segregations will thus have to await studies taking the Bunsen-Roscoe law into account. There will, in any case, be individual differences, but the evidence for an *ordinal* progression of energy extraction as we ascend the perceptual hierarchy is established by these threshold studies.

[3] Let us keep in mind that a millisecond is one-thousandth (0.001) of a second.

Perceptual Differences Based on Sensory Receptors or Affected by Experience

A very interesting experiment illustrating the role of the sensory receptors in perception and also suggesting their limitations was reported by J. L. Brown, Duhns, and Adler, 1957. Using the method of constant stimuli and dark-adapted subjects, the authors determined ALs of light energy (also called luminance thresholds) for the resolution of parallel-line-grating test patterns, which are simply sets of parallel lines forming patterns. The space between the lines can be made rather large, requiring low visual acuity, or very small, requiring high visual acuity. At different times the dark-adapted subjects looked at these patterns through different filters which would variously refract relatively pure spectral bands, from the blue to the red colors. The task required of the subjects was essentially to state whether any pair of patterns they looked at were the same or different. The results are interesting and informative.

For a *low order of visual acuity,* it was found that *blue filters produced lower luminance thresholds* relative to the other filters. On the other hand, for a high order of visual acuity, the lowest luminance thresholds for all the filters were essentially the same.

Other data indicate that the receptors closer to the periphery of the retina (*rods*) are more sensitive in night vision than are the receptors closer to the fovea or center of the retina (*cones*). Furthermore, the cones responsible for the transduction of blue light are more sensitive in twilight than those responsible for red light. (This is related to the Purkinje shift, discussed in Chapter 4.)

A reasonable deduction from the study is that even under dark adaptation visual function shifts from rod to cone function as the task becomes more demanding. Since cone adaptation is less complete under dark adaptation than is rod adaptation, the higher tasks (from our task 3 upward) are poorly performed under conditions of dark adaptation. Related data are reported in a follow-up study (J. L. Brown, Phares, and Fletcher, 1960).

A second group of investigators has verified the importance of cone vision for the adequate performance of the higher perceptual tasks. The study was done by Zigler, Cook, Miller, and Wemple (1930). In an attempt to determine whether qualitative differences in the perception of form could be found at different regions in the peripheral field of vision, 48 patterns, which included geometric figures, familiar figures, and unfamiliar figures (some were outlined, and others were incompletely outlined), were moved from extreme peripheral vision to the center of the visual field. The method of minimal changes was used with 11 subjects. Four different modes of appearance were reported as a figure was moved in over the visual field in any meridian.

1. The figureless field. There is no figure; only the background is perceived.
2. In the adjacent zone formless figure occurs. An unorganized mass of marks or lines which are meaningless is vaguely seen, and the principal dimension of the figure may be reported.
3. Formlike figure is the report for the next zone. There is a figure formation which suggests several names in succession.
4. Clear figure occurs in the innermost region. Here the details of the figure are accurately perceived.

Since more information is extracted as we go from the low to the high end of the hierarchy, it is not surprising to find a similar pattern emerging as we proceed from peripheral to central vision. In the last-mentioned experiment an interesting side issue was the emergence of increasing specificity of name classification. First the figure appeared, formed but unfamiliar, then the general class name was suggested, then the specific name appeared, and finally the figure was positively identified and recognized.

A third study, performed by Craik and Vernon (1942), throws further light on the relevance of sensory mechanisms for individual differences in the lower perceptual tasks and the increasing relevance of experience for individual differences in the higher perceptual tasks.

The 18 subjects used in this experiment were first completely light-adapted. Then ALs for various light stimuli were obtained continuously during 55 min of dark adaptation. Three results of this experiment are of interest for our present concern: (1) The subjects exhibited characteristic individual differences in cone and rod adaptation. Those who showed relatively high thresholds after cone adaptation showed relatively low thresholds after rod adaptation. Correspondingly, those who showed relatively low thresholds after cone adaptation showed relatively high thresholds after rod adaptation. (2) The low-cone-threshold subjects were better at performing simple perceptual functions, such as reading the position of a dial hand. This shows again that, under dark adaptation, the cones are capable of transducing lower amounts of figural information at the level equivalent to our task 2. (3) The ability to perceive more complex patterns, such as silhouetted pictures, was only partially related to the ALs for cone vision and even less closely related to the threshold for rod vision.

The third result brings us directly to the role of experiential factors in higher-order perceptual tasks. Craik and Vernon state that the perception of more complicated material was affected by a "variety of purely psychological" factors, such as intelligence, education, familiarity of the particular type of material and situation, and emotional attitudes. As the reader can anticipate, it is our view that the "psychological" qualities listed above represent the area of learning and experience which is important for the performance of tasks 4 and 5 in our hierarchy and that the emotional attitudes would be of particular interest in social perception (a division of task 5), as we shall see in Chapter 12.

Before going into greater detail about the other evidence suggesting the importance of organismic and experiential factors for the performance of higher-level perceptual tasks, we should perhaps refer to some representative studies indicating the intricate complexities of form perception. In one such experiment Bitterman, Krauskopf, and Hochberg (1954) demonstrated the kinds of mistakes people make in the identification of forms under dark adaptation. In this experiment each observer was dark-adapted for 10 min and then shown geometrical figures, each of which was illuminated for 0.5 sec. The typical mistakes were of the following kinds: A square was usually called a circle; a triangle, a circle; a cross, a diamond; an X, a square; and so on. A circle was usually identified correctly.

It is of significance that angled shapes were more confused than circular shapes. This fact is verified by the experiments of Hochberg, Gleitman, and MacBride (1948) and Krauskopf, Duryea, and Bitterman (1954),[4] who found that there is a higher threshold for visual form of shapes which have higher ratios of perimeter to area than those which have lower ratios.

Determination of the Perceptual Order

Thus far we have examined two kinds of evidence suggesting the hierarchy: (1) More energy is required to invoke the higher perceptual tasks. (2) Sensory factors are dominant in the determination of the two lower-order tasks, while experiential factors contribute increasingly important effects as the third to the fifth level of the perceptual tasks is reached. This suggests that the perceptual system is not determined by a single sensory mechanism but by at least two separate mechanisms which are somehow integrated in the complex task of form perception. The complexities involved in this integration are difficult to unravel. The following set of studies and theoretical interpretations may help to clarify some of the problems involved.

First of all, let us keep in mind that the subtasks reported in this chapter were obtained under relatively short durations of exposure. Bartlett (1916) reported that visual perception of form varied with the variation in the material given to perceive. When the material was simple in structure, when parts were so related by connecting lines that they formed wholes, when material was familiar to the subject, or when it carried a common representative meaning, the subject's approach was to make out the whole at a single glance. When these conditions were not present, the tendency was toward a more analytical method.

In an excellent and extensive treatment of form perception, Hake summarizes work on thresholds as follows: "The evidence shows a complexity of action including the ability to *detect the mere presence* of light, to *discriminate difference in the brightness of large areas of the target,* to *resolve*

---

[4] See also Gaito (1959b) for the importance of critical details in circles and angles.

fine details of the target, and to *appreciate the form or general shape of the whole target.* These several functions are not related to any useful degree. That is, the evidence does not permit the description of the visual system in terms of any simple sensing mechanism designed to sense or appreciate visual patterns" (1957, pp. 6–7).[5]

The four tasks enumerated by Hake correspond to our first four tasks. As we mentioned earlier, task 5 is an extension of task 4. Clues to the kinds of organization involved at the different task levels came from Hebb (1949), who suggested three levels of perceptual organization.

1. A primitive, sensorily determined unity, which refers to the unity and segregation of a figure from a background. The emergence of the figure seems to be a direct product of the pattern of sensory excitation and the inherited characteristics of the nervous system upon which it acts.
2. The nonsensory, figure-ground organization, which is defined as one in which the boundaries of the figure are not fixed by gradients of luminosity in the visual field. This organization is affected by experience and other nonsensory factors and is not inevitable in any perception.
3. The identity of a perceived figure, which refers to the properties of association inherent in a perception. It, of course, is affected by experience.

Hebb's first level of organization could be extended downward to include our tasks 1 and 2. Then his second and third levels would include our tasks 3 and 4, the latter again being extended to task 5. If this were the case, we would expect a higher correlation between performances on tasks 1 and 2, since they are more sensorily determined. Correspondingly, we would expect a higher correlation between tasks 3 and 4, since they are more affected by learning and experience. This is exactly what the literature indicates. Thus many studies report a very low, insignificant correlation between the thresholds for light and those for form (Craik and Vernon, 1942; Miles, 1953).[6]

Other studies (see, for example, Hyman and Hake, 1954) indicate that the threshold for light (task 1) is closely related to the thresholds for the orientation of the gratings of a parallel bar. A similar correlation is reported between light thresholds and those for designating the location of an object, especially in the gross up, down, left, right position (Leibowitz, Myers, and Grant, 1955). Finally, A. J. Marshall and Day (1951) reported that for the crudest type of pattern discrimination (probably analogous to task 2; let us recall also the work of Brown et al. on differences between red and blue light perception for low-acuity tasks) the light and form thresholds practically coincide.

While there is a lack of similar studies on the correlation between tasks 3 and 4, we at least know that they do not correlate with the lower two tasks. Furthermore, the work of Hake and of Hyman and Hake, cited

[5] Italics mine.
[6] Ives and Schilling (1941) report a correlation of only 0.179.

earlier, throws some light on what might be involved in the higher two tasks as opposed to the lower two.

First of all, these authors' report and data of Drury (1933) verify that many interacting factors, which are difficult to differentiate experimentally, are involved in the determination of the nature of form perception. These factors include the method of study, the number of forms used, the nature of the task as envisaged by the subject, and his interpretations, preferences, and guessing habits.

With respect to guessing habits, an interesting difference between lower and higher tasks occurs. It has been found that while the biases of subjects are not systematic for the detection of orientation, they are more so for the discrimination of patterns. In the latter case some forms are more likely to be selected by the subjects than others (Bitterman et al., 1954; Casperson, 1950; Helson and Fehrer, 1932; Hyman and Hake, 1954). These systematic biases may be related to the experiential development of perception, a topic to which we now turn for deeper discussion.

Phylogenetic and Ontogenetic Differences and the Role of Learning: Organismic Factors

Our third criterion for judging the existence of the hierarchy is concerned with the extent of phylogenetic and ontogenetic differences in the discrimination of the various perceptual structures. It will be convenient to discuss this evidence in conjunction with the fourth criterion, which concerns the role of learning, since the ontogenetic differences, to a large extent, involve the modification of perceptual discrimination through learning. (It should also be kept in mind that the brain organization changes with experience.) The meaning of these differences and the possible course of learning should be very carefully considered because of their implications for perceptual theory.

Observations which Köhler and other gestalt psychologists rely on heavily in support of their position are those initiated by Wertheimer (1923) and studied by Gottschaldt (1926; 1929). The latter found that mere *repetitive* experience with inspection of a form does not increase the probability of identifying it if it is embedded in a more inclusive whole. He concluded that the structural factors prevail over the effect of repetitive previous experience. After discussing these results, Köhler has asserted further that "whoever defends the *automatic* influence of past experience upon our seeing definite forms will have incumbent upon him the task of supporting his theory by other experiments" (1929, p. 208).[8] Contrariwise, Djang (1937) and N. G. Hanawalt (1942) have shown that experience does affect the task of looking for hidden figures under certain situations, but their results do not necessarily refute Köhler's statement concerning automaticity.

[8] Italics added.

The key to Köhler's argument lies in two factors. The first is his insistence on the importance of structural relations in the stimulus field; the second, his rejection of the *automatic* influence of past experience. As far as the first factor is concerned, it seems that we must accept the fact that perceptual forms are structurally determined; i.e., physical form is determined by internal physical relationships. These relationships remain invariant with respect to time and space; otherwise we cannot talk about a physical form at all. Certainly the gestalt psychologists have amassed a large body of data to demonstrate this fact; these experiments will be examined later. Köhler's rejection of the automatic effect of past experience is important, but—and this is an important "but"—we must ask a further question: If the percept is governed by structural factors and if past experience does not automatically modify these factors, does this mean that the organism responds innately to these structures without any influence of learning? Obviously this conclusion does not follow unequivocally from the premise or from the contrary results cited above.

We might ask, in fact, whether discriminations of some of these stimulus structures are not improved, or at least modified, by learning or practice. After we have considered this question, we shall be able to see more impartially whether all perceptual phenomena are pure "sensory facts" or whether some require learning for adequate unfolding. Let us then go ahead and examine the phylogenetic and ontogenetic evidence which suggests that perceptual phenomena can be ordered from primitive to complex, learning being unimportant in the primitive but becoming a more and more important determiner as we ascend this ordinal scale. We shall begin with the work of Hebb on rat perception, not only because Hebb has dealt with perceptual ordering but also because he has been most influential in redirecting our interest toward necessary modifications required in perception theory.

Hebb (1937a; 1937b) compared the discrimination ability of rats who were reared in the dark with that of rats who were normally reared. He found that the two groups did not differ in brightness discrimination but that the dark-reared animals were inferior to normally reared animals in pattern discrimination. If we assume for the moment that the absence of light did not impair the optical mechanism (we shall have more to say about this later), then these results suggest that brightness discrimination is a more primitive phenomenon than pattern discrimination. This assumption is in keeping with the order effect to which we have been exposed throughout this chapter. Hebb's finding is further corroborated by Lashley's study previously cited (1938), which found that after rats have learned to discriminate between two forms, the discrimination is completely lost if the brightness relationships are reversed. Thus, after a rat has learned to respond positively to a white triangle, no amount of training will produce a positive response to a black one alone. Brightness cues are dominant. In the rat, reaction to brightness appears to be largely innate, whereas form perception probably requires simple concept formation and has low availability for the rat.

Similar results have been obtained with primates and human beings. Thus Riesen (1947) compared the discrimination ability of four dark-reared chimpanzees with normally reared ones. He found that there were only little differences in brightness and color discrimination. When it came to pattern and form discrimination, however, the dark-reared animals were markedly inferior. In some cases the chimpanzees required weeks to learn to discriminate between different identities. Some critics have argued that the visual nervous system of the animals reared in the dark was probably damaged, but more recently Riesen (1958) reported similar trends when rats were reared under a dome which transmitted only unpatterned diffuse light. The case for the learning of pattern perception appears to be well established. Senden (1932) collected similar reports from clinical observations of human adults who were given vision for the first time in adulthood after congenital cataracts had been surgically removed. Again discrimination of brightness appeared fairly normal, whereas discrimination of forms required much learning, sometimes lasting two or more months. A recent study (Gregory and Wallace, 1963), which we shall discuss in Chapter 9, analyzes in depth a case of recovery from blindness.

It does seem quite definite that brightness discrimination is a positive sensory phenomenon, and it is doubtful whether anyone would want to argue for the significant importance of learning in brightness perception after considering the evidence. (In Chapter 5, in which systematic treatment of brightness constancy is given, we shall examine additional evidence relevant to this point.) But the issues with respect to the role of learning in form perception are much more controversial. We have mentioned Köhler's strong denial of the role of past experience in determining the perception of structural forms and the contrary results. There is other evidence, some not very reliable but some coming from well-controlled experimental studies, which strongly suggests that form perception is affected by learning. This evidence is derived from both human and comparative research.

For example, Piaget and Inhelder (1948) found that there was an age progression in the development of form perception which involved increasing levels of abstraction. While children could differentiate, by drawing, curved from rectilinear figures at about four years of age, the discrimination between triangles and squares followed a gradual development and did not become accurate until a later age. The studies of Riesen and Senden, cited above, also show the importance of learning in form perception.

We come lastly to a group of comparative studies on the problem of learning to perceive form. Gellerman (1933) compared the form-discrimination abilities of chimpanzees and two-year-old children. He found that both could differentiate triangles from other forms, such as rectangles and trapezoids, even when the triangles were turned upside down. This generalization was possible even when the brightness relationships were reversed. It should be remembered that rats found this kind of generalization impossible. So it is clear that we have a phylogenetic development, which is revealed in the fact that chimpanzees and man can learn to abstract form, despite brightness reversals, whereas rats cannot. Furthermore, when it came to generalizing continuous forms, like crosses and triangles, to the same forms produced by dots or placed on a variety of background shapes, the children were superior to the chimpanzees. Thus we find a phylogenetic hierarchy of form concept formation, which operates so that rats are inferior to chimpanzees in simple form conception, with the latter, in turn, being inferior to human children in more complex abstraction or generalization of form.

We might ask which factors determine this phylogenetic difference. The answer seems to involve the question of what is generalized: concrete parts or relationships. Lashley (1938) reports that rats will generalize from a triangle to a horizontal line if the line is about the same length as the base of the triangle. Moreover, although rats readily learn to differentiate triangles and squares, they find it almost impossible to differentiate circles and squares of comparable area. It would seem that the difference between the base of the triangle and the lower arc of the circle is too small to be effective. Furthermore, Fields (1932) reports that rats will not generalize a learned form discrimination of a triangle if the triangle is rotated as little as 25° to the right. In order to get the rats to generalize, the triangle must be gradually rotated a couple of degrees at a time. Subsequent studies by the present author (Forgus, 1954; Forgus, 1956) have shown that rats who were exposed to a complex form environment during their rearing were superior to cage-reared animals in both form discrimination and *generalization*. The perception of form identity and its generalization evidently require a fairly high level of learning. This learning probably results in changes in the cortex. Thus we know that human beings who have sustained damage in certain parts of the brain show greater visual impairment than chimpanzees, who, in turn, show greater impairment than rats who are brain-damaged.

Summary

By using such criteria as the amount of energy required, the relative importance of sensory and central functions, the influence of experience, and ontogenetic and phylogenetic development, we have established an order of perceptual segregation. This hierarchical order consists of the following subtasks: (1) detection of light and change in light energy, (2) the gross discrimination of a figural unity, (3) the resolution of a more clearly differentiated figure, (4) the identification of form, and (5) the manipulation or modification of form, as in social perception and problem solving.[9]

In this relative order, tasks 1 and 2 are more strongly determined by sensory factors, while the progression from task 3 to task 5 requires the increasing involvement of the brain (especially the cortex), learning, and experience.

---

[9] Since this chapter was written, an article based on the ideas developed here was published by a former student and colleague, Gaito (1964).

3

Some Methodological Considerations

This chapter has one main purpose, to provide a methodological context for the remaining chapters. At the outset it should be noted that the earliest investigators who developed methods for measuring perceptual phenomena were concerned primarily with the first level of our hierarchy. The determination of how small a stimulus a person could detect and how small a change he could discriminate raised the question of what kind of measuring *scale* we could construct in perception.

In trying to develop such a scale we inevitably encounter the problem of what kind of mathematical function will describe accurately enough the nature of the relationship between the perceptive or psychological scale, which is subjective, and the physical scale. This is the question to which the classical psychophysicists addressed themselves. For the sake of historical continuity, we shall briefly describe these basic psychophysical methods. There are a number of reasons for not discussing them in detail. Three of these reasons follow.

1. Psychophysical methods will have been encountered in standard courses and texts dealing with experimental psychology.
2. Since the classical methods have, for one reason or another, recently been challenged on *methodological* grounds, we want to give some attention to these objections and to the suggested alternatives which have been proposed.
3. While the methods of classical psychophysics have been adapted or modified to study the nature of the higher-order perceptual tasks, the investi-

gation of such hierarchical phenomena as figure, identity, and social perception presents problems which require innovative methods for solution. Thus the usual methods are too *limited* to help us uncover the nature of the variables defining the characteristic shape of an identifiable form or the direction of the subjects' biases in social perception.

Because of these considerations, this chapter will be organized into the following three divisions, each having the specific purpose designated:

1. The essentials of the most common psychophysical methods will be described. After each method has been presented, we shall list some of the perceptual problems to which it has been applied. The specifics of the application or the nature of any modification or adaptation will be left to later chapters dealing with the particular perceptive tasks.
2. Since traditional psychophysics concerned itself primarily with the determination of thresholds and perceptual scales, we shall discuss two alternative approaches to the measurement of these variables which have been contributed by modern theorists and experimenters.
3. Finally, we shall present a short section listing some of the important problems in perception for which traditional methods, even in modified form, are hardly of value. Alternative approaches will again be named, leaving their actual analysis to the appropriate later chapters.

We should perhaps emphasize our reason for choosing this strategy. Some purpose will be served by discussing the determination of thresholds and scales, since we shall not deal with these phenomena, as such, again and they are important for the first part of the hierarchy. We shall, however, encounter the higher-level tasks consistently. While it is necessary to point out the limitations of classical psychophysics in this chapter in order to place the newer methods in proper perspective, the real value of these newer tools can best be appreciated when we see how they help to clarify the conceptualization of perceptual problems. As in all branches of science, the method follows from the problem, and its value is to be judged as a function of how much light the data it generates throw on our understanding of the problem. Hence the relevant methods are discussed after a description of the conceptualization of the appropriate problem.

Traditional Psychophysics

The psychophysicist has set himself a most difficult task: the measurement of sensation or, more specifically, sensation as a function of stimulation (sensation is psychological, and stimulation physical). Sensation, as we know, is an internal psychological event. Therefore, direct knowledge of this event can only be attained by the person experiencing the sensation. Throughout the discussion this person will be referred to either as the observer (O) or the subject (S). The experimenter (E) must design his experiment so that he may obtain a dependable measure of this internal experience. This can be done by allowing O to report internal conditions with reliability through the institution of procedures to help E check O's reliability or through the manipulation of conditions which obviate the problem of reliability. How E decides to handle the reliability dilemma is a theoretical decision and one on which contemporary psychophysicists disagree.

It is sometimes frustrating to attempt to demonstrate to the beginning student of psychology the need for the measurement of sensation. To the student it seems that merely specifying the physical magnitude of the stimulus should be sufficient. If we know the physical brightness of a light, for example, that should tell us everything we wish to know about what is happening with respect to O's sensation. We may, however, have a few basic questions which are not answered by reference to the physical-magnitude measurements. For example, is the light bright enough to be seen by O? For the answer to this question we must appeal to O to introspect the contents of his consciousness and see if the sensation aroused by the light is there. Another question might be: "If I double the intensity of the light, will it seem twice as bright to O?" or "If I move the light to illuminate a different spot on O's retina, will it seem brighter to him?" These are psychophysical questions, and for their answers we must turn to a report from O. It might make things very much easier if we could specify the intensity and organizational properties of the sensation by knowing all the relevant aspects of the stimulus. It is this task to which the discipline of psychophysics directs itself.

Methodology of Psychophysics

In psychophysics, as in many branches of psychology, the methods an experimenter uses to investigate problems are determined by the opinions and the theoretical position he holds. In this section we shall survey three methods of collecting psychophysical data and the theoretical positions which underlie them. First, however, we shall examine the kinds of questions we seek to answer by using psychophysical methods. Essentially, there are two basic psychophysical questions: (1) How intense must a stimulus be to be perceived? (2) What is the relationship between physical stimuli and the corresponding conscious sensation?

The first question directs us to locate the *absolute threshold,* the minimum amount of energy of a particular type which allows the subject to perceive a stimulus (the dimmest light he can see, the least intense sound he can hear, etc.).

The second question, which is more complex, may be stated in a variety of ways. The classical formulation of the problem directs the investigator to locate the *differential threshold.* In this case the subject is already being stimulated. The question therefore is: How much additional energy must be added to the prevailing energy for him to notice a change? Given a light of 100 mL (millilamberts), how much must we increase the intensity for the subject to notice that the light is brighter? If the subject is hearing a 10-db tone, by how much can its loudness be increased before he notices a difference?

Actually, of course, the bulk of everyday perception involves much grosser discriminations than *O* is asked to make in experiments determining his absolute and differential thresholds, but the most basic psychophysical data provide useful information regarding sensory function.

Classical Psychophysical Methods

The three psychophysical methods which we shall discuss here may be used for both absolute- and differential-threshold measurements. We shall treat them in the context of absolute-threshold measurement, but the reader should easily be able to perceive their potential usefulness in determining differential thresholds.

METHOD OF LIMITS. In determining absolute visual threshold by the method of limits, the first step is to choose a graded series of intensities ranging from a light too dim to be seen to one just sufficiently bright that it may be seen 100 per cent of the time. These lights are presented to *O* in regular order on alternately ascending and descending trials. After each stimulus flash, *O* reports whether or not he saw it. Trained *O*s, who are more reliable, are usually employed in studies of this kind. After a large number of trials have been presented, the data are summarized and plotted as shown in Figure 3-1.

The convention in psychology has been, for the most part, to locate the threshold at the stimulus value perceived 50 per cent of the time. In this example the threshold is at an intensity of 50 units. Modifications of the

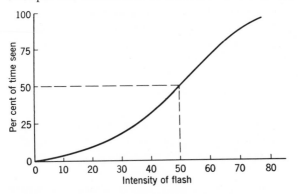

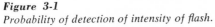

Figure 3-1
Probability of detection of intensity of flash.

method of limits, such as fractionation, have been used to study such perceptual phenomena as the scaling of visual distance reported in Chapter 10.

METHOD OF CONSTANT STIMULI. To determine the threshold by this method, it is again necessary to choose a graded series of stimuli. For the method of constant stimuli, the stimulus values are randomly ordered rather than presented in order. Again, data are tabulated in terms of the probability of detection for each of the stimulus values, and a curve like that in Figure 3-1 is constructed. Many of the experiments on the nature of shape perception reported in Chapters 6 and 7 have used this method. For example, in some experiments on shape constancy, the subject must choose, from a series of shapes varying on some dimension, one that looks like the standard shape which has been tilted through space. A number of such equality matches for each position of tilt are made, using a randomized order. From such data we can calculate the degree of shape constancy and, conversely, the average amount of error in the perception of each shape at each position of tilt. This method is essentially an adaptation of the method of constant stimuli.

METHOD OF ADJUSTMENT. Another measure of absolute threshold is more direct. In fact, during the previous discussion the reader may have wondered why the experimenter did not merely hand the subject the knob that controls the intensity of the light and ask him to adjust it so that he could just barely detect the stimulus. Such a procedure is called the method of adjustment. Since the subject will be somewhat variable at this task, he should be asked to set the knob several times so that the experimenter can average a number of values. On alternate trials the subject will "descend," that is, start with the knob at its full intensity, decrease it until he no longer sees the light, and then eventually "zero in" on the threshold value. On other trials he will start with the knob at its minimum intensity and ascend. Most of the experiments in the area of brightness and size constancy, reported in Chapters 5 and 6, use the method of adjustment. For example, the experiment by Gilinsky described near the beginning of Chapter 5 applied this method when the subject was asked to adjust the height of a near, variable triangle to equal that of the far, standard triangle.

Location of Differential Threshold

The second question we asked under "Methodology of Psychophysics" directs the classical psychophysicist to locate the differential threshold, the minimum change in intensity of a prevailing stimulus which can be detected by the subject. This is called a *just noticeable difference* (jnd). In the early 1800s E. H. Weber noted that a just noticeable difference was always a constant fraction of the prevailing intensity. If the intensity were high, a great deal of change had to be effected for the subject to notice a difference. If the intensity were low, only a small change was necessary to produce a jnd. He stated this relationship in the form of an equation known as Weber's law:

$$\frac{\Delta I}{I} = K$$

In this equation ΔI means the minimum necessary change in stimulation needed to cause the subject to say "I detect a difference"; I means intensity; and K is a constant. In other words, the minimum amount of change in intensity divided by the prevailing intensity equals a constant fraction for any one sensory system.

Perhaps some examples will make Weber's law more than a mere abstraction. If a man who makes 100 dollars a week is given a raise of 10 dollars a week, this change is, let us assume, just barely noticeable to him. If he were making 1,000 dollars a week, a raise of 10 dollars would be unnoticeable. If Weber's law held here, he would need 100 dollars more (one-tenth of the amount he is currently making) for him to notice additional spending money. For this particular system, $\Delta I/1 = \frac{1}{10}$. If he were making 200 dollars a week, he would need an additional 20 dollars; if he were making 10 dollars, one additional dollar would be noticed.

To apply this law to our differential-threshold case, we might use the method of limits. Beginning with a light of 100 mL, we would ask our subject to compare this light with another. We would then raise the intensity of the other light until he noticed that the two were different. If, upon locating the threshold, the comparison light were set at 120 mL, then $\Delta I = 20$. Twenty additional millilamberts of luminance were needed to cause the S to notice that the light was appreciably brighter. The Weber fraction at this level, then, is $\frac{20}{100}$, or one-fifth. Weber's law would then predict that this fraction would be the same regardless of how bright or how dim the standard light was. If the standard light were set at 1,000 mL, S would make the comparison light 1,200 mL bright. The curve relating I of the comparison light to $\Delta I/I$ would resemble that in Figure 3-2 if Weber's law held all the way across intensity.

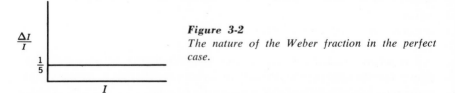

Figure 3-2
The nature of the Weber fraction in the perfect case.

The actual techniques involved in the classical psychophysicists' approach to the differential-threshold determination are similar to those discussed in the section on absolute threshold. Our final graphic output of the experiment, however, plots ΔI, the change in energy on the horizontal axis, against the percentage of time this change was detected by *S*, as in Figure 3-3. The differential threshold in this case is 18.

We may in determining the differential threshold utilize the method of limits, the method of constant stimuli, or the method of adjustment, as in our previous example. Always, however, as classical psychophysicists, we must ask our subject merely to report "yes" or "no" as his response, regardless of the level of his certainty.

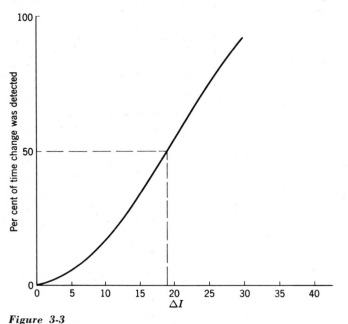

Figure 3-3
Percentage of time change was detected as a function of the magnitude of the change.

Alternative Approaches to Threshold Determination and Scaling

Now that we have examined some of the important methodological considerations of the classical psychophysicist, we may turn to an examination of some of the newer, alternative approaches to the same problem. Primarily, we shall summarize the arguments of two of the newer psychophysical investigators, examining their objections to the older approaches and their ways of dealing with the same problems.

Detection Theory

Tanner and Swets (1954) and others exemplify the general trend within contemporary psychophysics which is labeled detection theory. Their principal objection to classical psychophysics is directed toward the kinds of decisions classical psychophysicists make about the yes-no response. One objection of the detection theorist is to the so-called false-positive response, i.e., the response "yes" made by *S* when no stimulus has actually been presented. The detection theorist holds that the yes-no response is an impossible decision. What *S* really wishes to say, as we have seen, is that he is not sure whether he saw the stimulus or not. Detection theorists point out that when "catch trials" are interspersed in absolute-threshold determination, some subjects will give false-positive responses. On the other hand, more conservative subjects may adopt a higher criterion and *never* say yes until they are absolutely certain that a stimulus was presented. This practice increases the threshold value, and the number of false negatives may also be greater. False negatives are defined as failures to report a stimulus that was really detected by *S*. Of course, the psychophysicist never knows when a false negative occurs since in this instance he must rely completely on *S*'s word. On the other hand, false positives are easy to detect when stimuli have not been presented. Detection theory, however, also seems to imply that false positives may occur when stimuli have been presented, that is, stimuli below the value at which *S* actually perceives the stimulus. We may view these possibilities in the form of a 2 × 2 matrix (see Figure 3-4).

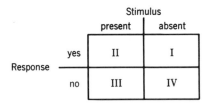

Figure 3-4
Four possibilities for a simple psychological threshold experiment.

This matrix examines an *S*'s yes-no responses as a function of whether or not a stimulus was actually presented. A subject with a high criterion will have few responses in cell I, the false-positive cell. On the other hand, he may have many responses in cell III, some of which may be false negatives. A subject who has adopted a low-criterion value may have many responses in cell I, indicating that he is answering "yes" sometimes when he does not see the stimulus. Further, he will have more responses in cell II than does the *S* with a high criterion. Consequently he will have a lower apparent threshold value, not because of his actual threshold but because of his lower criterion.

Detection theorists have had to devise methods for determining threshold which do not require the classical psychophysicists' naïve (to the detection theorist) acceptance of S's response. One of their methods may be called *forced-choice* technique. Let us use the method of constant stimuli in which stimuli ranging between some value below threshold and some value above it are presented to the S in a random order. Using a forced-choice technique, intervals of time are marked off (by a tone, for example). In one of these intervals the stimulus appears. S is asked to indicate which interval contained the stimulus. Let us suppose that we marked off four intervals. On the basis of chance, then, even if no stimulus were presented, S would pick the correct interval 25 per cent of the time. We must correct for the possibility of his guessing, since we wish to examine his responses which differ from chance. At a stimulus value which was clearly below the level which he could detect, he would correctly choose the interval once in four times. He would be wrong, on the average, three out of four times, or 75 per cent. Our formula for correcting for chance is:

$$\frac{per\ cent\ correct\ -\ per\ cent\ chance\ correct}{per\ cent\ chance\ incorrect}$$

If S gets 50 per cent of the intervals correct on a four-choice design, the formula would be (50 per cent − 25 per cent)/75 per cent. This level on our first graph, then, would be 33⅓ per cent. Seventy-five per cent is a divisor to help account for the decreasing role chance plays as the possibility of detection becomes higher. Thus if S gets all of the intervals correct (100 per cent), the formula would be (100 per cent − 25 per cent)/75 per cent, which equals 100 per cent. By computing these values for each stimulus intensity, we may construct a graph similar to that shown in Figure 3-1. The ordinate would contain the percentages as corrected for chance by the formula. The threshold is still taken as the 50 per cent (corrected) value.

The detection theorist uses similar techniques for locating the differential threshold. An increment is added to a prevailing stimulus, and S is asked to tell in which interval the increment appeared.

Stevens's Power Law

Another divergent trend from classical psychophysics involves the construction of the scale for sensation. Following Weber, G. T. Fechner's method of finding this scale was to locate the differential threshold all the way up the intensity scale and to consider these jnd's units of measurement. S. S. Stevens of Harvard has what he feels is a better method of scaling sensation.

When Fechner added up his jnd's across the scale of intensity, he derived a function which related intensity to sensation in a logarithmic fashion (see Figure 3-5). That is, the distance in jnd's from 1 to 10 intensity units is the same as the distance in jnd's from 10 to 100, from 100 to 1,000, or from 0.01 to 0.1, etc. Fechner's revision of Weber's law states: $S = K \log_{10} I$. He believed that he had constructed a useful interval scale, at the very least. Stevens (1957), on the other hand, thinks differently. He believes that what Fechner was doing in constructing such a scale was "quantifying error." At the time that Fechner was writing his *Elemente der Psychophysik* (1860), another psychophysicist, J. A. F. Plateau, was using a much different technique for relating the strength of a sensation to the intensity of the stimulus which arouses it. Plateau's technique, which is akin to that used by Stevens, is a far more direct method, calculated to produce a ratio scale directly by asking the subject for a ratio judgment. Stevens's subjects are given one stimulus and asked to set another stimulus so that it appears twice as intense or half as intense to them. For example, S is confronted with two lights, a standard and a variable. He can adjust the variable and is asked to do so. His task is to set the variable light until it appears half as bright as the other light. Stevens has shown that subjects can give remarkably reliable judgments on this task, using the "method of bisection."

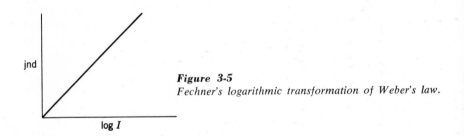

Figure 3-5
Fechner's logarithmic transformation of Weber's law.

If the larger problem, that of relating intensity to sensation, is examined, what kind of results does Stevens obtain? He finds that sensation rises as the power function of intensity. Mathematically stated, $S = KI^n$. We need not be concerned about K, which is an arbitrary constant that varies from sense to sense. I^n is the important element. As intensity is raised to the nth power, sensation is linearly changed.

At best, this situation is very complicated. A "decision" between Stevens's power law and Fechner's logarithmic law would require a great deal more information than we are prepared to give in this limited space. Suffice it to say that Stevens has collected some extremely convincing evidence in favor of the power-function shape of the relationship between sensation and intensity and that it appears that contemporary psychophysicists will increasingly adopt his point of view and techniques in investigations of this difficult topic.

Recent Innovations in Studying Higher-order Perception

Traditional psychophysics and even the recent change by such persons as the detection theorists and Stevens deal with a limited problem, namely, the construction of a psychological scale which bears some functional relationship to an obvious physical dimension, the scale of which is already known.

There are some important perceptual parameters which traditional psychophysical approaches are not designed to measure. We shall discuss the two important areas which are beyond the reach of classically oriented methods and state some of the recent innovations which show great promise in helping us to understand the determination of the variables.

Motives, Expectations, and Other Subject Variables

In describing the use of the forced-choice method by the detection theorists, we mentioned that this method was adopted to correct for the guessing habits of those *S*s using high or low crtieria in deciding whether the stimulus exists or not. In other words, the subject is considered an extraneous variable to be controlled.

Other investigators have deliberately been concerned with how subject variables such as motives, incentives, and expectations alter the value of the differential threshold. Thus, if *S* receives 25 cents for correctly detecting its presence and 10 cents for correctly detecting its absence and if it costs him 10 cents for each error, the number of false responses increases and the size of the threshold changes. Similarly, if the monetary rewards and penalties, called the *payoff function,* are held constant but the number of catch trials is increased, the threshold will also change. A very clear discussion of the application of this method, which is a derivation of *decision theory* and the theory of games, is presented by Galanter (1962). In Chapter 12, "Social Perception, Motives, and Personality," we shall discuss in detail and attempt a systematic theoretical synthesis of a number of studies dealing with the effect of motives on perceptual discrimination.

Another problem involves the measurement of such subjective variables as cuteness, beauty, and sexual attractiveness, for which no known physical scale exists. Attneave (1962, pp. 629–630) alludes to attempts by himself and Hochberg to develop complex psychophysical matrices to measure the relatedness in physical stimulus patterns which correlate with these subjective and esthetically important dimensions.

Measurement of Patterns

Beside the problem of measuring subjective variables for which a physical-scale parallel is unknown, we also must go beyond traditional psychophysics to measure the determination of how we perceive patterns of stimulation or combinations of more than one dimension. The gestalt psychologists in the early years gave us a qualitative set of principles to describe the grouping of stimulus elements or dimensions into a form, a gestalt. More recently such persons as Attneave have shown us how the application of such mathematical systems as information theory and set theory can be made to quantify the gestalt laws and other laws describing the determination of such perceptual segregations as recognizable form.

Attneave discusses the problem of multidimensional psychophysics in the publication just cited, on pages 631–633, and we shall describe much related work in detail in Chapters 7 and 8. These techniques have also been applied to studying concepts and thinking and other cognitive phenomena, as we shall see in later chapters. It is interesting to note that in Attneave's 1962 article he also discusses the intrinsic relatedness between perception and the other cognitive phenomena.

Summary

This chapter consisted of three broad sections. The first described briefly the classical psychophysical determination of thresholds and single-dimensional scales. The second discussed some modified methods designed to study the same problems investigated by traditional approaches. Finally, we mentioned the fact that recent innovations in methodology now give us an approach to the measurement of more elusive subjective variables, such as beauty and familiar identities.

4

Basic Psychophysical Functions

Before moving to a study of higher perceptual processes, it is desirable that some of the more basic visual data be examined. In Chapter 3 we discussed some of the common psychophysical methods. This chapter will concern itself with a discussion of some of the visual data which have been collected and systematized by using psychophysical methods.

It is not within the scope of this book to discuss the physics and physiology of the visual process. Most good introductory psychology textbooks cover this topic adequately, and we leave it to the reader to decide whether he needs a review of this information before proceeding with this chapter.

In the discussion which follows, we shall examine some of the important variables bearing on the transformation of light energy into neural energy. Some of these variables relate to the *state of the organism;* most relate to the *nature of the stimulus.* In the majority of the studies our dependent variable will be a threshold stated as it was defined in Chapter 3. We shall organize the discussion around *the major independent variables which affect visual thresholds.* It should be noted that we shall be examining numerous different types of threshold measurements. In many cases, we shall be using absolute threshold as our measure. In others, the dependent variable, threshold, will refer to somewhat higher processes, for example, the rate at which a flickering light appears steady or the minimum separation between lines in a grid which O can perceive.

There is one concept that we shall repeatedly employ in the discussion which follows, and perhaps it is well to define it at the outset so that the discussion will not be interrupted. The concept is that of the *visual angle*. It should be apparent, after some introspection, that a target which is approaching the eye projects a larger and larger image on the retina as it comes closer. Therefore, it makes no sense to report the size of a target independent of the viewing distance. To say that a target is 5 by 5 in. does not give any information about the proportion of the retina being stimulated until we know whether the target is being viewed at arm's length or from a distance of 500 ft. Consequently, a convention is adopted which makes the absolute size of the target irrelevant and expresses all target sizes in comparable units.

If the eye is taken to be a perfect orb, any distance on the orb may be expressed by a certain number of degrees, minutes, and seconds. For any target area, if we know the distance from the eye, it is possible to calculate the angle subtended by the image on the back of the retina. As the distance from the eye to the target increases, the visual angle decreases. Similarly, it is possible to speak of a stimulus location on the back of the retina, using the center of the fovea as a reference point, as being a given number of degrees from the fovea in a specified direction. This concept will prove most convenient in the ensuing discussion.

State of the Organism

While there can be no clear-cut separation between the receptor state of the organism and the nature of stimulus (the very fact that the latter stimulates the former implies an interaction between the two), we can nevertheless for systematic reasons separate the component parts. We shall begin with the effect of the state of the organism on the threshold value, then move to the effect of the kind of stimulus used, and finally deal with some effects of spatial and temporal patterning. In all these cases we shall try to give the reader an idea of the major variables affecting the sensory coding or transduction of visual information.

Retinal Locus

It is well known that the retina varies in sensitivity in its different parts. Mostly, this variation is due to the differential distribution across the retina of the rods and cones, which are the receptors for vision. Since rods have a lower threshold than cones, spots on the retina which are rich in rods should yield a lower threshold than the all-cone fovea. The anatomical distribution of rods and cones in the human retina was plotted by Østerberg (1935), who took a single human right eye and laboriously counted the rods and the cones from various sample locations in the retina. For the horizontal meridian of the eye, his data are plotted in Figure 4-1.

The fovea, as had been predicted from behavioral evidence, is devoid

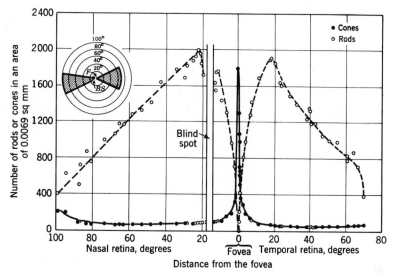

Figure 4-1

Distribution of rods and cones throughout the retina. The number of end organs per unit-area from the fovea to the extreme periphery has been plotted. Cones are represented by solid, rods by open, circles. The inset shows the regions sampled by Østerberg (1935) in obtaining the counts. (From Chapanis, 1949.)

of rods, whereas the cone density reaches 147,000 cones per square millimeter. The cone population drops sharply as one moves in any direction away from the fovea. The rod population, absent in the fovea, rises to a high level about 15 to 20° on either side of the fovea. Østerberg's data indicate that the nasal retina (the side nearer the nose) is more richly supplied with rods than is the temporal retina (nearer the temple). In many of the following studies, the effect depends upon the portion of the retina stimulated, since it is determined by the type of receptor stimulated.

State of Adaptation

As we may recall, both rods and cones contain chemical substances which break down as a function of exposure to light. When these chemicals are left in the dark for a period of time, a regeneration occurs which makes the concentration higher and, consequently, the cells more sensitive to light. Both light and dark adaptation have been studied, and they may be conceived as roughly opponent processes. For any given amount of light stimulation, an equilibrium is achieved in the photochemical substance. A decrease in light intensity results in a regeneration process and in a consequent increase in concentration and decrease in visual threshold. An increase in stimulation bleaches a greater number of molecules of the substance, decreases the concentration, and raises the subsequent threshold.

The dark-adaptation curve which is usually presented in introductory textbooks is generated in the following way. Using a trained *O,* visual threshold is taken as the dependent variable, and time in the dark becomes the independent variable. *O*'s eye is exposed to a bright visual field for a few minutes, and he is then placed in a dark room where his visual threshold is measured immediately and at successive intervals until the threshold reaches a stable, low point (about 40 min). Obviously, in determining *O*'s threshold, it is necessary to present several stimuli of near-threshold intensity. These test flashes have some effect upon *O*'s threshold, but their effect is ignored in the plot of the curve since any experiment attempting to control the effect of the flashes would be very tedious and probably not worth the additional effort. The usual dark-adaptation curve is shown in Figure 4-2.

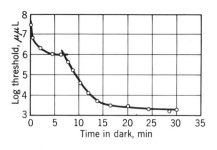

Figure 4-2

The course of dark adaptation following a high level of light adaptation. The first section of the curve is for the cones; the second, for the rods. The test light was restricted to the shorter waves, below 460 mμ, and appeared violet to the cones. (Reproduced by permission from Geldard, 1953, p. 35.) Threshold values are in micromicrolamberts (μμL). (From Hecht and Schlaer, 1938.)

It can be seen that the curve clearly is divisible into two parts. The first portion of the curve is referable to adaptation processes in the cones. Adaptation in the cones is complete in about 10 min. The second portion of the curve represents dark adaptation in the rods which has been occurring since the onset of the experiment. The cone curve obscures the effect of rod adaptation during the first 10 min, however, since the cones are adapting at a faster rate. The entire process is complete in 30 to 40 min and represents a 100,000:1 increase in sensitivity. It should be noted that the curve in Figure 4-2 does not depend upon pupillary dilation. *O* views the test flashes through an aperture which is smaller than his pupil, so that pupillary dilation and constriction can have no effect.

The curve in Figure 4-2 was generated by using a test flash presented at about 15 or 20° in the nasal retina. If the flash had been confined to the fovea, where only cones are present, only the first portion of the curve would be produced. The typical rod-cone break is present only if both rods and cones are being sampled.

Of course, the variable of preadaptation has an important effect upon the shape of the dark-adaptation curve. If *O* were subjected to an intense preexposure field for a long time prior to being placed in the dark, the cone segment of the curve would be more prominent. On the other hand, if *O* were adapted only to a feeble light prior to the test, the cone curve would be missing altogether.

Nature of the Stimulus

While areal and temporal summation effects on intensity as well as the wavelength composition must interact with such organismic factors as retinal locus to affect the threshold, we shall now consider the stimulus side of this relationship.

Effect of Stimulus Area

Under certain conditions, the eye appears able to summate energy across an area. *Ricco's law* states: $I \times A = K$. That is, the product of area and intensity yields a constant effect for a constant product. If intensity is doubled and area is halved, the effect remains the same. To *O* an increase in area would appear the same as an increase in intensity if Ricco's law holds. Another law, *Piper's law,* pertains to the peripheral retina. It states $I \sqrt{A} = K$. A phenomenon apparently related to areal summation is Abney's effect. If a large patch of light is illuminated all at once, the light appears to come on first in the center of the patch and then spread to the edges. Similarly, if the patch of light is extinguished immediately, the last sensation to fade is that associated with the center of the light. The edges disappear first, and the sensation appears to shrink to a central spot. This effect was at one time rather difficult to account for.

Exploration of area effects (Graham, Brown, and Mote, 1939) has shown the situation to be more complicated than either Ricco's or Piper's law would suggest. Ricco's law has been shown to hold, both for the fovea and the periphery, for very small flashes (up to about 10′ visual angle). Piper's law is in effect, in the periphery, between about 2 and 7° visual angle. In explaining their findings, Graham et al. hypothesized that each retinal element contributes to the total excitatory effect at the center of the stimulation by a factor of $1/r^p$, where r is the distance of the receptor from the center of the stimulation and p is an exponential constant. This hypothesis can handily account for Abney's effect. Since the receptors near the edge of stimulation are contributing less excitation and, in general, are less excited by neighboring receptors, they are expected to stop firing soonest. The last receptors to stop firing are near the center of the stimulation because they are receiving the excitation from neighboring receptors and because, according to the Graham, Brown, and Mote hypothesis, they are contributing the greatest excitatory effect to the total. In short, there is more summation at the center of stimulation and in the foveal area.

Effect of Duration

The retina is able to summate temporally as well as spatially up to a certain critical duration. After that duration, intensity becomes the sole determiner of threshold.

There is a general law which holds for many photochemical processes. This reciprocity equation, called the Bunsen-Roscoe law (see Chapter 2), states: $I \times T = K$. That is, intensity and time are interchangeable in the same way that intensity and area are related in Ricco's law. The Bunsen-Roscoe law is a surprisingly general law, predicting well in many kinds of photochemical reactions. It holds for the exposure of film in a camera, the germination of plant seedlings, etc. Since the initiation of the visual response is a photochemical process, one would expect the Bunsen-Roscoe law to hold here also. It does, up to 0.1 sec, the so-called critical duration. All light arriving in that first 0.1 sec is summated by the eye, so that it does not matter whether the light is spread evenly across the interval or most of it arrives in the last instant of the interval.

Apparently, the critical duration represents the time at which back processes begin in the eye. Temporal summation has been most adequately investigated by Graham and Margaria (1935) in a classic paper. Examining the relationship between critical duration and area subtended by the flash, they found, with very small areas, a clear break at about 0.1 sec. As they tested with larger areas, the break was less distinct, although it was still evident.

Effect of Wavelength

Figure 4-3 demonstrates the dependence of the threshold upon the wavelength of the light being used to stimulate the eye. Two curves are presented, one taken with relatively bright lights in the fovea (the cone curve), the other with dim flashes in the periphery of the eye after dark adaptation is complete (rod curve). Examination of the rod curve shows that maximum sensitivity is at a wavelength of about 511 mμ. The cone curve has a maximum sensitivity at about 555 mμ. The difference between these two curves accounts for the Purkinje shift, the shift in relative brightnesses of various hues or wavelengths of light as the observer switches from rod to cone vision. Let us examine an idealized experimental demonstration of the Purkinje shift.

Using a psychophysical observer who has had some experience in making judgments of equality between two stimuli, we place before him two relatively bright lights of different wavelengths. For example, let us give him a light of 511 mμ and one of 555 mμ. We set the 511-mμ light at a brightness of 100 units. We now ask O to make the 555-mμ light equal in appar-

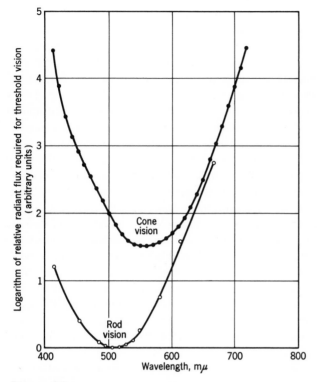

Figure 4-3
Photopic (cone) and scotopic (rod) visibility curves compared. The relative amounts of energy needed to reach absolute threshold as a function of wavelength. The cone curve is derived from the data of K. S. Gibson and Tyndall (1923); the rod curve, from those of Hecht and Williams (1922). (From Chapanis, 1949. Reproduced by permission from Geldard, 1953, p. 32.)

ent brightness. As we can deduce from his spectral sensitivity curves, as shown in Figure 4-3, he is less sensitive to light at 511 mμ than to light at 555 mμ (cone function). As a consequence, it takes less light at 555 mμ to appear equal in brightness to a light of 511 mμ. Let us say that O sets the 555-mμ light at 80 units.

Now, let us take the same observer and ask him to make a similar adjustment in very dim light, too feeble to excite the cones. Again, we set the 511 mμ light, this time at 10 units, and we ask him to make the 555-mμ light appear equal in brightness. Our subject, who is operating with the characteristic of the lower curve in Figure 4-3, is most sensitive to a light of 511 mμ and somewhat less sensitive to the 555-mμ light. As a consequence, he requires more energy at 555 mμ for the light to appear equal in brightness to the standard.

If we ask O to make this brightness match, using either photopic (cone) or scotopic (rod) vision, and then change the intensity until the other curve constitutes his operating characteristic, the lights no longer appear equal in brightness. This is the phenomenon known as the Purkinje shift. To restate the effect, it is the change in relative brightnesses of stimuli of differing wavelength as a function of the state of dark adaptation, or the shift from rod to cone vision, when making the brightness comparison.

This phenomenon can be observed under more naturalistic conditions. We may note two patches of color—flowers, for example, of differing hue— to be of equal brightness in the daytime. As sunset approaches, however, the relative brightnesses of the flowers changes until, by moonlight, the two flowers are quite different. If, for example, one of the flowers were red in the daytime, it would now be nearly invisible, while a blue flower, which was identical in brightness, would now appear gray.

There are basically three aspects or psychological attributes of color, each of which is related to a change in the physical dimension of light wave: (1) Changes in hue are directly referable to changes in the wavelength of the stimulus. (2) Changes in brightness are related to changes in the amplitude of the stimulating wave, the amount of energy contained in the wave. (3) Changes in saturation are effected by the addition of white light to the stimulus. The more white light is mixed with the stimulus, the less saturated is the resulting color. Figure 4-4 shows one way of representing this state of affairs.

The vertical axis of the color spindle in Figure 4-4 ranges from black to white through a series of discriminable differences in gray. This is the brightness dimension. The radius of the spindle represents the dimension of saturation. Hue is represented on the perimeter of the spindle. When we examine the largest portion of the spindle, it is clear that the greatest saturation may be obtained with colors which match this middle gray in brightness. As brightness is either increased or decreased, less range is possible in saturation.

The perimeter of the spindle, representing hue, contains all the visible wavelengths, plus some wavelength combinations not in the spectrum. "Fire-engine" red, for example, which is considered psychologically "pure" red, is, in reality, a mixture of red and purple. All the spectral reds appear somewhat yellowish to the observer. If a straight line is drawn from any point on the perimeter through the central axis to the other side of the perimeter, the two points opposing one another across this diagonal will constitute complementary colors. The mixture by addition of these two colors in equal proportions will produce the *gray* at the central axis. When we say "mixture by addition," we are referring to spectral mixing which occurs, for example, when colors are mixed through filters. Another way to get the same effect, as we remember from introductory psychology demonstrations, is to mix two color disks on overlapping color wheels. When the two colors are complementary, the observer will see gray. The most notable

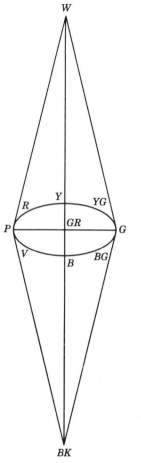

Figure 4-4
The color spindle in its simplest form. (Geldard, 1953, p. 52.)

pairs of complementary colors are red and blue green, green and red blue, and blue and yellow. It is clear that the gray obtained from additive mixture of these complementaries is quite different from the intermediate blends obtained by mixing pigments of these colors. Pigment mixing is a subtractive process. The existence of complementary colors and other color phenomena have raised the question of the nature of color sensation. The theoretical debate which has been waged for many years cannot be gone into here. A theory which survived for a long time was the Young-Helmholtz theory, which postulated three primary physical colors—red, green, and blue—and three types of corresponding receptors. The psychological color, yellow, came from a mixture of red and green. This theory could handle the three sets of complementary colors mentioned in the last paragraph as well as certain phenomena of color adaptation.

A theory developed more recently, called the opponent-color theory, which is based on the views of Hering, who opposed Helmholtz, can be studied by the interested reader in the original publication (Hurvich and Jameson, 1955). While the controversy has not been completely resolved, this theory, which proposes four colors in two pairs—yellow-blue and red-green—accounts well for the facts of color mixing, color blindness, and other phenomena. In any case, it is astounding that 350,000 jnd's of hue can be distinguished.

Patterning

Up to this point, we have been speaking of relatively low-level processes, but there are two important areas which we should discuss before leaving the topic of basic visual data. These involve a higher level of recognition on the part of *O,* at least in terms of the perceptual hierarchy. Both processes are a kind of acuity. One is the more familiar visual acuity, by which we mean spatial acuity; the other involves the ability to resolve temporal patterns. The latter is therefore a kind of temporal acuity and is measured by critical flicker frequency (CFF).

Spatial Acuity

How well the eye is able to resolve patterns is, in part, determined by the method we use to measure acuity. There are several different measures, and the amount of resolution possible depends upon the way acuity is measured.

The most common measure of visual acuity is the familiar eye chart utilized in testing for visual anomalies. The chart usually has rows of letters with the elements of the letters (the bars of an E, for example) separated by a known distance, yielding a known visual angle from the point of the observer. Probably the crudest measure of visual acuity, the eye chart is seldom used in laboratory situations because context effects (the known shape of the letters, for example) interfere with accurate measurement. The resolution defined as "normal" is 1' of visual arc, and the person who is just able to resolve this angle is designated as having 20/20 vision. That is, he is able to resolve at 20 ft what the average or normal person is able to resolve at 20 ft (this was the distance originally used in standardizing acuity data). If the subject is not able to resolve that well, he may, for example, receive a score of 20/40, meaning he is able to resolve at 20 ft a gap that the average person is able to resolve at 40 ft.

In the laboratory setting, many different types of targets are used. One common target is the Landolt C, a circle with a gap located at some point on its perimeter. Such circles differ in both size and location of the gap. *O*'s task is to indicate the position of the break.

Another type of pattern is the grid target, which is constructed of a series of closely spaced parallel lines. If *O* is unable to resolve the grid pattern, it appears to him as a homogeneous gray surface.

The method which yields the lowest estimate of acuity is the measurement of vernier acuity. Two fine vertical lines, one projecting downward and the other upward, just meet at the tips. The lower line may be moved out of position so that the tips of the lines no longer meet. *O*'s task is to adjust the lower line until he just perceives a discontinuity. With vernier acuity measurements, *O* is able to discriminate approximately 2″ of visual arc.

There are two variables which make a significant difference in spatial acuity. One is *illumination*. In general, the brighter the target, the better the visual acuity, up to some upper limit at which additional increases in brightness have virtually no effect. The other variable is *position* of the image upon the retina. As we know, when we wish to examine an object closely, we direct the image of that object so that it falls on the fovea of the eye. This is the best-seeing part of the retina, probably because the cones there are extremely densely packed and consequently slender and because they have a one-to-one correspondence at the retinal level. That is, they are not richly interconnected, as the receptors in the periphery are. Acuity measures taken at different points on the fovea reveal a sharp drop in acuity just a few degrees from its center. Acuity in the periphery is extremely poor. Of course, there is one case in which the fovea is less acute than the periphery. If the intensity of illumination is too weak to excite the cones, then all the vision must be mediated by rods. As a consequence, the stimulus falling on the fovea is invisible.

Temporal Acuity

In introducing this section, we mentioned the CFF as a measure of temporal acuity. If a light is turned on and off at a high rate, it appears to be steady and is said to fuse. The rate at which the light is flickering when it first appears to fuse is called the *critical flicker frequency*. The CFF, then, is taken as a measure of temporal acuity, or the ability to resolve short durations. The higher the CFF, the greater the temporal acuity. This phenomenon has been extensively studied by investigators, varying such parameters as brightness, light-dark ratio, retinal position, area, etc.

INTENSITY. There is a general law, called the *Ferry-Porter law,* which relates intensity of the flickering light to CFF. It states that CFF is a linear function of the intensity of the flickering light. As intensity is increased, the CFF should similarly increase linearly. For a 50:50 light-dark ratio, the Ferry-Porter law appears to hold very well, although the straight-line relationship has a different slope for the rods than for the cones.

AREA. In general, increasing the area of the target appears to raise the

CFF, although the relationship is not a simple one. Apparently, both the variable of brightness and the variable of area may be assumed to affect the CFF through a general increase in energy present during the "on cycle." The more energy present during the on phase, the greater the difference between on and off phases. If this difference is a large one, O should be better able to discriminate it.

APPARENT BRIGHTNESS. One variable which has been well systematized is the apparent brightness of the flickering light. Talbot's law establishes a straightforward relationship between the brightness of the flickering light, the proportion of time the light is on, and the proportion of time the light is off. It simply states that the light will be totally utilized. One form of Talbot's law is

$$B_a = \frac{B_o A}{A + B}$$

where B_a is apparent brightness, B_o is objective brightness, A is the proportion of time the light is on, and B is the proportion of time the light is off. According to Talbot's law, therefore, a light which is flickering in a 50:50 light-dark ratio should have the same apparent brightness as a steady light of half the intensity. Talbot's law is quite accurate under most circumstances, although Bartley (1951) reports an "enhancement effect" at around 10 cps. Lights flickering at around this rate appear brighter than Talbot's law would predict. Bartley hypothesizes that the enhancement at this frequency bears some relationship to the alpha rhythm of the brain, which for most Ss is about 10 cps, but evidence for this speculation is lacking.

Summary

In this chapter we described some of the major variables which determine the precision with which the eye as a sensory receptor can perform perceptual task 1, i.e., the detection of light or change in light. We grouped these variables affecting threshold into three classes, which, of course, have interacting effects. Under the heading "State of the Organism" we examined effects of retinal locus and receptor adaptation. Under "Nature of the Stimulus" we dealt with the factors of spatial area, temporal duration, and wavelength composition. Under "Patterning" we described the phenomenon of spatial acuity and a kind of temporal acuity measured by the CFF.

5

A Context for
Brightness Constancy

The world which we see does not consist simply of a collection of scattered light intensities and nuances of hue. Rather, it is organized into certain units and patterns, which we call attributes and which seem reliable, orderly, and dependable. That is to say, the perceptual world seems to remain fairly constant in spite of large-scale variation in the energy patterns which reach the retina.

Some of the kinds of things we see in the environment, therefore, maintain certain *invariant properties* with respect to changes in physical energy. We refer to these perceived invariant properties as the perceptual constancies. percep is same, stim. change.

The Perceptual Constancies

The first constant property of perception is organized at the level of task 2 of the hierarchy [1] and therefore primarily at the sensory level. This property is brightness constancy, which is part of the larger class called color constancy (color refers to both brightness and hue). The brightness of an object is not determined simply by the energy level of the source illuminating it but by the proportion of this incident light it reflects, relative to the proportion of the incident light reflected by comparison objects in the environment. We all know that the white, gray, or black of the vari-

[1] We define more fully the nature of brightness, size, and shape constancy as we go along in this chapter and Chapter 6.

ous objects we see in the everyday world remains fairly constant in spite of variations in incident illumination caused by such natural phenomena as strong sunlight, shadows, clouds, or twilight. This invariant property of object brightness is called *brightness constancy*.

There are other constancies, namely, shape and size, which are organized at the levels between tasks 3 and 4. A comparison of the two experiments in the next section supports this statement. *Shape constancy* refers to the fact that the perceived shape of an object remains relatively invariant with respect to changes in retinal image. Thus a rectangular book tilted away from the observer still looks like a rectangle even though its retinal shape becomes trapezoidal. *Size constancy* is seen in the following situation. We all know that the retinal size of an object decreases as its distance from the eye increases; yet the perceived size does not diminish with distance. In fact, it remains close to objectively measured size.

We can see why these three phenomena were traditionally grouped under the rubric "constancy," for each consists of a situation in which the perceived or psychological dimension does not follow change in the physical dimension. But we shall also see that the organization of brightness constancy is based primarily on retinal distribution of light energies, while size and shape constancies are influenced also by experience, attitude, and therefore, presumably, the mediational role of the cortex. First, we shall compare two experiments which indicate this difference.

This chapter goes into greater detail than the others since brightness-constancy investigations are typical of how perceptual studies have progressed. First, we ask quite naïvely (but with a disciplined attitude) the nature of the phenomena as they are revealed in perceptual experience and reports. This is called the phenomenological method. Then, we ask what the relationship is between the perceived phenomena and the physical-energy scale. This question takes us into the realm of the experiment, where we try to make our approach more quantitative and look for the source and magnitude of error.

Two Illustrative Experiments: Organization of Size Constancy at a Higher Level than Brightness Constancy

The purpose of the first experiment (Gilinsky, 1955) was to determine the effect of *attitudes* on the reported sizes of objects. A standard isosceles triangle was located at various distances directly in front of the subject; and a variable triangle, i.e., a triangle whose size could be altered, was located at a distance of 100 ft from the subject and at an angle of $36°26'$ to the right of the line of sight. The triangles, which were made of white-colored sheet aluminum, were seen against a background of grassy terrain, remote trees, and buildings at the far end of a field. There were four standard triangles, whose heights varied in 1-ft steps from $3\frac{1}{2}$ to $6\frac{1}{2}$ ft.

The subject judged the height of one standard triangle at a time, the height of the variable being altered until he considered it equal to the height of the standard. This was done by instructing the experimenter to lower or raise the variable in a pit in the ground. Such judgments were made of the four standards, located at distances up to about 4,000 ft. The method of adjustment was thus used.

Judgments of height at each distance were made under two sets of instructions. Under one set *S* was asked to alter the variable until it equaled the size of the standard, despite appearances to the contrary. These judgments were called *objective* matches because they were estimates of the actual size of the object. Under the second set of instructions *S* was told to alter the size of the variable until it equaled the size of the standard as it appeared at the moment, even though he knew it was bigger. These judgments were called *retinal* matches because *S* was instructed to follow as closely as he could the reduction in retinal-image size with distance. The average results of Gilinsky's experiment are shown in Figure 5-1.

It is quite clear from an inspection of Figure 5-1 that the two sets of instructions led to different sizes of matches. We know that the size of the retinal image of an object decreases as its distance from the eye increases. This is shown in the retinal-size curve in the figure. We see that the retinal matches follow this curve very closely. It would be safe to say that the retinal matches resulted from the discrimination of immediate sensory stimulation on the retina, with little intervention from central processes. But what about the objective matches? Here we see that size constancy closely

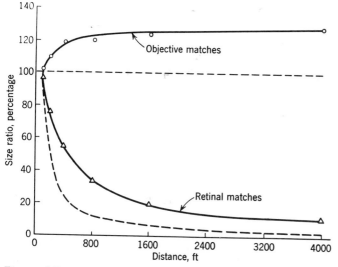

Figure 5-1
Objective and retinal matches plotted as ratios of the size of the variable to the size of the standard. (*After Gilinsky, 1955, p. 183.*)

followed the object-size level; in fact, there was overconstancy—i.e., *S* overestimated the size of the distant standard. It is indeed remarkable that the human organism is able to give two widely differing reports of size under the same condition of retinal stimulation. In fact, Jenkin and Hyman (1959) in a separate study concluded from a factor analysis of their data that perceptual judgments under retinal and objective attitudes were independent of each other. Further verification comes from V. R. Carlson (1960), who found no relationship between judgments of apparent and objective size.

We turn now to a brightness experiment (Gelb, 1929) in which the observer cannot make two highly distinct discriminations under the same pattern of stimulation. In a room where several objects are faintly lit by a ceiling light, a rotating *black* disk, illuminated by an intense but concealed lantern, is placed in the foreground. The beam of the lantern falls exactly on the area of the disk, no additional light being cast on the background. Observers report seeing a *white* disk standing in dim light, and this impression is very compelling. A small piece of white paper is then brought into the rotating disk. Instantly the disk is reported as "turning into" its objective black color, and the beam "becomes" very intense. When the white paper is removed, the disk dramatically changes back to white. These sudden reversals of perceived brightness can be induced with perfect consistency merely by moving the white paper in and out of the beam. Knowledge makes no difference in the perception.

In comparing these two experiments, we should note that in the first one the subject could ignore the relationship between size and distance if he wished, whereas in the second he could not ignore the relationship between the light reflected by the black disk and the light reflected by the white paper.

We use these two experiments to introduce a discussion of the perceptual constancies. The first example is an illustration of size constancy, which refers to the fact that the perceived size does not regularly follow changes in the retinal size of the object, providing there are adequate cues to distance. But it is very important to keep in mind that the observer can give either constancy or retinal matches under these conditions of adequate cues to distance perception. When cues to distance have been removed, he naturally can give only a retinal match. In the case of brightness constancy, however, as shown in the second experiment, the subject can give only one discrimination in each of the conditions: a sensing of illumination intensity when he is not able to compare the brightnesses of objects and a perception of objective brightness when he can compare the brightness of an object with that of at least one other object.

Brightness constancy thus refers to the fact that the perceived brightness of an object does not regularly follow changes in incident illumination, providing the subject is able to observe the total conditions of illumination.

As we have seen, however, the observer cannot ignore these illumination conditions as he can under one of the conditions in the size-constancy experiments. This suggests that a judgmental process is more deeply involved in size constancy than in brightness constancy. Brightness constancy, we shall attempt to show, is determined by built-in programming, whereas size constancy is also influenced by modified programming. We shall then take a look at shape constancy to round out the picture.

We proceed first to a fuller examination of the most primitive of the constancies, brightness constancy.

Brightness and Color Constancy

David Katz (1935), in his famous work on the phenomenal appearance of color, noted that there was a tremendous dissimilarity between the scale of perceptible illumination changes and the scale of detectable whiteness differences. In fact, the ratio of the highest illumination in which objects are detectable to the lowest illumination in which they are noticeable is of the order of several thousand to one. The corresponding ratio of the whitest white to the blackest black is only 60:1. Although Katz pointed out this important fact, that there was a difference between the illumination scale and the whiteness-constancy scale, he actually referred to the latter phenomenon as brightness constancy.[2]

It is now customary to treat *brightness* and *whiteness* as synonymous terms and to use the terms *luminance* (physical) and *luminosity* (psychological effect) to refer to changes caused by variations in illumination. Actually, brightness constancy is an aspect of what is more generally called color constancy. Hue constancy and brightness constancy together constitute color constancy. In this chapter we shall deal primarily with brightness constancy. Toward the end of the chapter, however, we shall relate it to other aspects of color constancy, including color contrast, adaptation, and induction.

Nature of Brightness Constancy

Katz was one of the first psychologists to give a good phenomenological description of the modes of appearances of color under a variety of physical conditions. The first important distinction he made was between *surface* and *film* color. The latter refers to color or light which seems to be amorphous and unattached to any object. Surface color, on the other hand, is seen as "belonging" to the surface of an object (Katz, 1911). In surface color, for example, the brightness is seen as an integral part of a *segregated*

---

[2] Koffka (1935) has stated it would be more accurate to speak of whiteness constancy.

unit or figure (task 2 in our hierarchy). Thus brightness constancy will hold only for surface colors, and a surface color must have a constant physical property to correspond to its psychological counterpart. In the case of brightness constancy, this constant physical property is termed *albedo*.

ALBEDO. Every object which has any reflecting surface has a property, an index of reflection, which we call its albedo. The albedo is a measure which tells us which proportion of incident light the object will reflect. Thus, a good white has an albedo of 0.85 or 85 per cent, which means it reflects about 85 per cent of the light that it receives. Similarly, a dark gray or a black has an albedo of 0.14 or 14 per cent, and intermediate grays have albedos which range between these limits. (Theoretically, a pure black does not exist since it would have an albedo of zero, and we would not see it at all.) We can express albedo in the formula $A = R/I$, where A is albedo, R the intensity of reflected light, and I the intensity of incident light. Thus, if an object receives light with an intensity of, say, 200 ft-c and reflects 160 ft-c, it has an albedo of 0.80 or 80 per cent. If it receives 150 ft-c, it will reflect 120 ft-c.

In everyday life the objects around us are numerous and have varying albedos, ranging from very low to very high. Even though the illumination which falls on them varies from bright daylight to the shadows of twilight, they will, under ordinary conditions, maintain their relative brightness because they always reflect a constant proportion of the light they receive; that is, the *ratios of the light they reflect must be constant because their albedos are constant.*

Prevalence of Brightness Constancy under Known Illumination Conditions

The three techniques described in this section show the general conditions which must be met if brightness-constancy perception is to prevail.

THE STANDARD EXPERIMENT: THE SHADOW METHOD AND ITS IMPLICATIONS. The experimental situation is illustrated in Figure 5-2. The observer sits in the experimental room as shown. Color wheel *A* contains a white disk. Color wheel *B*, which is in good daylight illumination, contains a white disk and a black disk which overlap so that the proportion of white in relation to black can be varied before the wheel is spun. In an application of the method of adjustment, the observer instructs the experimenter to change the proportion of white on *B* until it appears equal in whiteness to *A*. Katz reports the results for typical observers. In situation II, in which the reduction screen [3] was used, B typically contained only about 4.2° white; i.e., there was almost a complete lack of whiteness constancy. In situation I, however, when the reduction screen was removed, the amount of white

---

[3] A reduction screen obscures the surround or background.

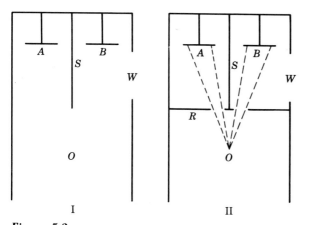

Figure 5-2
Plan of an experiment in brightness constancy, viewed from above.
(After D. Katz, 1911, p. 181.)

on *B* increased to 116°, or a fair amount of constancy. (Degrees can be converted to percentages or proportions, with 360° equal to 100 per cent or 1.) With the reduction screen the brightness match in *B* is much lower than the albedo equivalent in *A* because the latter is in a shadow. In other words, we get a match according to luminance or luminosity. But when the reduction screen is removed, the brightness match increases sharply, indicating a brightness-constancy perception. An explanation of these results will be given after related data have been described, but a clue already suggests itself. The destruction of constancy caused by the reduction screen must have affected the obscuring of the background as a reference source.

Exposure time also influenced constancy. The best results were obtained for an observation duration of 3.4 sec. As Katz lowered the duration of observation to 1.7, 1.1, and less than 1 sec by using tachistoscopic exposures, there was a corresponding decrease in the proportion of whiteness perceived in situation I. But even with an exposure time of 0.0017 sec, during which the shadowed disk was hardly perceptible, the proportion of white was appreciably higher than with the reduction screen present. There was still some constancy. Katz believed that the lowering of observation time had the same effect as the reduction screen; i.e., it reduced the surface color to film color by preventing a good survey of the illumination conditions and the general surround. We shall refer later to the significance of the work of Leibowitz, who found that reduced exposure time actually enhanced the brightness effect if a different method, namely, that of simultaneous contrast, were used (Leibowitz and Chinetti, 1957).

Comparable results are found when a black disk at *A* is exposed in intense illumination and *B* is exposed in mild illumination. Without the reduction screen the match is a fairly black color; with the screen it is transformed to white. The other general relationship reported above also holds.

Gelb (1929) reports analogous results with chromatic disks and chromatic illumination. At different times color wheel *A* contained a white disk and various chromatic disks (red, blue, green, etc.). These disks were seen in variously colored illuminations. Again there was a fair degree of color constancy without the reduction screen but essentially no color constancy with the screen. Constancy was destroyed in the former case only under very intense chromatic illumination. The explanation for this is rather obvious. For a hue to be reflected, its physical counterpart, the wavelength, must be present in the light composition. If a relatively pure spectrum band were illuminating a disk, it would be impossible to get hue constancy unless the wavelength band matched the reflecting capability of the disk. It is worth noting here that Helson found that achromatic surfaces retain their object (surface) color even until as much as 93 per cent of the incident illumination is chromatic (Helson, 1938).

In his first book Katz developed a theory of whiteness constancy which he later modified significantly following experimental and theoretical criticisms by Gelb. As a result of the modification, the theories of Katz and Gelb became quite similar. Both men realized that it was the conditions of viewing the illumination that exerted the primary effect on color constancy. In general, if the viewing conditions are such that the retina receives a pattern of reflected light coming from the object as well as from at least one other object or some constant frame of reference, like a common background, constancy is present. Here we get a direct sensing of relative albedos. But if the common background is removed, as by a reduction screen, the incident illuminations are different, the subject cannot get a direct comparison of albedo, and constancy is lost.

Let us take a specific example, inserting values for the albedos of the surfaces in Figure 5-2.

Albedo of *A* = 0.80
Matched albedo of *B* without the reduction screen = 0.60
Albedo of background = 0.40
Intensity of incident light to *B* = 100
Intensity of incident light to *A* = 20

Therefore

Intensity of reflected light from *A* = 16 (0.80 of 20)
Intensity of reflected light from *B* = 60 (0.60 of 100)
Intensity of reflected light from the background behind *A* = 8 (0.40 of 20)
Intensity of reflected light from the background of *B* = 40 (0.40 of 100)

Consequently, *A* reflects twice as much light as its background (16:8), and *B* 1½ times as much light as its background (60:40). If the ratio in both cases were 2:1, we would have perfect constancy, and a fair amount of constancy is therefore present. But if the reduction screen is used, the retina can only respond to the relative luminances of *B* and *A*, which have a ratio of almost 4:1 (60:16); hence *B* looks much brighter than *A*. Constancy is destroyed because the retina responds to absolute luminosities, not relative albedos.

METHOD OF ILLUMINATION PERSPECTIVE. Katz used this method while distinguishing the second of his phenomenological categories, which he referred to as the psychological qualities of the *pronouncedness* and *insistence* of brightness. The observer sits in a dark room under a high-powered lamp. An ordered series of 18 achromatic colors, from white to black, is presented in front of him at a distance of 1 m. Farther away, at approximately 5 m from the observer, various grays, white, black, etc., are presented to him one at a time in random order. His task is to equate one of the colors in the near series with the one presented farther away. When the far color was white, the subject chose a white from the near series which reflected approximately twenty times as much light (absolute intensity) as the distant white. In other words, despite the fact that the far color received one-twentieth as much illumination as the near color, the subject perceived the two whites as being almost equal; i.e., there was a high degree of *whiteness constancy*.

There were, however, two differences in appearance. The nearer white seemed "lighter" or "livelier." Katz called this a difference in insistence. Some observers also reported that the nearer white appeared more genuine, whereas the distant one appeared "darker" or "veiled in darkness." Katz referred to this as a difference in pronouncedness. The white in the better illumination is therefore both more pronounced and more insistent. This distinction between pronouncedness and insistence is even more vividly demonstrated when the distant color is black. Again the observer chooses a black from the near series which is close in albedo to the distant black, but now the distant black looks more pronounced; i.e., it is a better black. The near black, reflecting absolutely more light, is still more insistent. Thus a constant brightness, with a fixed albedo, always looks most insistent in strongest illumination. But there is an interaction between albedo and illumination. In general, the whites and light grays look more pronounced in *better* illumination, whereas the blacks and dark grays look more pronounced in *poorer* illumination.

The distinction that Katz made between insistence and pronouncedness is important for at least two reasons. First, it is an excellent demonstration of the value of phenomenology in research. The earlier psychophysicists had approached their investigation of the world of color with the bias of physics and consequently were looking for psychological correlates of accepted physical dimensions. Katz, going beyond the bias of physics, reported psychological dimensions for which there were no known physical correlates unless we considered the relationship between at least two physical dimensions. This, of course, poses the difficult problem of how to measure insistence and pronouncedness.

A search for the physical determinants of insistence and pronouncedness leads to the realization of the second reason why Katz's research was important. His research indicated that we cannot explain color perceptional phenomena simply in terms of one physical dimension, like wavelength or intensity, but must seek its determination in the relationship between physical factors, such as that between albedo and intensity of illumination. Some of the psychological correlates of color are subjective dimensions, and we must attempt to determine the nature of these scales. In the case of insistence and pronouncedness, the scale values are presumably determined by the interacting effects of albedo levels and illumination intensity, but the nature of this function requires experimental determination.

Not only are insistence and pronouncedness subjective phenomena, but the entire perception of whiteness and hue is also a subjective phenomenon. Katz's work therefore advanced our research on brightness constancy by pointing our search toward its relational determiners.[3]

SEPARATELY ILLUMINATED SUBFIELDS. The technique of separately illuminated subfields was introduced by Hsia (1943). The observer is seated in front of two separately illuminated open-ended chambers, at his right and at his left. At the back of the chambers, some 5½ ft distant, a heavy black drapery is drawn across to provide a common background and eliminate any direct contrast effects. This is a variation of the shadow method, in which the two chambers receive different incident illuminations.

A number of "standard" grays were used in this experiment. The standard gray disk was located in one chamber, and the intensity of the illumination reflected from it was varied by lowering or raising a ceiling light which illuminated this chamber only. The comparison gray disk was always presented in a constant "reference" illumination which was provided by another ceiling lamp. The observer, who could not see the sources of either light, had to make a brightness match of the comparison gray with the standard gray. This was done by adjusting the brightness of the variable disk with the aid of a spotlight. Four experiments were presented under varying illumination intensities, and 12 individuals served as observers.

A typical result obtained with a standard gray of 0.12 albedo is presented in Figure 5-3. It is clear that the actual match fell between the expected whiteness match and the expected illumination match. Although there were wide individual differences, with some observers closer to an illumination match and others showing greater whiteness constancy, the

---

[3] For more information on Katz's work, see Katz (1930; 1935); MacLeod (1932).

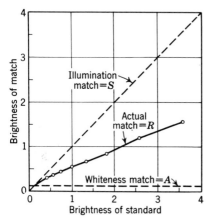

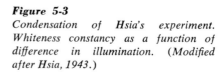

Figure 5-3
Condensation of Hsia's experiment. Whiteness constancy as a function of difference in illumination. (Modified after Hsia, 1943.)

average was about midway between the two. If the perception of the standard followed changes in illumination directly, then the actual match should have been close to the illumination match. If constancy were perfect, then the actual match should have followed the whiteness-match curve. Neither of these results occurred. Instead, we again find partial constancy.

Hsia's data are very important for at least two reasons. First, constancy was demonstrated in situations varying from the classical cases. Instead of merely comparing "normal" illumination with a shadow or intense illumination, he compared one illumination with many others. Yet constancy was observed even under these more variable conditions.

The second fact of importance is the study's indication that perceived whiteness is a *multiplicative function* of albedo and general illumination, provided there is a fairly constant reference for determining the latter; if not, a perception of illumination results. It would indeed be informative to ascertain what results would be obtained if either or both the reference illumination and the background were more variable. We would expect that there would be less whiteness constancy. The actual matches should follow the changes in physical intensity more closely.

The shadow method, separately illuminated subfields, and the method of illumination perspective all show that moderate whiteness constancy can be obtained if the observer has a constant frame of reference which indicates that the incident illumination on the two objects is different. In such cases the observer does not compare the two objects directly but judges each one relative to its background. Since the ratio of the object's albedo to its background albedo is constant, the whiteness ratios also are constant. But if the backgrounds are hidden, the subject lacks a constant frame of reference. He then has to compare the absolute reflected light of two objects directly. These brightnesses change with changes in incident illumination, and there is no basis for a constancy response. We now turn to the conditions producing such effects.

Destruction of Brightness Constancy under Obscured Illumination Conditions

Katz had argued that constancy is destroyed when surface color and film color are not distinguishable. A more general way of stating this proposition would be to say that constancy is destroyed or greatly reduced when the stimulus conditions preclude a perceived separation between the illumination reflected from the total field and that reflected from a specific object. Six of the techniques by which unification of general illumination and object color can be achieved are described in this section.

HERING'S FLECKSCHATTENVERSUCH (SHADOW SPOT EXPERIMENT). This research on shadow spots was first reported by Ewald Hering. When a small shadow is cast upon a piece of white paper, it looks like a fuzzy gray shadowed spot, the part of the paper under it retaining its white color. The gray shadow is clearly seen as superimposed on the white paper. But if we now draw a heavy black line around the shadow so that the contour coincides with the shadow's usual penumbra, the white paper in shadow instantly "turns" gray. Removing the penumbra apparently makes it difficult to detect the shadow as special low incident illumination. Thus the shadowed part is actually seen as having a darker color; an illumination match is made.

UNRECOGNIZED SHADOWS. Extending the shadow spot experiment, MacLeod (1940) obtained results which support this interpretation of Hering's findings. In an experiment modifying the classical procedure, the illumination source and shadow casts were concealed so that it was extremely difficult to judge either shadow as such. A color wheel with a disk of 180° white was exposed in a *natural shadow* (step 1). The albedo on a second wheel with a *circled shadow* was changed until it appeared as intense as the first disk (step 2). At this point the experimenter explained the entire setup, and *O* was allowed to examine the apparatus. Then whiteness matches were again made (step 3). The data were broken down on the basis of whether the observer saw two colors, two colors in shadow, or a color and a shadow.

The results showed that the uncircled disk appeared whiter than the circled one since the latter required more white for equivalent appearance. Furthermore, knowledge of the existence of the shadow made no difference: it is not what an observer knows or infers that counts, but direct effects of the stimulus pattern. It is interesting to note that the majority of subjects saw colors in both cases. Irrespective of what the observer thought he saw, however, the effect of lining the shadow was unequivocal: it decreased whiteness constancy. MacLeod reports that any object which is seen as standing in front of the illumination (be it called shadow or color) is distinctly brighter than when it is seen as part of the illumination.

Finally, it was found that whether the observers were instructed to assume a physical attitude or were told to observe naïvely made little difference in the results.

MacLeod's experiment demonstrated very potently how the perceived whiteness is dependent upon stimulus conditions. Knowledge or attitudes are unimportant in whiteness constancy. This is one difference, among others, between the various constancies which has apparently been overlooked in the literature when these phenomena have been classified together.

INUMBRAL SHADOW METHOD. This method, using a shadow without a penumbra, was developed by Kardos (1934) and extensively employed by MacLeod (1932) before the former published his experimental results. The apparatus setup, which differs only slightly from Katz's shadow method, is shown in Figure 5-4.

S and *M* can be either color wheels containing disks or disks alone. There is a white disk at *S* which receives the shadow coming from the concealed caster; the area to the left of *S*, of course, reflects more intense light. *M* stands in a general shadowed surround. If the shadow falls exactly on *S*, it appears black. If the caster is moved so that the shadow falls on part of the surround as well as the shadow, *S* immediately turns white, but it immediately returns to black if the shadow is made to fall only on it again. The experimenter can change the subject's perceived whiteness at will merely by changing the extensity of the shadow in this way; knowledge of the situation makes no difference in the results.

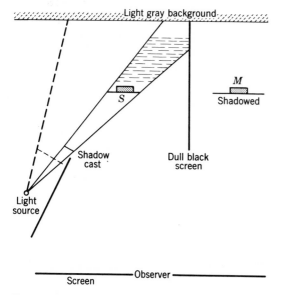

Figure 5-4
Inumbral shadow paradigm as used by Kardos and MacLeod. (After MacLeod, 1932, p. 14.)

The subject can also be asked to match the two albedos quantitatively by using color wheels. In this case, M contains much less white when the shadow falls only on S than when it falls on S and part of the surround. The differences are comparable to those obtained with the spot shadow, which were reported in the preceding section. In an experiment which is discussed in the section "Critique of Contrast Explanation of Constancy," MacLeod showed that the results hold even when contrast effects are controlled. Conceivably, the results are to be explained in terms similar to those used in our interpretation of the other shadow experiments.

Thus far we have dealt with situations in which the dimensions of a shadow are changed by manipulating its physical extensity directly. Similar results are obtained more indirectly by leaving the shadow alone and varying an aperture through which it is seen. The two instruments used to achieve this variation are the episcotister and the reduction screen.

EPISCOTISTER. The episcotister is a darkened rotating disk which allows light to pass through it during various fractions of the time. This, of course, assumes that the disk is so dark that it will not reflect any light into the eye. If the rotation speed is high enough to avoid flicker, the *Talbot-Plateau law*, which states that under this condition intermittent light stimuli produce the same sensation as a continuous flux of light applied uniformly to the eye, holds. Thus, if an individual looks at a 100 per cent white object through a rotating episcotister with a 10° opening, his retinas receive the same amount of light as that coming from a 2.75° ($^{10}\!/_{360}$) white disk viewed openly.

REDUCTION SCREEN. The results obtained with a reduction screen are actually similar to those found by MacLeod when he varied the size of the shadows. In the standard shadow method whiteness constancy is fairly good. If the disk in the shadow is viewed through a small hole in a screen, however, constancy is almost destroyed: a retinal brightness match results. But here again, whiteness constancy increases up to a point as the aperture in the screen is enlarged. This result follows because the observer now gets a better view of the surround and its reflected light pattern.

It will be remembered that Katz theorized that constancy was destroyed with the reduction screen because the latter had the effect of transforming surface color to film color. This hypothesis and his earlier theory of central transformation led to Gelb's critique and classic experiment on concealed illumination.

CONCEALED ILLUMINATION. This technique, used by Gelb, was discussed at the beginning of this chapter. Two modifications of the basic experiment produce similar results. Should the beam fall on more than the disk, constancy will prevail; i.e., the disk will look black. If we start with the first condition and then gradually increase the area covered by the beam, the change from white to black will be gradual. With a sharp increase in the beam, however, the disk will suddenly appear black. The same reversal from white to black will also occur if we stand fairly close to the disk and start and stop the rotation.

Constancy operates only when the illuminated field is heterogeneous enough to allow for the detection of the object color as separate from the illumination. As Gelb stated when he applied his hypothesis to the reduction-screen experiment: "When the disks are seen without the screen, we perceive, as Katz said, the entire conditions of illumination." That is to say, we see the *whole* visual space and its subsidiary wholes, their various shades and brightness. "When the reduction screen is used . . . it is to be noted that only unification not a reduction to a more retinal seeing has occurred" (Gelb, 1929, p. 676).

Contributing Field Factors

We have seen how Gelb accounted for whiteness constancy in terms of the articulation of the perceptual field. Objects maintain their color if the structure of the stimulus allows for their separateness. Under conditions which lead to unification of the field, constancy is lost since the object color becomes one with the general illumination. Recent research has attempted to determine more systematically what these factors are and how they interact to determine the nature of the perceptual field. Before discussing this research we should describe the general phenomena of color contrast since the studies, by and large, are related to this area.

COLOR CONTRAST, ADAPTATION, AND INDUCTION. In Chapter 4 we discussed sensory adaptation and color combining. In this section we want to relate the fact of adaptation to the effects called _color contrast_ and _color_

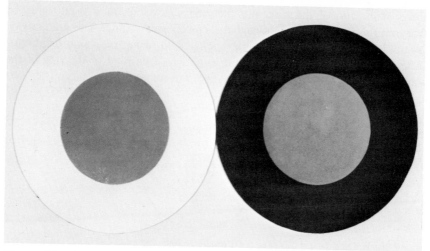

Figure 5-5
Brightness contrast.

induction. Let us look first at Figure 5-5. Although the inner circle in both cases has the same albedo, it looks brighter against the black surround and darker against the light surround. This is an example of brightness contrast. The determination of brightness contrast has caused theoretical debate, and it is not simply explained in terms of differential adaptation of the receptor cells in the area of the surround.

We find contrast in hue as well as brightness, as seen in the photograph on the front endpaper. In both cases we see that the complement of each color is induced into the inner gray circle.

That the phenomena of color contrast and color induction are not this simple can be seen by inspecting the photograph on the back endpaper. If we break the continuity of the gray ring where it intersects the border of the blue and yellow colors by drawing lines at the intersection, the complements are seen in each gray half, that is, blue against the yellow and yellow against the blue. Somehow the figural integrity of the gray ring resists the contrast effect.

Relation of Contrast Effects to Constancy

Some significant studies deal with this complex interaction. First of all, Wallach (1948) and Wallach and Galloway (1946) have attempted to explain brightness and color constancy as aspects of contrast phenomena. A schematic representation of Wallach's experiment is shown in Figure 5-6.

In general, the experiment proceeds in the following manner. By using sensitive episcotisters and projection lanterns, the standard, which consists of a light disk surrounded by a light ring, is presented to the observer. The brightness ratio of the disk and the ring can be set at a fixed value by varying the intensity of light and the episcotister setting. The comparison stimulus is projected on the same background, using the same technique. The comparison ring has a different brightness from that of the ring of the standard, and the observer has to vary the comparison's episcotister set-

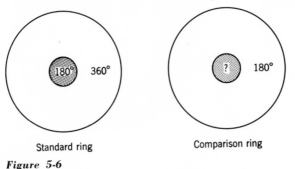

Standard ring   Comparison ring

Figure 5-6
Example of Wallach's experiment (1948).

ting until the disk appears as bright as the standard. The rest of the room is dark.

In the example shown in Figure 5-6, the ratio of ring to disk was 360:180, or 2:1, for the standard. Wallach predicts that the same ratio should hold for the comparison. Hence, since $2:1 = 180°:X$, $X = 90°$. Four observers actually gave a mean of 85°, which is fairly close to the expected 90°. A number of variations were performed, but the results were basically similar. Thus, our example is fairly typical of Wallach's general findings.

For example, in another experiment in which the rings had the same brightness, the standard disk was set at 90°. The ratio was 4:1; hence the expected setting for the comparison disk should be one-fourth of 180°, which is 45°. The obtained mean from four subjects was 47°, which again is fairly close to the expected 45°.

Wallach concludes that brightness constancy and the formation of surface colors are strictly a function of the *intensity ratios* because he found that he could change perceived brightness. merely by changing the ratios between two spots of light. If the ring was darkened, the disk appeared to be brightened, and vice versa. Wallach appears to be explaining brightness constancy in terms of contrast factors, as do he and Galloway in their experiment on hue contrast, the situation of which is depicted in Figure 5-7.

The first projection lantern P_1, partly shielded, flooded the entire space except the gray color wheel with green light. The second lantern P_2 cast a flux of white light which fell on the gray color wheel. The first match was

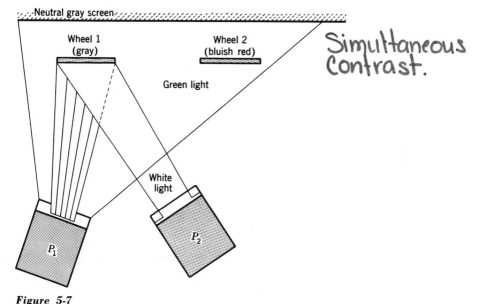

Figure 5-7
Experimental conditions for color-contrast experiment. (Wallach and Galloway, 1946.)

made through a reduction screen. Since green is the complement of bluish red, the bluish-red disk appeared gray through the reduction screen. The intensity of light coming from P_2 was varied until the two wheels appeared equally gray; but when the reduction screen was removed, the second wheel returned to its true bluish-red color while the gray wheel appeared to turn to an identical bluish red. The latter phenomenon results from simultaneous color contrast; i.e., the surrounding green light induces its complementary color, which is bluish red, into the gray color. The fact that the bluish red maintains its color only when the reduction screen is removed results from a view of the special green illumination which also falls on a background; hence, color constancy is evident.

These two parallel demonstrations led Wallach and Galloway to conclude that constancy and contrast phenomena stem from equivalent processes, but there are difficulties in this interpretation. First, what did the second experiment show? It demonstrated that perceived color is strongly determined by contrast phenomena when the illumination conditions are *obscured*. This demonstration was made in the first part of the experiment by using the reduction screen. In the second part the constancy of the second wheel was restored, but contrast then operated on the gray wheel. It is to be noted that the gray wheel and its surround received different kinds of illumination. What would happen if the experiment were carried out as before but with the white light also falling partly on the surround of the gray wheel? It is to be expected that the contrast effect would be lowered and constancy of the gray wheel would be improved.

It thus seems that Wallach and his coworkers have shown that brightness contrast and color contrast do affect perceived color but have not shown that contrast is the necessary condition for constancy to occur. For another recent attempt to interpret Gelb's results on brightness constancy as a contrast effect, the reader should see Stewart (1959).

In the other study (1948), previously referred to, Wallach himself seems to imply that he might be dealing with a special case. He says that "deviations from proportionality which occurred in our experiments are by far too small to account for the usual lag in constancy." A clue to these differences in deviations might be that Wallach was not dealing with whiteness constancy in the usual sense but with illumination ratios and luminosity matches.

CRITIQUE OF CONTRAST EXPLANATION OF CONSTANCY. In the studies just reported, Wallach wondered about the generality of his findings. He also stressed the importance of close contact between the two patches of light for the intensity ratios to be effective. While close contact does enhance constancy, other studies (Henneman, 1935; Hsia, 1943; Katona, 1929; MacLeod, 1940) have found that the surround affects constancy even if the figure and ground are not in direct contact but fairly close together.[4]

[4] See also Leibowitz, Mote, and Thurlow (1953).

Furthermore, the magnitude of the effect of the surround also depends on its energy level in relation to that of the figure, the sharpness or gradualness of the brightness gradients between the figure and ground, and related factors, as seen in the following experiments.

Following his earlier work on the importance of field organizational factors, MacLeod investigated the effect of the magnitude of the brightness gradients between the object and its surround on perceived whiteness constancy (McLeod, 1947). In his experiment, two overlapping color wheels, the inner one smaller than the outer, were rotated behind a neutral gray disk. A cross-sectional view of the stimulus is shown in Figure 5-8.

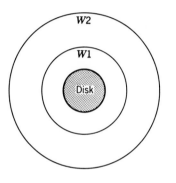

Figure 5-8
MacLeod's experiment on brightness gradients (1947).

$W1$ and $W2$ refer to wheel 1 and wheel 2, respectively, and appear as ring 1 and ring 2 around the disk. The physical brightness of $W1$ was periodically varied, while $W2$ was held constant. When the variation of $W1$ was gradual so that there was a gradual increase in brightness from the disk through ring 1 to ring 2, whiteness constancy was fairly high. When, however, there was a sharp increase in $W1$ so that it was much brighter than either the disk or $W2$, whiteness constancy was significantly lowered. Ring 1 was then seen as a sharply demarcated contour around the disk, which appeared to be darkened.

This experiment shows that when brightness changes of area between object and general background are gradual, constancy is fair; but when a sharp brightness gradient intervenes between object and background, this gradient creates contrast effects which depress constancy.

The problem of the enhancement or depression of brightness due to the inducing effects of the surrounding field has been more fully investigated. In one report, Diamond (1953) reasoned that previous studies on contrast were harder to assess since the stimulus was presented to both eyes; hence any interaction between the eyes would complicate the data. If one object and its surrounding field were presented to one eye and the comparison object and its surrounding field to a noncorresponding part of the other eye, then interactions between the two retinas could be controlled. Heinemann (1955) used this method in a study diagrammed in Figure 5-9.

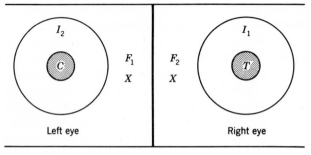

Figure 5-9
The comparison field C, the inducing field I₂, and the fixation point
F_2 *are presented to S's left eye only; the test field T, the inducing*
field I_1*, and the fixation point* F_1 *are presented to S's right eye only.*
(After Heinemann, 1955.)

The two stimulus patterns are presented monocularly. The luminances of the central parts and inducing fields (surrounds) are produced by techniques similar to those employed by Wallach. The test field T and the inducing field I_1 are presented only to the right eye, and the comparison field C with its inducing field I_2 only to the left eye. The observer has to match the apparent brightnesses of C and T as I_2 and I_1 are varied. This technique was used by Heinemann.

In the earlier study, which was similar, Diamond had found little inducing effect if the inducing-field luminance was less than the test-field luminance. For example, if C and I_1 were held constant and I_2 was varied, the expected variation in the equality brightness match on T did not occur if I_2 remained below the luminance of C. In other words, the constancy of the brightness ratio $T/I_1 = C/I_2$ breaks down if the luminances of the inducing fields are below those of the center fields. Conversely, the depression of test-field brightness by the inducing field occurs when the luminance of the inducing field is greater than that of the test field.

This result was verified in Heinemann's extended study,[5] which also pointed to new complexities. When the luminance of the inducing field is below that of the test field, the brightness of the test field is increased very slightly. With equality of luminances, the brightness of the test field starts to decrease progressively as the luminance of the inducing field continues to rise. What is most puzzling is that if we start with a lower inducing-field luminance and gradually increase it, the test field begins to show a depressed brightness even before the inducing-field luminance reaches the level of the test field. In a second study, Heinemann found other complicating factors, such as how much higher the luminance of the test field was and whether the comparison field had an inducing field at all. He concluded that the function relating the inducing-field luminance and test brightness is not

[5] See also Leibowitz, Myers, and Chinetti (1955).

linear but curved. That is to say, a unit effect is not obtained on the brightness of the test field for every unit change in the luminance of the inducing field. Rather, sometimes there is a very slight change, sometimes no perceptible change, and sometimes a corresponding change. What happens seems to depend, in the first place, on the size of the difference between the two luminances and on whether the inducing field is bigger or smaller than the test field. But the more precise nature of the functions relating these variables needs to be determined empirically. Heinemann concluded that an explanation of these effects should probably be sought at a level above the retina.

The information to be gained from these simultaneous brightness-contrast studies is that their effect on perceived brightness depends not only on intensity ratios but on many other organizational features of the stimulus structure. Thus far, it would seem that the effect of the surrounding luminance on the brightness of an object is greatest *if the surrounding luminance is greater, if the differences in luminance are marked, and if the contact between the two fields is close.* A theory trying to relate these data was more recently suggested by Diamond (1960).

REFLECTANCE RATIOS IN THE CONTEXT OF ALBEDO. Most of the preceding studies, and especially Wallach's, dealt with contrast effects and reflectance ratios without relating them to albedo. Hambacher repeated Wallach's study in part but varied the albedo of the disks (1956). The experimental arrangement is shown in Figure 5-10. Note that the illumination intensity of the variable color wheel and its surround was only half as great as that of the standard disk and its surround. The rest of the room

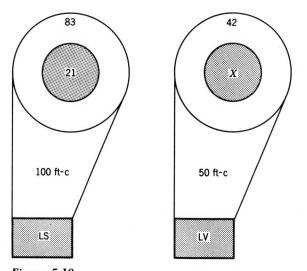

Figure 5-10
Experiment varying brightness and albedo. (After Hambacher, 1956.)

was dark. The distance between the centers of the two wheels was only 18.25 in. The three numbers refer to the albedos. The observer instructed the experimenter to vary the percentage of white of the variable wheel until it appeared to be as white as that of the standard. If constancy were perfect, X would be 21. If Wallach's brightness ratio holds, we should have $X/21 = 21/83$ (not $X/42$ since the variable receives only half as much incident light as the standard does). Hence, $X = 5.25$ ft-c (approximately).

In Hambacher's experiment, the albedo of both the standard and the variable stimulus was obtained by overlapping white and black disks. Using an illuminometer, Hambacher stated that a brightness of 5.25 ft-c from the variable disk would require a white sector of 10.56 per cent. The mean obtained by eight subjects was actually 15.01 per cent. The difference between Wallach's prediction and the obtained value is highly significant and much larger than any reported in his own study. Hambacher thought that the results could be handled better in terms of *whiteness ratios* rather than brightness ratios.

It is an established fact that the function relating perceived whiteness and reflectance (albedo) is not linear. The Munsell achromatic series of equal-whiteness steps takes this relationship into account.[6] The approximate relationship expressed in Table 5-1 contains 11 equal steps of apparent

Table 5-1

Relationship between Reflectance (Albedo) and Whiteness.
(After Newhall et al., 1943.)

Whiteness	Reflectance	Whiteness	Reflectance
0.0	0.00	6.0	0.29
1.0	0.01	7.0	0.42
2.0	0.03	8.0	0.58
3.0	0.06	9.0	0.77
4.0	0.12	9.5	0.88
5.0	0.19	10.0	1.00

whiteness. If we transform the albedo values in the table into whiteness steps, we have:

Standard disk $= 21 = 5.13$
Standard background $= 83 = 9.20$
Variable background $= 42 = 6.95$

Now the ratio is $\dfrac{X}{6.95} = \dfrac{5.13}{9.20}$

X is 3.88 whiteness, which, when converted back, is 0.1123 reflectance (albedo). Now, the obtained mean white sector on the variable wheel was 15.01 per cent, the black disk taking up the remaining 84.99 per cent.

[6] See Newhall, Nickerson, and Judd (1943).

The fused albedo of this variable wheel was 0.1224, which is not significantly different from the calculated 0.1123.

It is not surprising that albedo plays the vital role in whiteness constancy, since without it we would not have whiteness constancy at all. It is the albedo which is the constant property of the object.

Organismic Factors

We have mentioned that Heinemann, among others, thought that brightness is organized at levels above the retina. A relevant study was performed by Hochberg and Beck (1954), who found that a fixed intensity looks brighter if it comes from a surface parallel to the line of sight as opposed to a surface perpendicular to the line of sight. Evidently the brain codes retinal brightnesses within a field context based on experiences in the natural world; but in this coding it cannot break up the sensory pattern, as it can in certain conditions of size and shape. How high a level of organization is represented in this coding of the sensory pattern in brightness?

Most of the phylogenetic and ontogenetic data indicate that whiteness constancy is organized at a fairly primitive level (Brunswik, 1929), for example, it is present in fish and very young children. As shown by Brunswik, however, some developmental modification does take place. What the organism possibly learns can be inferred from a comparison of two studies performed by Burzlaff (1931).

In the first study Burzlaff used the method of illumination perspective, just as Brunswik had done. Forty-eight grays, ordered in equal-brightness steps, were placed far from the window. Each of the better-illuminated grays was designated as the standard at different times. Using the method of constant stimuli, the observer considered all the grays of the near series, comparing their whiteness with that of the distant series. Despite the fact that the distant grays received only one-twentieth as much illumination, the matches showed near equality. About 90 per cent constancy was obtained for all subjects, and there was no difference between four-, five-, six-, and seven-year-olds and adults. The curve relating age to percentage of constancy was practically a straight line, parallel to the age scale. Two features of this experiment should be noted: (1) The observers had an immediate scale on which to base their discrimination, which is probably why the percentage of constancy was unusually high. (2) The gray paper had good microstructure.

In a second study Burzlaff used a similar method but this time employed color wheels for the standard and the variable; i.e., he used the method of adjustment. In this case he found two important results. When the standard was more than 6 per cent white, constancy was low for both children and adults: about 22 per cent for the six-year-olds and younger children and about 32 per cent for the seven-year-olds and adults. But when the standard was 51 per cent white, there was a sharp increase, ranging from 30 to 85 per cent, in whiteness constancy for the five- to seven-year-olds and adults. Whatever development took place in whiteness constancy was completed by the time the child was seven years old.

What are the differences between the first and the second study, which was the only one to show the effect of development? The main difference appears to be the use in the second experiment of color wheels, which make more difficult the separation of natural contour and therefore of surface color.

Summary

The studies reviewed, which used primarily the psychophysical methods of adjustment and constant stimuli, suggest that whiteness constancy operates because the organism responds innately to differences between the intensity of reflected lights relative to the intensity of pooled reflected light coming from a common background or frame of reference.

If the common background is missing or illumination conditions are such as to preclude this relative perception, then illumination matches based on absolute differences between the intensities are made.

The theory offered to explain these facts is based on the ratios of reflected light, taking into account albedo and absolute intensity. It also subsumes color-contrast phenomena.

Whiteness constancy is a sensory fact, not appreciably affected by learning; that is, the organism does not have to learn to respond to *relative differences* between the reflectance of each object and its background (instead of absolute differences between the two objects). Although the observer responds innately to this relation between the object and background reflectance, the accuracy with which the ratio is matched is affected by field experiences in the natural world.

6

Size and Shape Constancy as Mediated Phenomena

We all know from experience that a house viewed at a distance does not appear to be a dollhouse any more than a coin located close to the eye seems bigger than a plate viewed from a greater distance. Actually, as objects recede from our eyes, they should appear to get smaller since the retinal-image size decreases as the distance from the eye increases. The fact that the perceived size does not regularly follow changes in retinal size is called the phenomenon of *size constancy*.

Another fact which we have all experienced is that the top of a classroom desk still looks fairly rectangular even if we view it from the side instead of from the top. Again, if we rotate a circle so that it lies obliquely to the line of sight, it still looks circular although the retinal image has become more elliptical. The fact that the perceived shapes of objects do not change as much as the shapes of their retinal images change is called the phenomenon of *shape constancy*.

It would be easy to argue that we see the sizes and shapes of objects in a constant way because we remember from past experience what their true sizes and shapes are. Such an assertion would be a gross oversimplification, however, and does not really explain what is happening. In any case, while constancy might be better for familiar objects, it also exists for unfamiliar objects. So, as in the case of whiteness constancy, we must look deeper to ascertain the important psychophysical relationships which underlie size and shape constancy. But when we do this, we shall see that the similarity between size and shape constancy and whiteness constancy ends with the demonstration that each does not follow regular changes in the physical dimension. The psychological factors underlying these constancies appear to be quite different, as was suggested by the comparison of the experiments at the beginning of Chapter 5.

Nature of Size Constancy

The objective match in size constancy that we introduced at the beginning of Chapter 5 appears to be an estimation in which judgment plays an important role. In this judgment or estimation, S must be relating visual angles to some other variable which he ignores in the visual-angle match. This something which he takes into account appears to be the fact that the apparent size decreases as a function of distance. If this statement is correct, then we can predict that objective-size constancy should *decrease* as we decrease cues to the estimation of distance. The reliability of this statement can be determined from the experimental facts presented below, which also indicate how complex the phenomenon is.

Determination of Size Constancy

The diagram in Figure 6-1 may help us to understand the situation in size constancy. Let us suppose that a stake whose *objective size, AC,* is 20 ft is moved from a spot just in front of S so that it is four times as far away. Since its distance has increased by four times, its *relative retinal size* will have been reduced to one-fourth of its original size, that is, from AC to AR, or, in our example, from 20 to 5 ft.

C

P

Figure 6-1
R   *Schematic representation of the size-constancy situation.*

A

Clearly, if S judges the new size to be only 5 ft, then constancy would be 0. If he judged it to be 20 ft, then constancy would be perfect. In our diagram AP represents the perceived or judged size. As AP approaches AR, constancy approaches 0; and as AP approaches AC, constancy approaches 1. If P is midway between R and C, then constancy is 50 per cent.

It is not necessary to think that S first senses the retinal size and then converts it to the objective size by taking distance into account. In fact, this probably does not happen, since Brunswik (1944) has found that there is more variability in retinal than in objective judgments. We simply mean that the subject can separate retinal-size stimulation from distance stimulation even though the ordinary experienced viewer does not usually do this. Certain individuals, such as artists, who adopt a more analytical attitude, do frequently separate retinal size and retinal distance. We shall return to this point later.

MEASUREMENT OF SIZE CONSTANCY AND THE BRUNSWIK RATIO. In Figure 6-2 we have schematically diagramed the typical size-constancy experi-

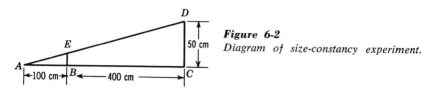

Figure 6-2
Diagram of size-constancy experiment.

ment. The subject, who is located at *A*, observes an upright standard stake, 50 cm high, situated at *C*, 500 cm away. A series of stakes of variable height is located at *B*, 100 cm away. The subject has to judge which variable stake has the same height as the standard stake; he chooses a stake of 46 cm. This is an application of the method of constant stimuli. How much constancy exists?

Brunswik (1929) has developed a method for measuring the amount of size constancy in such a situation. This quantitative measure, called the Brunswik ratio, is expressed below:

$$\text{Brunswik ratio (BR)} = \frac{P - R}{C - R}$$

where R = relative retinal size
  C = objective (or constant) size as measured physically
  P = perceived or judged size

Thouless (1931a; 1931b) uses logarithmic transformation of these values.

While these ratios have also been applied to brightness constancy, it seems more logical to talk about "phenomenal regression" to real object size, as Thouless does. Let us remember the two functional relationships obtained by Gilinsky in the same physical situation. Thus the Brunswik and Thouless ratios attempt to measure the extent to which the subject approximates the objective size C in his perceived size P. As P approaches C, the ratio approaches 1. The Thouless ratio may be a more accurate measurement since there is some evidence to indicate that judgments of distance follow a logarithmic distribution (see Chapter 10). Leibowitz (1956) has discussed the complexities involved in applying the Brunswik and Thouless ratios to constancy data in general.

Let us apply the Brunswik ratio to measure the amount of constancy obtained from the hypothetical experimental data for Figure 6-2. We know what P and C are but must determine R before we can compute the ratio.

One way of doing this would be to look into the retina and measure the retinal-image size. Although this can be done, it would be rather impractical, and there is a much easier way of finding R by using perspective geometry. Since we are comparing an object at 500 cm with one at 100 cm, we are interested in knowing how much *smaller* the retinal image is at 500 cm as compared with 100 cm; i.e., we want to know the relative sizes of the retinal image projected by an object at 500 cm and by one at 100 cm. In this example it is clear that since the object is five times as far away at 500 cm, its relative retinal-image size must be one-fifth as large, or one-fifth of 50 cm, which is equal to 10 cm. Another way of finding R, in general, is to draw the projection of CD, the object height at 500 cm, to A. This line represents the light rays reaching the eye from CD.

The corresponding or relative size at B is represented by EB. EB would then represent the relative retinal image of the standard CD, projected at 100 cm. By using the principle of plane geometry, we can compute EB, which is R, as follows: ABE and ACD are two similar triangles, since they are two right-angled triangles with the common angle at A. Therefore, $EB/CD = AB/AC$; and

$$EB = \frac{AB \times CD}{AC} = \frac{100 \times 50}{500} = \frac{5000}{500} = 10 = R$$

Therefore

$$\text{Brunswik ratio} \frac{P - R}{C - R} = \frac{46 - 10}{50 - 10} = \frac{36}{40} = 0.9, \text{ or 90 per cent}$$

We might also use the Thouless ratio to measure the index of phenomenal regression by merely taking the logarithms of the values in the ratio.

We pointed out that the individual can make an adequate judgment of object size only if he has some way of estimating the relative distance of the object from him. We must now examine this important aspect of size constancy.

Relationship between Perceived Size and Physical Distance

As we have noted, it is an established fact that the retinal size of an object is inversely proportional to its distance from the eyes. Hence, if R equals the retinal size, C the object size, and D the distance, then $R = C/D$, or $C = RD$.

If the subject has no way of estimating D, then C will be judged in terms of R, the retinal size, and constancy will be poor. The better his estimation of D, the distance, the better should he be able to judge the true objective size C. Of course, there are two ways in which S could judge the size of the object. The first is to judge the size of a familiar object. In this case D would be unimportant since S would be judging from memory and not from the perceived relationship between R and D. (We shall have more to say about this later in this chapter and in Chapter 10.) The other condition exists when S judges the size of an unfamiliar object. In this case he must use D if he hopes to judge C fairly accurately. This is neatly shown in a very ingenious experiment performed by Holway and Boring (1941). The experimental arrangement is shown in Figure 6-3.

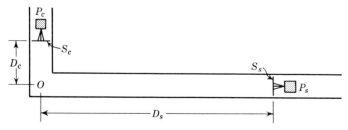

Figure 6-3
Plan view of the corridors. S_c indicates the position of the comparison stimulus located at a constant distance ($D_c = 10$ feet) from O. S_s at a distance D_s from O, indicates one of the positions occupied by the standard stimulus. The standard stimulus subtended a visual angle of 1°. Distance from O to the standard was varied from 10 to 120 ft. Pc and Ps indicate the positions of the projectors. (After Holway and Boring, 1941.)

The experiment was conducted as follows: O, the observer, sat at the intersection of two corridors. Down one corridor he could see a spot of light Ss, which was projected by the projector P_s. This spot always subtended a visual angle of 1° even though its distance from O was moved between 10 and 120 ft. This could easily be done, of course, merely by altering the opening of the projector. The spot of light on the variable Sc was adjusted to match the apparent size of the standard S_s at each distance of the latter. Functions relating apparent size to distance were obtained from five subjects, using the method of repeated adjustments, under four sets of conditions. The conditions were created to produce successive decreases in distance or depth cues, as follows: (1) binocular regard, in which O viewed with two eyes; (2) monocular regard, which reduced depth cues by eliminating binocular disparity; (3) monocular regard through an artificial pupil (the latter, cutting down the surround, reduced depth cues further); and (4) monocular regard through an artificial pupil and a long black reduction tunnel, stretching from O to the standard stimulus and eliminating most of the visual spatial frame of reference. The results of this experiment are presented in Figure 6-4.

Let us see what is actually happening in this experiment. Since the visual angle was held constant, one would expect the function relating size to distance to be a line parallel to the abscissa, as shown in the lower dotted line in the graphs of Figure 6-4. This would hold if the apparent size were based only on the visual angle or the size of the retinal image. If O cor-

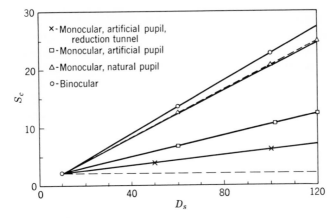

Figure 6-4
*Apparent size as a function of distance for four sets of conditions.
The figure is based on the averages of all the data obtained in the
present experiment. The slope of the function relating apparent size
to distance diminishes continuously as the mode of regarding the
stimuli is altered from direct binocular observation to monocular
observation through the artificial pupil and a long black reduction
tunnel. As the number of extraneous cues is diminished, the slope of
the function approaches zero as a limit; i.e., it approaches the law of
visual angle. The top broken line represents prediction from the law
of size constancy, while the bottom one represents prediction from
the law of visual angle. (After Holway and Boring, 1941.)*

rected the retinal image for distance, however, we would expect the apparent size to be bigger as distance increased, since the visual angle or size
of the retinal image remained the same. For size constancy, therefore, the
function relating size to distance would be represented by the upper dotted
line in the graphs of Figure 6-4. This line is derived from trigonometric or
geometric functions, from which it can be shown that a 1° angle will be
projected from a size of 8½ in. at 40 ft, 17 in. at 80 ft, and 25½ in. at
120 ft. We are now ready to interpret the results, which is quite a simple
matter.

With binocular regard, in the presence of good depth cues, size constancy
was very good; in fact, a slight overconstancy existed. But as depth cues
were progressively reduced, size constancy diminished until there was
almost a size match on the basis solely of the visual angle or the size of the
retinal image. We can thus conclude that the unobscured judgment of
distance is a necessary condition for adequate size estimation. In other
words, in the first two conditions in which O can make a fairly accurate
estimation of distance, he can approximate the object size from the equation
$C = RD$. (This does not mean that he actually solves the equation but
that this relational perception is taking place.) In the third condition his
estimation of distance is much less accurate, since an artificial pupil, which

decreases the size of the visual field, has the effect of greatly reducing perceived distance. An unobscured spatial framework is apparently one of the most important conditions for adequate distance judgment and even appears to be more important than the cue of binocular disparity. Finally, in condition 4, the surround is reduced even more. Under this condition the perceived distance is almost zero, and the perceived size is almost the same as the calculated retinal size; i.e., we have almost no constancy function.

Hastorf and Way (1952) were concerned that Holway and Boring obtained any constancy at all in condition 4. The actual computed constancy ratios were 1.09, 0.98, 0.44, and 0.22 for conditions 1, 2, 3, and 4, respectively. Hastorf and Way attempted to set up a situation in which condition 4 could be changed to give zero constancy. They noted that the reflected light present in the Holway and Boring experiment might have produced some cue to distance. Consequently they conducted the experiment under monocular regard in a black-painted, unilluminated room. In their first experiment they presented circular light areas at four different distances but with the same visual angle as in the Holway and Boring experiment. The match followed the law of visual angle. In experiment 2 the light at four different distances had the same objective size. Again the matches followed the law of visual angle. In both experiments the authors were successful in reducing the constancy ratio to zero. In a final experiment they found that, by using binocular observation, the matches approximate size constancy.

The fact that almost perfect constancy exists in conditions 1 and 2 of the Holway and Boring experiment probably does not surprise the reader, who is aware, from his own experience, of how well he can estimate object size. In addition, the whole process appears to operate very automatically. The reader may wonder why the experimental psychologist makes a problem of this "obvious" fact. But then, if we look again and see how poor constancy is in conditions 3 and 4, we may appreciate how complicated the mechanism underlying size constancy must be despite its automatic ongoing. We often do things without knowing how we do them, but the scientist wants to know the mechanism involved. In the case of size constancy, we are interested in understanding how this works not only because we are curious about scientific facts but also because of the obvious practical value of knowing under which conditions size estimation and distance judgment are most accurate. The author recently worked on a government project for the Army in which this problem was being investigated. Needless to say, the judgment of the size and distance of targets is a matter of life and death to the artillery gunner.

To appreciate further how important distance cues and a visual framework are for size judgment, we should examine the work of Brunswik. From this work it is again apparent that the cues provided from distance and the spatial framework are operating even though the observer is not necessarily aware of them.

Brunswik's Ecological Research

Brunswik (1944) performed some experiments which he termed *ecological*, since they represented a sampling of sizes of various objects in different "real-life" environments. In such situations he and another subject made independent estimates of the sizes of 180 different objects, varying from printed letters at short distances to buildings a few miles away. For each object they made judgments of each of the three terms in the size-distance equation, i.e., of C, the object size; D, the distance; and R, the retinal-image size. The first two estimates were made in meters, while R was judged in terms of the size the object would appear in a camera compared with the scale markings on a meter stick situated 1 m from the lens.

The results indicated that the size of the average error was much greater for estimates of retinal-image size than for estimates of distance and true object size. It would thus seem that, in actual fact, O was not solving the equation $C = RD$. How could the estimate of C be so accurate when the estimate of R, on which it presumably depends, was so inaccurate? This is another instance in which a perception of relations appears to be taking place without O's being aware of it; but this does not, of course, mean that O was not taking distance into account because, as we have pointed out, if distance cues are removed, size constancy breaks down. It is misleading to break down a relational perception into its component parts. In the example presented here we must remember that O is making judgments in absolute terms. The subjective scale of judgment might be different for the different terms, or the subject's *error* for the naming of the absolute judgments might be different for the larger sizes than for the smaller ones, or both things might be happening. Yet the overall judgment of the relationship might have dependable validity. This appears in fact to be the case. Through experience we might become so used to perceiving the integrated relationship that it becomes more difficult to sift out one of its component parts; hence retinal matches are more variable. This problem will crop up again when we discuss shape constancy.

Gruber made essentially the same point after reporting an experiment which tested the relationship between perceived size and perceived distance. He deduced from the size-distance hypothesis that if the distance of an object is overestimated, its size will be overestimated, and vice versa (Gruber, 1954). His stimulus objects consisted of two triangles. The standard triangle was suspended from a wire and located at variable distances. The nearer variable triangle was displayed on a large black screen at a fixed distance from the observer. The size of the standard at different distances was judged by telling E to adjust the variable triangle to equality.

The subjects were also asked to judge the distances from the observer to the triangle by estimating the distance relative to a known marker. The different constant errors for size and distance estimation were not in accordance with the size-distance hypothesis. Size was underestimated, and distance overestimated. It should be noted, however, that again different ways of measuring size and distance were used. More recently Wallach and McKenna (1960) have shown that even with reduced cues to distance, the size of the comparison stimulus and the methodology used influence the results obtained. In fact, they could not obtain retinal matches. Gruber himself concluded that both perceived size and perceived distance "emerge from a common matrix of on-going stimulus processes and moving traces, but this may be related to that matrix in different ways" (1954, p. 426). In other words, size and distance are related, although the constant errors made in judging each may be different.

In an earlier study (1940), Brunswik showed more directly that there is a high correlation between perceived size and distance. He asked one of his students at successive times to estimate the size of an object. Successive estimations were made at random and with the object at different distances. Brunswik found that the correlation between estimated size and objective distance (as *measured*) was between 0.95 and 1.00, suggesting that although the correlation between estimated size and estimated distance is low, the correlation between estimated size and real distance is almost perfect. This lends support to the argument presented above, in which we said that individuals might be responding quite accurately to a relationship without being able to give an accurate absolute judgment of one of the variables (in this case, distance).

Dukes (1950; 1951) performed a real-life experiment which was very similar to those reported by Brunswik. He stopped a six-year-old boy at random and asked him to point to five objects which looked "just as high" as the one at which he was looking. The heights of 67 such objects were estimated, and a correlation of 0.0991 between objective size and estimated size was obtained.

We have had some experiments which verify these naturalistic or ecological findings. First of all, we are reminded of the Gilinsky finding (see the beginning of Chapter 5) that subjects can give separate estimates of objective size and retinal (apparent) size. (Let us keep in mind that Brunswik found that objective-size estimates are more accurate than retinal-size estimates.) Jenkin and Hyman (1959) have established the independence of retinal judgments and objective judgments. By correlating and factor-analyzing the judgments given under retinal instruction and objective instruction, they found that there was no significant relationship between the two sets of judgments. A further verification of this finding was reported by V. R. Carlson (1960). An additional finding of interest from Carlson's experiment was the fact that both objective-size judgments and projective size correlated with distance judgments. But again the correlation between distance judgment and apparent-size judgment was nonexistent.

We might stop for a moment to consider what we have learned thus far about size constancy. The data which were discussed have shown that although individuals can make matches in accordance with visual angle, they usually do not, providing they have good cues to distance. Thus, if distance cues are present, the estimated size will be very close to the true object size. This is size constancy. On the basis of these findings—e.g., the lack of relationship between objective size and apparent size but the presence of a correlation between objective-size judgments and real physical distance— Brunswik (1940) has suggested that it might be better to measure size constancy by computing the correlation between estimated size and distance or between estimated size and objective size than by using his constancy ratio. This is a better measure since it eliminates constancy measures of more than 1 (overconstancy). The correlation technique is satisfactory if we have a sufficiently large number of estimates to permit the calculation of a correlation coefficient; if we have only one or a few estimates, however, the constancy ratio should be used. In any case, if the correlation between estimated (perceived) size and object size is high, the constancy ratio will also be high.

The logic underlying Brunswik's preference for the correlation measure is based on his assertion that human judgmental functions are probabilistic. We ask what the probability is that a response (e.g., judgment of size) will approximate a dimension in the remote physical environment. The probability depends on the extent to which cues provide information about the physical dimension. We have seen that the essential information-giving cues in size constancy are distance cues, but the information obtained depends on more than the actual physical distance. In fact, it depends on a subjective scale of distance, which may or may not approximate the physical distance, depending on certain conditions which we must now examine.

Organismic and Situational Factors Affecting Size-distance Perception

If an observer has some knowledge of the size of an object when it is close to him, then he will estimate its size from memory when the object recedes in the distance. If he does not have some familiarity with the object size, then he must have some way of estimating its distance. The degree of size constancy thus depends on the information received about the actual size or distance of the object. Many experiments which deal with the informational aspects of both distance and size have been performed. We shall discuss distance perception at length in Chapter 10, but we must review some of the relevant experiments here.

SITUATIONAL FACTORS. The first set of experiments deals with the importance of *three-dimensional cues*. All show that size constancy is better with three-dimensional objects. Weber and Bicknall (1935) report that the size constancy of photographs is better if they are presented stereoscopically than if they are presented nonstereoscopically. More recently, Leibowitz, Bussey, and McGuire (1957) have reported that both size and shape constancy are poorer when photographic reproductions rather than the actual situations are judged. (See Chapter 10 for a discussion of stereoscopic vision.) Finally, D. Sheehan (1936) found that size constancy was better for cubes and triangles than for circles.

Other experiments have shown that size constancy is not always related to actual physical distance but to the perceived distance, which is subject to varying degrees of error, depending on the conditions of the experiment. We have already mentioned in this connection the experiments of Brunswik and Gruber. Thouless (1931b; 1932) had argued that the perceived size lies somewhere between the retinal size and the objective size; i.e., it is never perfect. He called this phenomenal regression to the real object and stated that this regression or approximation was never complete. Subsequent experiments have shown, however, that this is not the case. As a matter of fact, there often is a tendency to overconstancy; i.e., the perceived size is frequently bigger than the object size. Moreover, this overestimation is even greater at relatively longer distances, i.e., distances over 800 ft. (See Figure 5-1 in Chapter 5.) We are more likely to get constancy values of 1 or less at shorter distances and of more than 1 at longer distances. The fact that there is a greater constant error for size estimation at longer distances is probably related to the fact that the constant error for distance judgment becomes greater as distance increases.

Representative of the experiments which report overconstancy are the following ones. J. J. Gibson and Glaser (1947) performed a field experiment in a natural setting. A standard stake of unknown size was located at distances up to ¼ mile, and a number of variable stakes were placed 14 ft from the subject at right angles to his line of sight. *S* had to choose one of the nearer stakes whose height was judged equal to that of the variable. In general, he chose a stake which was slightly higher: overconstancy prevailed. Similar results were obtained when the sizes were judged from photographs of the field setting. This similarity is used by Gibson to support his notion that density *gradients* are more important for estimating distance than retinal-disparity cues.

Piaget and Lambercier (1943a; 1943b), using a similar procedure of comparing near with far stakes, found similar results with adults. When the standard was far, it was again overestimated; when it was near, it was underestimated. Clearly, then, it appears to be the farther object which is overestimated. That this seems to be a result of learning to judge distance is suggested by the fact that children do not show overconstancy even when the object is far away.

Piaget and Lambercier also performed an experiment in which the horizontal angle between the standard and the variable was increased from trial to trial. They found that if the angle separating the standard and the variable was so great that the two could not be seen at a single fixation, the standard was overestimated. It is to be expected that when judgments cannot be made with one fixation, errors of estimation will increase.

EYE MUSCLE FACTORS. The experiments of Piaget and Lambercier point to another factor influencing size and distance judgments, namely, the effect of *eye muscle adjustments.* As a matter of fact, the transactionalists (see Chapter 10) have presented a series of experiments and reviews criticizing the size-distance hypothesis and emphasizing the importance of *convergence, accommodation,* and *other organismic factors.* Representative of this approach is the work of Kilpatrick and Ittelson (1953). These psychologists submit that the invariance hypothesis $(R = O/D)$ holds *only* when the visual angle, apparent size, and apparent distance are held constant. They offer other evidence which indicates that the hypothesis is too simple to account for all the cases. Thus, if distance and visual angle remain constant but normal accommodation is interfered with, perceived size changes. These authors present the following evidence relevant to this point: (1) Hering had noted that if accommodation is varied (by changing the fixation point) in monocular vision, the apparent size of the object changes; and (2) if accommodation is paralyzed by atropine injection, there is a reduction in apparent size. Illustrations of some of their demonstrations relating to both space and size perception are presented in a unified section, "Three-dimensional Space: Experiments and Principles," in Chapter 10.

Hermans (1940) also reports experiments which demonstrate the importance of accommodation and convergence. When the eyes are crossed (crossed free vision), the apparent distance of two cards is reversed. If the cards are then separated, increasing the convergence causes a shrinkage of apparent size. When two objects are so placed as to form the same visual angle and viewed with cross vision, they appear as one object with a size slightly smaller than the nearer one. This last demonstration gives us a clue to what is happening in experiments like those reported by Hermans and the transactionalists. These experiments show that in the size-distance invariance hypothesis, distance is not necessarily the actual physical distance but the apparent distance, which is determined by many factors, including accommodation and convergence. Thus, if the visual angle is constant and convergence is increased, we would expect a reduction in perceived size since the increased convergence is a cue for decreased apparent distance. This is what happened in the Hermans experiment. $(O = R \times D$; if D is smaller, then O is smaller if R remains constant.)

This conclusion is further substantiated in another experiment reported by Hermans (1940), who used three conditions of observation—binocular, monocular, and monocular through a pinhole—in a method similar to that of the Holway-Boring experiment. The subjects had to match the size of a standard lighted aperture. Perceived size ranged from smallest in the pinhole condition to slight overconstancy in the binocular condition. Hermans concluded that pinhole and monocular regard reduce the cues of muscular adjustment since in pinhole vision both convergence and accommodation are impossible and in monocular regard no convergence is possible. He verified the fact that pinhole vision destroys accommodation by showing that the image size was the same for both 20 and −20 diopter lenses.

Finally, there is the experiment by V. W. Grant (1942), in which he found that an increase in accommodation, convergence, or both leads to a decrease in the perceived size since such an increase produces a decrease in apparent distance.

We thus conclude that apparent distance which affects perceived size depends not only on true physical distance but also on other cues, such as those received from eye muscle adjustment. It would seem that, in any judgmental situation, the subject thus forms a subjective distance scale, which is determined by the interaction of a multitude of psychophysical factors. Let us look at one attempt to measure this subjective scale of distance.

PSYCHOLOGICAL DISTANCE SCALE. Gilinsky (1951) [1] pointed out that the psychological scale of distance is always dependent on the particular situation which is present. She has suggested that the subject always proceeds as if his horizon (infinite distance) were quite close. This horizon, which sets the limit of distance, lies somewhere between 50 and 300 ft, depending on the situation and the particular individual. In her experiments, S stood at one end of an archery range and directed the experimenter to mark off successive distances of 1 ft. She found that the "psychological feet" actually increased as the true distance from S increased. This can be seen from Figure 6-5, in which the data for one of her two subjects are produced.

We notice that if perceived distance were equal to physical distance, we would have the straight line. Instead we get a curved line, which is expressed by the equation $d/D = A/(A + D)$, where d = perceived distance, D = physical distance, and A = the horizon limit. In this experiment the horizon equals 94 ft (determined operationally). In any situation we can calculate d if we are given A:

$$d = \frac{A \times D}{A + D}$$

[1] We have already mentioned Gruber's plausible suggestion that perceived size and perceived distance are related to real distance but not to one another in a regular way. This point comes up again in Chapter 10, in which we discuss J. J. Gibson's work.

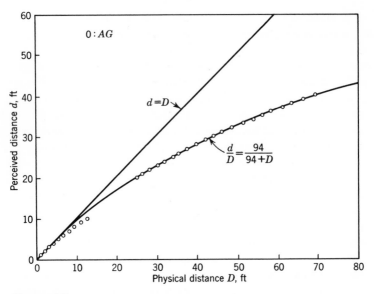

Figure 6-5
Perceived distance as a function of physical distance. (After Gilinsky, 1951.)

In other words, the psychological equivalence d is bigger than the physical distance D, or physical distance tends to become depressed.

The accuracy of the psychological scale of distance can also be increased if a frame of reference is provided. Thus, Piaget and Lambercier (1946) asked subjects to equate one of a series of wooden stakes of variable height, situated at 4 m, to a standard stake at 1 m. It was found that size constancy increased in adults when four stakes, known to be the same height as the standard, were placed between the standard and the variable. Constancy was increased to a lesser extent when the intermediary stakes differed in height from the standard.

We have seen that psychological distance is determined by the actual distance, the assumed horizon, cues to distance, and organismic factors, plus the frame of reference. A final condition which determines size constancy can be classified as personal, subjective, or attitudinal factors. Work on this point was performed mainly by the transactionalists. Hastorf (1953) placed a cutout circle at a distance. Under some conditions he said that the circle was a billiard ball; under others, a tennis ball. He found that when he "increased" the subjective size, while the visual angle remained the same, the subject reported an increase in distance, and vice versa. Other experiments dealing with personal, social, and attitudinal factors will be discussed in Chapters 11 and 12 on social perception.

Summary of Size Constancy

We have noted a very important difference between size constancy and whiteness constancy. In whiteness constancy the perceived whiteness is immediately determined by the stimulus conditions: there will be either an illumination or a whiteness match but not both, depending on the conditions. On the other hand, in size estimation we can get either a constancy or a retinal-stimulus match in the same stimulus situation, depending on the instructions or the attitude of the subject. If he is told to report the size as it appears, he follows closely the law of visual angle; if he is told to report the true object size, then perceived size follows closely the law of constancy. This suggests that size constancy is not purely a response to a sensorial process but involves judgment. The only condition producing one kind of response occurs in a situation in which cues have been eliminated or seriously reduced.

When S makes an accurate judgment of objective size or exhibits good size constancy, the following equation appears to be operating: $C = D \times R$, where C is the perceived object size, R the retinal-image size or visual angle, and D the distance. The subject appears to be responding in terms of this equation even though he is not able to specify the parts independently. Nevertheless, there is a high correlation between perceived size and distance but not between perceived size and visual angle. The subject is thus responding to a total relationship.

Apparent distance is dependent on a number of interacting factors. Experiments have shown that apparent distance is influenced by actual distance, the assumed horizon, distance cues, and attitudinal and organismic factors, plus the frame of reference which is provided. Under natural viewing conditions there is a close relationship between judged size and physical distance. When the subjective scale of distance is distorted from the physical distance, this distortion usually shows up in the perceived size.

Shape Constancy: Methods, Data, and Theory

Shape constancy refers to the fact that if a flat or a solid object is tilted so that it no longer is perpendicular to the line of sight, its shape is perceived as approximately the same as it was in the vertical position even though the pattern of its retinal image has changed considerably. This phenomenon holds when the object is rotated either vertically or horizontally in space. Thus we have all observed that a desk top looks rectangular even though the retinal image is not. Or if a square is tilted away from the observer, it still looks square even though the retinal image becomes trapezoidal. As a concrete example, let us suppose that the subject is observing an upright equilateral triangle from a distance of 5 ft. If the triangle is now tilted, say, 45° from this vertical position, the retinal image of its *altitude* becomes much smaller than it was when the triangle was upright. It is generally found, however, that if *S* is asked to equate the altitude of a variable triangle to that of the tilted standard, the equated altitude is closer to the true physical height than to the relative altitude of the retinal image.

Application of the Brunswik Ratio in Determining the Index of Phenomenal Regression

The index of phenomenal regression in shape constancy can be experimentally determined as follows, applying either the Brunswik or the Thouless ratio. The *standard* consists of an equilateral triangle outlined in a white or a black panel, which can be clamped to a ring stand in such a way that the triangle is viewed at an angle to the subject's line of sight. The *variable* triangle is outlined by white metal strips against the black background of a second panel. These strips can be adjusted to produce a continuous series of triangles with a constant base (equal to that of the standard) and two equal angles.

S sits with the standard triangle and the variable triangle 5 ft from his eyes. The experimenter tilts the standard triangle through a predetermined arc by tipping the top edge of its board away from the subject. *S* then directs the experimenter to raise or lower the adjustable screen until the variable triangle appears to have the *same shape* as the standard. When he announces that the shapes have been equated, the experimenter reads the altitude of the variable from the scale on the back of the apparatus. This procedure is repeated a number of times, and the average of the equated altitudes of the variables is computed.

The procedure for computing the index of phenomenal regression can be followed with the help of Figure 6-6. *A* represents the location of the subject's eyes. *BC* is the altitude of the standard triangle when it is perpendicular to the line of sight, and *BD* the altitude of the triangle when it is tilted through θ degrees. The relative change in the retinal-image shape is

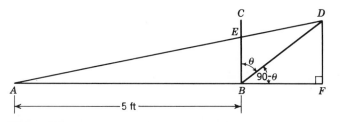

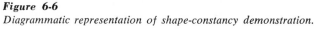

Figure 6-6
Diagrammatic representation of shape-constancy demonstration.

represented by the relative change in the altitude; we compute the projected altitude at the vertical plane, i.e., *EB* in our diagram. The reasoning here is quite simple and very similar to what happened when we calculated the relative retinal size in the size-constancy example. Since the base and bottom angles of the standard triangle remain the same, the change in its shape, as it is tilted, is represented by a change in its altitude; i.e., the triangle becomes "flatter." We are interested in knowing how much flatter the triangle becomes as compared with its shape in the vertical position. If we therefore compute the projected altitude from the tilted position to the vertical position, we have the relative retinal altitude. So we must first compute *EB*. We drop a perpendicular line, *DF,* to *ABF.* Applying the principle of trigonometry, we have

$$\frac{DF}{BD} = \sin (90 - \theta)$$

Therefore

$$DF = BD \sin (90 - \theta)$$

Second, we must find *BF*:

$$\frac{BF}{BD} = \cos (90 - \theta)$$

Therefore

$$BF = BD \cos (90 - \theta)$$

Now we have *BF*, and we are then able to calculate *EB* as follows:
Let *ABE* and *ADF* be two similar triangles. Then

$$\frac{EB}{DF} = \frac{AB}{AF}$$

Therefore

$$EB = \frac{DF \cdot AB}{AF} = \frac{DF \cdot AB}{AB + BF}$$

Therefore

$$EB = \frac{BD \sin (90 - \theta) \cdot 5 \text{ ft}}{5 \text{ ft} + [BD \cos (90 - \theta)]}$$

in our example.

Since *BD,* the true physical altitude of the standard triangle, and θ, the arc of tilt, are both known, the equation is easily solved. The index of phenomenal regression can now be determined by applying the Brunswik ratio,

$$\frac{P - R}{C - R}$$

where P = the average of the equated altitudes of the variable triangle
   C = BD, the object or physical altitude of the standard triangle
   R = BE as calculated above (the relative retinal stimulus)

From this it can be seen that the index of phenomenal regression can easily be computed for any degree of tilt. In experiments similar to the one just described, it is found that with normal viewing conditions the index of phenomenal regression lies between 0.60 and 0.80.

Dependency of Shape Constancy on Spatial Cues

We saw in the case of size constancy that the extent to which an individual can estimate the actual physical size of an object depends on the number of distance cues. We might expect a similar relationship in the case of shape constancy. Since the retinal shape changes as the object's *spatial* orientation is changed, it follows that shape constancy should be reduced as cues to spatial orientation are reduced or distorted. Many experiments have dealt with this problem.

Some of the earliest and most extensive work in this area was performed by Thouless (1931a; 1931b; 1932). In his first experiment he used as the standard a circle which was placed obliquely to the subject's line of sight. Under these conditions the retinal shape would be elliptical. The variable consisted of a series of ellipses between a "flat" ellipse and a circle, which was placed at a right angle to the line of sight. The subject had to choose one of these variables which he thought had the same shape as the standard circle. In general, it was found that the subject chose an ellipse which was less elliptical than the calculated retinal shape; i.e., he chose a shape which approximated that of the circle. Indices of phenomenal regression ranged between 0.60 and 0.80. Under these conditions, where the subject could clearly observe the differences in spatial orientation, shape constancy or phenomenal regression averaged about 70 per cent. Similar results were later obtained with squares and other shapes.

In subsequent experiments, Thouless found that if spatial cues are eliminated, the index of phenomenal regression can be reduced to zero. Thus, if the standard shape was viewed monocularly against a black-velvet background, the perceived shape approximated the retinal shape: there was no shape constancy. Monocular perception reduces the depth cues of retinal disparity and convergence, and the black-velvet background reduces texture cues to space. It thus seems that when depth cues, which provide cues to the spatial orientation of the object, are eliminated, then shape constancy is eliminated. A similar demonstration was provided by Ames (1946), who rotated a window in its frame until it appeared almost end-on to the observer; i.e., its retinal shape had almost no width. Nevertheless, it still looked like a rectilinear window. But when the image of the same rotating window was cast on a photographic plate so that most depth cues were eliminated, its shape changed continuously, always approximating the retinal shape.

The fact that shape constancy is dependent on depth cues was used by Koffka (1935) to expound his theory of shape constancy. As in the case of size constancy, he used the invariance hypothesis. He postulated that there exists a tendency to perceive the shape the way it is at a "neutral level," i.e., the way it appears in the frontal-parallel plane. In other words, he is asserting that shape remains invariant with respect to its shape in the frontal-parallel plane.

If Koffka was on the right track, then we might deduce that the degree of shape constancy is related to the subject's apprehension of its spatial orientation. Thus, shape constancy would be higher if the opportunity for judging the relative tilt or rotation of the object were increased. Conversely, shape constancy should decrease if the subject had difficulty in perceiving the relative tilt or rotation in space.

A direct test of Koffka's hypothesis was conducted by Eissler (1933). In the vertical plane he tilted the standard object at varying degrees, and the subject had to judge both its shape and the relative amount of tilt. The prediction, based on Koffka's assertion, was that the amount of shape constancy shown would depend on the accuracy of judging the tilt; i.e., as the accuracy of tilt judgments increased so would shape constancy increase. Eissler obtained three results of relevance. First, he found that phenomenal regression increased as tilt increased; i.e., the subject continued to correct for tilt as the latter increased. Second, regression was not complete because the discrepancy between perceived shape and real shape increased as the angle of tilt became more extreme. Third, he did find some degree of relationship between perceived shape and judged tilt; i.e., shape constancy did sometimes increase as the amount of judged tilt increased. This relationship, however, was by no means linear. In other words, improvement in shape constancy was not always accompanied by an increase in the amount of judged tilt.

Derivation of Cue to Shape from Perceived Orientation to Surround

Koffka has criticized Eissler's somewhat inconclusive data by pointing out that some of his subjects were one-eyed and could not therefore perceive space very well. More recently Stavrianos (1945) repeated a modification of Eissler's experiment. Her experimental design was superior, and her controls were better. Again she found little relationship between the perception of shape and the judgment of tilt. Whereas shape constancy was generally good, judgment of tilt showed more fluctuation and error.

With a few subjects, however, there was some relationship between the perception of shape and that of tilt under monocular vision, although this relationship was not present for normal vision. Other experiments by Stavrianos showed closer relationships. One of these experiments, using the method of average error, was concerned only with monocular vision. In another experiment binocular vision was employed, and the subject selected appropriate shapes from a number of rectangular forms varying in height and width (rather than using the method of average error). The results seemed to indicate that under some conditions the correspondence between the perceived shape of an object and its perceived tilt was marked but not perfect. The subjects appeared to be accepting a relationship between shape and tilt and to see the objects as three-dimensional identities which remained the same even though the spatial coordinates changed. Work by Langdon (1955c) tends to corroborate the latter statement. He found that forms which can be modified so as to change their shape are perceived as three-dimensional objects of fixed shape which are changing their position. We can now interpret the superiority of shape constancy in the monocular condition of Stavrianos.

Apparently the natural preference in perception is to maintain the integrity of the object's shape and to change its perceived orientation if necessary. Since perspective shape undergoes less change in monocular than in binocular regard, the subject responds more strongly to the change in orientation in the former case and less strongly to a change in perspective shape. Evidently the cue to perceived shape and perceived tilt comes not predominantly from changes in perspective shape but rather from perceived changes in orientation relative to the spatial surround.

Other experiments by Langdon (1951; 1953; 1955a; 1955b) verified this aspect and added some interesting information concerning perceptual cues. In one experiment performed in the dark, he used a fluorescent circular outline of wire rotating on a vertical axis from the direct line of vision through various angles to 90° and then back to direct vision again. The subject compared the shape of the rotating circle with 15 different outline ellipses representing various rotations of the circle to his line of regard. These matches were compared with the condition in which the circle did not rotate spontaneously. In this case the subject could rotate the circle so as to equate the circle with the ellipses. There was practically no constancy present with the circle stationary, but constancy was found with the moving-circle condition; the constancy increased with increasing speed of sweeps of the circle, up to 10 sweeps per second. The deformation of the stimulus as the circle moved enabled the observer to perceive the outline as a three-dimensional form having spatial orientation.

In one experiment Langdon (1955b) located two sets of standard outline circles and comparison ellipses in a distorted room. One set of circle and ellipse was undistorted, but the other set was distorted so as to appear undistorted in the distorted room. He reported that estimates of the perceived shape of the distorted forms corresponded to the characteristics of the room and not to the space occupied by the shape itself. This conclusion arose because the subjects were able to match the distorted circle and ellipse, which would have been impossible if the estimates corresponded to the space occupied by the shape.

The overall results of the Langdon experiments showed that the degree of constancy can be reduced by the removal of such perceptual cues as movement, texture, and shadows. These results remind one of the Holway and Boring experiment, cited earlier, in which size constancy was systematically reduced by gradually reducing the number of cues available to the subject.

Further verification that the shape of an object is determined by the spatial framework is provided by an experiment of Beck and Gibson (1955). These investigators found that the phenomenal (perceived) slant and, therefore, the shape were determined primarily by spatial frame of reference provided by a textured background surface. This conclusion held irrespective of the physical slant of the object.

We see here a problem similar to the one we faced in size constancy. There it was noted that while size constancy depends on distance cues, it does not depend on the accuracy of distance judgments; but if distance cues are removed, size constancy breaks down. Here we see that shape constancy does not always depend on the accuracy of judging spatial orientation; but, again, if spatial cues are reduced, shape constancy breaks down. It is clear therefore that both size and shape constancies depend on depth cues even though the subject has difficulty in giving an absolute judgment of the relative depth. This difficulty may merely indicate that the absolute-judgment task is more precise and demanding of the subject than is that of stating the size or shape.

We recently noted this discrepancy in the following experiment (Forgus, 1957). The standard object was located in a big box, and both the object and the box could be rotated. If the object were rotated 30° clockwise, the subject could see this change in orientation; but if the box were also rotated 30° clockwise, the object tilt appeared to be reduced almost to zero. In this way we were able to *distort* the apparent orientation of the object. In general, we found that the shape judgments followed the *directions* of tilt judgments. For example, in the case given above, in which tilt was grossly underestimated, shape constancy was reduced. It seems clear that shape constancy depends on the availability cues to spatial orientation: the better the cues, the better the constancy. Although shape constancy thus depends on an apprehension of the general direction of spatial orientation, it is not correlated with the accuracy of absolute judgments of the tilt of the objects.

Finally we have the work of both Thouless (1932) and Klimpfinger (1933), who showed that artists, who possess a more analytical attitude, have poorer shape constancy than average individuals. Moreover, both Klimpfinger and Brunswik (1933) found that shape constancy can be improved by instructing subjects in the synthetic or objective attitude and lowered by instructing them in the analytical attitude. This finding is very similar to that of the experiment on size constancy and attitudes performed by Gilinsky. Once again we see that shape and size constancies are more similar to one another than they are to whiteness constancy.

General Summary and Comparison of the Perceptual Constancies

The point stressed throughout this chapter, namely, that it is incorrect to combine whiteness, shape, and size constancies under a unitary trait, is strongly supported by the extensive study of M. R. Sheehan (1938). This investigator compared the responses of a group of young college women in a variety of color-, size-, and shape-matching tasks to determine the extent to which consistently high or low perceptual constancy characterized their judgments. The intercorrelations obtained were universally low and for the most part negligible. Only in the case of size and shape constancies did she sometimes find a positive correlation. This finding is probably related to the fact that both these constancies are dependent on depth cues, such as convergence and accommodation. Thouless (1932) found a small positive correlation between the constancies. Sheehan therefore asserts that it is logically and experimentally indefensible to use the term *constancy* if it implies the existence of a unitary trait. She concludes that "apparent size, shape, color . . . seem to be determined for any individual by a combination of the *objective* and *subjective* factors operative under the particular conditions of the judgment situation" (1938).

Furthermore, Leibowitz, Mitchell, and Angrist (1954) and Leibowitz, Chinetti, and Sidowski (1956) found that under reduced exposure time brightness constancy is improved, size constancy unaffected, and shape constancy destroyed.

Influence of Age, Development, and Learning on the Constancies

We have shown earlier in this book that subjective factors have a negligible role in whiteness constancy but a signifiicant role in size constancy. Furthermore, the cue to albedo, which is crucial for whiteness constancy, derives from a statistical averaging of the background illumination. For this reason whiteness constancy is usually subject to a large error. Moreover, we have also shown that it is relatively easier to judge the distance of an object than it is to judge its spatial orientation. From these facts we can make three other important deductions. First, size constancy should be better than whiteness and shape constancy, irrespective of age. Second, size constancy should show rapid improvement with age and experience. Third, shape constancy should also show some improvement with age and experience, whereas whiteness constancy should show less improvement.

These predictions are generally supported by Brunswik's comparison (1956), in which he compared his work on whiteness constancy with

Klimpfinger's work on shape constancy and Beyrl's work on size constancy. In this work it was found that in the two-year-old size constancy is 90 per cent complete and that it improves with age until it is 100 per cent complete in the seven-year-old. Shape constancy, on the other hand, is less than 15 per cent in the three-year-old and improves to almost 60 per cent in the fourteen-year-old. Finally, whiteness constancy is almost 30 per cent in the three-year-old and improves only slightly, to about 44 per cent in the sixteen-year-old. Thus size constancy shows a rapid increase to 100 per cent, whereas shape constancy improves by 45 per cent until it reaches 60 per cent in the fourteen-year-old, and whiteness constancy improves by 15 per cent until it is 44 per cent in the sixteen-year-old. Since size constancy is 90 per cent complete by age two, it probably showed more learning before that age. Data related to the fact that shape constancy continues to develop into a later age come from the work of Ghent. In one study (1960) she presented mono-oriented forms (forms usually seen in a particular orientation) in various orientations. She found that three- to seven-year-old children were most accurate in judging objective shape when the forms were presented in their characteristic position. The older subjects did equally well for all orientations of the shapes. In a second study (Ghent and Bernstein, 1961) it was observed that preschool children express strong preferences for orientation in the perception of geometric forms.

Many other studies support and clarify Beyrl's work on size constancy and age. Burzlaff (1931), for example, believed that size constancy was as good in children as in adults. Perhaps the most definitive work in this area was performed by Cruikshank (1941), who worked with 73 infants whose ages ranged from ten to fifty weeks. The standard stimulus consisted of a *large* rattle, which was always located at a distance of 75 cm from the infant (condition C). The variable consisted of a *smaller* rattle (one-third as big as the standard), which was sometimes located at a distance of 25 cm (condition A) and sometimes at a distance of 75 cm (condition B). The three rattles were presented one at a time, and the reaction of the infant was noted.

Now, it would be expected that if conditions B and C elicit the same reaction, then size constancy (distance relationship) is operating. If conditions A and C exhibit the same reaction, then the visual angle rather than size constancy is determining the responses. Some of the results follow. Up to twenty-two weeks of age A was responded to more frequently, followed by C. Thus, size constancy is poor during the early age period. Between the ages of four and five months A and B began to confuse the infants. Finally, at the age of six months a differentiation between A and C developed, with a more similar response between B and C. Thus, much learning of size constancy takes place very early, and Cruikshank concluded that size constancy occurs as early as in the six-month-old infant. Learning of size begins at six months, shows very rapid learning up to two years, and then shows slower learning until it is nearly complete in the six-year-old.

Zeigler and Leibowitz (1957), however, reported a more recent experiment on the difference between children and adults with respect to size constancy. Their studies indicated that learning continued to a later age. The children consisted of eight boys between the ages of seven and nine years, while the adults consisted of five men between the ages of eighteen and twenty-four years. These subjects matched a comparison with one of a series of standard objects located at various distances up to 100 ft. The sizes of the standard objects were so adjusted as always to subtend a constant visual angle. The results are contained in Figure 6-7. It is clear from inspection of this figure that the adults exhibited almost perfect size constancy, whereas the children showed much poorer constancy. It seems that learning of size constancy continues beyond nine years of age when longer distances than those employed by Cruikshank are used.

Finally, we have the observation of Akishige, reported by Lambercier (1946). He studied two congenitally blind children who at nine years of age were given temporary vision by means of a mydriatic, which dilates the pupil and thus allows some vision. Akishige found that the children's size constancy was only about 25 per cent as good as their whiteness constancy; and we know that, except for young infants, size constancy is much higher than whiteness constancy.

Unfortunately, few studies in which a typical learning situation in the constancies was set up have been performed. But it seems reasonable to infer from the developmental studies included in this section that learning

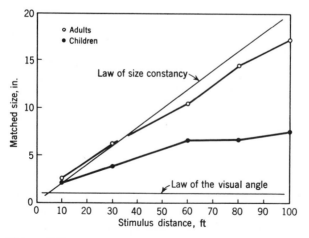

Figure 6-7
Mean matched size as a function of stimulus distance for a group of adults and a group of children. The size of the test object was adjusted so as always to subtend a constant visual angle. (Zeigler and Leibowitz, 1957.)

plays a major role in the development of size and shape constancies but not in the development of whiteness constancy.

In sum, it seems that whiteness constancy is almost complete in the three-year-old. Size constancy shows rapid learning and is almost complete in the two-year-old, although it does continue until about the age of nine, while shape constancy shows slower learning and is almost complete in the fourteen-year-old. In any case, while size constancy develops to 100 per cent, shape constancy reaches only about 60 per cent and whiteness constancy about 45 per cent. Since size and shape show the most learning and whiteness the least and since shape does not develop as much as size, we can order these three constancies from primitive to complex, in which case whiteness is most primitive, size in between, and shape the most complex. The same ordering is found if we use phylogenetic development as a criterion.

Comparative Data

Whiteness constancy has been found in very primitive animals. Locke (1937) found that it was high in monkeys, as did Burkamp (1923) for fish. David Katz and Revesz found that it was present in hens. The fact that it is present in such a wide variety of species supports Burzlaff's finding that whiteness constancy is as great for children as for adults when they have to match a standard against a series of variables. It again points to the primitiveness and stimulus-boundedness of whiteness constancy. Size constancy has also been found in subhuman animals. Thus Köhler (1915) found that size constancy is present in chimpanzees and hens.

Little work has been done on shape constancy in lower animals, although Fields (1932) found that after rats had learned to choose an upright triangle from a circle, they were unable to choose correctly when the triangle was rotated as little as 10°. To establish such form constancy (or a generalization or concept formation) he had to rotate the form through very small areas in a continuous way; learning was slow. Furthermore, the writer (Forgus, 1954) found that rats will show form constancy only after special upbringing, during which they are exposed to a variety of visual stimuli in their home cages. Finally, Lashley (1938) performed an experiment in which the rat could learn a discrimination on the basis of either brightness, size, or form cues. It was found that responses to brightness were primary and most dominant, with size next, and form last. Again the order is established.

Finally, it seems that once constancy has been attained, it is difficult to break under ordinary circumstances. The extent to which it is broken depends on how analytical the thinking and intelligence of the viewer are. Leibowitz and his collaborators at the University of Wisconsin (Leibowitz, Waskow, Loeffler, and Glaser, 1959) have found that rhesus monkeys exhibit high degrees of shape constancy. The following order in terms of decreasing constancy was found: mental defectives, slow learners, college students in elementary psychology courses, Ford Foundation scholars!

Summary Comparison of Constancies

In Chapters 5 and 6 we have attempted to point out the ways in which whiteness, size, and shape constancies differ, although we are a long way from clearly explaining these differences. Leibowitz and his associates at the University of Wisconsin have recently begun a systematic attack on the relationships between the constancies. They have also come to the conclusion that the constancies are affected by different mediational processes.

We should remember that the Wisconsin group has found that when observation time is lowered, brightness constancy is improved, size constancy is unaffected, and shape constancy is destroyed. More information is apparently needed for the perception of shape constancy.[2]

The results referred to at the end of the last section, however, indicate that perceptual constancy is not an intellectual process. This suggestion is strengthened by more recent work from Wisconsin and Jenkin (Leibowitz, 1961), which showed that size constancy is just as good in feebleminded persons and chronic schizophrenics as in normal subjects.

We can thus conclude, following the criteria used in this book, that brightness constancy is determined by the most primitive process, shape constancy by the most complex, with size constancy intermediate. But an understanding of the precise nature of this hypothetical process awaits further research.

General Conclusions on the Constancies

Whiteness constancy is determined by the reflectance ratios of the stimulus field. The role of learning is small.

Size and shape constancies show improvement with learning. In size constancy the individual learns to respond to the relationship between size and distance; in shape constancy, to the shape as determined by its spatial orientation. Thus depth and distance cues are important in size and shape constancies. Size constancy shows more rapid and complete learning than shape constancy.

The perceptual constancies can be ordered from primitive to complex, using energy-level, ontogenetic, phylogenetic, and learning criteria. (These appear to be similar to the criteria used in Chapter 2, and more research in the area seems needed and promising.) When this is done, we find that whiteness constancy is the most primitive, size intermediate, and shape the most complete. In children and

[2] See also Leibowitz and Bourne (1956).

primitive organisms the response to whiteness is most accurate (and dominant), while in adult human beings the response to size is most accurate, with shape in between.

Once established, the constancies are more readily broken down by analytical and intelligent organisms.

While a similarity exists, a theory of size and shape constancy must extend beyond a theory of whiteness constancy.

7

The Emergence
and Stabilizing
of Figure

Two broad objectives will be attempted in this chapter. First, we shall look at the conditions which are necessary for a total figure to be seen as emerging from a ground. Then we shall investigate the conditions which determine the relative instability, stability, and shape of the figure.

We began to consider this problem in Chapter 2 when we traced the hierarchy. Then in Chapter 4 we looked at the psychophysical functions which relate the factors determining the detection of changes in light energy and the discrimination of brightness and hue. Thus Chapter 4 dealt primarily with perceptual task 1 and, to some extent, perceptual task 2. In Chapter 5 we continued the analysis of task 2 when we investigated brightness constancy and showed why it is organized at a lower level than size and shape constancies, which were treated in Chapter 6.

Now we shall continue with the progression from task 2 to task 3, leaving task 4 to Chapters 8 and 9. Let us keep in mind that the perception of constant brightness has already introduced us to task 2 since it involves the discrimination of a unit. As the gradient of a brightness difference between any area and its surround becomes sharper, the area takes on a contour which shapes its figure. This figure can be quite unstable, the parts being seen as figure and ground frequently interchanging, or quite stable, depending on the relationships between the conditions of *stimulation,* the *receptors,* and the prior *experience* of the perceiver.

The discrimination of stable or definite figure takes us to task 3 and involves the extraction of more information. Perhaps this statement warrants amplification. If the figure becomes more stable, it means there is less uncertainty in the perceptual process. If there is less uncertainty, it means that less information from the input side is lost and more is transmitted. Hence the channel, or the organism, transmits or extracts more information. Whenever we reduce uncertainty, we leave less information in the stimulus and thus assume that more has been extracted by the organism.

Our discussion will be organized around three topics. Section 1, a short section, will deal with what happens when there is no heterogeneity in the stimulus. Section 2 will describe the nature of the unstable or ambiguous figure and its ground. It leads into a discussion of the conditions which make the figure more stable and definite. This will take us to section 3, which deals with the gestalt laws of perceptual organization and the subsequent innovations and theory to which this approach gave rise.

The Homogeneous Field or Ganzfeld

If the entire field which stimulated the receptors consisted of a homogeneous distribution of energy, it is obvious that no segregations could be perceived. Some differentiation in stimulus energy is necessary for a figure to be seen as separate from a background.

A field which gives a homogeneous distribution of energy is called a *Ganzfeld*. While it is technically difficult to achieve a completely homogeneous field, some investigators have succeeded in producing adequate *Ganzfelder* (W. Cohen, 1957; 1958a; Hochberg, Triebel, and Seaman, 1951). Hochberg et al. did it by having each subject wear half of a table-tennis ball over one eye. In this way they could study, for example, certain color phenomena in such a monocular *Ganzfeld*.

Cohen constructed a *Ganzfeld* which consisted of two intersecting translucent spheres. Each sphere had the following characteristics: (1) it was painted white on the inside, and (2) it was so constructed that any light entering it was evenly diffused over the entire inside surface through multiple reflections. If the illumination in the two spheres is identical, *S* sees a uniformly illuminated field if he looks with one eye into this *Ganzfeld* through a small opening in the first sphere.

Using this apparatus, Cohen reports some interesting findings. For example, if the *Ganzfeld* is uniformly illuminated with a highly saturated hue, the color gradually fades. First, the subject reports seeing a poorly saturated, diffuse hue which, within about 3 min, becomes a gray. Very often the gray is seen as denser and nearer than the hue. Thus we note that the *Ganzfeld* not only gives a perception of uniform light energy but also makes the ground unstable, that is, changes some of its characteristics, such as distance and hue.

For color to be maintained, some heterogeneity had to be introduced. One way to do this was to introduce an *achromatic* stimulus into a *chromatic* field; e.g., a gray disk introduced into a red *Ganzfeld* would be seen as a blue-green circle in a red background. It is interesting to note that the figure (disk or circle) took on the complementary color of the *Ganzfeld* and was seen as more saturated than the ground.

Another way of producing heterogeneity was to introduce *intensity differences*. Thus, if the second sphere had a lower luminance than the first sphere, a dark circular area was seen where the spheres intersect. In the phenomenon reported in the last paragraph, an intensity difference produced both a spatial separation of the circle from its background and a sharpening of its contour.

To show further that *Ganzfeld* stimulation produced the same effect as if there were no stimulation at all, we turn now to a brief description of the autokinetic effect. The purpose in introducing that phenomenon at this point is to demonstrate that while the autokinetic effect is usually produced in a dark room, a similar condition can be created in a *Ganzfeld*.

THE AUTOKINETIC EFFECT. The subject is located in a completely dark room, into which we introduce a spot of light. This can usually be done by placing a light source in a completely black box that has a pinhole through which the spot of light is seen. The subject is told to fixate the light, and after a short while he reports that he sees the light moving. The perceived motion of a light under such conditions, where there is no background, is called the *autokinetic effect*.

While no fading of the stimulus occurs, as was true of the *Ganzfeld,* the two phenomena appear to be related. First of all, the autokinetic effect also represents a case in which the percept is unstable: the light wanders in many directions which are not systematically predictable. Furthermore, Cohen (1958b) reports that a similar phenomenon occurs in a bright *Ganzfeld*. A stationary target was located in the Cohen *Ganzfeld,* which was homogeneously illuminated. The subjects saw the target as moving. Finally, Luchins (1954) found that the standard autokinetic effect could be reduced by making the background more heterogeneous. He did this by gradually increasing the background intensity in a modification of the typical autokinetic demonstration. As the brightness of the background increased, thus bringing more differentiation of the background into sight, the amount of autokinesis decreased until finally no, or very little, movement of the spot figure was seen.

The findings from these experiments on the *Ganzfeld* and the autokinetic effect suggest that the perception of *stability of both the figure and its background* requires heterogeneity in stimulus energy. This heterogeneity can be produced by differentiation in *intensity* (or, more fully, *energy level*), *wave composition, spatial extensity,* or *temporal sequence.* We shall return to this subject later. First, we go on to see what happens when a figure is shaped only by contour, with little else to differentiate it.

Figure-ground Phenomena: Primitiveness and Instability of Figural Unity

The discrimination of a figure from an amorphous background occurs at a higher threshold than that required for the discrimination of a formless brightness difference. We like to think of this event as being due to the greater amount of information which must be extracted in figure-ground differentiation. The many studies reviewed in Chapter 2 are relevant here. As an example, let us refer to the study of Freeman (1929). Inkblots and silhouetted outlines were exposed from short durations to longer durations in an ordered sequence. At first the observer saw only the brightness differences, followed by vague figural impressions. It was only when the exposure time was increased that the figure became focused, developed a definite contour, and emerged from the background.

The development of the figure goes through stages from instability to greater stability. These stages are illustrated in the experiment of Wever (1927), who exposed nonsense forms tachistoscopically from short to longer time intervals. When the figure-ground stage was reached, it appeared to have two steps. First, the figure was simple and not very stable, and then it developed into a better figure which had a primitive type of location.

The fact that figure-ground perception can be stable as well as instable may be shown in other ways. If one looks at a Necker cube, which is produced by an outline perspective drawing, the perception is very unstable. The cube fluctuates in the third dimension, now coming toward the observer and then receding from him. Similar demonstrations were made by Rubin (1921), using the ambiguous figure, an example of which is given in Figure 7-1. Looking at this picture leads to fluctuations in perception.

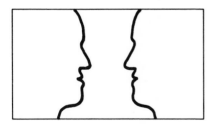

Figure 7-1
Ambiguous figure to illustrate fluctua-tions in figure-ground.

Sometimes the middle vase is seen as a figure with the rest the background; at other times the two profiles emerge as figures with the middle receding to the background. Such reversals in figure-ground are spontaneous and very difficult to control. We note that in these stimuli the brightness is fairly homogeneous, *with the only differentiation existing at the contours.* Such figures are quite unstable, with much ambiguity or fluctuation between figure and ground.

Attempts to Make the Figure More Stable

Rubin tried to show that the figure-ground relationship would be more stable if the brightness differences between two areas were more marked and the observer attended to one of these as the figure. By using a projection lantern, he was able to project on a screen a green irregular shape surrounded by a black area or a black shape surrounded by a green area. These stimuli were exposed for 4 sec. In one experiment the observer was first given 9 of these fields and told to see the enclosed figure; then he was given 9 more and asked to see the enclosing figure. In the critical test these 18 fields, now with reversed figure-ground relationships with respect to color, were randomly presented with 9 more fields, and one observer was asked to look at the *enclosed* field only while another was asked to see the *enclosing* figure only. The results indicated in general that the observer had difficulty in recognizing the figure when the color relationships were reversed. Apparently the organism had been responding to specific color patterns, so that reversing the color relationship impaired recognition. This statement is verified in another experiment in which Rubin found that figure-ground relationships were moderately persistent even at these lower exposure times. On successive exposures, the observer reported seeing the same part of the figure about 64 per cent of the time.

A modified replication of Rubin's research throws some light on the probable cause of his results (Rock and Kremen, 1957). A comparison between the two experiments and an understanding of the significance of the results will be aided by reference to Figures 7-2*a* and 7-2*b*. In Rubin's experiment the entire figure was exposed during the training period, and the subject was instructed to look at one part, either the figure or the sur-

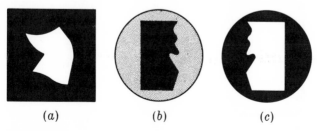

(*a*)   (*b*)   (*c*)

Figure 7-2a
(*a*) *One of Rubin's figures; the surrounded part was green.* (*b*) *The black training figure corresponding to test figure 13.* (*c*) *The white training figure corresponding to test figure 13 in Figure 7-2b.* (*After Rock and Kremen, 1957, p. 24.*)

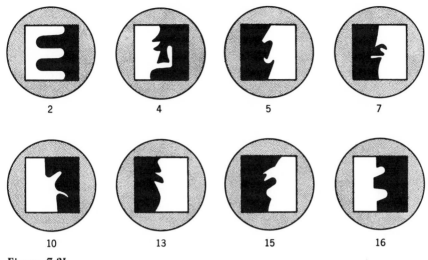

Figure 7-2b
The 8 critical test figures. (After Rock and Kremen, 1957, p. 25.)

round. In Rock's and Kremen's experiment only one-half of the test figure was presented during the training period. If it was the left half (see *b* in Figure 7-2*a*), it belonged to set A; if the right half, to set B (*c* in Figure 7-2*a*).

Since only 8 of 18 figures gave a 50:50 split in choice between A and B in a control group, only data from these 8 figures were used to analyze the results obtained from the experimental groups. The figures are shown in Figure 7-2*b*. In looking at the results, we should keep the following points in mind. For the 8 critical figures there were 76 responses to set A halves and 71 to set B halves. Counterbalancing for black on the left and black on the right, and vice versa, was followed. In the test figures 4 had black on the right, and 4 had black on the left. The number of subjects (out of 15 in each experimental group) who showed a preference for either the training half or the nontraining half, together with the control data, is shown in Table 7-1.

The difference between the distribution of results for group A (56:51) and the distribution of the control group (76:71) and that between the distribution of results for group B (63:48) and the distribution of the control group (71:76) are not statistically significant. Comparisons of the total number of responses to the figures exposed during the training period with the responses to those not seen during the training period (119:99) for the combined experimental groups were also not statistically significant. In both cases the chi-squared analysis gave chance probabilities exceeding 20 per cent.

The significance of the difference between results of Rubin and those of Rock and Kremen lies in the following fact: Rubin tried to "influence" his

Table 7-1

Responses to the Critical Figures. The Numbers in the Body of the Table Refer to the Number of Subjects Who Chose the Particular Half in Their Responses. (After Rock and Kremen, 1957.)

| Critical Figure | Groups | | | | | |
| | Control (N = 20) | | A (N = 15) | | B (N = 15) | |
	Set A	Set B	Training Half, Set A	Non-training Half, Set A	Training Half, Set B	Non-training Half, Set B
2	11 (B)	9 (W)	12	2	6	7
4	10 (W)	10 (B)	5	8	11	4
5	10 (B)	8 (W)	7	5	10	4
7	10 (W)	10 (B)	6	8	7	8
10	8 (B)	9 (W)	7	7	6	8
13	8 (W)	8 (B)	9	6	6	6
15	9 (B)	9 (W)	4	9	10	5
16	10 (W)	8 (B)	6	6	7	6
Total	76	71	56	51	63	48

subjects in the training period by exposing the entire ambiguous figure and instructing them to attend to one part. Rock and Kremen gave no instructions and used only half of the ambiguous figure for several exposures during the training. Rubin's method significantly increased the probability that a response would be made to the training part rather than the non-training part, while Rock's and Kremen's method did not. How can we account for this difference? In the first place, it is clear that mere *repetitive* sensory exposure is not sufficient to produce a consistent unity in figural perception, especially if the previously exposed unit becomes part of a larger, more inclusive composite. This conclusion is consistent with the findings of Gottschaldt, whose data and related work are placed in context later in this chapter.

The effect of presenting the entire ambiguous figure with instructions to attend to one part is to provide a *context* within which the figure is perceived. When the subject views the figure subsequently, he does not merely present a "blank" plate waiting for the stimulus to register sensorily. Instead he sends out *testing stimuli* or *sets* from the brain which select the part to be received and reacted to. This interpretation is consistent with our working model presented in Chapter 1.

Our interpretation is supported further by the following facts: The kind of results obtained by Rock and Kremen are believed to be determined by the crucial characteristics of the stimulus that the subject first saw. These authors also raise the question of how rewards and punishment can influence the probability of a perceptual response when repetitive exposure does not. The answer would seem to lie in considering whether repetition is enough to produce meaningful context, categories, or sets. Certainly verbal intent or some other motivational effect like reward or shocking is demonstrably more effective in accentuating certain classes of responses to stimuli.[1] We shall deal more fully with this problem of stimulus categorization and its determinants in discussing social perception and concept formation.

Suffice it to conclude this section by adding that other investigators have also shown that *learned* perceptual organizations influenced later perception significantly. When we discuss theories of perceptual learning in Chapter 9, we shall review the work of Leeper, who dealt with the genesis of meaning from poorly structured (ambiguous) stimuli through certain kinds of experience. He calls this process the development of sensory organization. We are, of course, suggesting that this sensory organization is guided by discriminating or "sorting" brain sets which develop after experience.[2]

EYE MOVEMENTS AS SET OR ATTENTION DIRECTORS. Eye movements are described in the directional sets discussed above. We should remember that Rock and Kremen believed that the results obtained depended on the crucial characteristics of the stimulus which was first seen by the subject.

Related to this fact are some interesting observations. Hochberg (1964), for example, notes that a contour can delineate only one of the two areas which it shapes. This is also true of edges in three-dimensional objects, but there is a crucial difference between a contour and an edge.[3] A contour can shift the direction of which side it shapes as the individual looks down it. This cannot happen when the individual looks at an edge. Thus the fluctuation in figure stability when there is only a contour to separate the figures can be caused by the ease with which the direction of shaping can change. One way of altering this condition is to make one side dominant. An edge does this; another way is to make one figure more articulated than the other. In an experiment on binocular rivalry, Breese (1899) showed this to be true. In an experiment of this type, two different targets are presented, one to each eye. The targets may merge or alternate, or one may "win out over the other" in the perception. In Breese's experiment the more articulate side won out.

In the contour situation, eye movements produce fluctuation. In the edge and Breese situation, normal eye movements are required for stability of figure. This fascinating and complex role of spatial and temporal change which is related to eye movements will be discussed again in Chapter 9 in connection with Hebb's developmental theory of perception.

[1] See, for example, Rock and Fleck (1950); Schafer and Murphy (1943).
[2] See Atkinson and Ammons (1952); Braly (1933); Leeper (1935).
[3] See also Penrose and Penrose (1958).

What we have essentially described thus far in this section is that, in the case of uncertain figure-ground relationships or ambiguous figures, the likelihood of producing a particular response to a perceptual stimulus can be increased by providing a subjective or organismic set. But the formation of one kind of figure or unity is also very definitely determined by the stimulus organization, as suggested by the last two experiments. In fact, the question of the relative influence of stimulus and subjective organizations in the determination of figure has been raised by many investigators whose work we shall now follow. It is logical to start this extension with the work of Wertheimer and the gestaltists, who were largely instrumental in raising the question of perceptual organization.

Gestalt Laws of Perceptual Organization: Grouping and Figural Unity

The question raised by Max Wertheimer in his classic article (1923) can be introduced by considering Figure 7-3. For perceptual discrimination to take place, the physical world of stimulation must contain some degree of heterogeneity. A homogeneous field or a *Ganzfeld* would produce very little articulation in the world of perception. At the other extreme, we encounter the fact that the number of segregations that the observer can perceive is limited by his capacity to process separate units. In *a* of the figure the individual cannot process the 42 dots at one glance; he would have to count them. Consequently he is just as likely to say, "I see a collection of dots" or "dots making up a square." In *b* the nature of the physical stimulus decreases the uncertainty or variability in perceptual reports. Most people are likely to report seeing three columns of dots and, in *c*, something like two columns of white dots bordering a column of black dots.

Since stimulus segregation is necessary for effective perception and since the observer cannot possibly discriminate all the segregations in the physical stimulus, the perceptual field tends to be organized into a limited number of wholes or units. It is to the question of determining the principles which

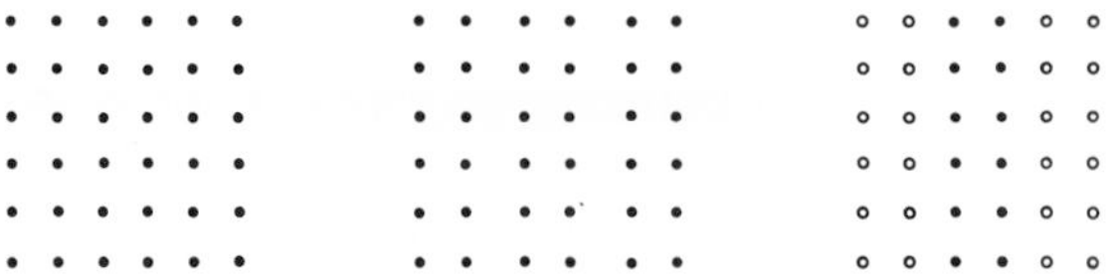

(*a*) A unitary whole

(*b*) Segregated into 3 units by spatial differentiation (proximity)

(*c*) Segregated into 3 units by brightness differentiation (similarity)

Figure 7-3
Illustration of the gestalt laws.

govern the grouping of the elements into these units or figures that Wertheimer addressed himself. The fruits of his insight were contained in gestalt laws of perceptual organization, the essence of which we shall now attempt to describe.

Law of Prägnanz

This is the basic law which governs the segregation of the perceptual field into separate forms. The elements of the field tend to segregate into forms which are most stable or which create a minimum of stress. To quote Koffka, the law of *Prägnanz* states that "psychological organization will always be as 'good' as the prevailing conditions allow. In this definition the term 'good' is undefined" (1935, p. 110). Nevertheless, when we study Koffka's examples and those of Wertheimer, it becomes clear that good or *Prägnanz* form is one which constitutes the simplest stable structure. The criteria for *Prägnanz* embrace such properties as regularity, symmetry, simplicity, inclusiveness, continuity, and unification. Examples of how the master principle of *Prägnanz* works are illustrated in Figure 7-4.

The remaining gestalt laws of organization essentially identify the principles governing the segregation of the stimulus complex into forms containing the greatest degree of *Prägnanz;* they are subdivisions under the principle of *Prägnanz.* We shall briefly discuss these principles here since both Koffka and Wertheimer have treated them fully with numerous illustrations. Furthermore, they are discussed and illustrated in elementary psychology textbooks. The laws are classified into intrinsic and extrinsic types.

INTRINSIC LAWS, OR LAWS OF CONSTELLATION. These are laws which are governed mainly by the constellation formed by the stimulus elements and purportedly operate independently of experience. The main idea expressed in these descriptive laws is that contour and color naturally arrange them-

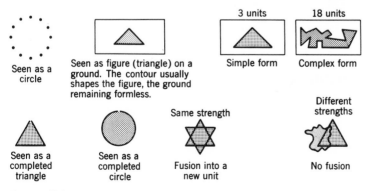

Figure 7-4
Illustration of Prägnanz in figural perception.

selves into certain patterns which compel the viewer to perceive the constellation in a certain way, i.e., in the direction of greatest *Prägnanz*. In other words, these laws describe how *Prägnanz* is achieved and should thus be considered subsidiary laws under the master principle of *Prägnanz*. Let us look at some of these laws which occur more frequently.

1. *Law of closure.* Closure is illustrated in Figure 7-5. Instead of breaking up the two figures at the points of intersection, the subject reports that he sees two unified figures, namely, an ellipse and a rectangle. That this is the result not necessarily of past experience but of figural properties was demonstrated by Wertheimer by controlling this factor. Thus when a W is presented above

Figure 7-5
An example of closure.

and adjacent to an M, the subject reports that he perceives not a W and an M but a diamond-shaped form enclosed by two vertical lines ▷◁ .

Koffka had stated that if the *external forces,* i.e., the objective stimulus conditions, are not organized to produce spontaneous "good" configurations, then the *internal forces* within the individual tend to modify the pattern of retinal stimulation toward a configuration with more "goodness." The effect of these internal forces on closure had been demonstrated by numerous investigations. Fuchs (1920) reported that if part of a circle was presented to hemianoptic patients [3] so that the incomplete part fell on the blind area of the retina, the patient would report seeing a complete circle. More recently, Bender and Teuber (1946) found that patients with lesions in the occipital cortex see a complete figure as such even when part of it falls on the blind area.

Factorial studies of closure carried out by such investigators as Thurstone (1944) and Mooney (1954) have found individual differences in the ability of individuals to "close" certain structures. One of the possible reasons for this difference is that the subjects bring differential effects of past experience to these unstructured figures. There is evidence to support this possibility in the study by Leeper (1935) on the development of sensory organization, which will be discussed in Chapter 9. These results show that learning does play a part, but a minimal one. As indicated earlier in this chapter, learning's dominant effect seems to be the production of directional sets.

2. *Law of inclusiveness.* That learning does not necessarily result from sheer frequency of exposure is seen in Gottschaldt's experiment (1926), performed to determine the effects of repetitive experience in viewing a form on the ability to identify it when it was later included in a more complex configuration. The subjects were permitted to study simple figures for 1 sec on each exposure. Some of the figures were presented 3 times only, while others were exposed 520 times. The observers were instructed to learn the figures. They were then presented with complex figures, each one containing only one of the simple figures. There were several complex figures for each simple one. The subjects

[3] Persons who are blind in one-half of each eye.

were allowed to examine the complex figures for 2 sec and merely told to describe them. In only 5 per cent of the cases in which the simple figure had previously been presented 520 times did the subject notice, or even guess, that the simple figure was contained in the complex one. Gottschaldt concluded that in this experiment *sheer* repetitive experience in perceiving simple figures clearly had no effect at all. The complex figures included the simpler ones to such an extent that the subject was not able to pick out the latter. The inclusion of the simple figure in larger structures had caused the former to lose its identity; it no longer existed phenomenally. The structural properties of the unified whole were so compelling that the subject was unable to see the parts.

This tendency, then, of the gestalt properties of a unified whole to change the identity of a subwhole contained within it has been called the law of inclusiveness. Added authority was given to this law by Köhler, who reports that even familiar figures such as numbers and letters which are firmly embedded in a larger configuration are difficult to detect. The researches of Djang and Hanawalt [4] showed that experience does affect the probability of detecting a hidden figure which is masked by a composite whole, but the figures used by Djang would probably not fulfill the criteria of *Prägnanz* in the view of Wertheimer and Gottschaldt. In the section of this chapter entitled "Experiential Factors," we present a comparison of the figures of Gottschaldt and Djang which illustrates the difference in strength of inclusiveness. (See also Figure 7-4.)

3. *Law of good continuation and direction.* This law merely states that forms which have continuous (and usually uninterrupted) contours are better configurations than figures which have discontinuous contours. Thus a trapezoid whose four sides constitute a continuous contour is more readily perceived than one which has two or more of its sides intersecting. This law is similar to the law of closure.

Figure 7-6
Example of good continuation.

Seen as a dimond in the middle of
:wo lines--not a W on top of an M

4. *Law of proximity.* This law and the law of similarity have received much treatment by Wertheimer and others and are illustrated in Figure 7-7 (see also Figure 7-3). If we present a row of equally spaced dots to a subject, he perceives them as a single row. If we now gradually decrease the distance between successive pairs, a point will be reached when the subject reports seeing groups of dots with two dots in each group. The spatial proximity which determines the grouping here has given rise to the name of the law.

[4] See Djang (1937); N. G. Hanawalt (1942).

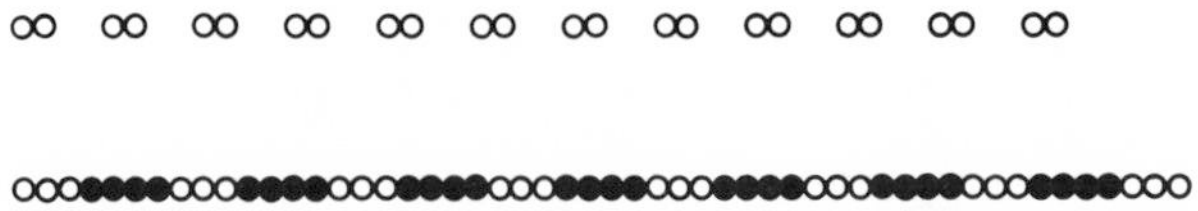

∞ ∞ ∞ ∞ ∞ ∞ ∞ ∞ ∞ ∞ ∞ ∞

○○○●●●○○○●●●○○○●●●○○○●●●○○○●●●○○○●●●○○○●●●○○○

Figure 7-7
In the top row, segregation is achieved by the law of proximity,
whereas in the bottom row the spaces between dots are uniform and
segregation is achieved by similarity.

5. *Law of similarity.* In Figure 7-7 we create more unities from a row of equally spaced dots by varying brightness in accordance with the law of similarity. We can continue with the dot demonstration. Suppose we present the subject with three rows of black dots and let the dots be spaced 10 mm apart in each row; then the subject reports seeing three rows of black dots in accordance with the law of proximity. If we now make the color of each alternate dot in each row the same, the subject reports seeing vertical columns of dots in accordance with the law of similarity. The dots in each row must now be brought much closer together for the law of proximity to win over the law of similarity.

By systematically altering the relations between the factors of similarity and proximity, the relative importance of these two laws can be ascertained under specified conditions. This procedure is very complex, however, and few conditions where these laws are opposed have been sampled. (A couple of these conditions will presently be considered.)

Other phenomenological principles, such as good curve, good contour, and common fate or common destiny underlying grouping, were specified by Wertheimer. But most, if not all, of them seem to be modifications or combinations of the principles of closure, continuation, proximity, and similarity. See for example, Figure 7-8.

EXTRINSIC LAWS. With regard to extrinsic laws, Wertheimer merely asserted that under conditions where the structural features of stimulus are poorly defined, the past experience of the individual may operate to produce one percept rather than another. For example, a series of words printed next to each other without spaces can still be separated and read, or exaggerated spacing can be ignored and meaningful words identified.

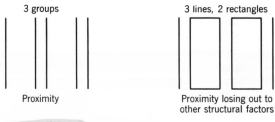

3 groups   3 lines, 2 rectangles

Proximity   Proximity losing out to
                            other structural factors

Figure 7-8
Competitive laws of organization.

Generalization of the Gestalt Laws

Although the illustrations presented by Wertheimer and Koffka (1935) are very striking, we might still wonder how general these principles of grouping are. That these laws operate to some extent has been demonstrated by the gestalt psychologists. But other studies have been performed to determine in a more experimental manner under which conditions they operate, and these indicate that the laws cannot act in a simple way. They interact in complex fashions, sometimes supporting each other and sometimes acting in opposition. Attempts have also been made to explain the nature of the effects of these principles.

EXPERIMENTAL EVIDENCE. At the turn of the century, Hempstead (1900) had shown that reproduced figures which were poorly apprehended as a result of exposure through an episcotister exhibited greater symmetry and regularity than the original. Perkins (1932) verified these results by showing that irregular-outline figures which were exposed for short durations showed greater regularity in reproduction. In another study, Bobbitt (1942) presented triangles tachistoscopically with varying degrees of incompleteness. He found that as the triangles became more nearly complete, a threshold was reached where the responses changed from perceiving separated parts to seeing a whole structure. Moreover, this tendency to closure was greater the more acute the triangle was. Closure occurred for even greater amounts of incompleteness in the more acute triangles than in the less acute triangles. Other experiments, such as those of Hochberg and Silverstein (1956) and Rush (1937), show that the gestalt laws operate in a complex way, with the grouping laws varying in strength, depending upon the direction from which we start (whether we start with similarity or with proximity). Furthermore, the laws are more prominent with older than with younger subjects, indicating a possible experiential or maturational effect.

Hochberg and his associates have particularly attempted to study the operation and strength of these laws quantitatively. In one experiment Hochberg and Silverstein tried to determine how much closer elements had to be (proximity) to overcome a stronger influence of brightness (similarity) which was pulling them in another direction. The stimulus material is presented in Figure 7-9.

The brightness of the squares in the rows was alternatively dark gray and light gray. The apparatus was so constructed that columns could be moved, bringing the second column closer to the first, the fourth closer to the third, and the sixth closer to the fifth. Correspondingly, the distance between the second and the third and between the fourth and the fifth columns would increase. That is to say, as the distance b decreased, the distance c increased. What these experimenters essentially did was to determine how much smaller the distance b (relative to c) had to be so that there would be

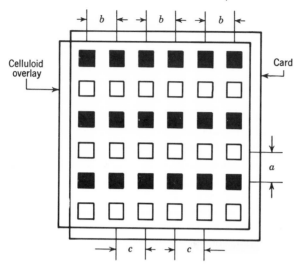

Figure 7-9
Stimulus material for Hochberg and Silverstein experiment.

vertical organization (seeing columns) which could overcome the force toward horizontal organization caused by differences in brightness between the rows. Hochberg and Silverstein found that when they increased the difference between the brightness of the rows, the difference between the columns had to be increased correspondingly to go from horizontal to vertical organization. A second result of perhaps greater interest is the fact that the amount of closeness depends on whether we begin with the presence of horizontal or vertical organization. Thus, if we begin with horizontal organization, we must move the columns to distance X to produce vertical organization. When we move the columns back, we have to go beyond X to produce horizontal organization again. This is called the *factor of direction,* which influences the relative strengths of similarity and proximity. To clarify this statement, if we start with a similarity, it tends to persist and is therefore stronger; on the other hand, if we start with proximity, it tends to persist and is therefore stronger.

In a further experiment Hochberg and Hardy (1960) found that as distance between rows decreased (proximity), there had to be a corresponding intrarow increase in brightness differences (producing alternating columns which were dark and light) to reorganize perception from apparent rows into columns.

In the final study to be referred to here, Hochberg and McAlister asserted that the utility of translating the organizational "laws" depends on the "empirical" determination of dimensions of abstraction along which "information" can be "scored" (such as number of angles, number of line segments, or some weighted combination of the two) and upon the "dem-

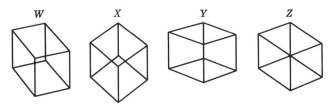

Figure 7-10
The Kopferman cubes. (After Kopferman, 1930.)

onstration of a quantitative dependence of response frequency on the 'information scores' " (1953, p. 361). In one experiment they presented tachistoscopically each of the Kopferman cubes a number of times and observed the frequency with which subjects gave bidimensional (as opposed to three-dimensional or depth) responses to each. The Kopferman cubes are presented in Figure 7-10.

The results are presented in Table 7-2. The two cubes (Y and Z) which require fewer lines, segments, and angles (the lowest "informational" scores of these two dimensions of the four cubes) to be seen as bidimensional gave rise to bidimensional responses more frequently than the other two cubes. This is an example of the operation of redundancy in the determination of figural goodness. We shall periodically examine the more formal approach to informational measurement and redundancy introduced by information theory.

Table 7-2

Bidimensional Responses to the Kopferman Cubes and Some Two-Dimensional Stimulus Characteristics of the Cubes.
(After Hochberg and McAlister, 1953, p. 363.)

Cubes	Bidimensional Responses (%)	Stimulus Characteristics		
		Line Segments	Angles	Points of Intersection
W	1.3	16	25	10
X	0.7	16	25	10
Y	49.0	13	19	8
Z	60.0	12	17	7

THEORETICAL CONSIDERATIONS. The stimulus pattern is the basis on which discriminating responses can be made. The arrangement of stimulus structures which presents the best possible cues for making discriminations will be followed. Thus, it is easier to respond to an array of elements by grouping the similar ones together than by grouping similar and dissimilar elements. This is a more efficient way of receiving information which is to a great extent redundant, and less effort is required. Likewise, it is simpler to differentiate structures which are spatially remote from those which are close together.

We know also that if forms are symmetrical, we have only to respond to one important feature since the two are "mirror images" of one another. If figures are asymmetrical, however, we must detect at least two, if not more, aspects. Thus, we must extract more of the available information.

Finally, it is clear that the essential features of a form are carried by the directional changes in its contours. These changes must be detectable if the form quality is to be fully comprehended. Is it surprising that when forms are poorly perceived or are reproduced the directional changes and discontinuities are minimized? Such principles as closure, good continuation, and good direction evidently operate to facilitate discrimination.

It is doubtful, therefore, that anyone would argue against the thesis that the gestalt laws facilitate perception. The controversy concerns the influence of learning and the relative strength of each law. While Wertheimer and others mentioned in this section have dealt with the latter question, the results are complex and generalizations can only be suggested with caution. Although the gestalt theorists asserted that the laws were not determined by learning, some of the work mentioned earlier suggests the possibility that the extent to which these principles operate may be influenced by previous experience. This is a very important problem which should be investigated further. A similar position was expressed by Attneave (1954a) in an ingenious application of information theory in an attempt to explain why the gestalt laws operate the way they do.

CONTRIBUTIONS FROM INFORMATION THEORY. Before we look at Attneave's results, let us see again what information theory is, although we return to it for a technical application toward the end of Chapter 8. (This approach was considered briefly in Chapter 1.) The theory was developed within communication engineering and was a systematic attempt to handle the transmission of messages through communication channels.[5] Psychologists, however, became aware of its application to the living organism as the communication channel (Quastler, 1955).

Messages of stimuli containing a certain amount of information are encoded (perceived) and transmitted through the channel. The decoding of the message or stimulus material is indicated by the responses of the organism. The communication channel for orthodox information theory is a static one, a "black box"; but when the living organism is the channel, the system must be treated as dynamic. Thus the encoding of the message is affected by the internal characteristics of the organism, namely, its physical characteristics and life experiences.

Attneave suggests how information theory might be used to quantify the

[5] See Shannon and Weaver (1949); N. Wiener (1948).

gestalt laws of organization. He begins, as Wertheimer did, with the fact that if the visual field were completely homogeneous, we would make no discriminations. The laws of organization are operating essentially to give *etc.* us information on the basis of which we make discriminations. Presumably a certain minimum amount of information is required before we are able to make visual discriminations. The articulation of the visual field is so constituted as to transmit a certain amount of redundant information. This ensures discrimination and the perception of certain forms or configurations.

Attneave presents some ingenious illustrations of how this information-transmission concept might be used to quantify the laws which govern the segregation of the stimuli of the visual perceptual field into certain good configurations. He begins by asserting that much of the visual information received by any higher organism is highly redundant; i.e., it contains unnecessary repetitive information. He gives examples of how this hypothesis might be tested by employing Shannon's "guessing-game" technique, which consists of presenting a series of elements to the subject at one time. The subject has to guess when the color, duration, or some other dimension of the stimulus will change. For example, if we were to present the subject with the diagram of a black ink bottle on the corner of a brown table against a uniform white background, he would be able to see this with little effort. The guessing-game technique, however, demonstrates that much of the information transmitted by such a field of stimuli is highly redundant. This redundant visual stimulation results from either (1) an area of homogeneous color or brightness or (2) a contour of homogeneous direction or shape. It can, therefore, be concluded that essential information is concentrated along contours (i.e., regions where color or brightness changes abruptly) and at those points on a contour at which its direction changes most rapidly, i.e., at angles or peaks of curvatures.

Symmetry constitutes another form of redundancy, since the information received from one side of a symmetrical figure is predictable from that received from the other side. Symmetry, it will be recalled, is one of the criteria of *Prägnanz*. In the same way the other gestalt laws of organization like similarity, good continuation, and proximity reduce uncertainty of perception by giving certain redundant information. The value of symmetry and redundancy is more complex than can be indicated here, however, and we shall return to the subject later in this chapter.

Furthermore, it would seem that the visual machinery is so constituted as to maintain redundancy at a certain level and not to overload the communication channel. Thus, the organism is required to encode little information. The gestalt laws of organization play a necessary role in this process, in which they operate to transmit economical information by providing a maximum amount of redundancy.

This work which Attneave has started seems very promising for the task of quantifying the gestalt laws of organization. The construct "economy of information transmission" seems to be a very useful tool to apply not only to principles of discrimination but also to concept formation and efficient problem solving. We have integrated such an application with our discussion of concept formation and thinking in the final part of this book, but here we should emphasize that the gestalt laws operate because they ensure minimize errors through redundancy. Thus we note that information can be quantified, with maximum information being transmitted when the great-minimize errors through redundancy. Thus we note that information can be qualified, with maximum information being transmitted when the greatest change occurs in contour direction and brightness. Furthermore, transmission of essential information is ensured by redundancy. Therefore, the various gestalt factors, including symmetry, good continuation, and other forms of regularity, may all be considered to constitute redundancy in visual stimulation (Attneave, 1954a, p. 209).

EXPERIENTIAL FACTORS. It has been postulated that the visual mechanism works in such a way as to ensure a certain amount of redundant information and also to encode essential information, thus providing for economy of efficiency in visual discrimination. It would be consistent to expect that the memory mechanism also works so as to make the "storage" of remembered forms more economical. G. A. Miller (1956a; 1956b) has considered how organisms tend to encode information in "chunks" so as to minimize strain. If encoding for economical memory functioning actually occurs, we would expect the brain to perform a certain amount of encoding in agreement with the gestalt laws. The effect of this hypothetical brain process should be evident in reproductions from memory of previously perceived forms. Some evidence relevant to such a process comes from the work of Wulf (1922).

Wulf presented various outline forms, one at a time, to observers and asked them to inspect these figures. The observers were then required to reproduce the forms at various intervals after the original exposure. The delay between inspection and reproduction consisted of such intervals as 30 min, 1 day, 1 week, a few months, and so on. Each observer made several reproductions of a specific form. Of interest is the fact that successive reproductions reportedly showed changes in the direction of the greater *Prägnanz*. The most important change appeared to be the accentuation of certain structural features. This accentuation, or emphasis, is illustrated in the principle of sharpening and the principle of leveling. Examples of these two principles are presented in Figure 7-11.

We may apply informational concepts to these principles. Thus it can be hypothesized that sharpening results from both redundancy and economical encoding, i.e., extracting the essential information into suitable chunks. Since the information is concentrated at the angles where the direction changes abruptly, encoding operates to accentuate the angles and make them sharp. This also results in a certain amount of redundancy since

Sharpening: Becomes:

Leveling: Becomes:

Figure 7-11
Changes in perceived form. (After Wulf, 1922.)

the angles become more or less equal. The redundancy which results from leveling is obvious. Through leveling the distance between the two lines becomes uniformly equal, and the essential information (curvature) carried by one line is repeated by the other.

Wulf also discussed the principle of normalization which is experientially determined. An example of this is what happens to the reproduction of a distorted W. On successive reproductions, the W becomes more regular and symmetrical.

The fact that we find these directional structural changes in the reproduction of perceived forms fits in with the premise that the field is structured to aid the efficiency of discrimination. But Wulf's studies raise an important question, which has to do with whether these changes operate independently of experience. He had theorized that the changes resulted from autonomous changes in the "memory trace" existing in the brain. These autonomous changes occurred in the direction of greater *Prägnanz* and operated independently of experience. Normalization is subordinate to these changes because, he postulated, the "normal" form is already a result of the operation of gestalt principles. Thus the W is symmetrical. Wulf is arguing that conventional forms are adopted because they represent better gestalts. The structural factors are the primary determiners of the perception and memory of forms.

Wulf's conclusions have been attacked on experimental grounds by E. M. Hanawalt (1937) and by Hebb and Foord (1945). If the forms are reproduced only once by a subject and if each subject reproduces the form at different times after exposure, there is no evidence of slow, spontaneous changes in the trace. That there is a change is apparent, but the subject who reproduces a form after 1 month, for example, does not necessarily show more change than one who makes a reproduction after 1 day. So what Wulf apparently showed was that the progressive changes were a result of the subject's trying to remember what he saw. It was easier to draw things more symmetrically or parallel to each other; it is easier to remember them this way. Again, we have maximization of redundancy operating to produce economical decoding of information.

The importance of making this distinction between what is seen and attempts to reproduce what is seen can further be appreciated by looking at the data from experiments of Rock and Engelstein (1958). Three separate experiments, each using different figures and different subjects, were performed. After a specified period elapsed since original exposure to the figure, each subject had either to reproduce or to recognize the original. Recognition response was made by choosing the match from 10 figures, which ranged in similarity from 1 to 10, 10 being identical and 1 being least similar to the original. This scale of similarity was obtained by pooling the judgments of many judges, and a different set of judges scored the reproductions. While some people might have questions about the compatibility of the data, since the judges were different, the results presented in Figure 7-12 are still informative. We note how the two recognition curves are very close to the original figure, even after 4 weeks, as opposed to the three reproduction curves, which deviate so greatly from the original.

It is to be expected that the stronger or simpler the original figure, the less the uncertainty and consequent room for change. Conversely, the weaker or more complex the original, the greater the uncertainty and room for change. It is in the latter cases that experience (the strength of its effect depending on whether there is more exposure or some deliberate training, practice, or biasing) usually shows up more strongly. Thus it is important to notice that *there is no reason to oppose structural (stimulus) factors to experiential ones.* They can, and usually do, work together. But having stated that experience influences perception and the reproduction of perceptions, we must go further and find out how the nature of the experiences affects the process. Such investigations are still being conducted.[6]

In his well-known work on remembering, Bartlett (1932) suggested, as

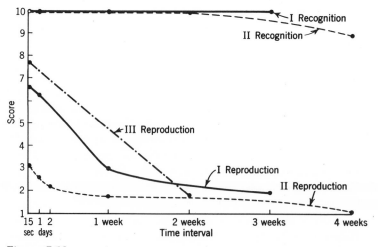

Figure 7-12
Curves of forgetting for recognition and reproduction. The Roman numerals indicate the experiment, each experiment using a different figure. (After Rock and Engelstein, 1958.)

[6] See Abe (1951); J. B. Carlson and Duncan (1955); George (1952).

a construct, "effort after meaning" to describe how a subject attempts to structure his experience into a consistent schema. Effort after meaning is an inferred process which states that the subject is always trying to get the most meaning from what he is perceiving. In one series of experiments Bartlett (1916) used a procedure different from Wulf's. He presented pictures of unfamiliar things, such as alien birds, to English students. Bartlett found that the reproductions showed changes in the direction of familiar things, such as domestic cats. In other words, when observers are shown unfamiliar things, they attempt to make them more meaningful by changing them into things with which they are familiar. Hilgard's achievement of environmental stability and clarity of perception (1956) and M. D. Vernon's schemata (1954) deal with similar processes, as suggested by Bartlett's concept, and are based on what we would say is a maximization of redundancy; so does Woodworth's motive to perceive (1947).

As mentioned above, an experiment by Gottschaldt (1926) demonstrated that mere repetitive experience in inspecting a figure does not increase its discriminability if it is part of a more inclusive whole (see Figure 7-13).

Figure 7-13
Illustration of inclusiveness. (After Gottschaldt, 1926.)

The experiment was conducted in following manner. The experience consists of inspecting a number of A figures, each of which is presented for 1 sec. Some of the figures were shown 3 times, whereas others were shown 520 times. During the test situation B figures, each containing an A figure, also were shown. The observer was merely told to describe the B figure. Only rarely did the observer mention that it contained an A figure. The results show that the A figure was mentioned in 6.6 per cent of the cases in which it had been exposed 3 times and in 5 per cent of the cases in which it had been shown 520 times. Gottschaldt concluded that the quality of the perceived form depends most strongly on the structural features of the stimulus: there is a very strong tendency to perceive the form which represents the "best" gestalt. Repetitive experience with a figure does not increase the probability of its detectability if it is embedded in a larger, more complex whole. It should be noted, however, that the directions given to the subjects were of a general nature. More than 6.6 per cent of the subjects might have noticed A in B but did not indicate this fact because of the generality of the instructions.

The limitation of this principle of inclusiveness is indicated in the experiments by Djang (1937) and N. G. Hanawalt (1942), previously cited. These experiments indicated that experience does play an important role in the hidden-figures task.

Djang's experiment is very instructive. It not only shows the kinds of forms in which experience does play a role but also deals with the complex nature of the various possible interactions between stimulus structure and learning. Let us first note the way Djang achieved inclusiveness, masking, or embedding from the examples in Figure 7-14 and then compare it with Gottschaldt's Figure 7-13. Next let us compare YOP with Gottschaldt's

YOP   ZIF

Figure 7-14
Examples of Djang's figures. (After Djang, 1937, p. 33.)

A figure and ZIF with Gottschaldt's B figure. Djang stated explicitly that he used figures in which many organizations are more or less possible. He not only compared the experimental groups that had previous experience with the masked forms with control groups that had not, but he also related the ease of finding the masked form in the composite to such factors as the ease of original learning of the masked form and the relative difficulty in learning the composite figure. It should be noted that the figures have nonsense syllables by which they were to be identified. Some of Djang's results follow.

1. The supposedly nonsense figures became meaningful in the process of learning.
2. The masked figures were seen as separate units in their composites (complexes) 20 times more often by the experimental group than by the control groups and 77 times more often on the first trial.
3. Some masked figures were more easily found than others.
4. The ease with which a masked figure was isolated was related to the complexity of the composite figure containing it, as measured by the number of trials required to learn that figure.

Although Djang concluded that a "search attitude" was not decisive, he thought it probably contributed to the discovery of the masked figures. In any case, the fact that the subjects had to learn nonsense-syllable identifications of these figures probably produced a different effect than the mere repetitive exposure in Gottschaldt's study. Furthermore, the equivocation of the organizations in the figures left greater opportunity for learning to influence the selection of structural organization.

Relevant to this last point are the results obtained in an experiment conducted by I. G. Campbell (1941), in which observers were asked to pick out a particular part of a whole design. He found that the observers could do this in about 3 sec if the part were regular or symmetrical, but it took them between 20 and 40 sec if the part had an irregular structure.

FURTHER EXPLORATION OF REDUNDANCY AND MEMORY FOR FORM. Now that we have seen the importance of structural organization and the way learning interacts with it, we might ask whether forms which are more definitively structured will be remembered more easily than forms which are more equivocally structured. A study which was designed to answer this question was performed by Attneave (1955). In this study, as in the earlier one cited, he attempted to quantify the gestalt laws by using the approach of information theory; but here he was interested in the memory of perceived forms. A total of 149 subjects was randomly assigned to one of five groups, each of which was shown 60 patterns of dot cells. Each pattern was shown one at a time, and the subject was required to reproduce the pattern afterward. There were five classes of patterns, as shown in Figure 7-15.

The figure contains one of the 60 patterns in each class. In the pattern 12R the dots were inserted into the cells at random. There were 12 "bits" [7] of information. The other two random conditions, 20R and 35R, contained 20 and 35 bits of information, respectively; but 20S contained only 12 bits since the pattern is symmetrical about the vertical axis. Likewise, 35S also contained 12 bits of information, since the pattern is symmetrical about

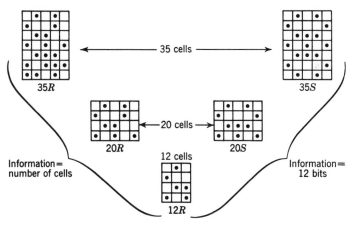

Figure 7-15

Examples of the five classes of patterns. The symmetrical patterns 20S and 35S are matched with the random patterns 20R and 35R. With respect to informational content, they are matched with each other and with 12R; i.e., 12R contains all the information necessary for the construction of either 20S or 35S. (After Attneave, 1955, p. 210.)

[7] The bit is the unit of information theory. The amount of information (bits) is defined as $\Sigma - P \log_2 P$, where Σ means the sum of and P is the probability of occurrence of each element of the stimulus patterns. If all alternatives are equally likely, the definition reduces to $\log_2 A$, where A is the number of elements.

both the vertical and the horizontal axes. Each group was presented with only one class of patterns.

EXAMPLE OF BITS. The reader may wonder why there are 12 bits of information in the 12 cells. If we apply the formula $\log_2 A$, each cell will have 1 bit of information, since there are two alternatives (a dot or no dot) for each cell, and $\log_2 2$ is 1. Therefore for 12 cells there are 12 bits of information, which seems to be true intuitively in any case.

As far as the 20*S* condition is concerned, the pattern simply contains two examples of the 12*R* condition in a symmetrical relationship. Hence Attneave feels no additional information is added. The same is true of 35*S*, which contains 12*R* repeated in horizontal and vertical symmetry. Attneave therefore concludes that the 12*R*, 20*S*, and 35*S* conditions each contain 12 bits of information. We shall question whether this is strictly correct after we have examined his results.

Three measures of memory were employed: (1) immediate reproduction, which consisted of reproduction of the pattern into blank cells immediately after exposure; (2) delayed reproduction, which consisted of reproduction 15 sec after exposure; and (3) identification, which consisted of learning the names of the patterns and then identifying them by their names.

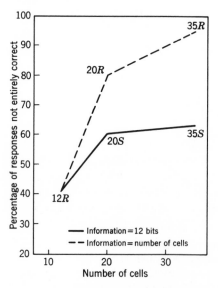

Figure 7-16
Delayed reproduction: percentage of imperfect responses for the five groups. (After Attneave, 1955, p. 217.)

The results of the three measures gave similar trends. We present the results of delayed reproduction in Figure 7-16. The patterns 12*R*, 20*S*, and 35*S* each contain only 12 bits of information, but 20*R* and 35*R* each contain more than do 20*S* and 35*S*. Two comparisons should be made on the graph in Figure 7-16. In all cases the errors were counted only from the

12 cells in each pattern which were identical. This was obviously done so that we could compare equal probabilities for making errors. The maximum number of errors which could be made is 12, with a chance probability of 6.[8] First we compare 12*R*, 20*S*, and 35*S*. Here we note that these patterns differ only in the number of elements but not in the amount of information concerned. It is clear from the graph that symmetry is not handled very effectively by the subjects as the pattern goes from simple to more complex; e.g., more numerous errors are made for 35*S* than for 20*S*. Similarly, we compare 20*R* with 20*S* and 35*R* with 35*S*. Here symmetry operates with a reduction in the amount of information from 35*R* to 35*S* and from 20*R* to 20*S*. In this case symmetry (redundancy) does make it easier to discriminate the patterns.

We should add that the effect of symmetry was greater in the delayed reproduction than it was in the immediate reproduction. Evidently the effect of redundancy in facilitating encoding has more chance to operate after delay.

A study by Adams, Fitts, Rappaport, and Weinstein (1954) found that subjects learn to identify symmetrical shapes more easily than asymmetrical shapes when the two are matched with respect to number of lines and angles. Fitts et al. (1956), however, have indicated that symmetry of figures may either hinder or facilitate form recognition, depending upon the manner in which they are presented. Likewise, Rappaport (1957) has shown that redundancy (provided by figures with repetitious outlines) is effective only when "noise" [9] is present. More will be said in Chapter 8 about the structural factors influencing form identification.

These studies show that the factor of symmetry may improve or hinder information encoding and memory, with the possibility of symmetry and redundancy being more effective when noise is present. We do not, of course, know whether symmetry does this better than some of the other gestalt factors. In the Attneave experiment, simplicity appears to limit the effectiveness of symmetry (compare 12*R* and 20*S*), but this might not happen in other situations.

Relative to the Attneave study, however, we might add that the assumption that no further information is generated when the symmetrical portion of a pattern is added may be questionable. Intuitively we see that the information content should not double, but it appears reasonable to assume that some small amount of information is added. If this were not so, the two patterns would be identical, which is definitely not the case. If we allow for an addition of a minimal amount of information (beyond that of 12*R*) for the symmetrical figures 20*S* and 35*S*, the results are more understandable. We can then say that the number of errors tends to increase with increasing amounts of information contained within the stimulus pattern

[8] The probability of being correct by chance is one-half.

[9] Noise is provided by distracting but irrelevant figural aspects.

and conclude that symmetry does improve information encoding and memory. What we need are studies to determine how the mechanisms operate and interact. The studies reported here serve to clarify the gestalt principle that figural goodness may be favorable to memory.

The case for the importance of structural features has been made. It appears that experiential factors do interact with *Prägnanz*. Köhler, in his rejection of the premise that learned experience can lead to structural changes, has stated that *Prägnanz* dictates the course experience will take. But other experiments (e.g., that of Djang) have warned that we must be more cautious in our interpretation; figures poorly structured from the standpoint of the criteria of *Prägnanz* can develop the status of identities after appropriate experience.

An intriguing experiment relevant to this point was performed by Razran (1939), who presented some of Wertheimer's figures to observers while they were eating. The figures, made up of flashlight bulbs (like Wertheimer's dots), consisted of a complex whole which contained subparts, some of which were "simpler" than others. The experimenter attempted to avoid intentional learning by telling the observers that the effect of eyestrain on digestion was being investigated. Subsequently, the subparts of the whole were presented, and the strength of a conditioned-salivary response was measured. It was found that the conditioned response was stronger for the simpler parts. It took much longer for a conditioned response to the more complex part to reach the same maximum strength, but the conditioned response to the simpler parts showed more rapid extinction. Thus, while responses to simpler forms are initially more dominant, *responses to more complex forms may become stronger after they have been well learned.* Does effort increase resistance to extinction? Although the simpler forms contain less information and are attained quickly, it is probable that with learning the subject encodes the complex forms in chunks which are as easily "stored" as are the simpler forms.

A somewhat similar position is reached by Thurstone in his factorial study of perception (1944).[10] He reported a number of factors operating in perceptual discrimination, of which two are relevant here. One factor, which is more primitive, is the ability to close and perceive configurations. The other, which is more cultivated, relates to the flexibility in breaking up configurations and going from one form to another.

In summary, it appears that responses which are primitive or initially more dominant are not necessarily the ones which remain dominant in the repertoire of the adults' behavior. Experiential factors can compensate for a lack of structural factors and can in certain cases become more dominant than responses to unlearned forms, possibly through an encoding process involving chunks of information rather than bits or pieces of information. "Doing what comes naturally" may be true for the naïve child, but after

[10] See also Guilford (1947); Roff (1952).

the experienced organism has learned the functional utility of responding to certain forms, the latter become important cues to behavior. As a matter of fact, the whole question of how experience influences form discrimination is a very complex one which cannot be answered by one overall principle, as Köhler has tried to do. In the next two chapters we shall present recent views and research on the effect of controlled practice on perceptual discrimination.

Summary

This chapter was divided into three main sections. Section 1 described data which show that a certain amount of heterogeneity in stimulation is needed for the perception of figure. Demonstrations within the homogeneous field or *Ganzfeld,* known as the autokinetic effect, show that a differentiated ground is necessary for the emergence of a figure. Section 2 dealt with conditions determining the relative stability and instability of figure-ground phenomena. A description of the gestalt laws of visual perception, especially as initiated by Wertheimer, was then presented in the third and largest division.

Recent attempts using information theory to clarify why gestalt laws work the way they do, especially the pioneering work of Attneave, were introduced to throw light on the organization of elements into figures, patterns, groupings, or configurations. The thesis is that gestalt laws operate to establish a certain amount of redundancy which in turn ensures us against maladaptive error in perception. The channel capacity of the human organism as a processor or transmitter of information is limited. While the amount of information we transmit is relatively low, we can rely on that information for effective behavior.

The relative importance of stimulus factors and experience in the determination of figural detection and recognition was assessed. Figures which are relatively simple (have *Prägnanz,* according to gestalt principles, or are redundant, according to Attneave) are more readily perceived and recognized. It is in the case of more complex stimulus patterns that the role of experience becomes more important in the establishment of a stable, more permanent figure.

8

Information Extraction
and Sensory Experience
in Form Identification

In Chapter 7 we dealt with the way stimulus elements tend to segregate or organize themselves in perception. We looked at Attneave's suggestion that the principles of grouping are governed by the limitations of the human organism as an extractor and transmitter of usable information. Furthermore, the amount of information contained in the stimulus is much greater than the amount the organism can actually use because of this limited channel capacity. This *redundancy* evidently exists to ensure us against mistakes; i.e., while we do not extract most of the potential information in the stimulus, what limited amount we do transmit we can use with meaning and reliability.

Having considered the emergence of unity or figure from a ground, we now want to see how that unity becomes a stable, meaningful *identity* or *form*. For example, a human face not only sticks out from a background but also carries certain meaningful information to the observer after the latter has had some sensory experience in looking at that face. The human face is extremely complex when considered from the standpoint of the potential information it contains. Despite the fact that the organism cannot possibly extract or process all the stimulus information because of its limited channel capacity, it is nevertheless remarkable that the perception of form identity is as accurate as it is in experienced human beings. During our everyday experience, for example, we come into contact with literally hundreds of faces, essentially all of which are different, and yet we come to recognize each identity with reliability. Clearly there must be a certain limited number of points at which the information is concentrated. Somehow the organization of these concentrated points of information provides the essential definition of the form. Two problems, to which we partly address ourselves in this chapter, are raised. How can we determine the *number* of these concentrated informational points in a particular pattern or form, and what is the *content* of these points which determines the definition or meaning of the identity? This takes us to a third problem, *sensory experience,* which significantly influences the way the contents of a form are structured.

Measurement of Information

The concepts of information theory [1] have been applied to the first problem, namely, that of determining the amount of information transmitted or the number of elements processed by the organism. While this does not tell us what the nature of the information is, it is at least an important beginning. Once we determine, for example, what the number of concentrated points of information is for a particular form, we can go ahead and explore precisely what these points are and how they happen to be the conveyors of the definitive information.

Perhaps it will help us to understand what follows if we begin with a look at some conceptions of the model. In Figure 8-1 we have the sequence of communication. Applying this sequence to the process of form perception in human beings would lead to the following considerations. Let us note first that the amount of information transmitted depends upon the correspondence between the symbols transmitted and those received and on the amount of noise in the channel. The source of the information exists in the array of physical energy which stimulates the sense organs. The information transmitted through the channel depends on the amount of information the organism can process (the channel capacity) and the way this process is modified by organismic sets and irrelevant stimulation (noise). The component of noise coming from organismic set, which would be regarded as a nuisance by the communication engineer, is an important determiner of how information is coded by the human organism. The human perceiver in the communication channel cannot be regarded as a perfectly predictable system. Differential effects resulting from the way past learning

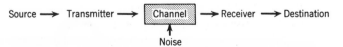

Source ⟶ Transmitter ⟶ | Channel | ⟶ Receiver ⟶ Destination

↑

Noise

Figure 8-1
The communication system.

[1] See, for example, Shannon and Weaver (1949).

interacts with the built-in programming ability of the nervous system produce modified programs in individuals.

We shall first look at the nature of the method for measuring the amount
of information transmitted in general form perception. Then we shall
inquire into the content of such information, i.e., where informational
points are concentrated, what determines the nature of such concentration,
and how experience and learning affect this process.

Amount of Information Transmitted

Let us consider the pattern in Figure 8-2, which consists of 32 cells.
Suppose we play a game in which the subject is required to discover which

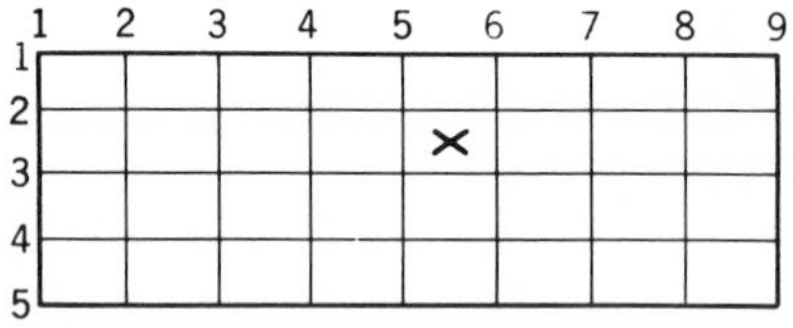

Figure 8-2
A pattern of 32 cells for illustrating the strategy in information extraction.

one of these cells we have previously decided to be the "correct" one. If *S*
transmits information most efficiently, he will be able to discover this cell
with the minimum number of questions. He could proceed by eliminating
one cell at a time, but intuition tells us that this would obviously not be the
economical way of selecting a strategy. A more efficient way of extracting
information would be to elicit answers which would eliminate the greatest
number of alternatives for each question asked. The strategy might proceed
somewhat as follows.

Question 1. Is it to the left of column line 5? Answer: no.
    Hence it must be to the right of this line.
Question 2. Is it above row line 3? Answer: yes.
Question 3. Is it to the left of column line 7? Answer: yes.
Question 4. It is to the right of column line 6? Answer: no.
    Therefore it must be in one of the two cells bounded by column
    lines 5 and 6 and row lines 1 and 3.
Question 5. Is it above row line 2? Answer: no.
    Therefore it must be the cell marked by *X* in the figure.

By using the procedure outlined above the subject was able to eliminate
half of the number of alternatives by asking each question in such a way
as to elicit the most informative answer. Measurement in information theory
is based on some operation of a binary choice (such as using the yes-no
questions above). The unit of measurement is called the *bit,* which is a
contraction of *binary digit.*

How do we go about measuring the bits of information? Let us look at
the example above. We started with 32 alternatives, and by five questions

reduced the alternatives to 1. Since each question involves the choice between 2 alternatives, we can measure the bits by determining to what power 2 has to be raised to arrive at the number of alternatives. In the example above, $2^5 = 32$. Therefore 5 bits of information are contained in the patterns of cells. If all the information is transmitted, the individual will solve the game by asking only five questions. The general equation of measuring the amount of information in bits is:

$$A = 2^H$$

or

$$H = \log_2 A$$

[handwritten: $\log_2$ Binary choices]

where A represents the number of alternatives and H is the symbol for expressing the amount of information in bits. (In our example above, $32 = 2^5$, or $H = \log_2 32 = 5$.) This equation holds only when all As are equally probable.

INFORMATION WHEN CHOICES ARE NOT EQUALLY PROBABLE. The equation $H = \log_2 A$ may be written as $H = \log_2 (1/p)$, where p is the probability of any one choice's occurring (derived from $p = 1/A$).

Now, let H_i represent the information associated with the occurrence of a particular alternative i; then

$$H_i = \log_2 \frac{1}{p_i}$$

To find the total amount of information connected with the occurrence of all events we must take the amount of information of each event "weighted" by the probability of its occurrence. Thus

$$H = p_1 H_1 + p_2 H_2 + p_3 H_3 + \cdots + p_i H_i + \cdots + p_n H_n$$

$$= \sum_{i=1}^{n} p_i H_i = \Sigma \, p_i \log_2 \frac{1}{p_i}$$

And, since

$$\log_2 \frac{1}{p_i} = - \log_2 p_i$$

$$H = \sum_{i=1}^{n} - p_i \log_2 p_i$$

How can this way of measuring the amount of information be applied to the analysis of form or pattern discrimination? Let us consider the situation schematized in Figure 8-3. This schematization by Miller (1953) of the communication channel can be concretized in the situation of form perception in the following manner. $H(s)$ is the information generated by the stimulus, or the input information; $H(o)$ is the information in the perceptual process, or the output information; and T is the transmitted informa-

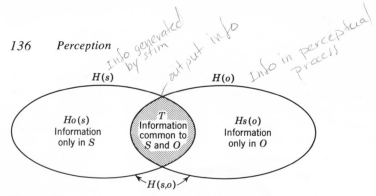

Info generated by stim *output info* *Info in perceptual process*

Figure 8-3
Schematic representation of the several quantities of information that are involved when messages are received from two related sources. (Modified from Miller, 1953.)

tion. The greater the overlap between $H(s)$ and $H(o)$, the greater the amount of transmitted information T. $Ho(s)$ is information which is put in at the senses but not recovered by the organism O. $Hs(o)$ is information added by the organism. T will thus be reduced by the presence of $Ho(s)$, which is called *equivocation*, and by $Hs(o)$, which is called *noise*. Equivocation can be regarded as information which the organism cannot discriminate reliably, and noise as irrelevant perceptual or "mental" sets. We can thus measure transmitted information by the formula

$$T = H(s,o) - [Ho(s) + Hs(o)]$$
total information — equivocation + noise

In other words the amount of transmitted information depends on the amount of input information which can be reliably coded by the organism, aided by relevant organismic sets.

We shall now present an actual example of measuring T, before we proceed to a discussion of the problems involved in discovering the factors which determine the transmission of information in form perception, i.e., before discussing the factors influencing the content of the information discriminated in form perception.

AN EXAMPLE OF MEASURING T (INFORMATION TRANSMITTED). The example which follows is intended to be a paradigm illustrating the measurement of presumably the number of concentrated points of information which are transmitted. It is representative of one kind of research currently being conducted by a number of investigators who are concerning themselves with measuring the amount of information transmitted in form and pattern discrimination. Credit is given to other investigators later in this section, but we have chosen our example from an experiment by Welton (1963) since the raw data were readily available, the research having been conducted in our laboratory at Lake Forest College.

Welton concerned himself with measuring the amount of information which is transmitted from a circular scale or a circular form. The purpose was to determine which segments of a circle transmit reliable information

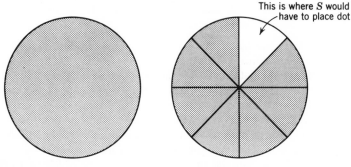

Figure 8-4
Welton's circle for the 8-division case. The figure on the left is the standard (inspection) circle, while the one on the right is the comparison circle. In the example given here, S would have to put the dot in the first division to the right of the vertical line of the second circle to be correct. (After Welton, 1963.)

to the subject. In order to determine this, a circle with a dot located $\frac{1}{16}$ in. from its circumference (on the inner side) was exposed tachistoscopically for 0.02 sec. The subject had to discriminate the position of the dot. Let us look at Figure 8-4. The procedure used for measuring the discrimination of the dot was as follows. First, it was possible for the dot to be in the center of any interval of four different sets of divisions: 4, 8, 16, and 32. The subject received 10 trials for each position in each set (10 for each position in the set of 4 divisions, making a total of 40; 10 for each position in the set of 8, making 80; 160 for the set of 16; and 320 for the set of 32). The order of presenting the stimulus cards with the circle was randomized for the subjects.

After preliminary training with a 4-division card (with the dot at the center) which was exposed for 2 sec and four practice trials with a test card, the experiment proper began. After each card had been exposed for 0.01 or 0.02 sec, the subject was required to mark the position of the dot on a replica of the circle just exposed. The circle was divided into the appropriate number of segments—4, 8, 16, 32—depending on which set the card that had just been exposed was drawn from.

The amount of information transmitted was measured by using a technique described by Garner and Hake (1951) for analyzing a data matrix. We should remember that for each stimulus the subject has to make a response, i.e., mark the position of the dot he has just seen. We want to know how accurate the response is for each position. Are some stimulus positions more easily discriminated than others; that is, do they lead to more reliable transmission? These positions we would call the *concentrated points of information*. How many of these "pregnant" points are there on a circle?

The mechanics involved in analyzing the data to answer this question is rather burdensome. Readers interested in using it can refer to the article by Garner and Hake. The brief steps are as follows:

1. First a data matrix has to be compiled. We record the response that was made for each of the stimulus positions.
2. By using the appropriate mathematical formula for calculating conditional probabilities, we determine whether each of the response portions (out of 4, 8, 16, or 32, as the case may be) has an equal probability of occurring. Applying these formulas, which are extensions of the equation for H, to the data, we find that the portions do not: some divisions are more likely to be chosen than others. The same stimuli are more likely to carry equivocal information. We calculate the amount of equivocation, which we call H_e. We already know how much information the stimulus contains by merely applying the formula $\log_2 A$ (e.g., 3 bits for 8 alternatives and 4 bits for 16 alternatives). We call this Hs.
3. Since in this experiment we have no way of measuring organismic set, we apply a simplification of formula 2 to arrive at the amount of information transmitted: $T = H_s - H_e$, where T is transmitted information, H_s is the information in the stimulus, and H_e is stimulus equivocation.

The results for all four sets and for each subject are presented in Table 8-1, from which we can see that the upper limit on the capacity to

Table 8-1

Summary of Results of Two Subjects on the Transmission of Information from a Circular Scale. (From Welton, 1963.)

Sets	S_{PK}				S_{KW}			
Number of Alternative Stimuli	4	8	16	32	4	8	16	32
Stimulus Information (bits)	2.00	3.00	4.00	5.00	2.00	3.00	4.00	5.00
Stimulus Equivocation (bits)	0.00	0.00	0.82	1.34	0.00	0.00	0.70	1.18
Information Transmitted (bits)	2.00	3.00	3.18	3.66	2.00	3.00	3.30	3.82

process the information given by the position of a dot on a circle approaches 4 bits. The graphs in Figure 8-5 indicate that the asymptote of the curve of the information transmitted is not fully evident, but it is clear that it is being approached.

How can the results presented in Table 8-1 and Figure 8-5 be interpreted? First of all, it should be noted that the number of bits which are transmitted varies somewhat from pattern to pattern, although there is some maximum limit. For example, Hake and Garner (1951) found the amount of information transmitted when the subject had to identify the position of

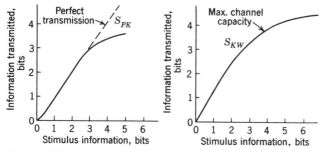

Figure 8-5

Graphs of information transmitted (T) plotted against stimulus information (H_s). Channel capacity appears to be approximately 4 bits. (From Welton, 1963.)

a point on a linear scale, where the number of alternative positions varied, approached an asymptote of 3.2 bits. Klemmer and Frick (1953) reported the maximum amount of information transmitted by a dot in a two-dimensional matrix to be 4.4 bits. In Welton's experiment, the asymptote was not reached for the 32 alternative conditions, although the amount of 3.82 bits was approaching an asymptote. Had he used conditions with a greater number of alternatives, the amount reported by Klemmer and Frick might have been obtained.

What is the value of knowing the amount of bits transmitted in the discrimination of form? Let us take the case of a circle as used by Welton. Essentially it tells us that there are probably four positions on the circumference of a circle which carry most of the information. It now remains for us to determine experimentally where these four points of concentrated information are. The inspection of Welton's data gives us a lead in this direction. These data show that there were more accurate responses to the *vertical* and *horizontal* positions, which give us two of the four pregnant points. In attempting to determine the other two points, we note further that there was a wider spread for responses to stimuli of the positions located 45° to the horizontal and the vertical. From these points equivocation is high, and they can probably be eliminated as highly pregnant. By thus experimenting, we can determine the points which, when combined, carry the essential form structure.

Now that we have seen how the amount of transmitted information can be measured, let us explore the possible factors which determine and limit this amount.

Contents of the Stimulus Which Influence Information Transmission

In Chapter 7 we described Attneave's examination of this problem by applying informational analysis to the gestalt laws. We now sample briefly from the work of other psychologists who have concerned themselves with applying informational techniques to the problem of form identification in general.

Let us recall that in the sections "Further Exploration of Redundancy and Memory for Form" and "Example of Bits" at the end of Chapter 7 we reviewed Attneave's report that, in forms with the same amount of alternatives, symmetrical patterns are more readily transmitted than asymmetrical patterns. It was also pointed out that Fitts et al. had found that the manner in which symmetry is presented influences its effect. Thus the situation is more complex. Since symmetry is one way of producing redundancy and since redundancy ensures us against errors in discrimination, while at the same time consolidating the transmission of reliable contents which determine the perceived form, it seems profitable to describe further some of the work on the role of redundancy.

The work of Rappaport (1957) is appropriate in this regard. We should keep in mind that the gestalt psychologists emphasized that *Prägnanz* facilitates figural perception. In informational terms this means, as Attneave stated, that redundancy makes form recognition easier. Rappaport, however, like Fitts, questions the view that redundancy always has an undirectional effect. He reports that the type of redundancy used and its interaction with visual noise alter considerably the ease with which visual forms are identified.

In the experiments performed by Rappaport the effects of two types and four levels (amount) of redundancy on the ease with which forms are recognized were studied. When background noise was present, redundancy *facilitated rapid discrimination,* but when the noise was absent, an increase in redundancy was accompanied by slower discrimination, that is, by an *increase in recognition time.* No differences in time to recognize the forms with the two different types of redundancy were found in the noise-free situation.

Inspection of the conditions used by Rappaport does not lead to a clear interpretation of why he obtained these results. He attributes the lack of differences between the two types in part to the nonutilization of redundant features by the subject when external noise was absent. As for the other result, he thought that the increased recognition time in the noise-free condition was due primarily to the difficulty the subject had in discriminating smaller details in the forms which were more redundant.

In conclusion Rappaport suggests that in some conditions a balance might exist between the facilitating effects of certain kinds of redundancy and the inhibiting effects caused by an excess of redundancy or its introduction in an ineffective way. It would be interesting to clarify the nature of this proposed balance in systematic parametric studies. A study by Attneave on the relationship between redundancy and the judged complexity of shapes is a step in this direction (1957).

In Attneave's study 72 shapes were judged for complexity by 168 subjects. The shapes were constructed so that certain physical characteristics were symmetrically varied and the remainder were randomly determined. Readers interested in the mechanics of constructing these shapes should consult an article by Attneave and Arnoult (1956). The forms were constructed by connecting a certain number of points according to specified rules. Some of the variables used in constructing the forms were the number of points (turns), symmetry, and the fact of whether the forms were angular, curved, or a mixture of angles and curves.

Attneave's analysis of his data led him to conclude that 90 per cent of the variance of the ratings of complexity could be accounted for by three factors. The first was the number of independent turns (angles or curves) in the contour. The second was symmetry. Symmetrical shapes were judged less complex than asymmetrical shapes when the total number of turns was constant but were judged more complex when the number of *independent* turns was constant (4- and 6-point symmetrical shapes were equivalent to 4- and 6-point asymmetrical shapes with respect to the number of independent turns but equivalent to 8- and 12-point asymmetrical shapes with respect to the total number of turns). The third factor was the arithmetic mean of algebraic differences, in degrees, between successive turns in the contour. The variable of angularity and vividness made no significant contribution to judged complexities. Six examples (symmetrical and asymmetrical) of the seventy-two shapes used by Attneave are presented in Figure 8-6.

Figure 8-6
Six of the seventy-two shapes used in the study. (After Attneave, 1957, p. 223.)

Now that we have been introduced to the apparent complexity of the role of *redundancy* in the determination of form, let us briefly look at some other factors which might have significant influence. We have seen that the *number of turns* and the *difference in degrees between successive turns* also play significant roles. Some other physical characteristics of forms have been studied by, among other investigators, Casperson and Attneave and Arnoult.

Casperson (1950) used geometric shapes, rather than the random shapes of Attneave, and measured recognition thresholds and the total number of correct identifications, instead of judged complexity, for his measure of discrimination. His stimulus shapes consisted of six basic classes: ellipses, rectangles, triangles, diamonds, crosses, and stars. There were five figures in each class, constructed by varying the three dimensions of area, maximum dimension, and perimeter. On the basis of the shortest recognition times and the greatest number of correct identifications, the following results were obtained:

1. *Area* produced the best measure of discriminability for ellipses and triangles.
2. *Maximum dimension* was the best parameter for discriminating rectangles and diamonds.
3. *Perimeter* gave the best discrimination for stars and crosses.

It would be a worthwhile exercise for the student to draw these figures, inspect them, contemplate why the three dimensions differentiated the shapes the way they did in this experiment, and then subject these contemplative hunches to experimental exploration. Evidently the subject relies on the best dimension available for making the most reliable discrimination. What this dimension is depends on the overall constellation, and to state that the rule is to follow the law of simplicity is to obscure the problem.

Besides the results for specific figures mentioned above, the following additional observations are of interest. The six basic forms can best be discriminated as a class when the maximum dimensions are known, while a prediction of discriminability for the total group of 30 forms can best be done on the basis of their perimeters.

Finally, Casperson compared the variances contributed by the 20 subjects with the variances attributable to form differences. His analysis supports the hypothesis that forms do differ in their discriminability and that individual differences among subjects are small compared with differences among the forms. For a general review of the complexities and differences among forms and for a further appreciation of the great variety of ways that they can be reduced to lower dimensionability, the reader should consult Attneave and Arnoult (1956).

We may grant the importance of the physical characteristics of the stimulus, but the organism is also a vital part of the communication channel. In fact, we have stated that the amount or the kind of information transmitted also depends on relevant organismic sets and the minimization of noise. This dependency raises the whole question of subjective experience, to which we now turn.

Sensory Experience and Learning in Form Perception

Some rather difficult methodological problems are involved in interpreting the effect of experience on perception. Since perception is a process which is inferred to intervene between stimulation and response, any change in the perceptual response after certain experiences can be accounted for in more than one way. The trouble arises when we try to determine which of these probable explanations is more nearly correct. In Chapter 7, we were exposed to the difficulties involved in such interpretations, and we shall meet them repeatedly in later chapters. In the present section, we want to consider some of the systematic ways in which the effects of learning on perception have been handled. This consideration involves a description of the experimental methodologies used, the results obtained, and the theoretical integrations attempted.

The typical experiments on perceptual learning involve manipulations of a number of varieties. Some experiments on so-called social perception have noted, for example, that the subject's recognition threshold is higher for certain "loaded" words than for certain neutral words. The usual explanation has been that the organism is "suppressing" recognition of these words. An alternative explanation is that these words are not as familiar as others to the subject and it is the lack of frequency which makes detection more difficult. A third explanation is that the subject has difficulty not in the sensory or motivational area but in the response area. Some sensory impulses call forth a greater number of responses than others, and these therefore lead to greater errors or higher recognition thresholds.

So we see that modification of discrimination can be accounted for in at least three ways. There is change in the receptive, mediational, or response systems or in all three of these, and to tease out the precise change is difficult indeed. Even studies which are experimentally well controlled encounter similar difficulties of interpretation. As an example, let us suppose we have two groups of matched animals. The experimental group is given certain training from birth, and the control group is not. We find at maturity that the experimental group is superior in form discrimination to the control group. Many factors could account for the difference. Here are some of them. (1) Training is necessary for the normal maturation of the sensory nervous system. (2) Learning is necessary for form discrimination. (3) Learning improves form discrimination. (4) What is seen early in life determines the course of perceptual development. (5) The frequency of practice accounts for the superiority. (6) Change in sensory encoding, mediational decoding, or motor responses, as mentioned above, accounts for the change in information processing.

It thus appears that the sensible way to approach the analysis of perceptual learning is to keep all these possibilities in mind and to look at the different kinds of training modifications which have been studied. We shall begin with an examination of imprinting, which seems to be the bridge between innate responding and instrumentally learned responding.

Imprinting

Let us start by trying to place imprinting in its proper context in the general information-extracting process. As we noted earlier, an organism might extract information by a built-in (innate) program or by learned programs. In the former case the following question is important. Will the organism always respond to a particular stimulus attribute in a fixed way or does the response depend on the time during his life-span when the stimulus was presented? Or maybe the particular form of the stimulus is unimportant as long as it is the first stimulus he receives during a critical period of early development. He will then develop a fixated response to that stimulus. This will be the most primitive kind of "learning," involving as it does an interaction between an innate maturational tendency and certain environmental stimulation. Imprinting appears to be an example of this kind of primitive, rigid learning.

Although the phenomenon was studied by others, Lorenz (1935) [2] was the first to call it imprinting. The term *imprinting* means simply that early social contacts determine the character of adult social behavior. Working especially with greylag geese, Lorenz postulated that imprinting occurs at a critical period early in the life of the animal.

Although there have been a number of studies reported since Lorenz's publication, especially since 1956, most of them have sought to link imprinting to associative learning. As we have said, however, imprinting appears to be an example of a much simpler, more rigid kind of learning. For this reason and also because he has dealt with some of the perceptual aspects of imprinting more systematically, we shall base our discussion on the more recent publication of Hess (1959).

Imprinting has been studied primarily in certain species of birds, like geese and ducks. Hess himself worked with relatively wild mallard ducks. The essential feature of the experimental imprinting procedure is quite simple. Duck eggs are hatched into a box in an incubator, and the young ducklings are carefully kept from viewing the outside world until they have been brought into the imprinting apparatus. The apparatus consists essentially of a circular runway around which a decoy duck can be moved. The duckling is placed in this apparatus, the decoy is set in motion (sometimes with duck calls, either pleasure tones or distress notes, and sometimes silently), and the experimenter observes whether or not the duckling starts to follow the decoy, i.e., starts to imprint. After initial training on this procedure, the strength of imprinting is tested by measuring the percentage of times the duckling follows the original decoy. A number of variables have been observed to influence effective imprinting. We shall give an account

---

[2] The releasing mechanism of the innate response by the stimulus (named by Lorenz) has been widely studied in many species by Eibl-Eibesfeldt.

of some of these variables which appear to be most relevant to the psychology of perceptual discrimination.

CRITICAL PERIOD. To ascertain whether there is a critical age period during which imprinting is more effective, the ducklings were imprinted at various hours after hatching. They were placed in the imprinting procedure, which contained a moving model of a male mallard. The sound emitted with the model was an arbitrarily chosen human rendition of "gock, gock, gock, gock." After imprinting the duckling was returned automatically to its box until it was tested for the strength of imprinting. The imprinting experience usually consisted of letting the duckling follow the model 150 to 200 ft around the runway for 10 min.

During the test, the duckling was given 1 min to make a choice between following the original male model making the "gock" sound or a female model giving the call of a real mallard female calling her young. The percentage of correct choices, i.e., following the male model on which the duckling had originally been imprinted, is shown in Figure 8-7.

Both of the graphs indicate clearly that while some imprinting occurs immediately after hatching, the optimum time for most effective imprinting is between the ages of thirteen and sixteen hours. At this age, the average imprinting score is between 80 and 90 per cent, and it steadily decreases to almost zero by the time the thirty-two-hour age group is reached. Ducklings between the ages of twenty-four and fifty-two hours who were first given imprinting experience in the presence of other ducklings who had already been imprinted at a younger age, however, obtained an average score of 50 per cent. But none of these ducklings obtained perfect scores even after the time and distance during imprinting experience were increased.

We might therefore ask why the strength of imprinting with older ducklings is significantly decreased. While this question cannot be answered

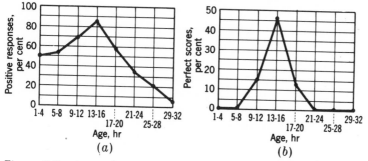

Figure 8-7

(*a*) *The critical age at which ducklings are most effectively imprinted is depicted by this curve, which shows the average test score of ducklings imprinted in each age group.* (*b*) *Another way of showing the critical age is by plotting the percentage of animals in each group that made scores of 100 per cent in testing.* (*After Hess, 1959, p. 135.*)

definitively, Hess has data which he interprets as indicating that the imprinting age is limited by the rate of maturation and should occur before the fear reaction sets in sometime after birth. Thus imprinting has some adaptive functions. Hess also found that the strength of imprinting increases with the distance traveled by the ducklings until an asymptote is reached between 75 and 100 ft. So the critical period is affected by *maturation, fear,* and *effort.*

COLOR AND FORM PREFERENCES IN IMPRINTING OBJECTS. In experiments with Vantress broiler chicks, imprinting experiences were given on one of the following moving spheres: red, orange, yellow, green, blue, near black, near white, and neutral gray. The imprinting was tested 24 hr later by seeing whether the chicks would follow the imprinting stimulus or one of the other forms in the case of a chromatic imprinting stimulus, or one of the other two in the case of an achromatic stimulus. To determine form differences, the same spheres were modified with heads, wings, and tails. The results show that the colors can be ranked from most effective to least effective in terms of imprinting strength as follows: blue, red, green, orange, gray, black, yellow, white. Hess concluded that the hue of a stimulus is more important than its albedo.

The complexity of the form had a definite influence on the ease and strength of imprinting. The plain ball was most effective, followed by the ball with wings and tail; and the ball with wings, tail, and head was the least effective. Finally, a stuffed brown Leghorn rooster was an even poorer stimulus. These results accord with the view that we have adopted about the informational aspects of forms.

In concluding this section, we shall summarize the comparisons that Hess makes between imprinting and associative learning. (1) With imprinting *massed* training is superior to spaced training; this situation is just the opposite of that found in associative learning. (2) In imprinting the *primacy* of experience rather than its recency is the maximally effective factor. (3) Punishment or painful consequences increase the effect of the imprinting experience; this violates the principle of reinforcement found in instrumental learning.

Hess concludes that imprinting is a "rigid form of learning, differing in several ways from the usual association learning which comes into play immediately after the peak of imprintability" (1959, p. 141). Imprinting permits the animal to learn the rough, generalized characteristics of the imprinting object. Increased specificity in discrimination comes later and probably follows the laws of conditioning.

Our next step is to examine these later experiences and see what they have to offer in helping us to explain how the discrimination of specific form identities develops. We proceed to an examination of figural aftereffects, which deal with the effect of relatively short experience in viewing forms.

Figural Aftereffects

Following his earlier work, Köhler has recently developed a theory of electrical conduction in the brain which he believes is the model for sensory and perceptual organization. This theory is based largely on his experiments with figural aftereffects.

The demonstration of figural aftereffects goes back to J. J. Gibson (1933), who reported the following set of experimental facts. The observer is presented with a slightly curved line in the vertical position, which he has to inspect steadily for 5 to 10 min. Toward the end of the inspection period, the line appears to be less curved; adaptation has occurred. The effect of this adaptation to curvature is so strong that if a straight line is now presented to the observer, it appears to be curved in the opposite direction. The adaptation had led to a negative aftereffect. Apparently, this was not a case of pure sensory (retinal) adaptation, for if the lines are inspected monocularly, the effect is only about half as strong. Evidently, summation occurs in the brain, the most likely area being the cerebral cortex.

This negative aftereffect has been verified with other stimulus material. Thus Gibson found that the same effect is obtained if the inspection line is bent in the middle. Again, after continued inspection, the line appears to straighten out, and a straight line presented after this inspection appears to be bent in the opposite direction. The size of the effect can be measured by asking the subject to adjust a flexible rod which can be made more or less straight by turning its parts through a middle axis. When this is done, it is found that the loss in bending during inspection is just about equal to the gain in bending of the straight line viewed after the inspection period. These quantitative aspects have been verified in an experiment by Bales and Follansbee (1935). Gibson himself has found similar results if lines are initially located in the horizontal plane. Moreover, the effect is also observed by tilting a vertical straight line through the vertical position. Thus if the inspection line is tilted 5° to the right of the line of sight, a vertical line, shown after inspection, will appear to be tilted as much as 5° to the left of the line of sight (J. J. Gibson, 1937a; Gibson and Radner, 1937).[3] The experiments dealing with the perception of the vertical are fully discussed in Chapter 10 in the section "Interaction between Visual and Proprioceptive Determiners of the Perceived Vertical and Horizontal," but here we must see how these studies on aftereffects influenced Köhler in the development of his theory.

Gibson himself had noted that the aftereffects, while strong at first, fade out gradually. As we have pointed out, it also seems that the cerebrum plays a large role in this effect. Gibson (1937b) did not offer a physio-

[3] See also M. D. Vernon (1934); Werner and Wapner (1949).

logical theory to explain the underlying "cause" of this effect, but he did relate it to the analogous adaptation effects which occur in other sensory and perceptual phenomena.

Köhler saw more in these effects, however, than an analysis of sensory adaptation. He applied them to develop a cortical theory of general form perception. This theory was first advanced in a paper by Köhler and Wallach (1944), in which they report a number of experiments on figural after-effects. The experimental paradigm is shown in Figure 8-8.

The inspection figure is exposed to the observer, who fixates the *X*. The test figure is so arranged that the left squares fall symmetrically above and below the area where the left inspection square had been located. Similarly, the right squares of the test figure fall in the area between the positions where the right inspection figures had been located. The result is that the observer typically sees the two right squares pushed together, whereas the two left squares are pushed farther apart.

Köhler and Wallach advanced the satiation theory of cortical conduction to explain these effects. They asserted first that "only things, figures, lines, patches, dots—i.e., particular visual entities cause such after-effects . . ."(Köhler and Wallach, 1944, p. 315). Any segregated entity in the visual field is associated with an electric current in the visual sector of the nervous system, and they stated that this "figure current polarizes the tissue through which it flows, and that the figural after-effects are observed; when later the current of a T-figure spreads in the affected medium, it is dispersed" (*ibid.*, p. 316).

Köhler and Wallach are dealing with the nature of direct currents. Their theory can be summarized as follows. The part of the brain which is polarized becomes satiated with current as a result of prolonged stimulation, and its resistance is consequently increased. When now the test figure is presented, the current which flows from the result of its stimulation will spread away from this satiated medium and be dispersed. The current will flow from the area of highest resistance to that of lowest resistance, i.e., from highly satiated areas to less satiated areas.

The application of this theory to the experiment which we just discussed

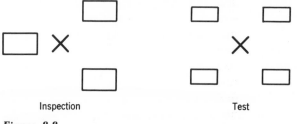

Inspection   Test

Figure 8-8
Demonstration of figural aftereffects. (*From Köhler and Wallach,* *1944.*)

is quite straightforward. The visual areas of the cortex which become satiated as a result of polarization are the parts which were stimulated by the contours of the inspection squares. When now the test figures are shown, the neighboring area of the brain becomes polarized and the current will flow from the satiated region to these neighboring areas. Thus it will flow outward on the left and inward on the right. This results in the left squares' being spread apart and the right squares' being pushed together. The demonstration can be verified in many other ways. Thus the inspection figure could merely consist of one outline square. If the test square is located outside the inspection square, it appears even bigger: its sides are pushed out. Similar results have been reported with the third dimension by Köhler and Emery (1947).

TEMPORAL FACTORS. The temporal course of the figural aftereffect has been investigated thoroughly. Hammer (1949) found that the magnitude of the displacement increased with the increase in the inspection period up to periods between 50 to 100 sec, at which point the displacement remained approximately constant. A number of Japanese investigators have been concerned with this aspect also. Oyama (1953) and Ikeda and Obonai (1953) were concerned with the magnitude or aftereffect occurring after inspection periods of 1 to 240 sec, with lags (between inspection and test) from almost zero to 125 sec. They reported that the aftereffect decreased with delay in measurement after the end of the inspection period, with the *rate of decay* varying directly with the duration of the inspection period; i.e., the decay was extremely fast for short inspection periods and very slow for long periods. In contrast to Hammer's results the length of the inspection period had little effect on the magnitude of displacement for all curves of decay which started from about the same level. Thus the effects of the length of the inspection period were present only for the rate of decay.

The difference in the results of Hammer and the Japanese may be partially or wholly due to different methodologies. Hammer (and Köhler, also) had used the method of average error, in which the subject adjusted the test figure to show the magnitude of the aftereffect. The Japanese used the method of constant stimuli, in which concentric circles were stimuli. One of the circles was presented as the test figure, and the subject reported whether the other circle (inspection figure) was equal, larger, or smaller. Further work by Oyama (1956), Obonai and Suto (1952), and Fujiwara and Obonai (1953) was not so definite as to the effect of the length of the inspection period. It appears, however, that the effect of the period's length has a greater influence upon the rate of decay of displacement than upon the magnitude of displacement which is present immediately following the period; furthermore, prolonged inspection of the inspection figure is not necessary for the aftereffect to occur. But again the delay between inspection and test does influence the measured size of the effect.

RELATION TO ILLUSIONS. A similarity between the concentric-circle illusion, shown in Figure 8-9, and the figural aftereffect has been pointed out by Ikeda and Obonai (1955a; 1955b). The small circle on the right is the same size as the inner one on the left, but it is perceived as larger. Ikeda and

Figure 8-9
Concentric-circle illusion.

Obonai showed that the aftereffect (a consecutive event) approaches the illusory effect (a simultaneous event) as the time interval between the inspection and test periods is reduced to zero, which indicates that both the illusions and the aftereffects probably belong to the same class of events, with time as the important variable. This effect is also related to the fusion of successively exposed lights into continuous movement as reported by J. F. Brown and Voth (1937), which is part of the larger class of spatiotemporal organizations in perception. This class of phenomena and difficulties in replicating them are discussed in Chapter 11.

The result of the work discussed above could be handled by the satiation theory. Furthermore, Köhler and Fishback (1950) have applied this approach to the destruction of the Müller-Lyer illusion, presented in Figure 8-10.

Figure 8-10
Müller-Lyer illusion.

Although the two lines are equal, the right one looks shorter than the left one. The Vs at the ends obviously have some effect in producing this illusion. It has been found that the illusion can be decreased by practice with illusions (Judd, 1902). Köhler and Fishback discovered that it can be decreased by about the same amount if only the end part of the line (with the V) is presented for continual inspection. The authors conclude that it must be the effect of satiation in the area inscribed by the V and not the result of direct comparison of the lines which lowers the illusion. The effect is explained as follows: since there is more satiation between the open part of the V than at its point, the V is pushed toward the point. This explanation accounts for the lengthening or shortening of the two lines which represent the decrease in the illusion. It is a challenge to the usual

explanation of learning, but Köhler and Fishback did find certain similarities between their results and normal learning, such as the fact that
distributed practice of inspection led to greater decrease in the illusion
than did massed practice. Furthermore, the aftereffects, if well established,
may last for months. The reader might contemplate how satiation could
affect the production and decrease of illusions shown in Figures 8-11 and
8-12.

SATIATION THEORY AND LEARNING. Notwithstanding these similarities
between learning and figural aftereffects, Köhler and his associates have
rejected the theory that learning influences the organization of perception.

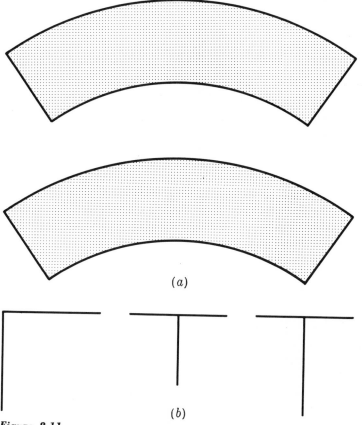

(a)

(b)

Figure 8-11

(a) *Jastrow illusion. The lower figure appears larger than the upper.*
(b) *The vertical-horizontal illusion. In the figure on the left the vertical
line appears larger even though the lines are of equal length. In the
middle figure the vertical line is shorter. The perception of equality on
the right shows that the illusions in the other two figures are related, at
least in part, to the intersections of the lines. How might satiation theory
explain these facts?*

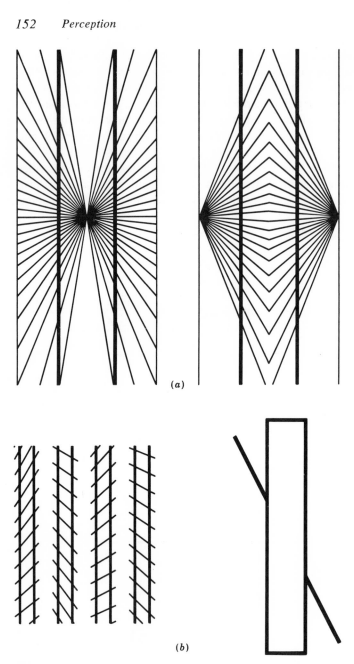

(a)

(b)

Figure 8-12
*Varieties of illusory effects. In a study by Gregory and Wallace
(1963) on the perception of a congenitally blind person who was
given surgery (see Chapter 9), interesting data were reported. The
normal reporting of curved lines in the Hering illusion (a), non-
parallel lines in the Zölner illusion and displacement of the slanted
line in the Poggendorf illusion (b), and the perception of depth and*

Rather, they suggest that the usual effects noted in learning experiments may be caused by satiation effects. This point of view is hard to accept since, as we noted, satiation effects are usually of a temporary nature. Nevertheless, the following statement is typical of Köhler's strong position against the effect of learned experience: "From these empiristic theories it would therefore follow that learning processes of the past are capable of causing satiation and figural after-effects in the visual brain. It will take an intrepid theorist to defend such an extraordinary view" (Köhler and Fishback, 1950; Köhler and Wallach, 1944).

Köhler may be right in stating that it would be rash to theorize that associative learning leads to these satiation effects, but the potency of his full argument rests on his assumption that the "figural-current" theory of brain action is correct. If it were not correct, there would be many other ways in which the effect of learning on perceptual organization could take place. The theory of Köhler has been challenged both experimentally and logically. We shall deal first with the experiments, interpretation of which is equivocal.

First of all, there is the fact that in Köhler's and Fishback's experiment, as pointed out by Woodworth and Schlosberg (1954), the Müller-Lyer figure subtended a visual angle of only 3°, as contrasted with the 26° in the Judd experiment. This could be one reason why Judd's observers had greater difficulty in overcoming the illusion. It is obvious that more satiation would be required for the larger figure, and it is possible that the effect would not be so great as Köhler and Fishback found. Whether satiation can be substituted for learning thus remains an open question which can be answered only after additional parametric studies have been performed.

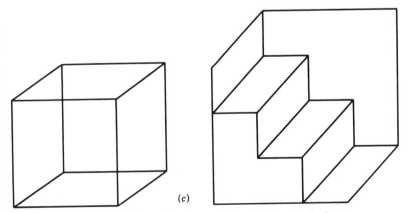

reversal in the Necker cube and staircase illusion (c) were all absent.
Instead, S reported these lines as straight and saw no depth or reversal.
The dilemma of choosing between satiation theory and a learning
interpretation is aggravated by data such as these.

More recently, Lashley, Chow, and Semmes (1951) attempted to put the satiation theory to an experimental test. They embedded gold pins in the cortex of one monkey and placed sheets of gold foil in the occipital surface of another. The monkeys showed no impairment in visual pattern discrimination on postoperative tests. The authors had reasoned that the gold would short-circuit the current and destroy the pattern set up by the stimulation of the forms.

Köhler has not as yet answered this criticism in print, although he did briefly refer to it in an invited address delivered to the 1956 convention of the Eastern Psychological Association. The present writer fails to see, however, that the experiment of Lashley et al. is a crucial test of Köhler's theory. Their assumption that the gold would short-circuit the current ignores one important axiom of the theory, namely, that figures are distorted only because the current flows from the highly satiated areas to less satiated areas. Now let us see what would happen in this experiment. It is known that the cortex is a highly conducting medium. Thus when the form impression stimulates the cortex, the figure current flows in the cortex. Anyone who claims that metal conductors implanted in the cortex would short-circuit this figure current must first prove that the metal has a resistance which is lower than any part of the cortex, since the direct current flows in the medium offering the lowest resistance. To prove that a metal is a better conductor than any part of the cortex would be almost impossible. This state of affairs indicates very potently how difficult, in fact, it is to put the satiation theory to a crucial test.

An experiment which attempted to test some of the implications of Köhler's theory was performed in a doctoral dissertation at the University of Pennsylvania. Moed (1959) was interested in testing some of the implications of the satiation theory for the destruction of the Müller-Lyer illusion. We shall report only a part of his findings here. Moed deduced from Köhler's theory that repetitive stimulation of the brain in the same way leads to faster satiation, and hence to faster destruction of the illusion, than stimulation in different ways. Let us look at the illusion stimulus again.

(*a*)   (*b*)

If we always present sections of *a* and *b* in the same orientation, then the illusion should eventually disappear. This is called asymmetrical satiation. On the other hand, we can present *a* on the left half of the time and *b* on the left half of the time, and vice versa. In this way, the satiation effects cancel out. We call this symmetrical satiation. In Moed's experiment he used these conditions of satiation: (1) completely asymmetrical, (2) partly symmetrical, and (3) completely symmetrical. From Köhler's theory, we expect (and Köhler himself has said) that condition 1 should show the greatest reduction in illusion, with 2 next and 3 last. Instead, Moed found that all conditions showed reduction in the illusion after repetitive exposures; there were no significant differences between conditions. It would be difficult for Köhler to handle these results, especially in view of the controls used by Moed.

We now summarize the satiation theory of form perception. The brain is considered to be a quasi-homogeneous conducting medium. Any stimulation of this medium (e.g., by contour stimulation) results in depolarization of brain tissue, which, in turn, leads to the flow of electrolytes. This flow of current limits the impact of successive stimulation. This limit, or increase in resistance, is called *satiation*. The perception of form and the various illusions result from what Köhler calls the pattern of *permanent satiation*. The more complicated the contours, etc., the longer it takes for permanent satiation to occur. This pattern accords with the fact that more experience is needed for identification of complex forms. Much work is required in this area. Thus we must know the effects of increasing intensity and contrast of the stimulating medium, for example; these higher intensities should lead to more rapid satiation and so on. The generality of the satiation theory is still debatable at this time, but these figural after-effects do exist. Their magnitude seems to be determined by *spatial proximity* and the *time lag between inspection and test*. The rate of decay is influenced by the length of the inspection period. These phenomena appear therefore to be of rather short-term duration and result from direct electrical effects on the brain, and it is doubtful that they are an adequate representation of the presumed associative learning underlying complex discrimination. They also appear to be part of a large organization, including illusions.

Statistical Theory

In view of the negative evidence and the rather unorthodox view of nervous function (e.g., minimizing the influence of the structure of the nervous system), alternative neuropsychological theories of form perception have been offered.

Other psychologists have particularly expressed great concern over, and dissatisfaction with, the satiation theory because it ignores the known facts about the neuroanatomy of the brain. Thus Day has stated that "an important objection to such a hypothesis can be found in the lack of correspondence between the alleged diffusion and satiation processes and the established evidence regarding neurophysiological events at the cortex" (1956, p. 139).

Day was specifically criticizing the interpretation of the experiment by Bitterman et al. (1954) which was discussed in Chapter 2. It will be remembered that various illuminated forms were presented against a dark background to the observers for 0.5 sec after they had been dark-adapted for 10 min; exposures were repeated every 2 sec. During the indefinite-figure stage the forms were confused. Thus a square was seen as a circle, a triangle as a circle, a cross as a diamond, and an X as a square. The same wrong percepts were made consistently. To explain these findings, Bitterman et al. suggested a "diffusion" model, a chemical analogy of the satiation theory which hypothesizes that chemical diffusion occurs at satiated points; the diffusion process thereupon reduces the accuracy of the perception. It is easy to see how they could theorize that satiation around the contour area would lead to the diffusion of current, which would push the lines in or out and thus lead to the misperceptions reported. Results in keeping with the diffusion model were obtained by Gaito (1959), who reported that at short-duration exposures straight lines were misperceived as curved lines more frequently than the reverse misperception occurred. While this would be predicted by the diffusion model, it would probably also be predicted by the satiation model.

The satiation theory, however, is not necessarily the most satisfactory way of explaining these results. We noted in Chapter 2 that many experimenters have found that there is an order effect in the emergence of various perceptual entities. Thus the stage of indefinite form is followed by the stage of definite form after the stimulus intensity has been increased. It therefore seems more plausible to suggest that the incorrect perceptions noted by Bitterman et al. are the result of inadequate stimulation, which accords much better with all the experimental facts reported in Chapter 2. Incidentally, Gaito observed that the order effect did appear with many of his subjects.

With similar misgivings, Day advanced a statistical theory of form determination as an alternative to the satiation theory. He argues that this theory, based on the work of W. A. Marshall and Talbot (1942) on the neurophysiology of vision, is in much closer and more realistic contact with neurological theory. This reinterpretation "has as its central notion a cortical representation of a perceived contour in the form of a Gaussian distribution of neural excitation in area 17" (Day, 1956, p. 139). This theory essentially states that neural impulses resulting from form stimulation are at their maximum along the contours and taper off in the areas around the contours. This tapering off of neural excitation, however, follows the normal probability curve of distribution with the contour as the midpoint:

If the physical stimulus is not strong enough, the peak of neural excitation will be below the threshold required for clear perception of contour. Since the distribution of neural energy around each contour will be rather flat, the combined effect results in a fairly even distribution of excitation. The somewhat higher level of excitation around the contour is not above the threshold required for clear detection of contour, and the form quality is confused. A graphical picture of what supposedly happens is presented in Figure 8-13.

A similar statistical theory has been suggested by Osgood and Heyer (1952) to explain the figural aftereffect. They maintain that the contours of the test and inspection figures produce a normal curve of excitation with the maximum at the contour point. The excitation curve for stimulation during the inspection period flattens with the removal of the inspection figure but is still present during the presentation of the test figure, and the contour of the latter falls to one side or the other of the previously inspected contour. The curve that would normally occur for the test figure is then modified by the residual inspection-figure excitability curve so that the maximum point of the modified curve (the perceived contour point) is to the right or left of the test-figure curve. The latter aspect accounts for the displacement effect.

A weakness of the statistical theory is that it is based on the theory of Marshall and Talbot, who assume that the magnitude of the neural excitation is related to optic nystagmus, which causes movement of the retinal image. Ratliff (1952), however, found instead that nystagmus acts to prevent total adaptation of receptors. Complete adaptation blots out vision completely. This result has been verified by Pritchard, Heron, and Hebb (1960).

At present there is little to choose between the statistical and satiation theories, except that the former is closer to the more accepted neurological functioning. A critical experiment has not been performed. Unfortunately, both theories appear to predict the same effects.

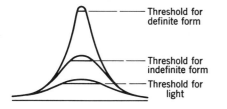

Threshold for definite form

Threshold for indefinite form

Threshold for light

Figure 8-13
The distribution of cortical excitation about the edge between stimulus figure and surround at the three stages of form perception. (After Day, 1956, p. 143.)

Where has this discussion led us? We have noted the difficulties with the satiation theory which led to the suggestion of an alternative statistical theory by Day and by Osgood and Heyer. If we accept the more conventional statistical theory of Day, we must still handle the problem of the modification of form through learning. The way to do this would be to specify which changes have occurred within the organism to lower the threshold for form. This is not the place to discuss the various theoretical accounts of the changes that result from learning, but it is necessary to test the key concepts and relevant experimental facts in order to develop the theme of this chapter.

Adaptation-level Theory

We shall end this chapter with a brief reference to the adaptation-level theory developed by Helson (1959). As in the case of the satiation theory, the adaptation-level theory treats the effect of prior experience on perception. Helson, however, dealt with a series of prior stimulations. As an example, let us suppose that a subject has to judge the brightness of a particular stimulus. We know that S is likely to judge the stimulus to be brighter if the background has a lower reflectance and darker if the background has a higher reflectance. Now, we can present him with a series of stimuli varying in brightness and then ask him to judge the brightness of a stimulus X. The judged brightness of X is affected by the state of adaptation created by the previous series. This adaptation level or frame of reference provides a context which can be quantified by using some weighted effect of the scale value of the series. For example, if the series effect is at some "high" level, the frame of reference depresses the judged brightness; if at a lower level, it enhances the judged brightness.

Helson has attempted to develop quantitative measures of adaptation level. In the case of kinesthetic perception, for example, the subject lifts a series of weights. If the weights were, say, 3, 4, and 12 g, then the adaptation level would be the geometric mean, which would be $\sqrt[3]{3 \times 4 \times 12} = 5 + g$. For examples of the extensive work related to the adaptation-level concept, a review of which is beyond the scope of this book, the reader should consult some of the following studies. Krantz and Campbell (1961) have shown the influence of language on the judgment of the length of lines. D. T. Campbell, Lewis, and Hunt (1958) have applied it to the auditory area of pitch perception. Finally, Helson (1964) has presented an extensive review of the wide range of phenomena from sensation to social behavior that have been investigated relative to adaptation levels.

Summary

This chapter dealt with the factors which determine the nature of form identification. The definition of a form requires the utilization of information. While the essential informational characteristics are carried by the stimulus, some of its aspects depend on the state of the organism. We must therefore look for both the stimulus and organismic determiners of how information is defined in a form.

The first task in the unraveling of this problem was to measure the amount of information extracted by the individual when he perceives any form or pattern. An example was given, using the applications of information theory as measuring tools. Having measured the amount, we went on to determine which parts of the stimulus are the carriers of this information; i.e., we looked for the pregnant points of concentrated information. The complexities of such factors as symmetry, redundancy, maximum dimension, and perimeter were investigated.

Finally, we considered how short-term sensory experience influences what is seen. This involved a discussion of imprinting, figural aftereffects, illusions, and adaptation level. Chapter 9 will deal with the effects of more long-term experience or learning.

9

Influence of Learning and Experience on the Development of Perception

In Chapter 8 we dealt with the role of sensory experience in perception. There also appears to be a more permanent effect on the perception of identity which results from practice, training, and learning. This kind of evidence has led certain psychologists to develop theories that prolonged practice in viewing forms leads to changes in the nervous system, particularly in the afferent branch, i.e., the nervous mechanism leading from the receptors to the projection centers of the cortex. Probably the best known of these theories is that of Hebb.

Hebb's Theory of Structural Changes in the Cortex

Hebb (1949) was one of the first psychologists to formulate a systematic theory to explain how associations in the nervous system are built through repeated form stimulation. Before reviewing this theory, let us describe the evidence supporting it, beginning with studies on the effect of sensory deprivation.

SENSORY-DEPRIVATION EFFECTS. An interesting group of experiments which are pertinent to the effects of sensory experiences on perception in general consists of the sensory-deprivation studies. In these experiments the quantity and quality of the sensory input of subjects are decreased. Usually the subjects are placed in small spaces, isolated from other individuals. Men have survived long-term confinement in relatively small spaces with a reduction in quantity and variability of sensory input (e.g., prisoners in solitary confinement, shipwrecked mariners, hermits) and in many cases with little adverse effect on behavior. These isolated events have not allowed quantitative specification of behavioral efficiency in various psychological processes, but recent studies at McGill University (Bexton, Heron, and Scott, 1954; Heron, 1957; Heron, Doane, and Scott, 1956) have been conducted to investigate the behavior of individuals confined to small spaces wherein sensory stimulation (visual, aural, and kinesthetic) is minimized. The subjects were paid 20 dollars a day to do nothing but lie on a comfortable bed in a small cubicle with eyes, ears, and hands shielded to reduce the sensory input from the environment. They wore goggles which admitted only diffuse light and had cardboard cuffs which extended below the finger tips. Auditory stimulation was minimized by the continuous hum of a fan, an air conditioner, and an amplifier. The individual left the cubicle only to eat or for elimination needs. Few subjects endured the task for more than 2 or 3 days, and 6 days was the maximum. The investigators maintained that even though the subjects were in need of money, they left this task for other jobs which paid much less but demanded much more in mental and physical activity, apparently indicating an overwhelming need to be exposed to patterned and varying stimulus input of almost any kind.

These investigations have indicated that decrements in performance and various abnormal phenomena may occur. Concentration, ability to carry on organized thinking, and various intellectual tasks were adversely affected. Visual, aural, and tactual hallucinations were reported. The hallucinations of some subjects involved sequences of geometric forms. In some cases the frequency of the spontaneous electrical activity of the brain decreased. Studies done by Lilly (1956) at the National Institute of Mental Health, in which sensory stimulation was reduced through immersion in a tank of water, reveal the development of hallucinations in a matter of hours. Only two subjects were employed, and the longest exposure was 3 hr. Lilly maintains that the human brain requires varied sensory stimulation for well-adjusted behavior.

Sensory-deprivation experiments performed at Princeton University and at the Air Force's Wright Air Development Center (WADC) in Dayton, Ohio, have not always reported the occurrence of hallucinations and performance decrements. J. A. Vernon, at Princeton, reports one experiment in which sensory deprivation facilitated the learning of adjectival lists (J. A. Vernon and Hoffman, 1956). Another experiment by Vernon and McGill (1957) indicates no difference in performance between deprived and control subjects. Some hallucinations, however, have been reported in other experiments lasting to 72 hr (J. A. Vernon, McGill, and Schiffman, 1958). These investigators maintain that the McGill University students are predisposed to report hallucinations because they wear translucent goggles which allow diffuse light to enter, whereas the Princeton subjects are maintained in darkness. They conclude that "the greater the reduction of stimulation the less the likelihood of hallucinations and . . . with increasing visual stimulation (short of pattern vision) not only the number but also the complexity of visual hallucinations may increase" (*ibid.,* p. 41).

Doane, Mahut, Heron, and Scott (1959) have checked the accuracy of this statement by having some subjects wear translucent goggles and others wear opaque goggles. The subjects wearing opaque glasses changed to translucent ones 1 hr before the end of the experiment. Of 11 subjects who wore translucent goggles, 8 developed hallucinations. Of the 2 subjects who started with opaque goggles, only 1 developed hallucinations, but both of them had vivid hallucinations upon shifting to translucent masks. This result appears to indicate that the *amount* of light allowed is not the complete determiner of the occurrence of hallucinations; lack of *variation* in the ongoing pattern of stimulus input seems to be a crucial variable.

Other experiments by Scott, Machen, and Baker (1955) have indicated that deprived subjects are more susceptible to propaganda (as well as showing other performance decrements) than are control subjects.

Air Force researchers seldom uncover hallucinations in their numerous investigations, which have ranged in duration from 4 hr to 7 days (Ruff and Levy, 1959), but some interesting changes have been reported in 52 experiments. At first most subjects report some anxiety. Later a loss of the sense of urgency to think occurs. If the experiment lasts long enough, anxiety reappears and thoughts may become completely disorganized. Schizoid subjects (determined by preisolation tests) have found the experience extremely stressful, and two of them terminated the experience within 2 hr. Compulsive individuals attempt to structure the situation around tangible bits of reality, e.g., counting respirations, folding paper, manipulating food, etc.

In regard to the infrequent occurrence of hallucinations in the WADC experiments, it is important to point out that the subjects were Air Force personnel, mostly officers in the middle thirties, who were probably quite different from the college students in the experiments at Princeton and McGill Universities. Some of the former subjects had actually been prisoners of war, and most had faced unusual situations.

At the Hehneman Medical College, Barnes (1959) has used rats and mice in sensory-deprivation experiments. He reports that after several days the animals showed neurotic symptoms, which involved great agitation, violent head twitches, and convulsions. Tranquilizing drugs were able to reduce the severity of the symptoms.

An interesting variation of the sensory-deprivation experiments has been provided by Wexler, Mendelson, Leiderman, and Solomon (1958), who confined subjects to a tank-type respirator (such as is used with poliomyelitis patients) for periods up to 36 hr. The arms and legs of the subjects were in cardboard cuffs, the repetitive drone of the respirator motor provided a masking sound, and the artificial light in the room was minimal and constant. All subjects showed impaired ability to concentrate, distortions in time judgment, and degrees of anxiety. A number showed pseudosomatic delusions, illusions, or hallucinations.

In evaluating the results of the sensory-deprivation experiments, a number of aspects must be considered. Kubzansky (1958) emphasizes that conflicting findings may be due to four important aspects, namely, definitions of sensory deprivation, subject variables, differential sensory modality preferences, and response measures. As we have indicated, different investigators have defined sensory deprivation differently. For example, Lilly was concerned with an absolute reduction of sensory input in his water-immersion experiment. On the other hand, the McGill group reduced the patterning and variation of the sensory input but retained the levels of input near normality. A third deprivation technique consists of providing a repetitive auditory experience and an impoverished visual field without goggles, or an absence of change of sensory input (Wexler et al.). These techniques are not necessarily exclusive, however, and the experiments of some investigators may consist of all three of them (e.g., the WADC group). The results of differences in the techniques used by the investigators at McGill and Princeton Universities have been considered above.

Of the other three aspects considered by Kubzansky, the effect of the subject variables obviously is to cause differences in response. The exact relationship between subject variables and responses has yet to be determined. Likewise, information on differential sensory modality preferences must await further research.

Kubzansky reports that four types of response measures have been used in deprivation studies, namely, length of stay, physiological change, behavioral change, and changes in thinking and increase of fantasy. Most individuals have used all four types of responses (e.g., the McGill group), while others have concentrated mainly on some of them (e.g., Barnes).

The WADC researchers suggest that seven classes of variables are important in sensory-deprivation experiments: (1) circumstances under which deprivation or isolation occurs; (2) subjects' background; (3) degree of "aloneness," considered physically and psychologically; (4) degree of communication between subjects and investigators; (5) degree of restriction in confinement; (6) perceptual space, or distance between the subject and the point at which the sensory input is affected; and (7) the modality, quantity, and pattern of the sensory input. As can be seen, some of these variables are similar to those of Kubzansky, and all are not mutually exclusive.

Thus in evaluating the results of sensory-deprivation experiments, a number of variables must be considered. The greater part of the research indicates, however, that overall behavioral efficiency, including form perception, does decrease. These results are consistent with suggestions from recent neurophysiological advances concerning the brainstem reticular system (Delayfresnaye, 1954; Fuster, 1958; Malmo, 1959), a relay site receiving fibers from lower centers and from the periphery, projecting them upward to the cortex (corticopetal), and projecting fibers from the cortex downward (corticofugal). The thalamus is in intimate relation with all parts of the cortex via these projections.

In recent years the brainstem has been receiving more attention. Scattered throughout the brainstem are clumps of reticule-shaped cells which have been given the name *reticular formation*. These cells are anatomically different but appear to be physiologically similar (Delayfresnaye). If an animal or a human being is resting or sleeping and the reticular formation is stimulated electrically, the animal or human being shows a "reactivation pattern." This is indicated in the EEG (electroencephalogram) by an increase in the frequency of the brain rhythms, beta activity being dominant. On the other hand, if destructive lesions are made in the upper mesencephalon or the diencephalon, the alert or resting animal shows a "deactivating pattern"; i.e., the animal shows brain waves which are characteristic of sleep or coma, the delta waves. Much research has indicated that the brainstem sends fibers to many cortical regions; some of these fibers relay in the thalamus before projecting to the cortex, while others go directly to the cortex. Likewise, the reticular system receives fibers back from the cortex. These up-and-down fibers are called nonspecific or diffuse tracts. Some individuals have attempted to localize a center for integration of the diffuse system in the thalamus (Penfield, 1954). It appears that this system contributes a facilitatory or tonic effect on behavior. Variations in activity of the diffuse system have been related to degrees of consciousness, low activity corresponding to the "unconscious" states, whereas greater activity is related to the active, conscious states. Furthermore, it has been indicated that there is an optimum activity level which is consistent with best performance (Fuster, 1958). When there is too little activity of these cells, the animal sleeps; when there is too great activity, he becomes emotional and rigid in his behavior. Fuster showed that perceptual discrimination was poor with little stimulation of the reticular system, was more efficient with greater stimulation, and finally was poor again with further increases in stimulation.

Although there are many problems to be solved, these studies on sensory deprivation do indicate that, in the adult organism, fairly continuous bombardment from the reticular system is required for the integrated activity of cognitive processes. This is necessary for integrated thought and the correct perception of integrated forms. Hebb would argue that such repetitive stimulation throughout the development of the individual, especially during the formative years, produces closed neurological systems, cell assemblies, which form the basic neurological units underlying the perception of identity. This is a group-structure theory (of nerve cells), as opposed

Droopy

to either the electrical or the chemical theories of the brain process under-lying form discrimination. What is more, it states that these structures are built up slowly after repetitive experience; it could be called a theory of neural learning. We shall discuss this theory again later.

Hebb (1960) draws further support for his theory from the work on stabilized retinal images (Pritchard et al., 1960), to which we now turn.

FORM DISCRIMINATION FROM STABILIZED RETINAL IMAGES. As we men-tioned in Chapter 8, optic nystagmus leads to a shifting of the image to different cells. These continuous small movements of the eyeballs are nec-essary for good visual acuity. If the image is stabilized, i.e., keeps stimu-lating the same cells, acuity is decreased and form discrimination becomes less effective, until finally the perceptual object fades out. Among others, Riggs, Cornsweet, and Lewis, (1957) and Pritchard (1960) have developed a technique for stabilizing the retinal image, which thus provides an excel-lent method for studying the temporal development course for the per-ceptual process and also for determining the basic units making up the total form.

Examples of the visual stimuli used by Pritchard et al. are shown in Figure 9-1. Employing the technique of stabilizing retinal images developed by Pritchard, the authors presented these visual stimuli to four experienced subjects. The reported phenomena have been confirmed. The figures would eventually begin to fade, come back, and fade again. The time before fading and the percentage of the time that the figure would remain intact depended on its complexity. Thus a simple figure like a line was visible about 10 per cent of viewing time, whereas a complex figure like an unconnected set of curlicues or a facial profile (figures 2 and 3) maintained at least one of its parts for as much as 80 per cent of viewing time. The authors state that "chaotic as the activity of the figure may seem at first, it still obeys some rules which relate to the form of the figure itself" (Pritchard et al., 1960, p. 71). Some of these rules follow.

1. Simple figures like straight lines and good (gestalt) figures act as a unit, while jagged diagrams are more active and less stable than rounded ones (figures 6, 13, and 14, for example). None of these data supports Hebb's earlier assumption that the angle or the corner is the perceptual element. Rather, the line seems to be the basic unit. Parallel lines are frequently seen together.

2. A field effect occurs. Thus in figure 17, parts of the triangle and circle which are close together are seen together. A little later an arc of a circle which is "parallel" to a line of the triangle is seen with it.

3. Figure 18, with the dotted line, is an example of closure. Certain other good figures like a circle, however, are often distorted, as in the reports of subjects who came out of the McGill isolation room previously re-ported in this chapter.

4. There are many experiences of depth effects, as shown in figure 7.

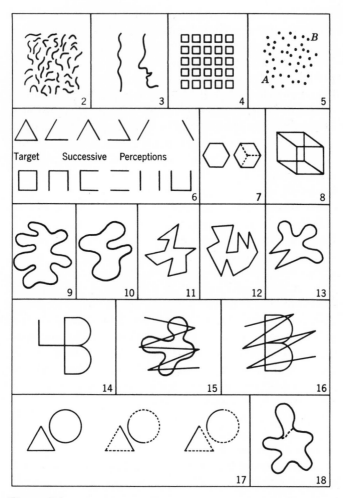

Figure 9-1
Examples of visual stimuli used (figures 6, 7, 17, and 18 also show successive perceptions). (After Pritchard, Heron, and Hebb, 1960, p. 71.)

The authors conclude that gestalt and elementaristic conceptions of perception are not as antithetical as was once thought. This complementarity is summed up in the following propositions:

1. Perceptual elements, as distinct from sensory elements in Hebb's sense, exist in their own right, but the wholes are simpler than usually conceived and consist of straight lines or short segments of curves.
2. "More complex wholes, such as squares or circles, are syntheses of simpler ones though they may also function as genuine single entities" (*ibid.*, pp. 75–76).

For evidence that these effects of stabilized retinal-image perception are caused by alternation in the semiautonomous process which is mediated in the association cortex, Hebb points to data of the following kind. First, a target as shown in Figure 9-2 was presented as a stabilized image to his subjects by Tees (1961). (The identifying letters *A*, *B*, and *C* were not present in the target.) What did the subjects see? If we designate the periods when the whole figure is seen or when none of it is seen, we find by taking the means for four subjects that *A* is accompanied by *B* 73 per cent of the time and by *C* only 22 per cent of the time. Since the parallel lines *A* and *B*

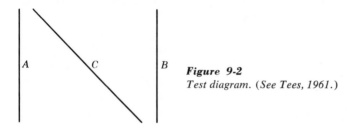

Figure 9-2
Test diagram. (See Tees, 1961.)

are farther apart than lines *A* and *C*, the correlated activity of *A* and *B* cannot be due solely to a field effect (such as spread of current to neighboring regions) either on the retina or in the cortex but must be caused by some activity in a system (Tees, 1961). Furthermore, the work of H. B. Cohen (1961) and Krauskopf and Riggs (1959) indicates that the system is located centrally, i.e., in the cortex. The data from Cohen are graphed in Figure 9-3.

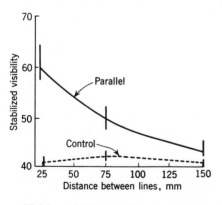

Figure 9-3
"Percentage of time a stabilized straight line is seen by one eye when an unstabilized parallel line is seen by the other eye, at separations of 25-, 75-, and 150-minute arc. (Broken line, percentage of time visible when the parallel line is not presented to the other eye.)" (After Hebb, 1963, p. 20.)

Hebb and his associates conclude that these phenomena and others "are intelligible in terms of a semi-autonomous activity of closed systems in perception but *unintelligible when perception is regarded as a simple input system*" (Pritchard et al., 1960, p. 76). [1] How the elements in this system are synthesized or segregated through experience is a difficult and unre-

[1] Italics mine.

solved problem to which we shall return after examining more evidence bearing on such an associative learning theory of the development of form perception. For a more recent discussion by Hebb of the issues that are involved in isolating these and other phenomena of how learning changes the cortical system which mediates the perception of identities, the reader should see his address to the American Psychological Association (APA) on receiving an award for distinguished scientific contributions (Hebb, 1963).

DEVELOPMENTAL STUDIES. Hebb also developed his theory to explain the results of research on the development of perception. The first study referred to is Von Senden's monograph (1932; 1960) [2] on the visual abilities of congenitally blind patients who were given vision for the first time at maturity by the surgical removal of cataracts. Since the monograph consists of a collection of case reports, the extent of scientific control is hard to determine, but many of the reports in scientific journals gave anecdotes and Von Senden evaluated them carefully. It is possible to summarize his conclusions by stating that all patients were capable of detecting brightness and color differences immediately but required some practice before they could accurately discriminate space, size, and identity (definite form). There were crude perceptions of space, size, and form, but these clearly improved with learning. It should be emphasized that reactions to visual stimulation were clearly present but visual discrimination markedly improved with practice.

Two studies performed by Hebb with rats fit in with Von Senden's data. Hebb reared rats in darkness from infancy until they were adults. In the first experiment he tested their abilities in brightness discrimination. He found that they were as good as normally reared rats in differentiating a white disk from a black one, and they responded readily to relative differences in brightness. In the second experiment he found that dark-reared rats had greater difficulty in discriminating horizontal from vertical striations. They were poorer in pattern vision than normal control rats used by Lashley (Hebb, 1937a; 1937b).

Riesen's work (1947) also provides relevant evidence. He reared two chimpanzees in darkness until they were sixteen months old. They were then tested on various visual discrimination tests. Brightness differences were readily discriminated, but depth and pattern vision improved with learning. Similar results were obtained with rats raised with diffuse rather than patterned light instead of in darkness (Riesen, 1961).

Two studies, published after Hebb's original book had appeared, are relevant to the immediate point at hand. Riesen et al. (1953) reared a

---

[2] Let us note that Gregory and Wallace (1963), referred to in Chapter 8, assert that it is not that clear that learning plays an important part in vision. They consider maturational variables and habit transfer from touch in their patient, who eventually died. Their findings on illusion, however, lend support to a learning interpretation.

group of cats in darkness until they were fourteen weeks old. They were then given diffuse light in one eye and patterned light in the other for 30 min daily until they were seventeen to twenty weeks old. Training of an initial visual-discrimination habit with the eye exposed to patterned light showed much slower learning for the experimental group than for the control group. When tested for transfer of the habit to the other eye, the experimental group took a significantly shorter time to relearn the habit than to learn it originally. The study not only showed that experiences with patterned light influence pattern discrimination, but it also indicated that perceptual discrimination is partly organized at a level higher than the receptor.

Siegel (1953) performed a similar study with two groups of ringdoves. The experimental group was reared with translucent hoods over their eyes which prevented them from having any pattern vision during development. The control group was reared normally. When Siegel tested the ringdoves for form discrimination with a modified Lashley jumping apparatus, he found that the experimental group was significantly poorer than the control group. Leeper's experiment mentioned later in this section supports Hebb's position.

From studies such as these, Hebb concluded that the perception of brightness and simple unity is innate, whereas the perception of identity is learned. Simple unity includes figure-ground and other nonconventional forms, such as those resulting from configurational principles.[3] Identity refers to a recognizable, meaningful, permanent form.

Hebb advanced a complicated and ingenious neurological theory to account for what happens to the brain as a result of learning to perceive identities. We shall summarize its main construct by giving the example of learning to perceive a triangle. Hebb starts by saying that the perception of a total triangle is possible only after repetitive experiences of viewing it. He refers, for example, to some of Von Senden's cases who followed the *corners* of the form with their eyes when they first saw it. Hebb concludes that repetitive fixation of these corners leads to *structural* changes in the cortical cells: they grow. After more experience these visual cell assemblies become connected to cell assemblies in other parts of the cortex, including the motor cortex, to form a complex *phase sequence*. This phase sequence operates so that stimulation of the central area representing one corner of the triangle sets the entire sequence in motion: the cells fire successively and rapidly, permitting immediate perception of form. The growth of the assemblies has essentially resulted in lowering synaptic resistance. Since the lines are the simple, innate perceptual element, containing redundant information, the critical information of identity is at the corners and curves. Somehow learning, repeated practice, produces neural (chemical or struc-

---

[3] These unities are simpler than these principles suggested, as Hebb himself has stated in his 1960 work reported earlier in this chapter.

tural) changes which link these elements at the corners and turn them into the complex form.[4] Thus the change produced by learning results in sequentially ordered activity in the cortex.

It should be noted that Hebb accounts for form perception as the result of building through an associationistic process which follows enriched experience. A similar approach, with neurological reference, especially by Bruner in 1957 and later, has been adopted by Bruner and Postman (1948), Postman (1953a; 1953b), and Bruner (1957). In the first paper the authors theorized that "perceptual accentuation" is a very important intervening variable in determining the percept. "Accentuation is the differential vivification of different parts of the perceptual field, and as such, can be considered part of perceptual organization" (Bruner and Postman, 1948, p. 100). Some of the variables which govern accentuation are the range of values of the attributes which the subject has experienced in the past, the frequency and amount of reinforcement associated with the object, and the availability of the object for manipulation and consumption in relation to the subject's need for the object.

In the second paper, Postman had changed his position somewhat. For one thing he suggested three hypotheses about *central mediators* of perception. First, the presence of stimulus discrimination initiates a process of sensory organization, an important determiner of which is associative learning of the type referred to by Hebb. Second, the context of the stimulus has a selective influence on its sensory organization. (Context refers to such stimuli as instructions and central attention.) Third, the sensory organization arouses other associated processes which determine the "meaning" of discrimination.

The experiments used by Postman to support his theory came largely from the area of social perception, which is discussed in Chapter 12. From these analyses, he concludes that "perceptual behavior may be usefully conceptualized in terms of learned response dispositions, whose acquisition and performance are governed by general principles of associative learning such as *frequency, recency, and effect*" (Postman, 1953a; 1953b). A similar type of theory dealing with the development of sensory organization was presented by Birch and Bitterman (1949). Hebb's theory emphasizes that perceptual consequences result to a large extent from learning and are thus subject to *set,* a view similar to Bruner's expressed in his theorizing on perceptual readiness (Bruner, 1957).

Response-specificity Theory

The data and theories which we have discussed thus far indicate that learning can influence perceptual discrimination in at least the following

---

[4] The last two sentences are very small modifications of Hebb, particularly by mentioning neurochemical instead of only neurological change.

ways: (1) Imprinting shows that certain experiences occurring in the short critical period during infancy lead to a rigid response to almost any stimulus taking place at that time. This is very simple, nonassociative learning involving a direct connection between a stimulus and a response. (2) Phenomena such as figural aftereffects show that fixation of forms produces a change, probably in the sensory area of the cortex, which leads to a change in the way a subsequent form is perceived. (3) The work on sensory deprivation and perceptual learning suggests that the discrimination of an identity develops after repetitive visual experience has led to the formation of complex closed systems of nerve-cell assemblies between the sensory cortex and the motor cortex.

The interpretation of these phenomena deals by and large with modification of the sensory medium or connections between the sensory and response mediums. We come now to a fourth effect of practice, namely, an increase in response differentiation. Theorizing in this area has been led by J. J. Gibson and Eleanor J. Gibson (1955; 1956). These authors contend that all existing theories of the perceptual process, including those based on association, "take for granted a discrepancy between the sensory input and the finished percept and they aim to explain the difference. . . . The development of perception must necessarily be one of supplementing or interpreting or organizing" (Gibson and Gibson, 1955, p. 33).

[handwritten margin notes: read exper. # mistakes for scale of complexity]

They propose an opposing view by presenting the results of an experiment. Human subjects were confronted with nonsense figures which looked like parts of human fingerprints. The figures could differ in three dimensions of variation: (1) number of coils (three, four, or five), (2) horizontal compression or stretching, and (3) orientation or right-left reversal. In all, 18 such items were printed photographically on cards and shuffled with 12 other cards which included some that differed in many dimensions. Each subject was first shown a critical item, another nonsense figure, exposed for 5 sec. Then the pack of 30 cards was exposed individually for 3 sec, and the subject was told to report which of them had the critical figure. The author found that there were generally no incorrect recognitions of the figures differing in many dimensions, but the other 18 figures were sometimes misperceived. The mean number of trials required to reach the correct responses ranged from 3.1 in adults to 6.7 in young children. Moreover, there was a difference in the magnitude of erroneous recognition, depending on whether the 18 figures differed in one, two, or three dimensions. Those differing in one quality led to a greater percentage of erroneous recognitions than those differing in two qualities, which, in turn, led to more numerous errors than those differing in three qualities. From this experiment and other evidence, Gibson and Gibson concluded that perceptual learning leads to increased specificity or differentiation of the perceptual act; i.e., the individual becomes more sensitive to the variables of the stimulus array.

After presenting an excellent review of the studies dealing with the effect of practice on perceptual judgment, including studies (Fehrer, 1935; Gilliland, 1925; Lawrence, 1949; 1950; 1952; Seward, 1931) on pattern discrimination which support their own results, Eleanor J. Gibson (1953) offers a theoretical suggestion as to how this increased specificity or differentiation of the perceptual response might take place. A schematic representation of that theory is presented in Figure 9-4.

A central discriminative feature between a theory like Hebb's and a theory like that of the Gibsons is that Hebb considers sensory stimulation to have invariant consequences, whereas perceptual consequences are variable and derive their stability from cortical sets resulting from learning; conversely, the Gibsons believe that sensory stimulation produces the changeable consequences, while the perceptual consequences contain invariant relationships which result from the properties of objects and which do not have to be learned. In a recent article J. J. Gibson states: "I submit to Hebb the suggestion that the first problem in perceptual physiology is not how the brain responds to form as such, unvarying form, but instead how it responds to the *invariant variables of changing form*. I think we should attempt a direct physiological theory of object perception without waiting for a successful theory of picture perception" (1963, p.

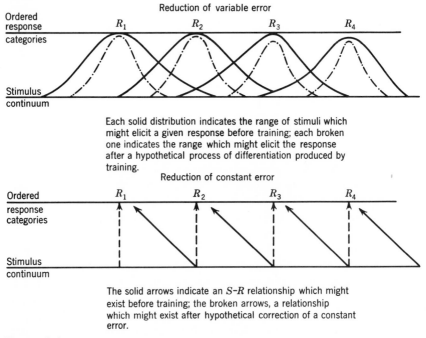

Figure 9-4

Schematic formulation of changes which may occur in improvement of perceptual judgments. (After Eleanor J. Gibson, 1953, p. 424.)

14).[5] It seems to me that this is precisely what Hebb is trying to do. Examples, among others, that Hebb cites are what happens when we learn to read mirror-image letters, such as FRANCE becoming ƎƆИAЯꟻ, or learn to adjust to a spatially reoriented world, a topic which we shall discuss in Chapter 10. In these cases, after making the initial readjustment of reading, for example, from right to left, the *sequential patterns* are identical. Thus it seems to me that the positions of Hebb and Gibson are not mutually exclusive but may in fact be considered complementary to one another. Before attempting a synthesis we shall analyze a recent study on the origin of form perception which throws some light on how perception develops from innate, wired-in reactors to modified (learned) programming.

A Comparative Study of the Origin of Form Perception

Fantz (1961a) studied the development of form perception in young chicks, chimpanzees, and human infants. The chicks, whose behavior is visually dominated, were presented with a number of different shapes, each enclosed in a clear plastic container to eliminate the influence of smell, taste, or touch. The number of pecks made on each shape was recorded by an electrical circuit attached to each container. More than 1,000 chicks hatched in darkness to preclude visual learning and withheld from exposure to real food were tested upon their first exposure to light. Some of the results follow for 112 chicks. During the first 10 min they pecked at a sphere 1,000 times, a cubelike shape 300 times, and a pyramid 100 times. Not only did the chicks peck at the sphere 10 times more frequently than at the pyramid, but they also consistently "preferred" a sphere to a flat disk. What appears to be a strong evolutionary development of form discrimination in chicks might not be true of higher animals. Consequently Fantz tried to tease out the roles of innate ability, maturation, and learning in monkeys, chimpanzees, and man. Taking off from Riesen's study, previously mentioned, he raised monkeys in darkness from 1 to 11 weeks. The monkeys reared under these conditions for the shorter period generally exhibited good spatial orientation after a few hours or days when brought into a normal environment, and they also showed a normal interest in patterned objects. Those left in the dark for the longer periods, however, exhibited almost complete spatial disorientation when brought into the light for the first time. "The older infant monkeys bumped into things, fell off tables, could not locate objects visually—for all practical purposes they were blind" (Fantz, 1961a, p. 5). Fantz reports that it sometimes took weeks for them to "learn to see." As contrasted with the younger ones, who preferred patterned objects, the older infant monkeys appeared to be more interested in color, brightness, and size.

[5] Italics mine.

From these results with the monkeys Fantz reasons in the following manner. Obviously innate ability cannot be the whole answer; otherwise the dark-reared animals would not be so highly disoriented. Maturation cannot stand alone either; otherwise the younger animals would not be superior to the older ones. Usually learning alone is inadequate as an explanation; otherwise the older animals would not require a longer time to learn to perceive than the younger ones. Evidently, following the wired-in reaction to certain stimuli (chimpanzees reared in darkness except when brought into a testing situation exhibited a definite preference for certain objects), there is an interesting interaction between maturation and learning in the development of pattern discrimination. The amount of training interacts with the time at which it takes place to produce the effect. There is much evidence, as we shall verify later in this chapter, to indicate the superiority of early over late learning (given maturational readiness, presumably).

While practical limitations preclude the use of experimental controls as adequate as those employed with the other animals, Fantz presents some interesting data on human infants. Infants between the ages of one and fifteen weeks were tested at weekly intervals in a "looking chamber." The infant was placed on his back and looked up at a chamber of uniform color and lighting. The experimenter placed two objects, slightly separated, at the top of the chamber. The positions of the objects were randomly varied. By looking through a peephole in the top cover of the chamber, the experimenter could see which object was reflected in the infant's eyes. In this way visual fixation, which was taken as an index of visual interest, was measured. The results for various patterns follow.

1. First of all, the infants preferred heterogeneous patterns over homogeneous ones. Thus, while no choice was shown between a large triangle and a small one or between a circle and a triangle, a checkerboard pattern was preferred over a homogeneously colored rectangle. Moreover, during a 1-min test, the infants would, on the average, fixate a bull's-eye pattern for almost 20 sec, while they would look at a horizontally striped pattern for only 10 sec. Although there was a preference for the stripes in infants under two weeks old, the preference gradually shifted to a bull's-eye, until the experimenter found a marked preference for the latter in the eight-week-old infants.

2. A second result showed that infants preferred looking at the pattern of a human face over printed matter and a bull's-eye over homogeneously colored disks (red, white, yellow), in that order. The pattern, not color or brightness, is important.

3. Finally, the adaptive significance of the form is indicated by the fact that the infant prefers a human-face pattern to a scrambled-face pattern, to an oval which was black at the top and reddish at the bottom, again in that order.

Fantz's work provides some fascinating insights into the complex interaction between innate, maturational, and learning variables in the development of form perception and its adaptive significance. One word of caution, however, seems in order. The fact that the infants prefer certain kinds of complex patterns to others does not necessarily mean that they can freely and completely discriminate their identity. It may very well be that the kinds of visual exploration revealed in such interest provide the very kinds of neural excitations which lead to the cortical organization of cells (Hebb's assembly and phase sequence) which then make the complete identification of forms possible. In this regard it is instructive to note that Gollin (1960) found that a greater amount of completeness was required for younger children to recognize incomplete forms than for older children to perform the same task. Then there is the work of Eleanor J. Gibson and Walk (1960) on the cues used in depth and distance discrimination and on which cues are innate and which require learning for effectiveness. This study is included in Chapter 10 in the section "Three-dimensional Space: Experiments and Principles."

Synthesis

We begin with the proposition that the foundation of perception consists of certain innate responses to sensory organization. Examples of such organization are those discussed in Chapters 5 and 6, certain gestalt configurations, and so on. A similar view has been expressed by Zuckerman and Rock (1957), who assert that it is illogical to say that learning improves perception unless there is some innate organization in the perceptual process to begin with. This follows; otherwise, adaptive behavior to a stable environment would be impossible. While this is so, we have just seen that there are four ways in which perceptual discrimination and judgment are modified after experience or practice. Finally, we want to deal with a fifth effect, which probably represents the highest order of perceptual learning, namely, learning to respond to relationships between different patterns.

Let us start by seeing what can happen in the course of perceiving the following ambiguous figure. The individual sees either a vase or two profiles

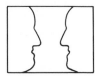

since the organization contains these segregations, but through training he could learn to see predominantly either the vase or the profiles. What then is the role of learning in perceptual organization? It is suggested that learning results in the differential sensitivity of the organism to various combi nations of sensory patterns. As a result of adjusting to the environment, the organism has learned the significance of various patterns of energy. In the past history of the organism, responding to a stimulus quality in one way has led to a particular kind of environmental feedback, which itself consists of stimulation. This feedback might strengthen or weaken the response to one kind of sensory organization, depending on how successful the response was in achieving a desired end. (Presumably, this appears in size constancy. The stimuli for retinal-image size and distance are both present, but initially the individual responds to the size. After learning, he responds to the relationship between size and distance; then constancy occurs.) As the environment becomes more complex, it is necessary to respond to relationships between dimensions in order to adjust adequately. In this way learning results in realizing the significance not of one dimension but of similarities and differences between various patterns.

We observe that a response is made to a particular external stimulus. We then measure this response. From subsequent training we find that the organism starts responding not only to one dimension of a stimulus but also to related stimulus patterns in various combinations. We find further that the particular index of response measurement—verbal report, matching, adjustment, etc.—produces similar trends. It seems safe to infer that the learning consists of differential sensitization to new combinations of patterns, and it is clear that the limitations to the number of sensory qualities which can thus be interrelated are determined primarily by the complexity of the organism.

Let us examine some experimental evidence in support of this theory, which demonstrates some of the ways in which differential sensitivity to complex stimulus patterns may arise. Leeper (1935) performed an experiment dealing with the development of "sensory organization." He used three experimental groups and one control group, and all subjects were human beings. All three experimental groups were given experience in perceiving certain ambiguous figures. Experimental groups A and B were given help when they could not see the object (they differed with respect to how soon the help was given), group C was not given any help but was told the class of objects into which the figure fell, and the control group did not have this preliminary experience. The four groups were then tested for their ability to identify new ambiguous figures, all of which were presented tachistoscopically. The three experimental groups identified a significantly larger percentage of figures than the control group did. Experimental group C was most superior. There was, however, some variation from figure to figure. Leeper concludes that habit-derived organizations win out over spontaneous organizing influences by various means. He further suggests that we turn our attention to the problem of classifying materials of learning on the basis of a "to-be-discovered" hierarchy of functional similarities.

It is our interpretation that these habit-derived organizations resulted from the fact that they achieved significance because the experimental task demanded that they do so. Is it clear that they won out over spontaneous organizing influences? Since the figures were unstructured, there was probably very little organization which resulted from structural factors, but it became necessary for the organism to respond to a pattern to solve the perceptual problem. This could only come about through learning to group various stimulation entities of the figure into a larger combination. Active attention and searching behavior must have played a large role (we note the superiority of group C).

This conclusion is strengthened by the work of Schafer and Murphy (1943), who have reported that the perception of ambiguous figures is influenced by the history of previous rewards and punishment for seeing either form. These results have, however, been questioned by Rock and Fleck (1950), who repeated the experiment and reported contrary results. Thus the evidence of the role of learning with ambiguous figures is not unequivocal, although there is no disputing the fact that learning does lead to increased sensitivity to certain relationships in the stimulus field.

A study dealing with the "assumptions" a chick makes in perceiving brightness is reported by Hess (1950). After two groups of chicks were hatched, they were reared under different conditions of illumination in their living cages. The experimental group had the light source coming from below, whereas the control had it coming from above. In the first experiment, the two groups were tested for their pecking responses to shaded representations of grain after 7 weeks in their respective environments. In the second experiment, weekly tests were made. The results, in part, are presented below.

The control chicks made their first pecks predominantly at photographs showing grain illuminated from above, while the experimental animals first chose photographs showing grain illuminated from below. Again we see that the chicks apparently learned to "expect" that significant light stimulation would come from a particular spatial direction.

Some of the experimental results obtained by the present writer appear to support the general position adopted here. From previous studies it was concluded that the influence of experience on perceptual discrimination and problem-solving ability depends on the relationship between the experience and the requirements of the test problem.

In one study two groups of rats were reared in complex environments from weaning until they were adults. Those in group VM were reared in a large box which afforded much opportunity for visual and motor experience with many inanimate objects. Those in group V were reared in an identical box, but living space was restricted to a plastic cage inserted inside this box so that they could only see, but not play with, these inanimate objects. When these animals were tested on a form-discrimination problem, with an open elevated maze, group V was superior to group VM (Forgus, 1954). In a second study, it was found that if similar animals partly learned to solve an open T maze with many visual cues present, group V was still superior, but when learning was completed in the dark group, group VM became superior to group V (Forgus, 1955a). In a third study, similar groups were trained to learn partly a multiple T maze which was closed off from the rest of the room. Visual aids were present at each bifurcation point so that an animal could immediately perceive the cue when he reached the choice point. If he pushed through a door containing vertical striations, he was "correct"; if he pushed through a door containing horizontal striations, he ended in a blind alley. Under these conditions the two groups were equally good in initial pattern discrimination, but when the visual aids were removed and learning was completed, group VM was once more superior to group V (Forgus, 1955b).

From these combined results we concluded that the animals were not learning to perceive forms as such in the test situation. The visual discrimination of form was equally good in both groups (the third study), but group V had become more highly sensitized to react to visual qualities. Thus when the problem situation was complex, containing many irrelevant stimuli, the rats of this group would attend more readily to visual patterns than those of group VM would. This would account for the faster rate of learning which group V exhibited under these conditions (studies 1 and 2). When visual stimulation was poorly differentiated, however, group VM showed the greater sensitivity in responding to nonvisual cues which was required to complete the solution of these problems. This tendency presumably results from the greater diversity of their experience (studies 2 and 3). The interpretation of these results is similar to Harlow's error-factor theory, discussed in Chapter 15.

Finally, we might refer to a study (Forgus, 1958a) in which litters of rats were randomly split into four groups after they had been weaned. The animals were then individually reared in separate cages. The cages of group T contained outlined triangles and circles on their walls. The walls of the cages of group A also contained circles, but *the sides of the triangles contained a gap in the middle,* although the angles were continuous. The cage walls of group S had the same circles, but the *"triangle" had no angles.* Group C, the control group, had no forms in its cages. The figures are shown in Figure 9-5.

The rats were reared in these cages until maturity, at which time they were tested on a form-discrimination problem. The two forms which they had to discriminate were identical to the triangle and circle contained in the cages of group T. (Of course, the three experimental groups had seen the same circle.) The results showed that group S was highly superior to all other groups, the only other difference being that group T was somewhat

Figure 9-5
*Triangles T, S, and A, which were located next to the circle in the
cages of group T, group S, and group A, respectively. The outlines of
the forms were white, and the backgrounds were black. (Forgus,
1958a, p. 76.)*

superior to the control group. We should mention here that Eleanor J.
Gibson and Walk (1956) also found that rats reared with forms in their
living cages were better able to discriminate them than rats raised without
the presence of these forms. But the striking difference was the superiority
of group S.

My interpretation of this experiment is that the differential sensitivity
to triangle vs. circle was greater for the side-form group S than for any of
the other groups. To explain this, we must specify what the differences in
the relationships between the forms were in the test situation as opposed
to the rearing situation. It has been reasoned that rats respond to differences
in form on the basis of differential cues from the *bottom* part of the figures
(Lashley, 1938). To ascertain the differences between the test and the
rearing, we must therefore ask how the relationship between the bases of
the two figures changed from the home cage to the test maze. Let us
examine this question for the three experimental groups. In their home
cages, the members of the side-form group were exposed to a triangle whose
base was clearly demarcated. This resulted from the lack of angles, which
led to discontinuity of both brightness and contour, while the circle was
continuous. When these rats were placed in the test situation, however,
they were faced with a triangle whose base was continuous in both brightness
and contour. The marked change in the stimulus relationship focused the
animals' attention on the stimulus cards, which in turn led to a faster rate
of discrimination learning. In other words, the side-form animals were
more sensitive to the actual problem situation because the change in the
stimulus relationship from rearing to test was greater for them than it was
for members of the other groups. This inference is tenable when we contrast the rearing and the test situations of the side-form group with those
of the other groups.

In the case of the true-form group T the relationship between the triangle and the circle was identical in the rearing and the test situations. As
contrasted with the experience of the first group, both forms were equally

familiar; therefore it was more difficult to develop a differential response to the situation.

The angle-form group A, like the side-form group, faced a new situation. But let us examine this statement more closely. The change from the home triangle to the test triangle was not nearly so great for this group as for the side-form group. Whereas the side-form group faced a change in the discontinuity of both brightness and contour, the angle-form group faced a change in brightness only. The continuity at the angles remained the same.

The control group presented a situation which was completely the reverse of that of the true-form group. Whereas the true-form group faced two equally familiar forms in the test situation, the control group faced two forms which were equally unfamiliar. Therefore, the animals of this group, too, would have great difficulty in developing a differential response between the two test forms.

In summary, the transfer from previous experience to test problems is based not so much on familiarity with the test stimuli as on the *extent to which previously learned relationships aid an animal in developing differential responses to the relevant cues in the problem situation*. It is true that familiarity made the true-form group superior to the control group, but the former was grossly inferior to the side-form group. It appears that such principles as frequency may be influential, but they do not tell the whole story.

An organism responds to sensory stimulation because it is sensitive to the energy pattern which results from such stimulation. The important fact about past experience seems to be that the individual has learned the significance of similarities and differences in patterns of stimulus organizations and the information they impart. This view has further experimental support (Forgus, 1958b). For one of the most recent reviews of perceptual learning, the reader should see Eleanor J. Gibson (1963).

A Word of Caution: Stimulus and Learned Factors in Set and Attention

The developmental studies just reviewed as well as the theories of such individuals as Hebb and Bruner emphasize the importance of learning in the development of perceptual set, but it is important to note that attention can also be directed by stimulus and situational factors. Thus, M. D. Vernon (1954, pp. 55–56) reviews some studies which show that a great number of elements can be apprehended if they are homogeneous but that accuracy in identifying them is facilitated by *heterogeneity*.

It is generally stated that such *external* factors (meaning stimuli) as contrast, size, movement, and emphasis enhance the attention-directing value of a stimulus. The work of Berlyne (1958) has linked these characteristics under the unifying label *complexity*. In one study it was found that, when given a choice, human subjects would spend more time looking at forms where there were more numerous rather than fewer elements, where the arrangement of elements was irregular, where the elements in a group differed in structure as opposed to being homogeneous, and where the shape of the form was irregular rather than regular. These are some of the ways in which complexity can be defined.

In other experiments Berlyne (1951; 1957a; 1957b) dealt with novelty of stimulus. In the first experiment the subject was first presented with one, two, or three stimuli during a familiarization stage. Then *S* was presented with, for example, three stimuli, one of which differed in color, shape, or both. This was the novel stimulus. *S* merely had to press a key corresponding to one of the stimuli. The novel stimulus was responded to more frequently. Berlyne's second study and some studies by other individuals show that novelty (or a stimulus which is different from the rest) attracts initial fixation and paces the directing of attention.[6]

This finding that attention is directed by a change in stimulation from a previous level is consistent with what is now generally believed about the way the nervous system functions (see Chapter 2). The writer's 1958 work, previously mentioned in this chapter, shows that even a change from a long-term learning set has greater attention-getting value.

Thus, attention is directed by the nature of the stimulus, by certain short-term effects of prior stimulation, or by long-term sets. The influence of set and motives arises again in Chapters 11, 12, and 13.

Summary

While reviewing the studies on sensory deprivation, stabilized retinal images, and the role of experience in the development of perception, we described theories which postulate that experience produces associative assemblies, increased specificity, and differential sensitivity. Thus, perceptual attention is influenced not only by the nature of the stimulus and short-term prior stimulation but also by long-term sets resulting from learning.

[6] See, for example, Dember and Earl (1957).

10

Space
Perception

In Chapter 6 we saw how important the *relationship* between visual angle and distance is in determining the perception of the size of objects. Distance, of course, is extended in the third dimension; hence, the perception of distance is part of the perception of three-dimensional space. In the last section of this chapter and in Chapter 11 it will also be shown that the spatial dimension is an important part of the relationship underlying the perception of motion and certain other physical and social events. As a matter of fact, it would be difficult to conceive of man's adjusting adaptively to his world if he did not respond to its spatial aspects in a relatively accurate way. The perception of space can be broken down into two areas:

1. *Two-dimensional space*. Here we are concerned with the fact that we can locate things to the left or right and up or down.
2. *Three-dimensional space*. We can also locate the distance of an object away from us; i.e., we can tell, within limits, whether it is nearer or farther from us along the line of sight. This is the third dimension, which itself consists of two somewhat separate, although related, issues. The first is the perception of the *depth* of an object like a cube or any other object which has volume. In addition to the object's height and width, which represents its two-dimensional area, we can perceive its depth or thickness. The second issue is the perception of the *relative distance* of objects from us along the third dimension.

When we consider the phenomena of space perception, as outlined above, we must examine the way the individual locates objects not only with respect to one another but also with respect to his own bodily orientation. So we become concerned not only with the spatial location of external entities but also with where we are, in what position (upright, to the side, etc.), and in which direction or directions we must go to get from here to there.

Formulation of the Nature of Space Perception in Historical Perspective

INFLUENCE OF THE CLASSICAL THEORIES OF SPACE PERCEPTION. As is true of most of the perceptual phenomena, the problem of space received its first extended experimental attack from the great German scientists Ewald Hering and H. L. F. von Helmholtz. Although many of their experimental findings and techniques have remained classics, it cannot be said that their theories of space perception were entirely satisfactory. It will be remembered from the history of psychology that Hering attempted to "solve" the problem of the visual perception of space with his theory of "local signs." This theory stated that each point on the retina has specific innate signs or values for height, width, and depth which correspond to specific heights, widths, and depths in the external world. It said in essence that space perception is innate because it is not experiential and then implanted a mechanism in the retina to "explain" the ongoing of this process. We note in passing that Rudolf Hermann Lotze's theory of local signs stated that the signs or values, which result from *intensity* patterns of stimulations, have to be learned; i.e., the individual learns what the sign means by learning to discriminate the intensity patterns. Thus, although the capacity to perceive is innate, the actual process is affected by experience. While this theory is less circular than Hering's, it still did not solve the problem because it asserted that the mind has the innate tendency to take these intensity patterns, which are nonspatial, and arrange them into spatial dimensions. How the mind executes this transformation was not known.

Helmholtz had a purely empiristic theory of space: the signs or cues to space have to be learned through experience. Once the learning has taken place, the process of space perception becomes automatic and we make "unconscious inferences" about spatial location from these cues. We shall consider what these cues are later when we discuss this very popular psychological approach more fully. At this point it should be stated that the kind of theory that Helmholtz presented does not tell us clearly how experience develops in the organism the ability to discriminate spatial dimensions in the stimulus complex; for example, does the organism begin with any innate reaction to spatial dimensions as such? There must be some basic innate reaction, or else adaptive behavior would be virtually impossible. The discriminative response is given out first and differentiates with practical experience. The evidence reported on the constancies by Leibowitz and his associates suggests that the development of size-distance relationships is not an intellectual process but is represented by a simpler mediational process.

The futility of the nativism-empiricism argument concerning space perception was well stated by Carr in his famous book on this kind of perception (his statement can be generalized to include all perception): "Insofar as a relation is natively conditioned, we are confronted with the further task of discovering the organic mechanism involved. Likewise, the ultimate objective is a knowledge of the developmental principles involved in the case of an empirical phenomenon. An adequate account of space perception can well be given without specifically mentioning the problem of nativism and empiricism" (1935, p. 6).

Although it has been stated that neither the theory of Hering nor that of Helmholtz is adequate, this fact should not detract from the great experiments they performed. After all, they were two of the first scientists to attempt a serious experimental attack on the problems of perception. Complete scientific theories are rarely developed by one or two men. Science is a cooperative adventure; usually, adequate theories are reached only after a number of progressive advances have been made by scholars over the work of their predecessors. Hering and Helmholtz made a good start in space perception. Although they differed in how they regarded the role of experience, both worked on the probable list of physiological changes which follow our viewing of, or adjustment to, the spatial characteristics of the world. They reasoned that these physiological changes provide cues—J. J. Gibson (1950) has stated that "clues" is a more meaningful word—to the perception of the spatial orientation of the individual and the things around him. As we have stated, Helmholtz thought that we have to learn to recognize these cues, whereas Hering believed that we have innate capacities to respond to them. But the approach of breaking down the total act of spatial perception into subprocesses involving the utilization of cues was common to both men. As a matter of fact, this general, analytical approach provided the directional set for experiments and theories of space perception from the nineteenth century up to recent times.

RECENT ADVANCES IN A THEORETICAL APPROACH TO SPACE PERCEPTION. The difficulties inherent in the "analytical-cue" approach were indicated primarily by two psychologists. Koffka (1935), representing the gestalt view, argued that the stimulus for space does not consist of a number of discrete elements but is a *whole* pattern consisting of interacting "forces." Gibson (1950) has pointed out that retinal stimulation coming from the spatial surround does not result from point-for-point stimulation of the retina but from *relational patterns* of stimulation on its surface. It would appear that two modifications of the classical cue theory were required to advance our theory of space perception. First, it is not necessary and is probably fallacious to assume that each point in space is represented by a point on the retina. *It is the relationship between the points and the energy patterns to which they give rise which seems to be the essential quality of the stimulation for space perception.* Second, we must remember that these cues are always interacting; under one set of conditions a particular cue may be more important, while under another set a different cue is dominant; quite often a number of the cues are working together. This was reported in experiments by Smith and Smith (1957).

Having emphasized the importance of considering interacting relations, let us now see what kinds of relationships have been established in the study of space percepion. We shall begin with a brief review of two-dimensional space and then go on to the more complex problem of three-dimensional space.

Two-dimensional Space: Experiments and Principles

The main coordinates of two-dimensional space are the gravitational *vertical* and the *horizontal* which is perpendicular to it. These two planes constitute the main frame of reference against which we ordinarily judge spatial direction that is located in two dimensions. Emphasizing the importance of the *visual* mechanism, the gestalt psychologists have traditionally argued that space is not located with reference to our bodies but with reference to the vertical and horizontal as perceived "out there." The two-dimensional field can be represented essentially by a right angle. When Wertheimer said that the lines which contain this right angle are *Prägnanz-stufen* (pregnant steps), he meant that they, the lines, provide a consistent anchor for judging the direction of other angles.

When Koffka invoked the principles of "invariance" to account for the accuracy of spatial perception, he was reasoning in a similar way. He postulated that the vertical and horizontal planes set up forces in such a way as to produce a neutral tension field, i.e., a field in equilibrium. This field provides a stable visual framework against which the directions of all other objects are judged. The reason we perceive spatial direction correctly is that the angles made by these objects with the framework remain invariant or consistent. If one axis of the framework is tilted without the observer's realizing it, the equilibrium is upset; consequently a compensatory force will be generated to restore the balance. Under such conditions the observer usually perceives a compensatory tilt, in the opposite direction, of other objects located in the field.

Since gestalt research does not fully explain the nature of this force or how it is generated, it should be used cautiously as a hypothetical descriptive concept. Furthermore, evidence which has recently been accumulating in United States Air Force literature demonstrates the importance and complexity of proprioceptive mechanisms in spatial location.

Both Carr and Gibson have argued that the placement of parts of the body in relation to external objects is an important aspect of perceiving direction. Carr has asserted that the visual detection by an individual of parts of his eyebrows, nose, cheek, trunk, arms, and legs is a necessary component of localizing an object in space accurately, while Gibson has stated that the inclusion of his own body in the perceptual process permits the individual to infer that he is "here" and the object is "there." Other investigators listed below have insisted on including the contribution of proprioceptive mechanism—i.e., labyrinthine (balance-sense) and kinesthetic (muscle-sense) sensation—if the individual is to achieve a more complete understanding of spatial perception. It seems quite reasonable to suppose that the visual perception of the gravitational vertical is at least partly determined by the fact that the human body normally provides an upright framework. What are the facts which will permit us to appraise this argument and thus develop an understanding of the perception of two-dimensional direction?

Interaction between Visual and Proprioceptive Determiners of the Perceived Vertical and Horizontal

The results of an experiment by J. J. Gibson (1933), which were verified by M. D. Vernon (1934) and Radner and Gibson (1935), suggested the conditions under which the perceived spatial direction remains invariant with respect to the vertical coordinate. The first two experiments showed that if an inclined line or shape is fixated for a long time and no other visual surround is present, the line eventually appears to be less steeply inclined; i.e., it begins to "approach" the true vertical. The third experiment, however, showed that if the tilt is very strongly perceived and verbalized as such, the inclination may even be exaggerated. Nevertheless, in all these conditions, after the perceived inclination has been diminished, a vertical line subsequently introduced appears to be tilted in the opposite direction. The amount of this compensatory tilt is usually related to the magnitude of the original inclination. (We note, in passing, the similarity of these findings to those of Köhler et al. on figural aftereffects, discussed in Chapter 8.) This appears to support the gestalt principle of invariance, as expounded by Koffka and supported by Köhler and Wertheimer. It should be added, however, that both Gibson and Vernon thought that the visual vertical is supported by the postural or kinesthetic senses (it should be noted that the subject was sitting upright and that there was no other visual surround available to affect his perception).

As early as 1912 Wertheimer performed an experiment which, he believed, supported gestalt theory. In this experiment observers were required to look at the reflection of a room in an *inclined* mirror through a tube which eliminated the rest of the surround. The observers reported that the room (not the mirror) appeared to be inclined and that the objects in the room were arranged in a disorderly fashion. During the early part of the observation the subjects were quite disoriented in space, but as time elapsed, the room was seen to recover its usual spatial framework and the subjects regained their orientation. This early experiment was one of the findings on which Koffka based the gestalt principle of invariance. The gestalt psychologists would argue that since the visual framework tends to remain constant, the inclined plane produces a compensatory force to right itself. This would account for the way in which the room gradually regained its normal upright position. We have mentioned that Köhler's theory of direct current flow in the brain, used to explain figural aftereffects, provides a possible mechanism for explaining the direction of the force. It would be difficult, however, for the satiation theory to specify why the current flows to the vertical and not to the horizontal in the case of the tilted rod, for example. Evidently the postural vertical plays an important role. Furthermore, the work on the stabilized retinal image and on the effects of experience and the use that Hebb makes of these kinds of data in his structural model of the brain provide other avenues for explanation. The adequacy of the view that two-dimensional space is primarily determined by direct visual sensory stimulation is thus questionable. The Innsbruck studies, presently to be discussed, in which subjects gradually adjusted to a world which was reversed by lenses, strongly suggest how judgment based on active learning can be used to adapt to a world where the usual visual framework has been rotated.

INDIVIDUAL DIFFERENCES IN VISUAL AND PROPRIOCEPTIVE DETERMINATION. Asch and Witkin (1948a) concluded that their experiment verified Wertheimer's results and supported Koffka's theory. The experimental task was similar to the one used by Wertheimer; i.e., the observer had to look at the reflection of a room in an inclined mirror through a tube which prevented direct vision of the room. In this experiment the subjects were blindfolded when they were brought into the room. After the blindfolds had been removed, the subjects immediately looked through the tube while they were in an upright position. Once this experiment had been completed, they were again brought into the room, this time without blindfolds, and were permitted to look at the mirror scene with free vision. In both conditions the subjects were required to adjust a line to their judgment of the vertical plane. Although five different effects, showing individual differences between subjects, were observed, one result occurred most frequently. This dominant effect was that most subjects set the vertical relative to the tilted plane in the mirror and not relative to the postural or gravitational vertical. The four other effects were observed less frequently. A few observers adjusted the line to the true gravitational vertical, presumably using their own bodies as a reference, and a few reported the room as upright even when they viewed it with unobscured vision. Some saw the tilt but thought that it was they who were tilted. Quite a few observers reported that the tilt was seen at the beginning but that it gradually disappeared in the perception. Asch and Witkin were impressed by the tremendous stability, or tendency toward stability, of the visual spatial framework.

The findings of Gibson and Mowrer (1938) and Mann (1952) suggest caution before we completely accept any theory which emphasizes the visual determiners of two-dimensional space to the exclusion of postural determiners. For example, in the experiment of Gibson and Mowrer, which was similar to that of Wertheimer, they found that while the room scene became less steeply inclined with continued inspection, the tilt was not eliminated completely. It appeared to them that the observers adapted themselves to the fact that the two main coordinates of space were distorted, which led to the disappearance of the feeling of disorientation. After reviewing the relevant data, Gibson (1952) urged that we do not argue over whether the visual or the proprioceptive factors are more important but emphasize instead the *joint interaction* of the factors in the visual-proprioceptive complex which determine perceived direction of two-dimensional space. This is indeed a good suggestion, for we have seen throughout our study that dichotomizing usually does not get us very far. Let us go ahead then and examine further the conditions under which visual or proprioceptive factors or both together determine the direction of two-dimensional spatial location. Under usual conditions these two factors operate together. We shall consider such factors as conditions of stimulation that favor visual determination, conditions that make proprioceptive determination more likely, and the effect of attitude, prolonged exposure, and so on. We shall begin to get a better understanding of these conditions when we examine additional studies in the series performed by Asch and Witkin.

THE DOMINANT VISUAL FRAMEWORK. In a second experiment, Asch and Witkin (1948b) varied both visual and proprioceptive conditions of stimulation (not only the visual conditions, as in the first study). This time the subjects were brought into a room which was actually tilted through 22°. As before, they were first brought in blindfolded and asked to adjust a rod to the vertical immediately after the blindfolds had been removed. They were then brought into the room with free vision, and the experiment was repeated. The results of this experiment, in general, verified those of the tilted-mirror experiment. While individual differences similar to those observed in the first experiment were obtained, the majority of the subjects again estimated the vertical to be roughly parallel to the walls of the inclined room rather than parallel to their upright bodies. Furthermore, when the subject was making his judgment from a tilted chair, the visual framework became an even stronger determiner of the estimated vertical. This was particularly true when the subject's body was tilted in a direction opposite to that of the room. A few of the subjects still found it possible to ignore the visual field and to use the gravitational sense (kinesthetic and labyrinthine stimulation resulting from the bodily tilt) in judging the vertical, but the majority could not do this even after a training and discussion period. It would seem that, under normal conditions and for most individuals, the visual framework is a stronger determiner of space perception than the postural framework. This tendency appears to be so strong that when the visual coordinates are distorted, the perceived vertical undergoes a comparable distortion. The importance of these visual referents becomes even greater when the postural balance (upright) is upset. This dominance of the visual sense is understandable when we consider how important vision is in everyday life.

In another experiment Witkin (1950a; 1950b) studied the effect of postural distortion on perceived space when the visual framework was in its usual position. Blindfolded subjects were placed in a cubicle which was moved around a circular track at various speeds. Proprioceptive stimulation was thus produced by the gravitational force and the centrifugal force caused by the rotation. When his blindfold was removed, each subject was required to adjust a rod to the vertical and horizontal position. He was able to do this with a very high degree of accuracy when the cubicle was lit, but he made a much greater error when adjusting an illuminated rod when the cubicle was dark (thus removing most of the visual framework). This was especially true after the cubicle had been moving at high rotation speeds. The error of estimation, however, was smaller than the angle of the resultant force (gravitational and centrifugal). As usual, a great deal of variability was observed between subjects in the dark-cubicle condition. Some subjects saw the walls of the cubicle as vertical, while others thought that they were tilted. Although visual cues were dominant, postural forces became more important when visual cues were reduced or removed.

INCREASING IMPORTANCE OF PROPRIOCEPTIVE STIMULATION IN A RE-DUCED VISUAL FRAMEWORK. Witkin and Asch (1948a; 1948b) in a final set of experiments required their subjects to inspect a luminous square frame which was tilted through 28° in a dark room. When their bodies were upright, the subjects generally set the vertical relative to their posture. Under these conditions, in which visual stimulation was extremely reduced, postural determination of the vertical was dominant. When the body was also tilted, however, the error of estimation became larger. Some subjects even became completely disoriented and lost all sense of direction in the room. Subjects who were strongly influenced by the visual frame under these conditions were quite unsure of what they were doing. But then, what else could be expected with both the visual and the postural senses disturbed? The positive point is that postural cues are reliable and become very important when the visual framework is reduced. Presumably this is one of the mechanisms utilized by blind people to orient themselves. This finding is further supported by the fact that the subjects in this experiment accurately adjusted a luminous rod to the gravitational vertical plane in a dark room, provided that their bodies were upright. Their judgments became less accurate when their bodies or even their heads were tilted.

A similar experiment, showing the conditions under which postural determiners become more dominant, was performed by Mann et al. (1949). The subjects were displaced from the gravitational vertical in a tilted chair in a dark room, which thus provided no visual framework. They were required to set two parallel luminous lines to the horizontal. Since their bodies were tilted, they generally set the lines at an angle to the true horizontal. But when they were next required to adjust the chair so that their bodies were upright, they were able to do this with considerable accuracy, despite the fact that they were looking at the tilted lines. This finding is not contradictory to that of Witkin. In Witkin's experiment the rotation produced a centrifugal force which was perpendicular to the vertical; this could have the effect of distorting postural cues considerably. In Mann's experiment a subject's body was tilted only to one side in a stationary position.

Thus far we have seen that the visual framework generally provides the dominant determination of two-dimensional space under ordinary conditions. It is only when visual cues have been reduced that postural or proprioceptive stimulation becomes a more important determinant of spatial orientation. These two generalizations are limited to some extent by consistent individual differences which we shall examine in greater detail later. This seems to be the place to introduce a discussion of a recent research program dealing with the interaction between energy received from sensory and from motor stimulation. These experiments, initiated at Clark University, have led the investigators to develop an organismic theory of perception called sensori-tonic theory.

SENSORI-TONIC THEORY. Werner and Wapner, the originators of this theory, begin by expressing dissatisfaction with the sensory approach of psychophysics because it relegates the organism to a minor role and thus undermines the importance of individual differences. These theorists believe that the narrowness of a sensory approach to perception can be overcome only if we consider the interactions between energy coming from the stimulation of the different senses and muscles and the relation of the stimulating objects to the organism. Since it is in the organism that these stimulations, coming from diverse sources, interact, the organism becomes the focal point for the study of perception; hence, the designation *organismic theory.* This organismic approach to perception, called the *sensori-tonic theory,* is described in three articles by Werner and Wapner (1949; 1952; 1955). Many experiments in support of the theory have also been published, and we shall refer to some of them as our treatment progresses; but the main theoretical assertions were presented in the 1952 article, on which the following discussion is primarily based.

The sensori-tonic theory is an attempt to combine both sensory and tonic (e.g., kinesthetic) factors into one explanatory system. Sensory factors refer to any experience derived from sensory qualities or sensory data which form a gestalt. Tonic factors refer to changes in muscular tension which result from any action (e.g., postural changes, motor inhibition, or phasic contractions) leading to actual movements. For a sensori-tonic "event" to occur there must be some functional equivalence between energy derived from sensory and from tonic stimulation. Only when there is some equivalence can sensory and tonic qualities interact and result in a perceptual event. The perceptual event results from an "organismic energy state," a "total dynamic process."

In an experimental demonstration of functional equivalence reported by Wapner, Werner, and Chandler (1951), 20 male and 20 female undergraduate students instructed the experimenter to adjust a luminescent rod in a dark room until it appeared to be vertical. The judgments were made under each of the five conditions listed below, in which mild electrical stimulation was applied to the neck and auditory stimulation was supplied by earphones.

1. Control (no external stimulation)
2. Auditory stimulation to the left ear
3. Auditory stimulation to the right ear
4. Electrical stimulation to the left side of the neck
5. Electrical stimulation to the right side of the neck

The results indicated that the perceived vertical was closest to the gravitational vertical when no external stimulation was applied. Moreover, the position of the rod was identical for auditory and electrical stimulation applied to the right side and also for auditory and electrical stimulation applied to the left side. The perceived vertical was displaced to the left under conditions of external stimulation to the right and to the right under conditions of external stimulation to the left. All these results are statistically reliable. This experiment demonstrates not only *functional equivalence* but also *dynamic equilibrium,* which is related to the construct symmetrization. In other words, it is postulated that the organism tends to establish and maintain a steady state of body equilibrium (dynamic equilibrium). When this equilibrium is disturbed, compensatory shifts in energy take place to restore it. Thus, when more stimulation (energy) was applied to the right side, the vertical was displaced to the left, and vice versa. Other experiments (e.g., Werner and Wapner, 1952) have shown that asymmetrical object stimulation induces a change in the organism so that a more symmetrical relationship exists between the stimulus object and the organism. This tendency is termed *symmetrization*. "That is to say, 'symmetrization' is an expression of the tendency of the organism to change its equilibral state in such a way that stimuli coming from the object will make for minimal disturbance of the organism" (Werner and Wapner, 1952, p. 333). This principle is related to the gestalt principle of invariance or *Prägnanz*.

To show further that the results observed above (e.g., electrical stimulation to the neck) are caused by an increase in muscle tonus, the following experiment was performed by Werner, Wapner, and Chandler (1951). It is similar to those performed by Mann et al. and by Witkin and Asch, previously discussed, and the observed effect is called the Aubert E phenomenon after the man who first reported it (1861). In the experiments, 40 students were required to adjust a luminescent rod to the vertical in a dark room. The judgments were made while the subject's body was tilted through 15 and 30° and while he was either supported or not supported by the back and sides of a chair. The results showed that the perceived vertical was displaced to the side opposite to the direction of body tilt and in proportion to the angle of body tilt. Moreover, *there was more displacement in the unsupported than in the supported body condition.* These results, which verify the previous findings, led the authors to conclude that it is not tilt per se but *the degree of muscular involvement,* causing tonic imbalance, that is the important variable in these effects caused by the interaction of sensory and proprioceptive factors.

By using such constructs as *dynamic equilibrium* and *minimal disturbance,* Werner and Wapner have attempted to explain perception as the result of an interacting "field" of energy. Although these investigators have dealt primarily with sensori-tonic factors, they believe that other factors, such as affective and attitudinal state, contribute to the organismic energy state.[1] They also theorize that if energy is locked in one system, e.g., by muscular inhibition, it will be released in another way. This is the construct of *vicariousness.*

While we must await more direct proof of functional equivalence and dynamic interaction through the actual measurement of energy systems, the sensori-tonic theorists have given us behavioral manifestations thereof. Moreover, they have again pointed out, quite dramatically, that space perception, like other perceptual phenomena, is very complex. Many variables—sensory, organismic, and situational—may contribute to the perceptual event, and we may even use the individual differences observed as an approach to understanding personality, a topic to which we shall return later. All of this leads to the hypothesis that the individual differences are partly a result of learned attitudes or sets, and the next section includes some evidence which suggests that this is the case.

[1] See, for example, Werner and Wapner (1954). This is related to *intermodal transfer,* which holds for the other senses, too (see Dember, 1960).

ZERO GRAVITY AND RELATED RESEARCH ON FLYING. When man goes out in a space-probing capsule, he encounters a number of problems, of which zero gravity is a major one. Let us see what zero gravity involves.

The normal gravitational force is that of 1 g, but the force can vary. During rapid acceleration and deceleration, higher g forces are encountered. On the other hand, when a force of 1 g is imposed upward so as to counterbalance the gravitational force of 1 g downward, the physical condition of zero gravity results. The psychophysiological counterpart of zero gravity is weightlessness. A body is weightless as soon as it is allowed to move freely under the influence of gravity and of its own inertia. This condition exists to some extent in a free fall but only for a few seconds. In space flight it is present during most of the flight.

Recently Air Force scientists have developed a technique whereby reduced gravity can be attained for periods up to 40 sec. Approximately half of this period consists of the zero-gravity state. These conditions have been attained by putting an aircraft into a power dive, pulling out, letting the aircraft rise for several thousand feet, and then allowing the plane to nose over once more. This is referred to as the Keplerian or parabolic trajectory. The parabola has a vertical axis.

Air Force scientists have conducted many experiments under virtual weightlessness (Gerathewohl, 1954; 1956; 1958; Gerathewohl, Strughold, and Stablings, 1957). When this condition is attained, all objects tend to float because they have no weight. Unless the individuals in the aircraft have their safety belts fastened, they float out of their seats. Objects as well must be secured. To be used, liquids must be encased in squeeze bottles.

In one experiment, Gerathewohl et al. had subjects attempt to hit a bull's-eye under 1-g, 0-g, and 3-g conditions. Under the 1-g condition the attempts were clustered around the bull's-eye; under the 3-g condition, below the bull's-eye; and under the 0-g condition, above the bull's-eye. The subjects under zero gravity learned, however, that they must compensate for lack of gravity and adjusted so well that *after about six trials of weightlessness they achieved about the same accuracy* as under the normal gravity condition,

This indicates the importance of the gravitational force as its affects the proprioceptive sense of the organism and also suggests that, with proper selection and training of candidates, individuals can adjust, both psychologically and in their performance, to this unusual condition.

Experiments under zero gravity have also been conducted with animals (cited by Gerathewohl, 1954; 1958). Mice were sent aloft in a V-2 rocket and two Aerobee missiles. Cameras recorded their behavior during weightlessness. Signs of disorientation were present, but the mice were able to maintain their coordination by clinging to wire mesh. In one experiment in an Aerobee missile a normal mouse and one that had lost the labyrinth mechanisms of the ear were launched. The normal mouse appeared to be confused during the weightless state, but the labyrinthectomized mouse was less disturbed.

Dr. von Beckh of Buenos Aires has reported similar results with a species of South American water turtle. These animals are very accurate in projecting their long necks at food. A normal turtle and one that had lost the use of the labyrinth were employed. The labyrinth had been destroyed by an accident, and the injured turtle required a number of weeks before it learned to compensate for damage to the labyrinth through visual orientation. Both animals were subjected to the weightless state in an aircraft, and their coordination was tested. The damaged animal was able to snap accurately at its food during weightlessness, *using the visual cues it had learned.* The normal animal was unable to coordinate its movements properly, but after 20 or 30 flights it began to regain its coordination.

Gerathewohl has also reported that the zero-gravity condition interacts with or completely negates the operation of the righting reaction in cats, a reflex behavior in which proprioception plays an essential part. These experiments indicate that animals can adapt to the weightless state if visual cues are present. It is interesting to note that the operation of the labyrinthine sense is a handicap at first under zero-gravity conditions. This is consistent with the experience of fliers, who report the occurrence of disorientation when flying under instrument conditions if visual cues are eliminated. These results are in keeping with our earlier statements concerning the dominance of the visual sense.

These experiments have been concerned only with short periods of zero gravity. With space flight, man undergoes this condition for long periods of time, inasmuch as the space ship is in a state of equilibrium between gravitational and centrifugal forces, and adverse effects may occur. Some medical men have feared that muscles might atrophy, coordination diminish upon disuse, and other deleterious neurological effects occur. The immediate and long-term effects on perception are conjectural. These fears of psychological and physiological impairment have not been substantiated (see discussion of Project Mercury below). It is interesting that the dog Laika survived seven days of complete weightlessness without ill effects in Sputnik II, according to Russian sources, and man eight days in the Gemini project.

The interest in this area should provide much research to advance our perceptual knowledge. For example, soon we should acquire information concerning the effects of loss of gravity on perceptual aspects involved in orientation in a diffuse open field—e.g., "space myopia" arising because of lack of suitable reference points on which to focus, effects of depth perception, orientation, etc.—as well as other information. In any event, the scant information which we have available indicates the importance of visual and proprioceptive stimulation in perception and behavior. For a vivid account of the importance of visual, labyrinthine, and proprioceptive cues in spatial orientation and the fatal accidents which occur when these cues are misperceived, see Cocquyt (1952).

But the available evidence which we discussed also shows the remarkable capacity man has to learn readjusting or adjusting responses to new cues. This is further borne out by a report from Project Mercury (*Mercury Project Summary,* 1963). The remarkable finding is that although there were perceptual disturbance and ego disorientation at first, United States astronauts could adjust completely, looking at space sights coming through a window and performing motor tasks involving concentration, and more recently, even walk in space.

Effects of Set and Experience

We shall start this section by referring to an experiment by Mann and Boring (1953) in which they demonstrated that the kind of experimental instructions given to the subject has a significant effect on his judgment of the vertical. The task consisted of setting targets to the gravitational vertical against a visual framework. Two groups of subjects were used. Members of the naïve group were merely told, without further elaboration, to set the targets to the vertical. Members of the sophisticated group were reminded, with explanations from time to time, what the nature of the task was. The results indicated that the judgments of the sophisticated group were more accurate than those of the naïve group. Mann and Boring warn that space perception is a selective process which depends on many factors, including such state (organismic) variables as purpose, mental set, training, and experience. No more dramatically has the effect of the state of the subject been shown than in a series of experiments dealing with adaptation following prolonged exposure to distorted visual fields.

SPATIAL ADAPTATION: THE INNSBRUCK STUDIES. Almost 70 years ago Stratton (1897) observed the effects on spatial orientation of wearing prismatic lenses which completely inverted the visual field. It is a well-known fact, of course, that under normal viewing conditions the retinal image is inverted with respect to the external stimulus; i.e., things are "upside down" on the retina and are probably transposed in the cortex. In Stratton's study the observer looked at the world through prismatic lenses which "rectified" the normal inversion so that the retinal image was upright. Consequently he saw the world as inverted. As we might expect, the observer was very much disoriented and disturbed at first, but after prolonged wearing of these prisms he was able to readjust to this new spatial world. Similar studies were conducted later by such investigators as Ewert (1930) and Snyder and Pronko (1952).

Ewert's three subjects wore the lenses for periods of 14 to 16 days, while Snyder and Pronko's one subject wore them for as long as 30 days. All these investigators report similar effects. At first the observers exhibited

complete spatial disorientation, were unable to make coordinate movements, and could not localize objects with any degree of accuracy. After a
while, however, they began to adapt themselves to the new situation and
gradually regained their spatial orientation so that they were finally able
to localize objects fairly accurately and move around with fair coordination.
It is clear that the retinal image did not undergo such a dramatic change;
*rather, the observers learned to adjust their kinesthetic responses to a
changed visual world.* Thus they would reach down if something appeared
up, and vice versa. A striking readjustment, indeed.

Similar effects were noted by G. G. Brown (1928), who produced
inclination of the visual field by 75° in the left-right plane, but the most
elaborate set of researches in this area was and is being carried on by
Kohler (1951) and his associates in the University of Innsbruck. Kohler
in 1953 studied the effect of left-right reversal plus many other spatial and
color distortions. The study reported below is typical of his findings and
should be regarded as the general paradigm. These results suggest implications which are supported by the other studies. To help understand the
nature of this experiment, a diagram of the results of one of Kohler's
subjects is presented in Figure 10-1. This diagram is representative of the
general results.

For 50 days the subject wore spheric "half prisms" which were attached
to a frame in such a way that if he turned his eyes upward, he looked
through the prisms, which distorted the visual field, whereas if he looked
downward, there were no prisms and hence the field was normal. The effect
on space perception of thus inducing two ocular-postural frames of reference (upward and downward) was measured by what Kohler called the
adjustment method; e.g., a curved line was varied in curvature until it
appeared straight to the subject; likewise, the angles of a rhombus were
altered until the figure appeared to be a square, and so on.

The graphs presented in Figure 10-1 represent the results obtained with

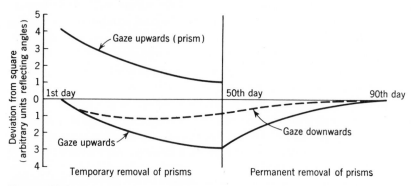

Figure 10-1
*Diagrammatic representation of effects and aftereffects of wearing prisms on percep-
tion. (Reproduced from Werner and Wapner, 1955, p. 131.)*

a rhombus. The abscissa indicates the number of days; the ordinate presents the angular deviations in arbitrary units of the rhombus from a standard square. For convenience the deviations of the lower left angle of the test rhombus are plotted. Points on the ordinate above zero mean that the deviation was in the direction of acute angularity, while points below zero mean that it was shown by the obtuseness of the angle. We note that effects were measured under four conditions: upward gaze through prisms, upward gaze with prisms temporarily removed, downward gaze, and upward gaze with prisms permanently removed.

The results are quite clear. During the 50 days when the prisms were worn the subject showed spatial disorientation at first; i.e., when he looked upward through the prisms, there was great distortion in spatial location. There was gradual adaptation, however, so that by the fiftieth day of wearing the error (deviation) was only 25 per cent as great as on the first day. This adaptation (or readjustment) is further indicated when we examine the upward gaze when the prisms were temporarily removed. Here we notice an aftereffect, which became increasingly strong as the number of days increased. In carrying over the adjustment from the prisms to free vision the subject, of course, made an error in the opposite direction, i.e., from acute to obtuse. During the first 3 days the magnitude of this aftereffect was the same for downward gaze, but thereafter it did not increase for the downward gaze as it did for the upward gaze with free vision. Finally, we notice that after the prisms had been permanently removed, the subject gradually readapted to the normal conditions of viewing. But again it required more practice to do this when looking upward than when looking downward. The aftereffect was still much greater in the former case and did not disappear completely until the ninetieth day, or 40 days after the permanent removal of the prisms.

The results of Kohler's experiments and inspection of the impressive adaptation curves (e.g., Figure 10-1) make it clear that training or preexposure does alter the way an individual responds to identical patterns of stimulation on the retina. Clearly the retinal pattern of stimulation did not change; rather the individual learned to make different responses to the same stimulus relationship so that his behavior became more adaptive. Moreover, this learning can become so differentiated that different responses are made to similar patterns of stimulation coming from different areas of the visual field.

In this section on two-dimensional space we have seen that the perception of the vertical and the horizontal is complex. Under usual conditions spatial orientation is determined by a joint interaction of visual and proprioceptive factors, although the visual framework appears to be dominant. It is when the visual field becomes impoverished that kinesthetic and labyrinthine stimulation becomes more important. Finally, it was also stated that such factors as set, attitudes, adaptation, and learning play an important role in spatially adaptive behavior. This suggests that the individual differences observed are, in part at least, a result of different past experiences or learning. Some psychologists have even theorized that these individual differences reflect differences in the personalities of the observers. This topic will be discussed in greater detail in Chapters 11 and 12. Right now we shall end this section by noting that Witkin (1950) and Sandström (1951) have suggested that, in Western culture at least, the visual factor in spatial perception is even stronger in women than in men.

Three-dimensional Space: Experiments and Principles

The one approach to depth perception which has remained most popular in psychology is the classical theory of cues, which was suggested by Helmholtz almost a century ago. Boring (1942) has noted that in American psychology the constructs *cue* and *clue* have been used synonymously to mean some sensory data on which perception is based. Although cue simply refers to the triggering of some response, while clue implies some reasoning process, the meanings of the two terms have never been clearly differentiated. The term *cue,* however, has become traditional and conventional.

The essence of the cue theory is based on a distinction between sensation and knowledge. All knowledge comes through the senses, but before the "mind" can know, it must act on the raw stuff of sensory experience; i.e., it must interpret sensory data. The sensory events which form the basis of this interpretation are the cues, and the mind thus acts as a computer in analyzing their significance. Because the analysis of cues is involved, we can talk of either the cue or the clue in the analytical theory.

One word of caution when conceiving of cues seems in order. While it is true that it is desirable to isolate these factors when studying them, such isolation does not tell us how the individual actually perceives depth in everyday situations when these cues are usually interacting in a complex whole. This warning has recently been given by two proponents of this approach, who stated that "the outcome is not necessarily a mere sum of the effects of single factors. . . . In general, known objects are surprisingly stable and often resist distortion by inappropriate accommodation, convergence, or retinal disparity" (Woodworth and Schlosberg, 1954, p. 464). They go on to point out that many of the discrepancies in the literature are due to the fact that the attempted isolation of any single factor was often not done with extreme care. The main point is that the perception of depth is the result of an interacting process, and a theory of depth perception must do more than specify the factors entering this interaction. Let us then examine the dimensions in the physical stimulus pattern which provide bases for discriminating depth.

The traditional list of visual depth determiners has been classified into primary and secondary cues.[2] The primary cues are effective in direct sensory perception, while the secondary cues are used principally, although not exclusively, to create depth effects in drawings and paintings. This distinction may have led to an unfortunate connotation since the so-called secondary cues, which must also have actual psychological effects in the real world, have been neglected in research. Yet they are necessary in the perception of especially large distances.

Primary Cues

We shall classify the cues into groups according to the relative distances at which they cease to be effective, i.e., distances where successive changes become too small (falling below the difference limen) to produce a change in discriminable depth. The distances still need to be more precisely determined, but some evidence exists to permit the classification of an ordinal hierarchy at least. The distances reported are thus intended as guides and are not to be regarded as firmly established.

EYE MUSCLE ADJUSTMENTS. These are the cues of *accommodation* and *convergence* which operate at distances up to 25 and 80 ft, respectively. Accommodation, which is the change in the shape of the crystalline lens to bring the object into clear focus as distance varies, was established as an experimental fact by Scheiner and thought to be a depth cue by Helmholtz. Since each eye has its own lens and since one eye can accommodate while the other is, for example, closed, accommodation is called a *monocular cue*. There are many other monocular cues, most of which are listed under the secondary cues, but accommodation and the principles of perspective geometry (visual angle and linear perspective) are the basic cues in the direct sensory perception of depth. Of course, the laws of perspective geometry are not limited to distances up to 80 ft but work for much greater distances.

The power of monocular cues in creating impressions of certain spatial arrangements is illustrated in the Ames demonstrations,[3] presented in Figures 10-2, 10-3, and 10-4. If brought to these rooms blindfolded, the subject immediately, upon opening one eye and placing his head in the correct position, sees rectangular rooms. If the subject starts to look with both eyes and then closes one eye, the room is first seen according to its distortion but gradually turns into a rectangular room after inspection periods of up to 30 sec or more. The reason the effect does not work with two eyes is because each retina receives a different image. This leads us to convergence and disparity, two *binocular cues,* which we shall discuss now before return-

[2] See Boring (1942); J. J. Gibson (1950).
[3] See Ames (1946); Ittelson and Kilpatrick (1952).

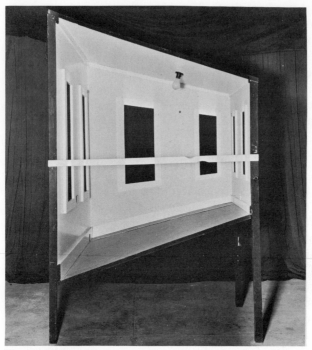

Figure 10-2
A monocular distorted room based on a 4- by 4-ft reference room.
When viewed with one eye with the chin in the hollow place on the
horizontal crossbar, the room is perceived as shown in Figure 10-3.
(After Kilpatrick, 1961, p. 165.)

ing to an evaluation of the theoretical significance of the Ames demonstrations as seen by the proponents of transactional theory.

Convergence and accommodation, thought by George Berkeley to be based on sensations of muscular strain from the eye muscles, were first investigated by Wilhelm Wundt in 1862 through his famous thread experiment. Wundt's one subject looked through a flat tube at the center portion of a single thread which was vertically suspended in the center of a room, at the far end of which was a smooth, illuminated wall. The subject's task was to look at the string, turn his head while the experimenter altered the distance, and then look at the string again and tell whether it was nearer or farther than before. Under monocular conditions the subject was able, after some practice, to compare the two distances of the thread with a difference limen of about 7 per cent. Under binocular conditions the DL was reduced to about 2 per cent. Wundt concluded that while both are functional cues, the sensations derived from convergence provide a stronger depth cue than those derived from accommodation.

Wundt's conclusion was criticized by Hillebrand (1894), a student of

Figure 10-3
A distorted room of the same size and shape as the one shown in Figure 10-2 but taken with the camera lens at the prescribed viewing point. (After Kilpatrick, 1961, p. 166.)

Hering, who also performed subsequent experiments, which were followed up by Bourdon (1902) and Bappert (1923). Hillebrand questioned whether Wundt removed convergence in his monocular condition since the muscles of the two eyes work together even when one eye is not looking at the object. He also thought that other cues, such as greater detail when the thread was nearer, might have operated. Using the sharp edge of a cardboard as a stimulus, which was moved back and forth, Hillebrand concluded from his experiments that neither accommodation nor convergence is an effective depth cue.

Bourdon used a lighted box with a circular window in it. When the distance of the box was changed, the size of the window was altered so that a constant visual angle was always presented. When the box was at a distance of 4 m, the subject judged it at between 3 and 10 m with binocular regard. For monocular regard Bourdon used two lights, one at a distance of 1 to 2 m and the other at 20 m. The subject was not certain which light was farther and which was nearer. Finally, Bappert thought that accommodation might work at nearer distances but found that the subject performed more poorly than chance when comparing lights at 25 cm and 16½ cm.

Figure 10-4
The large monocular distorted room. (After Kilpatrick, 1961, p. 166.)

These older experiments cast doubt on the reliability of accommodation as a cue but suggest that convergence may be more reliable at rather short distances.

The disadvantage in these experiments is that, by directly measuring the effect of accommodation and convergence, they must control so many other factors that the experiment becomes difficult to interpret. A more indirect approach was attempted by Chalmers (1952). In this experiment perceived size, instead of judged distance, was the dependent variable. The subject was seated in a dark room, and a luminescent strip (the standard) was presented to him at distances between 10 and 120 ft. He had to equate the size of a comparison strip to that of the standard under four conditions: when the comparison was at 10 and 120 ft, respectively, and under monocular and binocular observation.

Under the monocular conditions size constancy held up to 25 ft, while under the binocular conditions it held up to 80 ft. From the size-distance invariance hypothesis it was therefore inferred that distance was judged accurately up to 25 ft with one eye and up to 80 ft with two eyes. Since the subject did not know the size of the stimuli, it is doubtful that relative size was much of a cue. Similarly, binocular disparity could not have been too effective since the subject did not fixate one point constantly. Movement parallax was also not very important. The effect of any of the other possible cues, excepting accommodation and convergence, appears to have been negligible or nonexistent under the conditions of the experiment. Nevertheless, the distances of 25 and 80 ft are probably too large since it is probably impossible to rule out completely relative size and binocular disparity.

From what has been said, it can be concluded that accommodation is a very weak cue and breaks down at a viewing distance of 25 ft. Convergence is a little stronger but breaks down between 50 and 80 ft. If there is a gradient of muscular tension associated with increasing accommodation and convergence, therefore, it apparently reaches its effective limit at 25 ft in accommodation and 50 to 80 ft in convergence, or probably at somewhat shorter distances.

BINOCULAR DISPARITY. Binocular disparity is effective up to medium ranges of 800 to 1,900 ft. Since the time of Helmholtz a complicated conception called the *horopter* has been discussed in the literature.[4] A thorough understanding of this conception is important for a detailed mathematical analysis of certain aspects of depth perception, but for a psychological understanding of the general phenomena of depth and distance perception a definitive statement is sufficient. If an observer fixates a certain point in space, stimulation from certain other points produces clear corresponding images on the two retinas. These are called *corresponding points* since stimulation from them does not produce double images. The horopter is a theoretical line which connects corresponding points. It can be induced geometrically that "the *theoretical* shape of the horopter is a circle which passes through the point of fixation and the centers of rotation of the two eyes" (Woodworth and Schlosberg, 1954, p. 461). Stimuli coming from points outside the horopter produce disparate images on the retinas, and it is this disparity between the two images, called binocular disparity, which is considered a cue to relative depth or distance.

Ogle has stressed, with empirical support, that the horopter is theoretical and deviates from the Vieth-Müller circle described by Woodworth and Schlosberg. This deviation results from Panum's areas, where we get fusion of images falling on noncorresponding points and physiological nystagmus. A theoretical diagram of part of the horizontal horopter thus described is presented in Figure 10-5. Evidently the horopter is not just a line.

Furthermore, the asymmetry in function between the two retinas increases as visual distance decreases (Ogle, 1950). Presumably the tendency to fusion increases as distance increases, and hence the cue of disparity eventually breaks down. Fusion demands that disparity be suppressed, but when we measure stereoscopic acuity, we have a situation in which binocular vision with stereopsis demands fusion of disparate patterns from the retinas while information about their disparity is maintained.

[4] See Helmholtz (1924); Ogle (1950).

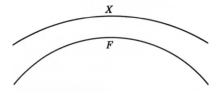

Figure 10-5
Region of binocular single vision and the longitudinal horopter. Data are from an observation distance of 40 cm; ordinates are magnified twofold. (After Ogle, 1950, p. 43.)

An example of how the sensitivity of binocular disparity can be measured, which is based on Helmholtz's three-needle experiment, is presented in Figure 10-6. An angle of disparity of only 2.0″ of arc is certainly small and corresponds to a distance of only 0.6 mm in the experiment described above, but we notice that the experiment was performed at a viewing distance of only 2 m. If we keep in mind the principles of geometry, it is quite clear the 2.0″ will correspond to increasing distances as the viewing

Figure 10-6
The Helmholtz three-needle experiment. (After Woodworth and Schlosberg, 1954, p. 470.) The dots A, B, and C represent vertical needles mounted on little blocks, which are placed on a level table. Only the needle shafts are visible to O, who is represented by the nodal points of his eyes, L and R. The needles are a few millimeters apart laterally. O must judge whether B is lined up accurately with A and C so that all three are equally far from him, or whether B is a little nearer or farther away. His average error is primarily measured in millimeters (ΔD), but such a measure cannot be compared directly with one taken with a different distance D from O to the plane of the needles A and C. A better measure is the angle of disparity, or angular measure of disparity, which is the convergence angle for the nearer object minus that for the farther object. In the figure, then, the angle of disparity equals the angle ∠ D minus the angle ∠ D + Δ D.

A method for computing these angles has been explained in Woodworth and Schlosberg, page 458, and will be applied here to a result of Bourdon (1902), who found one O successfully discriminating an offset of 0.6 mm at a distance of 2 m (2,000 mm), as indicated on the figure.

We have, in general, $\angle D = \dfrac{13,407,225}{D \text{ mm}}$

Therefore,

$$\angle D = \frac{13,407,225}{2,000} = 6,703.6''$$

and

$$D + \Delta D = \frac{13,407,225}{2,000.6} = 6,701.6''$$

Angle of disparity = 2.0″.

We usually consider 1° as a fairly small angle, but in this performance an angle of only $\frac{1}{1800}$ of a degree was perceptually utilized.

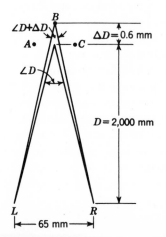

Binoc. Ret. Disparity.

B
∠D+ΔD
A•   •C   ΔD = 0.6 mm
∠D

D = 2,000 mm

L   R
|← 65 mm →|

distance is increased. At a certain point this difference threshold becomes large enough to make the disparity cue essentially nonexistent. Moreover, wide differences exist between individuals with respect to sensitivity to binocular disparity. That it is an effective cue in most individuals, however, has been established. Thus, Howard (1919) found that the average depth thresholds for nine subjects were only 14.4 mm for binocular vision, as contrasted with 285 mm for monocular vision. In this experiment also relatively short viewing distances were employed.

An interesting application of the principle of binocular disparity is again provided by Ames (Ittelson and Kilpatrick, 1952, pp. 52–53), using binocular rooms which are binocularly equivalent, i.e., which produce images on corresponding parts of the retinas. These demonstrations are presented in Figure 10-7, and it is very instructive to compare this photograph with the monocular-room demonstration and also to consider the reason for the magnification of the object in (*a*) relative to the one in (*b*).

SUBJECTIVE DISTANCE. Luneberg (1948) has presented a theoretical explanation of why the distorted rooms are perceived as rectangular and also of other spatial phenomena, such as Blumenfeld's parallel alleys, by developing mathematical equations expressing the transformation of physical space into psychological space. The equations are based on the notion of free motion, which is defined as point transformation that preserves spatial configuration, and on the view that psychological space is non-Euclidean.

Luneberg deduces that the relation of sensory (psychological) distance to physical distance is hyperbolic, i.e., curved and negatively accelerated. There is no infinity in sensory distance. These curves, which are called *Luneberg's circles,* differ for different observers and at different ages for the same observer. There are two subjective constants. One is related to the interpupillary distance of the eyes and determines sensitivity of depth perception which is greater than sensitivity of size perception. The second constant relates sensory judgment of size to actual physical size.

Luneberg's attempt to relate physical and subjective space, which has qualitative support in the evidence discussed although it awaits qualitative verification, brings to mind Gilinsky's attempt to relate physical distance to psychological distance, which we discussed in Chapter 6.[5] She also stated that the function relating the two was negatively accelerated and approached an asymptote at rather short distances. Her conclusion has been challenged by Gruber (1956) in connection with his work which we also discussed in Chapter 6. The magnitude of the problem is illustrated in Figure 10-8.

Gruber's data indicate that perceived distance d does not approach a maximum asymptotic function as physical distance increases since he failed to produce the negative constant error which would be expected if $d/D < 1$ for all values of D. Thus, while these attempts to develop mathematical relationships for distance perception are admirable, specification

[5] See also Blank (1959).

Figure 10-7
Small (a) and large (b) binocular distorted rooms, with the same Bisquick box appearing in both stereoscopic pairs. The box, by its apparent alteration in size and shape, reveals to some extent how different the two rooms themselves are in size and shape. These photographs may be cut out and mounted for stereoscopic viewing. (After Kilpatrick, 1961, p. 171.)

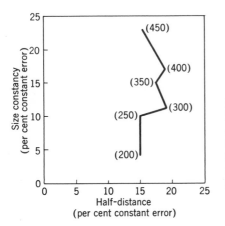

Figure 10-8
The lack of relation between perceived size and perceived distance. The figures in parentheses are the physical distances bisected in half-distance judgments, and the physical-distance judgments represent perceived size. (After Gruber, 1956.)

of the nature of the function awaits more empirical data. Gruber concluded that "the information we lack can only be supplied by concrete experimental analysis of proximal stimulus-correlates of physical distance" (*ibid.*, p. 475). Concerted attempts to find these correlates have been made by J. J. Gibson and his associates at Cornell University, who have launched a systematic attack on the problems of space perception. Gibson's work and gradient theory are discussed in the next section.

Secondary Cues

Those cues which are traditionally called secondary are effective at distances up to and beyond 600 yd. The upper limit at which these cues are useful has not been established, but studies have used distances exceeding 1,000 yd and, in one case, up to 8,000 yd. More work needs to be done on these cues to determine thresholds and the distances at which gradients approach their effective limits.

1. *Upward angular location of grounded objects.* As the angle of displacement of grounded objects from the horizontal line of sight appears to decrease, the objects appear farther away from the observer. Objects which appear to be vertically closer to the horizon are also farther away, given level ground, and this fact (i.e., differences in upward angular location) can be used as a cue to distance. Artists employ this cue very effectively. When they want to create the impression that something is farther away, they locate it higher on the canvas in the picture.

2. *Perceived size of familiar objects.* We have stated many times in this chapter and in Chapter 6 that the relative retinal-image size (visual angle) of familiar objects can be used as a cue to distance. Thus, Gilinsky (1955) has demonstrated that relative-size cues from objects which are only 3 to 6 ft high can be effective for differential range estimations up to 4,000 ft. Moreover, Holway et al. (1945) found that, when judging the distance of a familiar panel 8 in. wide by 14 ft high which was attached to the front of an automobile, sub-

jects made range errors of only 1 per cent under *monocular* viewing. These small errors held for distances up to 1 mile.

3. *Texture and density gradients.* If we look across a landscape (a patch of grass, a field of daisies, shrubs, or trees), we observe that the texture of the ground becomes finer (denser) as distance increases. Consequently objects located on a ground with finer texture appear to be farther away than objects located on coarser ground of the same type of texture. J. J. Gibson (1950) has stressed the importance of this gradient underlying the perception of relative distance, but the precision of this cue has not been established. Dusek, Teichner, and Kobrick (1955), for example, found that the variability of relative-distance discrimination is not significantly different for terrain of pavement, sand, or snow. They used distances up to 500 yd. Clark, Smith, and Rabe (1956) found that under monocular conditions outline gradients and texture gradients in a form lead to more accurate judgments of slant of the form than when the form is homogeneous.

GRADIENT THEORY OF SPACE PERCEPTION. As Gibson has stated, "the word *gradient* means nothing more complex than an increase or decrease of something along a given axis or dimension" (1950). An example is given: The gradient of a highway is its change in altitude with distance. The gradient may be zero, when the road is level or when it increases or de-creases at a constant rate; positive, when the inclination increases with distance; or negative, when it decreases with distance. Furthermore, the change (gradient) may be moderate or rapid, or it may change along the way, as is true when traveling over a hilly terrain. If the change is very abrupt, as it is when an inclination terminates at a cliff, it is called a *step*. Gibson has suggested that "these concepts appear to be admirably adapted for describing the retinal image since both gradients and steps of stimula-tion can be found within it" (*ibid.*, p. 73).

The concept of gradient thus defined is used by Gibson to develop a theory of space perception. In essence, the kinds of gradients he specifies are based on the two rules of perspective previously discussed. The first rule, the law of visual angle, states that the frontal dimension is projected as a size S which is inversely proportional to distance D; algebraically this means that S is proportional to $1/D$. The second rule is that the longitudinal dimension is projected as an altitude A which is inversely proportional to the square of the distance. The algebraic equivalent of this states that A is proportional to $1/D^2$. Thus it is the longitudinal dimension which is com-pressed relative to the frontal dimension. Gibson has applied these perspec-tive techniques to the *texture of a surface* instead of to the edges of a surface, as is usual. By so doing he has demonstrated that these perspective techniques can be used to construct such patterns as texture gradients and density gradients, which often underlie our perception of depth and dis-tance. Examples of gradients and steps of stimulation and the importance of texture perspective in giving impressions of receding, continuous, or abrupt changes in surface are presented in Figure 10-9.

Figure 10-9
Texture and density gradients and steps of stimulation giving impressions of receding, continuous, or abrupt changes in surface and distance.

It is apparent from the foregoing that the concept of gradient is a useful tool which aids in an explanation of depth perception. The validity of such an explanation is based on the assumption, which is geometrically and logically sound, that stimulus gradients give rise to *corresponding* gradients on the retina, which in turn lead to corresponding impressions of depth and distance in the psychological (more specifically, visual) world. In a more recent explication of his theory, Gibson (1958) emphasizes his belief that every phenomenal aspect of the visual world is represented by a corresponding aspect in the physical energy which influences the receptors. Instead of discussing inference, we should be looking for the determination of ability to discriminate these higher-order patterns of stimulation.

Other Secondary Cues

1. *Superposition* (*interposition*). This term means that a near object may partially obscure far objects. Such an interruption of the surface of one object by the boundaries of the nearer object is a cue to relative distance of the two objects. All of us have observed this interruption when looking at a distant mountain range. The question is how this becomes a cue. The hypothesis originally advanced by Helmholtz and later revised by Ratoosh (1949) had stated that the junction points between the two objects provide the only determiners of interposition; i.e., the contour which appears to be complete, regular, and

continuing in one direction is seen as nearer, while the contour which takes a sharp turn in direction is seen as farther away. This hypothesis was tested by Chapanis and McCleary (1953) in two experiments. These investigators found that in certain patterns of stimuli where the junction points could not have provided such cues, the subjects still gave unanimous judgments of depth. There was some evidence that the *relative sizes* of the elements in the pattern provided probable cues to depth in such cases. The authors concluded that the overall form or configuration of the elements is far more important than the junction points alone in determining the discrimination of relative depth. For an experimental approach to this cue, the reader should consult another of the Ames demonstrations (Ittelson and Kilpatrick, 1951).

2. *Aerial perspective.* As we look at objects in a distance, we frequently notice that the more distant objects appear to be bluer or more violet in color. Thus the green vegetation on a mountain nearer the horizon looks more bluish than the vegetation of a mountain closer to us. This observation of the change in color, which has not been measured, is a probable cue, called aerial perspective, and depends on the amount of haze in the atmosphere and the level of illumination.

3. *Filled and empty space.* It has been noted that a distance which is filled with objects looks farther away than one which is relatively empty.

4. *Light and shade.* It has been shown that the appearance of spatial depth of an object is lost when it completely lacks shadow. Thus light and shade patterns provide cues not to distance but to the depth or relief of a single solid object. A homogeneously illuminated flat drawing or painting of an object is seen in two dimensions (other factors being controlled); it has an illumination gradient of zero. If the illumination is sufficiently heterogeneous, there is an impression of solidity. Von Fieandt (1939) found that the appearance of bulges or dents in a surface can be produced by changing the apparent direction of illumination. Although there exists a tendency to see such lighted and shaded areas as convex rather than concave, a reversed impression can be created by bringing in the illumination from above. Lauenstein (1938) also reported that changes in the source, intensity, and direction of illumination of solid objects change their appearance and the direction of depth relief. An illustration of the use of lighting in producing a greater depth effect is shown in Figure 10-10.

Another example which not only illustrates the light-shade effect on depth but also shows that the depth effect is reversed when the image is inverted is presented in Figure 10-11. In order to get the reversal of depth relationship, the page should be turned upside down (Evans, 1948).

5. *Relative brightness.* Münster showed that if two equidistant bright surfaces are presented (one to each eye) and a dark filter is interposed between one eye and its corresponding surface, then the latter surface appears to be farther away. It is sometimes mistakenly believed that the more distant an object, the lower the intensity of its retinal image. Gibson has reminded us that relative brightness is only a cue of distance of point sources of light; it does not apply to *reflecting surfaces.*

6. *Size and perspective.* This cue is, of course, based on the law of visual angle, which we discussed in Chapter 6. Since retinal-image size is inversely proportional to distance, relative size as well as a continuous change in size

(a)

(b)

Figure 10-10a and b
The effect of lighting contrast on the impression of depth. Notice that low contrast reduces depth significantly.

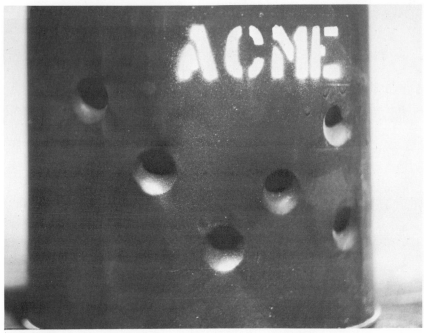

Figure 10-11
Light-shade effects on depth. Turn the page upside down and notice the reversal of depth effects.

with increase in distance may be a cue to distance. This is especially true when we are dealing with familiar objects or objects which have fairly constant objective sizes. (The reader is referred to the section "Nature of Size Constancy" in Chapter 6.) The geometry of perspective which approximately duplicates the retinal image is one technique which is used to create the third dimension.

7. *Linear perspective.* This cue is similar to relative size but applies to longitudinal rather than frontal dimensions. The law of linear perspective states that the retinal size of a longitudinal dimension is inversely proportional to the square of the distance from the observer. We have all witnessed the operation of this cue when looking at a straight highway or railroad and noticing the sides converge in the distance.

8. *Motion parallax.* This cue is defined as the relative apparent motion of objects as an individual moves his head or opens and shuts each eye in succession. Generally the nearer object appears to move faster than the more distant one.

Interaction and Utilization of Cues

Now that we have examined the various cues, we should remind ourselves that they do not work in isolation but generally interact to determine the extent and direction of spatial perception. Whether any of the cues are more important than any others has not been experimentally determined, but the evidence does indicate that the classical primary cues (accommodation, convergence, and binocular disparity) are not nearly so important as they once were believed to be. Thus the cues based on perspective, such as texture and density gradients and especially relative size, appear to be more important than the others, particularly where long distances are involved.

Kilpatrick and Ittelson (1953) and other writers in the same school, in summarizing the theoretical implications of the Ames demonstrations, have questioned the validity of the approach which maintains that these physical cues are as reliable as claimed by such people as J. J. Gibson and the gestalt psychologists. Instead, they reason that such relationships as size-distance invariance can be affected by a number of subjective (see previous discussion on subjective distance) and experiential factors, the organism being in a continuous *transactional* relationship with the objective environment. Schlosberg (1950), however, has pointed out quite logically that these objective physical factors must be the reliable bases of adaptive behavior in space. When these cues are distorted or conflicted, as in the Ames demonstrations, the organism is faced with ambiguous, unstable, or impoverished stimulation (Gibson has also stressed this fact) and is thus forced to rely on the cue in this situation which is most stable in that stimulus complex. Frequently objective size and shape constancy constitute the most stable cue. Let us remember the data of Brunswik, presented in Chapter 6, which indicate that whenever the physical condition permits, the subjective perception of size is determined by real physical distance as measured objectively rather than by apparent distance. In certain cases, however, as in the moon illusion, size is determined by apparent distance. Thus the moon looks bigger at the horizon than at the zenith since objects closer to the horizon always appear farther away and, because the visual angle is constant, the apparently farther moon looks bigger (Boring, 1943; Rock, 1962).

It would seem, further, that when many of these cues are operating simultaneously, they facilitate greater accuracy of depth discrimination since they transmit a certain amount of redundant information (signs) about depth. When we look at a spatial scene with both eyes and through an unobstructed visual field, depth perception is usually more accurate. If we look at a distant range of mountains, we can detect at least five cues— interposition, aerial perspective, linear perspective, relative size, and upward angular location—working together. We can gradually reduce the accuracy of depth perception by systematically reducing the cues until we reach the condition of monocular perception in the dark, in which depth perception is almost nonexistent.

A good indication of how, for example, the light contrast cue can strengthen the texture cue is illustrated in Figures 10-12 and 10-13. In Figure 10-14 we see how the cue of linear perspective, which gives the impression of receding distance and thus makes the higher man of any two look bigger, can be in conflict with upward location. When this picture is turned upside down, the illusion is decreased; i.e., the same man no longer looks that much bigger since he is now lower on the page.

DEPTH IN REPRODUCTIONS. An interesting description of the pattern of cues which make a considerable amount of depth perceivable in a picture was provided by Schlosberg (1941). He was referring to the "plastic" depth that can be obtained monocularly and is most striking when the viewing lens has the same focal length as the camera lens with which the picture was taken.

The perception of depth clues determines whether we see a picture as *representing* depth or as actual objects *deployed* in depth. Depth clues may include shading, clearness of outline, perspective, and superposition. Depth is immediately a way of perceiving, not merely the addition of something to a picture in varying amounts.

Clues for "flatness" [6] include identity of binocular fields, surface glare, the absence of monocular parallax changes when the picture is moved, cues from accommodation, and others. The perception of depth may take place in viewing a picture if the flatness clues can be eliminated or weakened and

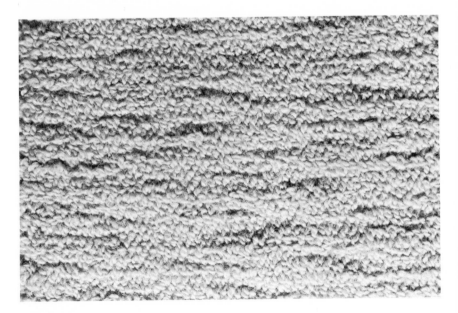

Figure 10-12
Texture gradient under high contrast.

[6] Both Schlosberg and Helmholtz consider flatness a special form of depth.

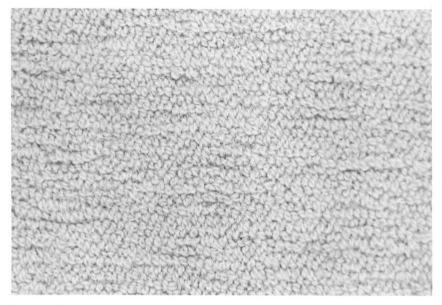

Figure 10-13
The same surface as in Figure 10-12 under low contrast. Notice the diminishing of texture gradient.

the depth clues exaggerated. The flatness clues, which cause normal binocular inspection of a picture to force the observer to see a flat picture, may be eliminated (thus permitting the plastic effect) by looking at the picture from a distance, monocular viewing (looking through a tube or a lens or looking at the picture monocularly in a mirror), partial binocular vision (blurring the image in one eye during binocular vision or using prisms to displace or rotate the image in one eye), full binocular vision through a large lens, and the use of the iconoscope.

The plastic effect has, according to Schlosberg, an "all-or-none" character: the effect is usually either clearly present or absent. He agreed with the gestalt psychologists that "depth perception cannot be considered as a mere addition and subtraction of factors of differing importance."

In a similar analysis, Evans (1948, pp. 141–142) shows how many cues combine with a total pattern to create the impression of depth in photographic reproductions. For good depth effects the visual angle or magnification should be high, the contrast high, the image sharp rather than diffuse, the tone continuous rather than grainy, and the surface glossy rather than matte. Furthermore, he points out how important viewing distance is as a determiner of good depth impression from a photograph. He states that the correct viewing distance for a print is the focal length of the lens multiplied by the number of times the print will be magnified. For example, if the focal length is 2 in. and the print will be magnified four times, then the

Figure 10-14
Interaction between linear perspective and upward angular location.
If we turn the page upside down, we notice that the illusion of size
is diminished.

correct viewing distance is 8 in. A comparison of the two photographs in
Figure 10-15 shows how a reduction of the viewing distance drastically
depresses the depth effect. Evans concludes by noting that the "correct
viewing distance gives the proper perspective; that is, the angular relations
seen between objects are identical in the picture with those of the original
objects as viewed from the position of the camera or lens" (*ibid.*, p. 143).

ORGANIZATIONAL FACTORS. Michotte (1950a) showed that the impression
of a three-dimensional cube could be changed to the perception of a two-
dimensional hexagonal by the introduction of a new brightness relationship.
An illustration of this change is presented in Figure 10-16.

(a)

(b)

Figure 10-15
(a) *Wide viewing distance.* (b) *Same scene as in Figure 10-15a but with a narrower viewing distance. Notice the reduction in the impression of distance.*

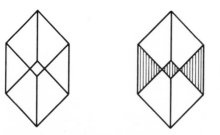

Figure 10-16
Three- and two-dimensional figures. (After
Michotte, 1950c.)

Certain other experiments have determined the relative effectiveness of
retinal (binocular) disparity under various field conditions. Thus, Schriever
(1925) found that experimental alteration of retinal disparity does not
change the perceived depth relief of photographs of solid objects provided
that linear perspective, shadow effects, and superposition (especially the
latter) are kept constant. Furthermore, Kopferman (1930) demonstrated
that disparity gradients [7] are ineffective if they conflict with configurational
forms. To his observers he presented glass slides, each with part of a straight-
line figure on it, one behind the other, so that parts of the line pattern
appeared continuous. Three different results were obtained, depending on
the structural continuity of the pattern of lines. A two-dimensional form
was seen if the parts formed a connected, continuous whole. Under other
conditions the observers saw either a three-dimensional whole or two
separate figures in different planes. Finally, M. D. Vernon (1937), among
others, has shown the existence of individual differences in stereoscopic
acuity and the importance of the total field. She found that the equating of
the distances of two white screens, each with a dot on it, is sometimes more
accurate in monocular vision when the surroundings are partly visible than
in binocular vision when the surroundings are obscured. Conversely, in
monocular regard with the surroundings visible, the correct relationship of
the object to its surroundings is often difficult to judge because the size
relationships of the two objects to each other and the total surroundings
are unknown.

In a very interesting and novel experiment Hochberg and Brooks (1960)
attempted to find a way of measuring the combined effect of a number of
variables on the perception of depth. After determining a multiple-regression
equation and after factor analysis, they reported that greater *complexity*
(the number of angles), *asymmetry* (the number of different angles divided
by the total number of angles), and *discontinuity* (the number of line segments which are not continuous) of the projection of a three-dimensional
object in two dimensions give a greater impression of a three-dimensional
object.

Our earlier reference to individual differences again raises the question

[7] In this regard it is interesting to note (Beck, 1960) that the addition of a binocu-
lar-disparity gradient to four different texture gradients does not remove all the
ambiguity in the dissemination of slant and recession.

of the extent to which spatial perception is learned. Piaget (1937) has observed that the accuracy of depth location undergoes much improvement in infants between the ages of three and nine months. Furthermore, Cruikshank (1941) has concluded from her experiments and those of others that children younger than six months make gross errors in reaching for objects. After that age an improvement in depth discrimination apparently takes place; e.g., a child ceases to grasp at far objects beyond his reach. Gesell (1949) and his coworkers have noted that improvement in the precision of depth location continues up to one year and probably beyond that age.

DISCRIMINATION OF SPACE AND EXPERIENCE. From the evidence examined in this chapter we may reasonably conclude that there exists an innate potential to respond to the various relationships which lead to our perception of space. Which of these factors becomes more functional to an individual as he develops probably depends to a large extent on experience and learning. Moreover, it has been shown that the accuracy of space perception can be greatly improved by training even in adults. Thus, Horowitz and Kappauf (1946) reported that a constant range error of 30 to 40 per cent was reduced to 20 per cent by training in serial range estimation. Other reports show that a probable error of 30 per cent was reduced to 17 per cent and that constant errors as well as variability of range estimation were reduced through training. Finally, Eleanor J. Gibson (1955) et al. have concluded that the most effective and general method of improving absolute judgment of distance is through a technique they call *scale training*. In this experiment the subjects had to learn to discriminate distances on a 300-yd grassy field. One reference point was located near the subject; the other was a hedge at the end of the field. Using the technique of fractionation, the experimenter required the subject to divide the 300 yd into successive halves, i.e., 150 yd, 75 yd, and so on. After repeated trials, the subjects' accuracy improved to such an extent that it even showed transfer of improved distance judgments to completely different grassy fields. It would seem that the subjects' difference threshold to the texture gradient had probably been lowered through training.

A thorough investigation of the development of depth perception has been undertaken at Cornell University by Eleanor J. Gibson and her associates (Gibson, Tighe, and Walk, 1957; Gibson and Walk, 1960). They constructed an apparatus called a *visual cliff*, which is depicted together with an explanation in the photographs in Figure 10-17. A number of species, including chicks, turtles, rats, lambs, kids, pigs, kittens, dogs, and human infants, were tested on this apparatus. Depth discrimination seemed to be present in all these animals, and the kinds of emergent behavioral patterns were characteristic of the way the particular species had adapted to its environment. Thus, chicks less than twenty-four hours old always hopped off the board on the "shallow" side. Kids and lambs one day of age never stepped into the glass on the "deep" side.

(a)

(b)

Figure 10-17a and b
The visual cliff. Note the baby crawling toward the mother on the
shallow side and staying away from the mother on the deep side.
(*After Gibson and Walk, 1960. Reprinted with permission. Copyright
© 1960, 1961 by Scientific American, Inc. All rights reserved. Photograph courtesy of William Vandivert.*)

To eliminate the effect of spurious variables, kids and goats were tested at the Cornell Behavior Farm in a modified experiment. The pattern was attached to plywood which could be moved from a distance just under the glass to distances farther beneath the glass. When the pattern was just beneath the glass, the animal would move around freely, but when the optical floor was more than 1 ft below the glass, the visual cliff was apparently too great: the animal would immediately freeze into a crouching, defensive position. "Despite repeated experience of the tactual solidity of the glass, the animals never learned to function without optical support. Their sense of security or danger continued to depend upon the visual cues that give them their perception of depth" (Gibson and Walk, 1960, p. 4).

Rats and cats, which are nocturnal animals, did not exhibit such dependence on vision. For example, hooded rats when placed on the glass over the deep side moved about freely provided that they could feel the glass with their vibrissae, but when the center board was raised several inches so that the glass could not be reached by the vibrissae, 95 to 100 per cent of the rats descended on the shallow side.

Human beings are, of course, highly dependent on vision. In one experiment Gibson and Walk tested 36 infants, ranging in age from six to fourteen months, on the visual cliff. Of the 27 infants who moved off the board, all crawled out on the shallow side at least once. Only 3 moved off the edge of the board to the glass on the deep side.

The results of Gibson and Walk confirm the belief that adaptive behavior and thus survival of a species require the ability to discriminate depth by the time the individuals locomote independently. The respective ages are one day for the chick and goat, three to four weeks for the rat and cat, and six to ten months for the human infant.

The data presented thus far do not tell us whether certain kinds of experience with light stimulation are necessary before these abilities to discriminate depth emerge. Therefore Gibson and Walk performed an experiment to test the variable of experience. One group of rats was reared in darkness, and another under normal conditions. When tested on the visual cliff at ninety days of age, the animals from both groups chose the shallow side. Then the experimenters manipulated two cues to depth perception. When the density gradient cue was eliminated, the dark-reared animals still preferred the shallow side, but when the motion parallax cue was eliminated, allowing only the pattern density to operate as a cue, no preference was elicited. Evidently motion parallax as a cue is innate, but pattern density is not.

Summary

In this chapter we saw how the perception of space is determined by the information carried in relational stimulation. Thus the perception of two dimensions and bodily orientation are affected by both external (e.g., visual) and internal (proprioceptive) referents.

The fascinating interaction between visual and bodily stimulation is indicated by such studies as the space-flight projects and sensoritonic investigations. These and other experiments also reveal the amazing adaptability of human space orientation when the normal frameworks are distorted.

In the case of three-dimensional space, we saw how a variety of cues produce a "field" effect which makes the perception of depth inevitable and not, for example, merely something added to a picture. These cues or their combinational effect must be destroyed or reduced for the impression of depth to be reduced or confused.

The function relating psychological distance to physical distance is problematical since there are at least two subjective constants which vary from individual to individual and within individuals at different times.

For adaptive behavior to take place there must be an innate reaction to some aspect in the energy flux carried to the receptor. With learning, experience, or training, however, the organism's sensitivity to a greater variety of these cues and to their interacting effects improves greatly. In rats, for example, the cue of motion parallax is innate, whereas density gradient does not become a cue until experience has taught the organism the "significance" of this variable. Training also leads to increased specificity or differentiation within a particular cue.

11

Motion, Event,
and Social Perception

In this chapter we shall examine some of the evidence which indicates that the perception of motion, events (interaction between classes of stimuli), and social phenomena, such as motives, is governed by certain *spatiotemporal relationships*.

Motion Perception

In various articles, J. J. Gibson (Gibson, 1954; Gibson, Olum, and Rosenblatt, 1955) stressed the fact, considered important by certain students of perception for some time, that the problems of motion perception involve to a large extent the problems of space. The full realization that efficient experimental headway in the investigation of motion perception requires that it be related to problems of spatial organization is an important methodological and theoretical advance. Prior theories suffered from lack of richness and generated little exciting research because they did not relate the different patterns of stimulation: witness, for example, the explanation of motion perception in terms of such physiological events as the sensations resulting from moving the eyes in pursuit of a moving object. One of the more apparent weaknesses of such a theory is that it fails to handle the striking parallel between the perception of real physical motion and so-called apparent motion. But the realization that we should start with the inclusion of space is only the first important step in understanding the psychology of motion. The difficulty comes when we look for the specific relationships involved.

In Chapter 10 we saw how the perception of space is crucially dependent on relations existing along many dimensions (e.g., gradients); in Chapter 2 we learned that spatial segregation of the perceptual field into separate classes is based on brightness gradients and configurational principles. In this section we shall see that the primary determiners of motion perception can also be classified into two classes which involve spatiotemporal functions and configurational principles.

Before discussing these two sets of principles, let us state at the outset that the experimental evidence seems to indicate that problems of so-called real movement and so-called apparent movement are similar. Real movement has been limited to the perception of movement when physical bodies are actually in motion, while apparent movement has been defined as the perception of movement of entities which are not in actual physical motion. This distinction stems from the orientation of physics which defines reality in terms of physical referents that can easily be effected. The organism's reality, however, is that which is psychologically real; let us keep in mind Immanuel Kant's admonition that phenomena are the only true reality in psychological experience. Therefore, all psychological motion is phenomenal, i.e., exists in the experience of the observer. Besides, we shall see evidence which suggests that a unitary set of principles can be developed to handle the phenomena of the perception of both real and apparent movement. We shall thus treat these two events as a unitary phenomenon, discussing evidence which points to their basic similarity. Gibson (1954) has already pointed to the way in which these two events are similar. In perception, what is real is that which is perceived as real, and no one who has seen a motion picture will deny that the movement he sees on the screen appears to be as real as actual physical motion.

STIMULUS FOR THE PERCEPTION OF MOTION. In a more recent article, Gibson (1960a) states that information about space, form, and changes in space is contained directly in light. The nature of the stimulus containing the information might consist of higher-order variables if only we would develop the appropriate mathematical function for describing them. For example, in the perception of change, e.g., of movement in space, the stimulus information would be indicated by some kind of optical transformation of the illumination pattern. What need to be determined are the mathematical functions describing these transformations. The functions describing the order and transformation of the stimulus should correlate or correspond across the four interrelated variables, namely, distal stimulus, proximal stimulus, brain field, and behavioral responses (perceptual world).

Since Gibson feels that the first link in the chain has been neglected in perceptual theory, he continues his admirable attempt to define the proximal energy stimulation and its relation to the distal stimulus and advises that "we must learn to conceive an array not as a mosaic of stimuli but as a *hierarchy of forms within forms,* and a flux not as a chain of stimuli but as a *hierarchy of sequences within longer sequences"* (Gibson, 1960b, p. 700). [1] Let us then see what the higher-order patterns of stimulation might be in the case of the perception of motion and related phenomena.

Spatiotemporal Relations and Motion Perception: An Interdependent Organization Effect

The perception of moving objects takes place in a spatial frame of reference, the stable visual environment. There are two questions concerning this phenomenon to which we need answers: (1) What determines the stability of the environment? (2) Under which conditions are points seen to move across it? These are questions of real importance which we can only attempt to answer at present.

The first point to note is that the part which is seen as the stable environment is not necessarily the part which is stationary. It is not clear what determines why one part is seen as moving while another is seen as stationary, but this phenomenon appears to be related to the perceived figure-ground relationship. Thus we know that the part of the field which meets the criterion of "figural property," e.g., the part which is smaller, is usually seen as moving, irrespective of whether it or the larger surround is actually moving physically. Under these conditions the physically moving surround is perceived as a stable, stationary ground. To illustrate this point, we might refer to the experiment of Duncker (1939) in which he studied the perception of two lights in a dark room where one light was in physical motion while the other was held stationary. When the subject fixated one light, it was seen as moving even when the other light was actually in physical motion, the fixated light being stationary. Duncker suggested that the fixated light was seen as moving because it stood out as a figure, the other light becoming part of the ground.

In the same study Duncker performed another experiment in which a stationary light was enclosed by a moving luminescent-outlined rectangle in an otherwise dark room. Again he found that the light was seen as moving while the rectangle appeared to be stationary, and again we note that the figure moved phenomenologically while the physically moving rectangle was seen as a stationary ground or stable framework relative to which the light was seen as moving. Evidently we perceive not absolute but relative motion. We do not see one point moving absolutely in space but rather something moving relative to something else. We are reminded of Albert Einstein's theory of relativity, in which motion depends upon the relative position of the observer and which is at variance with the earlier Newtonian ideas.

[1] Italics mine.

Let us now attempt to answer the second question. Specifically we want to know which factors or combinations of factors govern the perception of the motion of this figure. We shall see that the nature of motion perception is determined by relationships existing between spatial, intensity, and temporal factors. As we have said, the stimulation for the perception of motion is relational. The visual system responds to certain relationships existing between two or three of the factors listed above. If the perception of motion is to occur, these relationships must remain within certain limits.

One of the first psychological experiments designed to investigate these relationships was performed by Wertheimer (1912) in his classic study of the phi phenomenon, which is one kind of stroboscopic or apparent motion. (Anyone who has seen the lights moving on the marquee of a theater has seen an illustration of phi movement.) Two points of light, spatially separated in the frontal plane, were exposed successively to the subject, who was sitting in an otherwise dark room. The *time interval* between successive exposures of the two lights turned out to be a crucial factor. Wertheimer found that for "pure" or optimum phi to occur, i. e., for the perception of a spot of light swinging back and forth in unitary motion to take place without the awareness of two objects moving, an optimal time interval of constant duration was necessary. We now know that this value held only for the conditions, especially the distance separating the lights, imposed by Wertheimer.

Korte (1915) carried out a more extended and parametric study of the phi phenomenon. He found that the time interval was not constant but varied as the distance varied; i.e., if distance between the lights was increased, the time interval had to be increased for optimum phi movement to be maintained. By varying the distance between the lights, the time interval of successive exposures, and the intensity of the lights in his experiments, Korte obtained certain relationships for phi movement on the basis of which he formulated three laws which govern the perception of optimal phi: (1) the distance between lights varies directly with the time interval between successive exposures; (2) the distance varies directly with the intensity of the light stimuli; and (3) the intensity varies inversely with the time interval.

The first law seems to hold up well, but the effect of intensity is controversial. For example, Neuhaus (1930) reported results which conflicted with Korte's second law. This is not the place to repeat a review of this problem, which has been covered very well by Neff (1936), but one thing seems fairly certain, and that is the reported *relationship* which is necessary *between the spatial distance and the time interval* for the perception of optimal motion.

The phi phenomenon is not just an example of apparent movement but is related to a larger organizational effect concerning space-time relations. Thus modern Japanese work has shown, for example, that when the time relations between the lights are altered, a perceptible alteration in the distance separating them follows (Obonai and Suzumura, 1954).

To show the similarity of the space-time organizational effects in apparent and physical motion, we might note that J. J. Gibson in a study previously cited (1954) has pointed out that "stroboscopic stimulation differs from so-called real stimulation only in being discontinuous whereas the latter is continuous. The relations of order are the same in both." In the same article he reports that when a patterned surface on a moving belt is presented, the speed and direction of the linear motion are perceived with some degree of accuracy. The same thing holds in the perception of the rotary motion of the surface of a disk. Moreover, the perceived velocity of the moving surface tends to remain constant even at different distances from the eye, despite the fact that the retinal velocity of its image varies inversely with distance from the eye. The fact to remember, however, is that the retinal image of the distance through which the surface is moving also varies inversely with the distance from the eye. In other words, *the ratio between the retinal image of the distance and the angular velocity of the retinal image remains constant.* The resulting constant velocity, then, is in agreement with our hypothesis that motion perception is relational.

Another fact which accords with this position is the Aubert *Fleischl* paradox reported by J. F. Brown (1931a). The paradox is that the perceived velocity is somewhat slower when the subject's eyes follow the moving pattern to-and-fro than when he fixates a small aperture through which he sees the surface moving. This makes untenable any eye-movement or other elementaristic theory of motion perception. Again, what seems to be important here is the perceptible distance of the surface and the relation to its velocity. This generally fits in with Korte's law relating distance and time interval in the phi phenomenon since "real" velocity is obviously related to the *time interval between successive spatial stimulations.* These findings were corroborated in an experiment by Gibson, Smith, Steinschneider, and Johnson (1957), in which they found that the accuracy with which the speed of two moving surfaces can be matched is just as good with fixation of the eyes as with the eyes in pursuit.

We may summarize this section by stating that for the perception of motion $d/t = K$; that is, the ratio of distance to time must fall within a certain constant range. In the case of actual physical motion t is the velocity; in the case of stroboscopic movement t is the time interval. Of course, much research is needed to determine additional questions. We want to know, for example, what the ranges of K are, what neurological events underlie these perceptions, and the extent of individual differences. We must also know how other stimulus factors influence the range of K. With relevance to this question, we know that configurational principles have a significant effect on the perception of motion. To this subject we now turn.

Configurational Factors in Motion Perception

At the beginning of the section "Motion Perception," we mentioned how important figural segregation is in determining what is seen as moving and what is seen as the stationary ground. We now return to a consideration of this fact and to other structural features of the stimulus field which influence the perception of phenomenal motion.

Some of the earliest work on the configurational nature of motion perception was performed by J. F. Brown (1931a) and Metzger (1926), who studied the thresholds of velocity between the perception of change of position and movement and the perception of movement and of partial fusion of moving illuminated objects. Their moving objects consisted of such illuminated objects as a row of squares. They reported that two transformations in motion were evident: first, a change from shift of position to steady movement; and, second, a change from steady movement to a continuous circular path. The same "shrinkage" was reported when subjects observed four lights arranged in a cross as in Figure 11-1 and exposed successively (J. F. Brown and Voth, 1937).

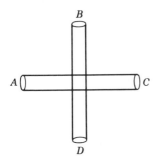

Figure 11-1
Arrangement of the lights in the experiment of J. F. Brown and Voth.

An interesting fact that this study found was that the shrinkage depended upon the time interval between successive exposures. It was only at particular time intervals (corresponding to the time required for optimum phi) that a band of light moving in a circle was seen. At time intervals lower or greater than this value either simultaneous flickering or successive flickering was seen. The results are summarized in Figure 11-2.

That the nature of the phenomenal motion is not fully understood is apparent from subsequent experiments. Sylvester (1960) attempted to replicate the experiment of Brown and Voth. After successively energizing the lights at the four corners (of a cross or diamond), as described by Brown and Voth, he did not obtain the reported movement of light in a circular path lying within the perimeter of the lights. Data of Christian and Weizäcker (1943), who extended the first experiment of Brown and Voth, may throw some light on what possibly is happening. The latter

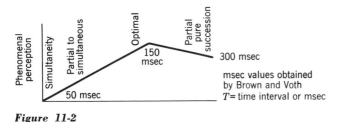

Figure 11-2
Perception as a function of the time interval. (After J. F. Brown and Voth, 1937.)

investigators found that sometimes shrinkage occurs, and sometimes "expansion," and that sometimes there is a fluctuation between the two. It would thus seem that the forces operating to pull a "circle of light" in or out depend on the relationship between the speed of movement and the circumference of the circle. Unfortunately, the exact relationships have not been determined. In our laboratory we recently found that instructions play a crucial role.[2]

An attempt to relate these organizational effects to the gestalt laws of configuration was made by Ternus (1926), who presented three points, lights *a*, *b*, and *c*, which were slightly separated along a straight line. This stimulus was shortly followed by three other light points, *b*, *c*, and *d*. The position of the *b*'s and *c*'s in the first and second stimuli were identical, and the distance separating contiguous points was constant. The subject reported seeing *a*, *b*, and *c* moving to the right despite the fact that the stimuli were not moving physically. This result is in agreement with the law of uniform direction or uniform density, which was referred to in Chapter 7. In a similar experiment the first stimulus consisted of three dots exposed as above, while the second consisted of three dots arranged in a straight line which formed an acute angle with the "line" of the first stimulus. The subjects reported that the three dots had moved through an arc. Ternus called these demonstrations the perceived movement of *phenomenal identity*. The reason for his choice of this term is self-evident. Spatial position of the dots (proximity) was obviously important in his experiment.

Fernberger (1934) described a situation in which the law of similarity can be considered to counteract the law of proximity in determining the perception of the motion of phenomenal identity. He exposed a pair of lines, a thin line and a thick one, which was shortly followed by a similar pair of lines, but in the second exposure the thin line was on the opposite side of the thick one. The subject reported that the thin line was jumping over or under the thick line; i.e., three-dimensional motion was perceived.

PHENOMENAL MOTION AS PART OF A LARGER ORGANIZATION. The relationship between spatiotemporal patterning and apparent motion is only

[2] Another relevant study supporting and extending J. F. Brown and Voth is reported by Mulholland (1956); see also Forgus and Strobel (1964).

part of a larger relation between space-time-brightness organizations and perception. The work of the Japanese on phi phenomena, that of Brown and Voth, and that of Weizäcker, referred to in the last section, show this to be true; so does the research of Johannson on the perception of events reported in the section "Configurations in Event Perception" later in this chapter. But it is the recent demonstrations of *meta contrast* which perhaps demonstrate this fact most clearly. The initial work by Scheffler (1951) defined meta contrast as the depressing effect by the second of two brief, adjacent, asynchronous excitations on the sensory impression introduced by the first. The term has since been applied to a variety of effects besides depression or inhibition, as can be seen from the article by Toch (1956).

In the original experiment by Scheffler two *a* squares were first presented, followed 1 sec later by three *b* squares, as illustrated in Figure 11-3. The

b	a	b	a	b

Figure 11-3
Diagrammatic representation of meta-contrast stimuli. (After Scheffler, 1951.)

a squares were seen as darker intervals between the visible appearance of the three *b* squares, which appeared in unison. The effect of *a* was not zero, however, since *b* looked different when *a* was omitted and since imperfections in *a* were incorporated in the appearance of *b*. The effects were variable, and sometimes apparent motion was seen. The similarity of the squares in terms of *pattern* and *intensity* was an important determiner of how the phenomena appeared.

Other studies showing how the depressing effect on the first stimulus is caused by its relation to the form of the second, into which it can be appropriated or evolved, have been reported by Schiller (1933) and Werner (1935). The variety of meta-contrast phenomena was more fully examined by Toch (1956), who dealt not only with the basic temporal pattern but also with figure-ground variation and complex elaborations of the basic pattern. Toch's basic pattern is shown in Figure 11-4.

b	a	b

Figure 11-4
The meta-contrast stimuli of Toch's basic pattern.

Some of Toch's observations follow. The basic three-square figure was perceived by all subjects as two squares, in most cases moving away from the center and otherwise showing movement. In the situation in which *b* squares alone were flashed on the screen, the squares were found to be stationary and brighter than those in which *a* preceded the presentation of *b*. When the *b* squares were changed to semicircles, they were seen as very bright and moving away from a dim gray square linking them. Finally, the use of two ¼-in. strips to separate the three squares enabled the middle square to appear visible, although it was reported as being dimmer and of shorter duration than the others.

The last report is related to the study of Alpern (1953), who found that the meta-contrast effect is increased as the *angular separation* between the two flashes in space *is decreased* and as the intensity or duration of the second *b* stimulus is increased.

Related reports came from the investigation of apparent movement by Sweet (1953), who found the marked variability between his subjects was lessened when the lights were adjacent. He also reports that the perception of movement was more precise in the periphery than at the fovea even though the subjects continued to see movement at longer delays between the first and second stimuli. When the lights were adjacent to one another, the movement was transformed into a streak of light. As the delay was decreased to about 5 msec, the fused light moved as a whole; it was finally stationary as the time interval approached zero msec. These findings seem to be related to the results of J. F. Brown and Voth when they found that the perception evolves from flicker through movement to a stream as the time interval between the exposure of successive stimuli is decreased.

From the foregoing experiments the following generalizations can be made. First, the effect of the second stimulus is not to produce an all-or-none inhibiting or depressing effect on the first. Second, the perceived information (e.g., movement, increased brightness, fusion) is a function of the first stimulus since the effect does not occur without it. Third, we conclude that the observed effect is between the first and second stimuli.

Toch theorizes that apparent movement in the spatiotemporal sequence results from the motion to which the retina responds, namely, adjacent and successive order. Thus, the stimulus for motion may be *ordinal*. The common denominator in all these phenomenal space-time experiences "would be the successive stimulation of adjacent portions of receptor surfaces" (Toch, 1956, p. 357). The explanation in terms of ordinal stimulation is related to J. J. Gibson's approach, which is restated at the end of this chapter.

Thus far we have seen how important configurational principles and space and time relationships are for the perception of phenomenal motion. We noted that the perception of constant velocity or motion depends on a certain relationship's holding between spatiotemporal dimensions and also that phenomenal motion is part of a larger organizational effect involving temporal relationships in space. We learned secondly that these relationships are modified by certain factors, such as intensity and configurational principles. In the next section we shall treat the perception of phenomenal events in greater detail.

Perception of Physical and Social Events

In this section we want to investigate further some of the phenomenal aspects of perception. We may term the perception of these phenomenal qualities the *perception of events*. We shall begin with an introduction to time perception and then proceed to a treatment of more complicated events, such as the perception of motivation, causation, intentionality, emotionality, and social events.

Perception of Time

We could begin a discussion of time perception by looking at Einstein's special and general theories of relativity, which have indicated that the fourth dimension of time is not independent of the three space dimensions, but these ideas would be of importance only when extreme velocities are involved, as when man ventures into space. This fascinating psychology of the future is just getting under way.

Let us start by considering the psychophysics of time perception or, more accurately, time discrimination. The perception of time has two aspects. One involves the estimation of time which has elapsed between the presentation of two successive stimuli; this is called the perception of *time interval*. Since the signal is not continuous but consists of two bounding stimuli, this phenomenon is also referred to as the perception of an "empty" interval of time. The second aspect involves the perception of a "filled" interval of time, called the *duration*. When we study the perception of duration, the stimulus which forms the time signal is, of course, continuous; i.e., it fills the entire interval of time to be judged.

We know that the experience of time intervals or differences between certain intervals is a fairly direct and relatively immediate process. For example, it was pointed out earlier along that the motion of pure phi can be removed merely by changing the time interval between successive exposures of the two lights. If this is done by controlling the conditions properly, then the change in experience is very compelling indeed. Under such conditions, then, where the distance between the two lights has remained constant while the time interval has changed, we find that phenomenal motion of the lights has either changed or ceased completely. We recall also that changing the time relationship can lead to a perceived difference in space between the lights. We must conclude from these facts that a significant change in the time interval has an immediate effect in altering the percept. The perception of differences in the duration of time is also an immediate process. Thus it is not difficult for an individual to tell that a light exposed, for instance, for 4 sec has a duration longer than that of one exposed for 2 sec.

Despite the immediacy of time perception, our discrimination of absolute magnitude of time intervals or time durations is relatively inaccurate under ordinary circumstances unless we have some external frame of reference against which our judgments may be made. This tendency to externalize any duration is very strong. Sturt (1925, p. 88) reports that when an ordinary person is asked to estimate a short duration of time, he adopts external criteria for his judgment. Thus he may count the period in what he believes to be seconds, or he may swing his hand in the manner of a pendulum.

In the same book Sturt reports two studies which may give us some indication of which factors are operating in situations like those mentioned in the previous paragraph so that discrimination of time is improved. In one study she asked subjects to estimate short time periods under two different conditions. Some subjects merely estimated the time interval, whereas others were permitted to tap their fingers during the interval. With a suitable method of tapping far greater accuracy was attained than for estimates without it. In some of her experiments the error was between three and four times as great when the subjects estimated the time as when they counted in taps. In the second study subjects were asked to estimate in seconds or minutes the time that a pencil was held up by the experimenter. The actual duration varied from 1 sec to 1 min on different trials. In most of the trials the subject merely estimated the duration; but in some of them the subject, who was smoking a cigarette, was told to burn his hand when the experimenter raised the pencil and keep the cigarette against his hand until the experimenter lowered the pencil. Contrary to what was expected, the average of the judgments when the hand was burned was one of the best set of estimates, and in it the estimated time showed the least bias in either direction. The experimenter's hypothesis, based on "everyday" experience, that there would be more numerous overestimations of time during the "unpleasant" period was rejected. The errors were both negative and positive, and the average accuracy was greater than for most of the trials which did not include the unpleasant experience caused by a cigarette burning the hand. The average error during the unpleasant trials was 19.4 per cent, as compared with an average error as high as 40 per cent in some of the other trials.

If we take the results of these two experiments of Sturt together, it would seem that the improved accuracy was a result of making the duration "stand out" more sharply in the two experimental conditions; that is to say, that burning or tapping had the effect of emphasizing the figural or unitary property of the duration, as it were. The tapping or burning focused the subjects' attention on the period of time during which these events were in operation. Thus these durations stood out from the background time in general. This interpretation, which is ours and not Sturt's, seems all the more plausible when we observe that all but one of her subjects in another experiment gave her a grossly inaccurate estimate (an overestimation) of how long it would take them to walk around the ordinary room in which they were sitting. The similarity between Sturt's results and visual figure-ground phenomena seems close enough to suggest a related interpretation. At least, it would seem profitable to put this hypothesis to further empirical tests and see whether there are similar principles operating in time estimation and in visual figure-ground perception. We have seen how important figural properties are in determining the perception of form and motion, and perhaps they have important effects on the perception of time as well.

In visual perception, if the figure becomes too big, it may not be seen as figure any longer and may merge into the ground. The same can be said if the figure becomes too small. Similarly, we would expect that there would be a certain time range within which the estimation of time intervals should be fairly accurate. Outside these limits accuracy should be progressively poorer. Some psychophysical experiments have established certain limiting values.

Blakely (1933), using the method of constant stimuli, studied the discrimination of empty time intervals which were bounded by two sound clicks. The just noticeable difference (jnd) was 8 per cent of the standard for intervals of 0.6 and 0.8 sec and 10 per cent for intervals of 0.2 to 1.5 sec. For time intervals above these values the percentages increased. Thus the jnd was 20 to 30 per cent of the standard for intervals between 2 and 30 sec. There were also great individual differences between the subjects. It is clear that time discrimination was most accurate at relatively short intervals, between 0.2 and 1.5 sec, and even more accurate when the range was narrowed. Similar results were obtained by Woodrow (1930), who asked subjects to reproduce short intervals of time by tapping a reaction key. The standard deviation of the reproduction was 8 per cent for intervals of 0.2 to 2 sec and 16 per cent for intervals of 4 to 30 sec. Thus, the most favorable stimuli, i.e., time intervals between 0.2 and 2 sec, are similar to the most favorable intervals found by Blakely.

Comparable results have been established for the estimation of the duration of time. Thus Quasebarth (1924), using continuous light stimuli, found relative jnd's ranging between 7 and 14 per cent of the standard for a duration of 2 to 8 sec. We note that the stimuli were presented visually in this study. Stott (1933) obtained similar results with a sound stimulus which consisted of continuous tones.

IMPORTANCE OF FILLING THE TIME INTERVAL. The results of these four psychophysical studies indicate, first, that the discrimination of time intervals is fairly accurate only for relatively short intervals, ranging between 0.2 and 2 sec. Second, it seems possible to discriminate somewhat longer time periods when estimating durations than when merely estimating empty intervals. This can be seen by comparing the results of Blakely and Quasebarth, which were discussed above. The jnd for the time interval of

2 sec was 20 per cent of the standard, as compared with 7 per cent for a duration of 2 sec. Even a duration of 8 sec had a smaller jnd than a time interval of 2 sec (14 per cent of the standard, as opposed to 20 per cent). I realize, of course, that this conclusion is tentative since it is dangerous to compare different experiments directly, but the differences are so striking as to suggest this conclusion. In any case, this conclusion fits in with our interpretation that the filling in of a duration increases its figural properties by making it stand out more definitely. The more clearly the time stands out, within limits, the better are we able to estimate its extent.

Psychophysical research has also shown that the discrimination of time is determined not only by the size of the interval but by the characteristics of the bounding stimuli. Thus Woodrow (1928) studied the effects of inequality in the length of the bounding stimuli on the estimation of empty time intervals. For one fixed interval he found that the estimate was 5 sec if a short stimulus was followed by a longer one. The estimate changed to 0.66 sec when the bounding stimuli were reversed, i.e., when a long stimulus was followed by a short one. We thus see that the estimation of time is influenced by stimulus conditions *surrounding* the actual physical interval. This is another similarity with figure-ground perception, in which we know that the figural property is influenced by the structure of the ground.

CONFIGURATIONAL ASPECTS. Other experimental evidence seems to indicate that the perception of time or, rather, the experience of it is influenced by field factors which ostensibly have no relation to time. Thus, J. F. Brown (1931b) found that the apparent velocity of an object in a brightly illuminated field is slower than in a darker field when, in fact, the objective velocities are equal. Since the distance traveled is the same in both conditions, we deduce that phenomenal time is slower in the brighter than in the darker field; i.e., a constant time interval is experienced as longer in the brighter of the two fields. Brown went further and put this hypothesis to an empirical test. Observers were asked to equate the duration of seen motion with that of a fixed time interval which could be marked off by two visual or acoustic signals. Two equations were made, one in a bright field and the other in a darker field. The two equations having been made, it was found that the required velocity in the brighter field was greater than that in the darker field. In one particular equation the ratio obtained from five subjects averaged 1.23. Although there were only a few subjects, the direction of the results was the same in all of them. We may therefore conclude that on the average, and in this experiment, a unit of time was experienced as flowing 1.23 times faster in the darker field than in the brighter field.

Koffka (1935, pp. 296–298), interpreting these and other experiments by Brown, asserted that if we include all constellations for which phenomenal velocities have been investigated, we may conclude that phenomenal *time flows faster in smaller, darker, and nearer fields* and on occasions when the motion is more vertical than horizontal. The relationship between perceived time and brightness lends support to the other studies previously cited which found that phenomenal velocity is faster in darker fields.

MOTIVATIONAL ASPECTS. William James suggested quite some time ago that the rapidity of perceived time passage is partly determined by the desire to have time pass. Despite this suggestion from James and observations from everyday situations, few studies have attempted to investigate the relationship between time perception and motivation. As we pointed out in the last section, most of the research on the perception of time has investigated psychophysical relationships. The fact that we know is that figure-ground and certain other configurational relationships influence the accuracy of time estimation.

A few well-controlled studies, however, have investigated the effects of some personality and motivational variables in time estimation. Thus, Filer and Miles (1949) found that subjects estimated a unit of time to be shorter when they were working under motivated conditions (e.g., during regular class periods) than when they were bored (e.g., at the end of the class period). This result is supported by Harton (1938), who found that time estimates are shorter when there is a greater degree of effort and persistence in task performance than when less effort and persistence are involved.

One of the most extensive pieces of work dealing with the relationship between time estimation and motivation was performed by Hindle (1951), who investigated the relationship between apparent time and apparent rate of progress toward a goal. She started with the accepted equation for the perception of velocity:

$$\text{velocity} = \frac{\text{distance}}{\text{time}}$$

She translated her terms to make the equation better adapted to her problem and predicted that

$$\text{perceived rate of progress} = \frac{\text{perceived distance traveled}}{\text{perceived time}}$$

Transposing terms, we have

$$\text{perceived time} = \frac{\text{perceived distance traveled}}{\text{perceived rate of progress}}$$

In her experiment Hindle used two groups of subjects, each of which was given simple tasks to perform. Group M, the motivated group, however, was instructed to attempt to achieve a specific goal, while group N, the nonmotivated group, was set no goal. Half of the subjects in each group were interrupted after they had traveled 67 per cent of the distance to the goal of group M, while the other half were interrupted after 90 per cent of the distance had been traveled. At these interruption periods each subject was asked to estimate how much time had elapsed since he had been working on the task. Hindle predicted that there would be differences between the time estimates of the two groups only in the last judgment.

Since group N had no specific goal, its members could not judge their rate of progress. Hindle expected, however, that when group M subjects were getting nearer to their goal, their perceived rate of progress would increase. Since perceived distance traveled was held constant, by applying the formula we would expect that time estimates would be shorter for group M on the last judgment. This would not hold for the first judgment, since the subjects would still be too far from the goal for this variable to be effective. Hindle's predictions were borne out in the experiment. Specifically, she found that in the *last* part of the task, when the activity leads to a clearly defined *end of a task,* ". . . estimates of time spent increase more slowly with increments in score than do time estimates for activities having no clearly defined goal." This statement does not hold in the earlier part of the task.

This interaction between time estimation and motivation was confirmed by Meade (1959), who found that such variables as perceived rate of progress and attractiveness of goal produce shorter time estimates for a group which is motivated but not for a nonmotivated group. De Wolfe and Duncan (1959) found that the amount of time a subject worked on a comparison task (rest, reversed-alphabet training, anagram solving) to equate it with time spent on a previous standard task varies inversely with the level of behavior required on the comparison task.

By way of summary, we note that Loehlin (1959) reports that the following factors significantly influence the perceived length of time intervals:

Filled vs. empty intervals
Activity vs. passivity
Amount of repetition of an activity
Interest vs. boredom

The implications of a decade of research on time perception are discussed by Wallace and Rabin (1960).[3]

Now that we have entered the area of the role of motivation in time perception, we should go further and study the perception of motivation and related phenomena. This whole area dealing with the effect of motivational and personal variables on perception has recently been termed *social perception* by some American psychologists. Before we deal with this work, however, we should investigate some of the European work on the perception of motivation and emotion since the European psychologists have approached the problem in a more orthodox psychophysical and configurationistic tradition.

---

[3] See also the book by Fraisse (1963), which was published just before this manuscript was completed.

Configurations in Event Perception

The work in this area was initiated by a Swedish psychologist, Johannson (1950), who was actually studying the perception of kinetic (motion) structures. His study differed from the usual motion studies since he was interested in the perception of groups or configurations of stimuli. The groups were called events, and the perception of a continuous and unitary change in these groups was called the perception of an event. His apparatus consisted of a series of mechanically controlled celluloid disks which could be rotated and otherwise moved in the frontal and horizontal planes. Figures painted on these disks were projected on a translucent screen. It was on this screen that the subjects actually saw the phenomenal movement of these events.

One of the most interesting phenomena studied by Johannson was motion synthesis, which is illustrated by the following experiment. By painting appropriate dots on the disk the following pattern is projected on the screen: Two points are viewed simultaneously, one (*a*) moving up and down at a constant rate, while the other (*b*) subscribes a circle, also moving at a constant rate. The subjects report seeing two separate up-and-down motions, with *b* having a slight sideways motion as well. Johannson called *a* the influencing element and *b* the affected element. We see in his work that configurational movement can be produced by arranging the elements in certain ways; the elements thus affect one another.

Gibson's Work on Optical Motion and Kinetic Effects

J. J. Gibson (1957) extended the experimental and theoretical analysis of events similar to those reported by Johannson. He concerned himself with the question of how perception can be aroused by stimuli. What comes from an optical motion? What is defined as a projection in two dimensions of a physical motion in three dimensions?

There seem to be two ways we can describe optical motion. One is to divide the moving pattern into convenient elements, describe the positions of all the elements of a coordinate system, and then describe the motion of all the elements by the successive values for each element on the coordinate system. This method is analytical. A second method, which Gibson prefers, is to accept the moving pattern as given and use the operations of defining perspective transformations in geometry to describe a family of changes of pattern.

There are two kinds of projection. One is parallel, as in the case of the blueprints of an architect's plans. Parallel projections, resulting in similarity transformations, differ only in size. The other kind, called central or polar projection, results in foreshortening. This is what we do when we draw scenes and objects in perspective, as the architect draws a view of the house for his client. Although both kinds of projection lead to a perspective transformation in geometry, the ordinary usage of the term *perspective transformation* is limited to the latter case.

In his theory Gibson states that motion can be described as a continuous series of perspective transformations. This series, which is a family of static forms of a temporal series, can be analyzed by six parameters: (1) vertical translation of the pattern in the plane; (2) horizontal translation of the pattern; (3) enlargement or reduction of the pattern (the first three are transformations of translation); (4) horizontal foreshortening of the pattern; (5) vertical foreshortening of the pattern; and (6) rotation of the pattern in the plane.

In one experiment J. J. Gibson and Eleanor J. Gibson (1957) applied this theory to analyzing the results of an experiment on the perception of rigid motion. The experimental arrangement is diagramed in Figure 11-5. The mount containing the shadow caster could be rotated on any of three axes or translated in any of three dimensions. The shadow was actually cast by opaque figures which were painted on a transparent screen on the mount. The size and shape of the moving image, the "virtual object" seen behind the translucent screen, changed as the mount moved. The order of transformation followed the spatial order or movement.

Similar empirical demonstrations were performed with nonrigid, elastic motion by Von Fieandt and Gibson (1959). In the latter experiment 940 changes from motion of rotation to motion of compression or the reverse were detected by any subject. Only once was there a false positive, i.e., seeing a change when no actual physical change took place. Unsophisticated subjects could distinguish this nonperspective transformation from continuous perspective transformation.

A final illustration will be mentioned. It is possible to cast a shadow on the screen through several parallel sheets of glass, each of which has been sprinkled with talcum powder. When the sheets of glass are stationary, a

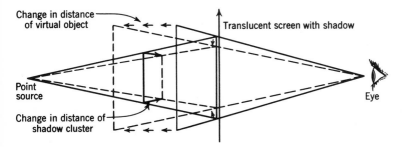

Figure 11-5
The shadow transformer. (After J. J. Gibson, 1957, p. 291.) The variables of form and transformation are thus isolated for study.

"Milky Way" effect is perceived, but if the sandwich of mounts is moved, a depth effect is produced, with each layer of nebulous material appearing to stand in front of its neighbor. This demonstration and its explanation are similar to the phenomena of the kinetic depth effect studied by Wallach and O'Connell (1953) and to stereokinesis reported by Metzger (1953).

Finally, we note that the synthesis of disjunctive, or separate, motion can also be related to this work. We have already seen this effect in the work of Duncker and Johannson. The laws defining their order and relation are more clearly seen in the work on phenomenal causality performed by Michotte, to which we now turn.

Michotte's Work on Phenomenal Causality

We saw in the work by Johannson and Gibson and the studies on meta contrast how one element can influence or cause a change in another element. The perception of causality and other phenomenal events have been studied extensively by Michotte. Michotte (1946) and his students were concerned with studying the perception of *functional connections* and the perception of causality. Using special technical equipment, such as that depicted in Figure 11-6, they were able to make two (or more) small colored rectangles 1 cm long and 0.5 cm wide move along a horizontal slot 15 cm long and 0.5 cm wide. These rectangles could be stopped at any position on the slot or made to move at any given moment. The direction, speed, and extent of movement of the objects could also be changed whenever desired. From this brief description of the apparatus it can be seen that an infinite variety of movement combinations could be obtained.

Using this ingenious technique, Michotte found that certain combinations of visual stimuli produce certain specific causal impressions. The effect of these combinations depends on such relational factors as (1) the initial spatial distance between the objects, (2) the time they begin to move, (3) their speed, (4) the time interval between the movement when the first

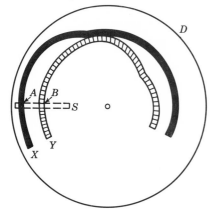

Figure 11-6
The causality phenomenon. (From Michotte, 1946.) As the disk D rotates, A and B are seen as the rectangles through the slot S.

object comes into contact with the second and the time the second object moves, (5) the nature of the contact, (6) the direction of movement, and (7) the distance moved.

In one experiment in which two rectangles *A* and *B* were presented, the different kinetic combinations caused such specific impressions as "*A* goes toward *B*," "*A* pursues *B*," "*A* joins *B* and unites itself to it," "*A* bumps *B*," "*A* chases or repels *B*," "*A* distorts *B* by exerting pressure on it," "*A* pulls *B*," "*A* goes to find *B* and takes it away," and "*A* pushes *B* with follow-up." Michotte calls any one of these events functional connections because the observer actually sees changes occurring in an object "in function" of another.

Let us examine these phenomena in greater detail to find out which conditions of stimuli lead to these different impressions. The main combinations and their effects based on their functional connections follow.

1. Object *A* alone moves and makes contact with *B*.
   a. The contact is of short duration.
      If the speed is slow, the impression is that *A* touches *B*, but when it is fast *A* is seen as striking *B*.
   b. The contact is prolonged.
      If the speed is slow, the impression is that *A* gently goes to *B* and unites with it, but when the movement is rapid, the impression is that there is a violent crash and that *A* and *B* become welded together.
2. *A* moves to *B* and stops while *B* begins to move.
   a. The contact is short (30 to 40 msec).
      If the speed of *A* is the same as or slightly greater than that of *B*, *A* is seen to propel *B*. If *A*'s speed is faster than *B*'s, *A* may be seen to throw *B* forward. When *B* moves faster, then it is seen to be released by *A* or to be running away from it but not to be propelled by it. In general, these events are called the *billiard-ball effect*.
   b. The contact is long enough for the objects to form a global unity.
      This is often interpreted as a momentary agreement between *A* and *B*, followed by disagreement and separation.
3. *A* moves to *B* and makes contact with it; then the two move together at the same speed and in the same direction in juxtaposition.
   a. When there is no pause at the moment of contact, the impression is that *A* carries *B* along with it. This is known as the *pushcart effect*. If a slow approach by *A* is followed by a rapid increase in the velocity of *A* and *B*, then the impression is that *A* carries off *B* by "brute force."
   b. When there is a momentary pause after contact followed by a movement of the two objects in the same direction, the impression is one of "going together." Michotte (1950c, p. 119) stated that "the unity is naturally accentuated by the similarity of their kinetic properties." The law of common fate, which was first stated by Wertheimer (see Chapter 7), is used by Michotte to describe this effect and many of the other phenomena of causality which he found.

These examples are sufficient to illustrate how the factors enumerated earlier determine the impressions of different kinds of causality, but the factors of direction and distances moved need more elaboration. After A touches B, the direction of movement of the latter must be similar to that of A; otherwise B appears to have its "own" movement, independent of A.

If, after being touched by A, B moves through too great a distance, the impression of a causal connection is absent. Michotte interprets this by saying that the impact has a certain *radius of action* within which it is effective. If B moves too far, it goes beyond this radius of action and thus appears to have its own power of motion. But increasing the length of B's path does not increase the number of reports of B's being released by A (Boyle, 1960). If we increase the velocity of both A and B, the radius of action increases.

Thus far we have seen that A appears to do something to B; i.e., A causes something to happen to B. A was thus seen to do one of the following: to "touch B," "strike B," "unite with B," "crash into B," "propel or launch B," or "carry off B." It should be stressed that the perception of causality (or the lack of it) is direct. As Michotte emphasizes, the impression "is not a 'meaning' *attributed* to literal, step-by-step translation of a table of stimuli; they are primitive, specific impressions which arise in the perceptual field itself" (1950c, p. 120). Which impression is perceived depends, of course, on certain relationships existing among the stimuli. In other words, it is the totality of the stimuli and their various interrelationships which determine what is seen. These phenomenal impressions are essentially dependent on the system of stimulation. Following the principle of concomitant variations, every appreciable modification of this system produces a change in the nature of the perceived connection. For example, the impression of "approaching" and "departing" occurs only when the distance between A and B falls within the radius of action. The radius of action is not fixed, however, but varies with the speed of the moving objects. Michotte thus deduces that the characteristic impressions he found must be considered gestalts, i.e., specific kinetic structures corresponding to the action of a group of successive interacting stimuli on the eye.

While Michotte asserts that the impression of causality arises spontaneously, experience merely serving to define more precisely the conditions under which mechanical causality is perceived, other investigators have seen an important *experiential* determiner of phenomenal causality. For example, Gruber and his associates (Gruber, Fink, and Damm, 1957) and Powesland (1959) studied the influence of practice on attributing the collapse of a model "bridge" to the prior removal of one of its vertical supports. "The 'temporal threshold of causality' was defined as the maximum value of delay (between removal of the vertical support and collapse of the bridge) consistent with reliable reports by S of an impression of causality." It was found that practice trials with longer delays increased this threshold value, whereas practice with shorter delays decreased this threshold value. Powesland found that these two kinds of practices had similar effects on Michotte's launching phenomenon. In his first experiment he found that the number of interpolated practice trials increased the value's effect. The effects of practice in his second experiment could be obtained only if the subject verbalized the effects during the practice trials. These results require further study for clear understanding. The reader should also see Olum (1956) on developmental differences in perceived causality.

The reader probably noted that some of the combinations reported earlier gave rise to the impression of intentionality. Thus we find such reports as "momentary agreements between *A* and *B*," "*A* carrying off *B* by brute force," "*A* and *B* go together," and "*B* runs away from *A*." All these statements imply that *A* or *B*, or both, wanted to do something; i.e., they had intentions. This, of course, gets us into the area dealing with the perception of motives, which is involved in social perception. We leave this topic to Chapter 12.

Summary

We might summarize this chapter by stating that we have seen that the perception of motion and kinetic events is determined by relations existing between elements of time, space, and brightness. Moreover, we have learned that certain configurational events, such as figure-ground, radius of action, and common fate, also influence the perception of motion and phenomenal events. In Chapter 12 we shall see that the analysis of the configurational aspects of kinetic events promises to be a good beginning for the study of social perception.

12

Social Perception, Motives, and Personality

In Chapter 11 we investigated the relational and configurational aspects of event perception. In this chapter we want to investigate the perception of the expression of such phenomena as intentions, motives, emotions, and personality characteristics. Conversely, we shall also be interested in the influence of such functional factors as motives and personality characteristics on perception. Investigations of these phenomena have been approached from two quite different viewpoints. The European psychologists have dealt with the first problem and have attempted to reach an understanding of the perception of personality variables through the study of kinetic events. The American psychologists, on the other hand, have been more concerned with the influence of personality variables on perception. Strange as it may seem, the European work in this area has thus been more operational. We shall deal with this work first and then proceed to the work being done in this country.

Perception of Social and Personality Characteristics

As we mentioned in Chapter 11, this work has received its greatest impetus from Michotte (1946), whose research represents the first concerted attack on the problem of assessing human personality through experimenting with the perception of kinetic structures. This he does by relating the perception of kinetic events to the perception of *emotional* expression.

First of all, we note that reports such as those mentioned at the end of the previous chapter occurred with such frequency that Michotte has linked them with human perception of emotions in other individuals. There was an obvious tendency for the observers to compare the actions of the objects with human or animal activities affected by emotional states or attitudes. This tendency to translate the phenomena into human characteristics created a problem which Michotte has tried to handle.

He starts by stating that our knowledge of the emotional states of other individuals is based necessarily on their perceptible reactions, such as their words, facial expressions, motor gestures, and simple movement of the eyes. Furthermore, emotions can be divided roughly into two classes, depending on whether they present an integrative or a segregative relationship between the individual experiencing them and the thing, person, or event which is their object. Examples of integrative emotions are sympathy, friendship, and love; whereas antipathy, disgust, anger, hate, and fear are segregative types. The motor reactions corresponding to an integrative emotion usually result in an approach, which may manifest itself in the positioning of an individual close to another or by establishing a contact more or less pronounced or more or less prolonged—a handshake or an embrace. The motor reactions corresponding to segregative emotions, on the other hand, reveal themselves in withdrawal behavior, such as running away from something we dislike or fear. Michotte's thesis is that *"the physical reactions which correspond to emotions fulfill in fact the conditions of stimulation which are necessary to produce in an observer the kinetic structures of the kind that we have studied"* (1950c).[1] Thus the integrative reactions have the effect of producing in the observer the impression that one individual is approaching another if the distance between them falls within the radius of action. Juxtaposition, contact, or association of movements (the law of common fate) produce new perceptual unities (gestalts) presenting various degrees of integration. On the other hand, the segregative reactions produce impressions of withdrawal, departure, repulsion, and violence.

Michotte illustrates how the factors in his experiments might play a role in the perception of integrative or segregative emotions. Speed of objects, for example, plays an important part. Rapid movement gives the impression of "violence," whereas slow movement leads to the perception of "gentleness." The interpretations of these emotional states were quite specific, and the reports of different observers were in general agreement with one another.

We might take one motive and discuss in greater detail how Michotte analyzed the kinetic structure underlying its perception. Let us take the case of perceiving a "friendly approach" and suppose that there are three objects (persons, for example), *A*, *B*, and *C*, all in sight of each other. *B* feels attracted by *A* and goes gently toward him but feels indifferent

[1] Italics mine.

to *C*. As far as the physical stimuli and their corresponding retinal stimulations are concerned, a diminution of the distance between *A* and *B* is accomplished by a corresponding increase of the distance between *B* and *C*; yet the observer might only report that *B* goes gently to *A*. *C* has no psychological relationship to *A* and *B* because he falls outside the radius of action. This fact alone is sufficient to illustrate the difference between the system of physical stimuli and the structural organization of the perceptual field. As Michotte says, "Because the structural organization is determined by various factors (radius of action, etc.), only the approach and union come into the perceptual field of the observer and the impressions he receives actually correspond to the sentiments of the agent. The principles which govern the structural organization come into play, and the emotional reactions of the agent evoke specific kinetic structures in the observer. . . . It is in this sense, and only in this sense, that one is justified in talking about expressive behavior" (1950c, p. 121).

Thus far we have seen that the perception of certain kinetic structures underlying the impression of causality, intentionality, motives, and emotional expression is governed by the organization of the perceptual field into specific structures or gestalts.

Now, the perception of social situations largely involves the perception of peoples' intentions and expressive behavior. We thus find Michotte generalizing his hypothesis to the social scene. He notes that the mutual reactions of two individuals often determine the reaction of other individuals present in the group. So if we observe one individual acting aggressively toward another, we may in turn behave aggressively toward him. The conditions of visibility are often deficient when we are observing social interactions. This might be a result of distance, poor lighting, or relatively insensitive receptors. In such cases the general outline of behavior revealed in the simple kinetic structures enables us to perceive the nature of the social situation with a fair amount of veridicality.

The work of Michotte promises to provide real insight into the way we perceive such personal attributes as emotions, intentions, motives, and interpersonal relationships. By continuing such phenomenological analysis we should be able to establish the functional relationships between certain organizations of kinetic structures and perceived personal characteristics. Of course, we hope then to be able to establish quantitative laws. For example, we shall want to know the exact nature of the relationship between space and time variables which determines the extent of the radius of action, and so on.

Studies similar to those of Michotte had actually been carried out earlier by Heider and Simmel (1944), who investigated the "apparent behavior" of inanimate objects. Presenting situations and activities of objects without human faces, they proposed to determine the dependence of the individual's response on certain stimulus configurations. The subjects were asked to interpret a motion-picture film (an animated cartoon) in which three geo-metrical figures (a large triangle, a small triangle, and a circle) were shown moving in different directions and at various speeds. As shown in Figure 12-1, the figures were moving around or in and out of a rectangle, a section of which periodically opened or closed like a door.

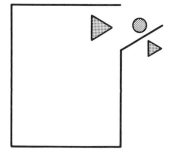

Figure 12-1
Exposure objects displayed in various positions and configurations from the moving film. The small triangle (hero) is seen as opening the door for the circle (girl), who is escaping from the large triangle (villain). (After Heider and Simmel, 1944.)

Of interest to us here are the results obtained from two fairly large groups of female college students. The first group was merely asked to describe the film as a *motion picture,* while the second group was asked to interpret it as if the objects were human beings. Despite the difference in the instructions, all but one subject in the first group also attributed human characteristics to the objects. We may thus treat the results of the two groups together. Three generalizaions from this study are of great interest:

1. The phenomenal relationship between the objects was determined by temporal succession, spatial proximity, and good continuation. For example, in one scene the big triangle was following the small triangle around until it touched the small triangle, which then changed its direction and came to rest. This scene was interpreted in general as follows: The big man was chasing the little man, and when he caught him, he hit the little man until the latter reeled back under the impact of his blow. This interpretation illustrated the principle of temporal succession and good continuation. The principle of spatial proximity determined "interpersonal" relationships between the three objects. Thus the little triangle and the circle, which were seen together frequently, stood out as a pair that was opposed to the big triangle. This pair was seen as a man and a girl in love. The big triangle was seen as a villain who fought with the little man and who chased or pursued the girl.

2. Phenomenal causality: First, it was found that the interpretation of simple movement combinations varied according to the unit seen as the origin. Furthermore, the movements were organized in terms of the acts of persons. Thus, when the big triangle moved to the little triangle and the latter changed direction, this scene was perceived as the big triangle's imparting energy to the small one. The interpretation was that the blow from the big man caused the small man to fall. Second, phenomenal causality was effected by the impact of one object on another. The impression of an

apparent movement of energy was very strong. Simultaneous movement with prolonged, not short, contact also gave the impression of one object's causing something to happen to the other. Thus each of the three figures sought to impart movement to the "door" of the rectangle ("house") when the figure and the door moved together in prolonged contact. The figure was said to push or pull the door.

3. Perception of "intentionality" or motive: It was frequently said that the big man "wanted" to hurt the little man or that he "lured" the girl in. Other words such as "forced in," "invited in," or "escaping" all carried the meaning of intention; i.e., certain motives were attributed to the objects. The classification of these motives was based upon the following factors:

   a. The person to whom the origin of the motion was attributed: For example, the big man wanted to molest the girl, whereas the little man wanted to rescue her.

   b. The sequence of events: For example, the big man chased the girl around the house and then went in to pursue and molest her. The motives were interpreted in terms of a succession of changes which became a *connected sequence*.

   c. Finally, the surrounding field determined the motives and thereby the meaning of the event, e.g., whether the figures were in or out of the house. This is related to the figure-ground phenomena.

The work discussed in this section suggests that such configurational principles as good continuation, proximity, and figure-ground effects play a significant role in organizing the perception of motivational and emotional expressions under certain experimental conditions. We see in the work of Heider and Simmel and of Michotte an interesting approach to causality and intentionality.

Evaluation, Implication, and Extension of Phenomenal Causality Studies

While Michotte and Heider have given us some of the phenomenological variables related to the perception of interpersonal relationships, the quantitative function of these relationships awaits further work. Moreover, once these relationships have been established, the question of whether these expressive behaviors operate independently of experience still arises. For example, Gruber et al. (1957) studied the effect of practice in the perception of phenomenal causality in a "collapsing-bridge" model. The bridge would collapse sometime after a vertical support had been removed. Needless to say, whether the collapse was attributed to the removal of the vertical support or not depended on the time interval between the two events. This time interval (threshold) could be altered by experience. Thus, if the practice trials interpolated between two estimates of causality consisted of long time intervals, the threshold was increased on the second trial, whereas it was reduced if the practice trials consisted of near-zero delay. Similar findings were reported by Powesland (1959).

Olum (1956) has approached the possible role of experience in phenomenal causality indirectly by studying the developmental aspects of the perception of causality. Using Michotte's techniques, she studied the pushing and releasing phenomena in seven-year-old children and adults. Two results of interest are relevant to us. First, the children frequently saw *A* passing *B,* although this did not in fact happen. Second, *B* was often seen to come and meet *A*. Olum interprets these results as possibly related to developmental aspects of perceiving configuration and stroboscopic motion. The reader should also consult Lacey and Dallenbach (1939) for informative treatment of how children learn causal relations.

The experiential aspects of the perception of personal attributes are of crucial importance since they conceivably are related to the nature of interpersonal relationships. It would take us too far afield to go into this area, but there are two sources which I can recommend to the interested reader. The first is a book by Heider (1958) on the psychology of interpersonal relations. The second consists of some interesting work at the University of Illinois by Fiedler and Steiner,[2] who show that the simple view which states that the individuals who are most accurate in the perception of others also have the best interpersonal relationships is an oversimplification. The variables are more complex. Finally, there is a good review of the work on the perception of people by Bruner and Tagiuri (1954).

Influence of Social and Personality Variables on Perception

While the European psychologists have been interested primarily in the perception of social events, the American psychologists doing research in this area have been interested chiefly in the influence of such "functional" variables as group membership, motives, attitudes, etc., on the nature of the perceptual act. Two broad classes of variables have been studied: (1) the influence of these social and personal variables on perception and (2) the influence of "loaded" stimuli on threshold values for recognizing them.

Influence of the Group on Discrimination

These researches on social perception began with the well-known experiment of Sherif (1935) on the influence of the group on the autokinetic effect. Before discussing the experiment, we should briefly describe this effect. If a point of light in an otherwise dark room is fixated by a subject, the light is seen to move around in various directions. This phe-

[2] See, for example, Fiedler (1953); Steiner (1959a; 1959b).

nomenal movement is called the *autokinetic effect*. It should be noted that light is presented without any other stimulation; i.e., it has no spatial background or frame of reference. In Sherif's experiment the spot of light was presented to a group of subjects in a dark room. Each subject publicly reported his judgment about the direction in which the light was moving. Upon repeated reports it was found that the individuals were converging upon a common report; i.e., their reports changed gradually so that each one said that he saw the light moving in more or less the same direction. The subjects were not aware that they were being thus influenced by group judgment. Sherif concluded that a *group norm* had been developed experimentally.

The experimental finding of Sherif captured the imagination of psychologists to such an extent that many saw in it the prototype for all perception. A great number concluded that all perception is the result of what we have learned to perceive from our culture and subcultural groups. Perhaps the excitement of this phenomenon blocked realization of the fact that the autokinetic effect is not an event produced by adequate stimulation but actually results from impoverished stimulation. So the first caution we must observe is that group influence on perception is limited by the nature of the distal stimulus. This is to say that Sherif's experiment demonstrated that in the absence of an external spatial framework a group norm provides a frame of reference. Although Sherif noted that his finding is more relevant for a theory of judgment and discrimination than for perception, our broad information-extraction conception of perception would consider judgment and discrimination processes as operating within perception.

The experiment does show that the group can influence the development of a frame of reference. This source of variance which was not attributable to the physical stimulus probably became more important as the physical scale became less reliable, and vice versa. Other work, such as that of Helson (1948), has also shown how subjective scales are developed, but a general satisfactory theory of the development of scales of judgment has not been thoroughly worked out. For an attempt in this direction the reader should consult Stevens (1957) and Volkmann (1951).

Although some limitations must be placed on the implication of Sherif's experiment, it did suggest how group membership might influence the discriminatory process. Following his work, it was natural that psychologists would become interested in doing more research on the influence of cultural, subcultural, and personal experience on discrimination. Anthropologists had already pointed out that the way various peoples regard and categorize their world is influenced by cultural experience, but little experimental work has been done to clarify this effect. A long and extensive series of researches followed the publication of an experiment by Bruner and Goodman (1947), who were among the first psychologists to put this social view of judgment to an experimental test. Scattered research findings suggesting these phenomena had been published earlier. For example, Ansbacher (1937) suggested that personal values would influence perception of size, and Stephens (1931; 1936) showed that personal interests could lead to perceptual distortion in the judgment of angle size.

Bruner and Goodman used two groups of subjects, one group consisting of ten-year-old poor children and the other of ten-year-old rich children. The children in each group were required to adjust the size of a circle of light to apparent equality with various coins and cardboard disks. The investigators found that all the children tended to overestimate the size of coins up to a 25-cent piece, but the sizes of the cardboard disks were estimated correctly. A 50-cent coin was not overestimated. Of particular significance was the fact that *poorer children overestimated the smaller coins to a larger extent than did the rich children.* Adults also overestimated the sizes, but this overestimation was present for 50-cent pieces as well. Bruner and Goodman concluded that the poorer children showed greater overestimation because they valued money more than the rich children did. Therefore, the poorer children showed greater sensitization to the value of money. This finding did not show up with the larger coins because "they were too valuable to be real." It is difficult to understand why there was a general error of overestimation, especially when we consider that this error held for all coins in the case of adults. Leaving aside this difficulty in accounting for the constant error, the authors thought that the experiment demonstrated that differential sensitization to value does influence the perception or judgment of size.

There are other difficulties with the preceding experiment, as has been pointed out by Carter and Schooler (1949) and Pastore (1949). In their experiment Carter and Schooler used a series of coins of various sizes as well as aluminum and cardboard disks. They found that the smaller coins and disks were underestimated while the larger coins (25 and 50 cents) and disks were overestimated. They had asked the children to estimate the sizes directly and also to reproduce their estimated sizes from memory. Only in the *recollection* of estimations did they find that the poorer children showed greater overestimation of the larger coins than did the rich children. Moreover, coins and aluminum disks were overestimated to a greater extent than the cardboard disks. Thus these authors and Pastore concluded that the results of Bruner and Goodman were caused by the fact that larger sizes are generally overestimated. It should be noted that the difference between the results of the two experiments were partly caused by the fact that *different children estimated the coins and disks in the Bruner and Goodman experiment, whereas the same children were used for both estimations by Carter and Schooler.*

Collateral evidence for Bruner's theory comes from other experiments. Thus Bruner and Postman (1948) found that disks containing a dollar sign, which represented positive value, were overestimated to a significantly larger extent than disks containing a swastika, which represented negative value. Although Bruner and Rodrigues (1953) did not find significant absolute difference between judgments of the size of metal slugs and coins, Vroom (1957) found that even coins which were completely defaced were significantly overestimated compared with aluminum disks with designs on them.

Most of the evidence tends to support the view that value influences size discrimination or estimation. It seems that where a constant error (e.g., overestimation) exists, the positive value has some effect on emphasizing this error, especially when judgments of size are made from memory. A direct experimental study of the influence of motivation on judgment was performed by Lambert, Solomon, and Watson (1949), who studied the effect of reinforcement on size estimation. Two groups of children, aged three to five years, were rewarded for turning a crank handle, the control group with pieces of candy and the experimental group with poker chips which they could subsequently put into a vending machine to obtain candy. When they were later required to estimate the sizes of the poker chips, the experimental groups showed significant overestimation while the control group did not; but when they performed the task without reward, the overestimation disappeared. Considering the results and issues raised by the experiments discussed in this section, we might tentatively conclude that value can have a significant influence on the judgment of size or other dimensions, especially when the distal stimulus is unclear or lacking in a reliable, concrete frame of reference.

Another demonstration performed by a member of a group of psychologists who have developed the transactional theory of perception also suggests the effect of value on the judgment of size. The transactional theory, which was developed by Ames, Cantril, Kilpatrick, and Ittelson, has as its primary assertion that perception is the product of past experience. This view has been developed from experiments performed under conditions of impoverished, distorted, or ambiguous stimulus fields. A thorough review, consisting of such experiments as the moving trapezoid window, is found in a monograph edited by Kilpatrick (1952). A rather fascinating demonstration in which a distorted room was used is reported in this monograph by Wittreich. If the individual looks through an opening into this room, the sizes of various objects are distorted; they appear either smaller or bigger depending on where they are situated. Wittreich asked each of a group of married subjects to view his or her mate and a stranger who were located in the distorted room. The Honi phenomenon, in which less distortion of size is reported for the valued object than for the nonvalued object, was observed. Thus, among the couples married more than a year, only one showed the Honi effect, while more than 50 per cent of the newly wed couples showed it. Wittreich is careful to point out that this is only a preliminary investigation, but it does suggest that personal factors may have some directing effect on judgment and perception when the visual field is distorted—or is it merely that newlyweds were judging from memory while the others were not? But if so, why? Other experiments dealing with the directing influences of emotions and other personal factors on perceptual discrimination have also been performed with impoverished stimulation.

Before turning to these studies, which deal primarily with threshold values, let us take a brief look at the broader aspects of *cultural* and personality variables in perception. A useful summary of this field is provided by Dennis (1951), and we shall merely point to some of the kinds of studies and ideas which have been generated. One kind of study deals with the influence of cultural attitudes and experience on perceptual discrimination. For example, it has been said that the natives of the Torres Strait area exhibit much less of the Müller-Lyer illusion than Europeans do (Seligman, 1901); and Malinowski has noted that Trobriand Islanders are much more likely to notice, even accentuate, paternal resemblance lines but to suppress maternal resemblance in perception (Malinowski, 1923–24a; 1923–24b).

In the area of projective techniques, Bleuler and Bleuler (1933) found that Moroccans give an inordinate amount of rare detail, while Cook (1942) reports that Samoans' Rorschach protocols are characterized by the predominance of wholes and space responses. Henry (Henry, 1941; Schachtel, Henry, and Henry, 1942) and his associates report that the Pilagá Indian children of Argentina also give much rare detail and many sexual responses. It has been theorized that the frequency of certain responses by particular cultures is related to the predominance of these kinds of visual experiences in the groups in question. For example, the Pilagá children have much sexual experience and sexual freedom. Similarly, the dominance of responding to the white spaces by the Samoans could be related to the fact that white is a favorite and symbolic color in their culture. Thus it is very important to establish cultural norms before we generalize from one culture to another. A high degree of space response or responses is considered a sign of hostility or opposition in a United States resident, but a serious mistake in diagnosis might be made if we generalized this view to a Samoan. Before we can discuss idiosyncratic or personality-directed perceptual distortion or accentuation, we must know what constitutes deviation from specific cultural or subcultural norms.

Besides the effect of cultural variables on such phenomena as illusion and projective technique, there is an interesting effect on perceptual meaning. Thus Bartlett (1932) found that subjects' memory of alien pictures and stories was always transformed to the familiar. We do not know from Bartlett's study whether the distortion took place in initial perception or in the meaning or reproduction. In any case, the variance in perception attributable to personal factors needs careful consideration. We shall now look more deeply at experiments in this area.

Personal and Emotional Factors as Directing Influences in Discrimination

Shortly after the publication of the Bruner and Goodman experiment, Bruner and Postman reported a number of experiments on social perception which also included theoretical analyses of perception.[3] This new theory was called by Krech the *new-look approach* since its innovators stated that they wanted to take a new look at perception. They were particularly critical of the classical gestalt approach, which they thought overemphasized the stimulus determination of perception at the expense of organismic or functional factors, such as past experience, motivation, set, and the like.

The main assertion of Bruner and Postman was that past experience selectively sensitizes the organism to different aspects of the stimulus complex. The differential "sensitization" acts as a set which selectively predisposes the organism to respond to different aspects of the stimulus complex and in different ways. This set is a function of prevailing needs, motives, attitudes, and personality structure, all of which result from interactions between the organism and his social environment. Thus selectivity in perception is determined largely by the positive and negative values of a person, his motivational structure, and the attitudes he has learned through past experience. With this main thesis in mind, Bruner and Postman contended that an adequate theory of perception must include a definition not only of adequate stimulation but also of the *creative role* of the perceiver. Perception is actually a result of the interaction between an active organism and his stimulus environment. The investigators thus developed a theory which was both organismic and functionalistic. They emphasized particularly the role of the perceiver (the functionalist aspect), postulating that he performs four functions during perception.

First, there is the function of *selection*. The organism selects the stimuli to which he responds since the stimulus potential of the environment is too great for him to perceive everything. Second, there is the function of *accentuation*. Some stimulus aspects are accentuated at the expense of others. This accentuation is a result of momentary needs and past learning. Third, there is *fixation*. What is "habitually" seen in a situation is a result of fixation of previous perceptual responses in that situation. Finally, the total perceptual act represents an *organized configuration*. These four functions are affected by the prevailing state of the organism, which "is compounded of the organism's needs, his values, his hopes, his past experience, his culture—in short, all those items of his past history which have gone into making him what he is" (Bruner and Postman, 1948, p. 84).

An experiment illustrating what these authors considered to be the effect

---

[3] See, for example, Bruner and Postman (1948).

of motivation on perception was performed by Postman, Bruner, and McGinnies (1948), who gave a group of subjects the Allport-Vernon test of values. By scoring the subject's responses to the items on this test, they were able to construct an order of six values, such as religious value, economic value, esthetic value, and so on. Thus they could determine for each subject his strongest value, his next strongest value, and so on down to his lowest value. After this test each subject was presented with words which were exposed for varying durations, from short to longer periods. Some of the words were closely associated with low values while others were closely associated with high ones. The testers recorded the time of exposure at which the subject clearly recognized the word. It was found that the recognition threshold was inversely related to the ordering of the six values; i.e., the high-value words were recognized at shorter time exposures than the low-value words. The authors had predicted, and their results supported, that *selective sensitization* would lower the recognition threshold for high-value words but that *perceptual defense* would increase the recognition threshold for low-value words.

The effect of perceptual defense was investigated further by McGinnies (1949), who presented tachistoscopically 11 neutral words and 8 critical words (whore, bitch, etc.) to eight male and eight female subjects. The critical or taboo words required longer exposure for recognition, and their prerecognition stage was accompanied by heightened emotional reactions as measured by the galvanic skin responses (GSR). McGinnies concluded that he had not only verified the existence of perceptual defense but also had shown that threatening stimuli arouse autonomic reactions before conscious awareness and that this emotional state is an essential part of the defense mechanism which increases the recognition threshold.

Subsequent researchers have questioned this interpretation of the data in terms of causal effect of emotional states. Diggory et al. (Aronfreed, Messick, and Diggory, 1953; Diggory, 1956) found that the recognition threshold and the emotional reactions were stronger if the subjects were female and the experimenter was male, and vice versa, so that at least part of the longer time could be attributed to the possibility that the subjects were embarrassed and surprised that such words were being used and wanted to be positive before reporting that they recognized them. This embarrassment and "shyness" would also account for the increased emotional reaction. Furthermore, Solomon and Howes (1951) have pointed out that the increased recognition threshold for the taboo words might simply be due to the fact that these words appear less frequently in print and are therefore less familiar and not so readily available for the subject to call up. Consequently they provide poorer cues for recognition, thus requiring longer exposure time. This view is supported by Solomon and Postman (1952), who found that when the subjects were required to guess what the word was during prerecognition periods, they guessed in the direction of other interests when the dominant interest word was missed but went far afield with low-interest or "dirty" words. Woodworth and Schlosberg suggest plausibly that the more extensive an individual's previous experience of an object, the greater the number of cues that can be reduced and still permit recognition. "This factor undoubtedly contaminates the results mentioned, but it does not explain away some of the observed facts." (We shall return to this subject later.)

We must, however, be very careful in interpreting these data. While the positive value may tend to accentuate a given dimension (e.g., positive size error), the negative value may do the reverse. Such observed effects as increased recognition thresholds and emotional reactions can be attributed partly to the effects of unfamiliarity and embarrassment.

In addition to perceptual defense, perceptual vigilance (similar to sensitization) has been discussed by Deese (1955). He prefers a concept dealing with an excitatory state, such as vigilance, rather than a concept dealing with inhibition, like perceptual defense. Accordingly, vigilance could be defined as the probability of a response to a given stimulus. Vigilance is increased by extrinsic stimulus conditions and familiarity from past experience, such as familiarity with highly valued objects. It is reduced by low familiarity, and so on (this accounts for some but not all of the data in studies of perceptual defense). In an experiment Deese states his main thesis in an "expectancy" hypothesis which asserts that "the feedback from a search task determines what the observer expects from further participation in the task in a single proportional relationship and that his vigilance will vary accordingly" (1955, p. 362). He is cautious to add that vigilance is not directly determined by task feedback but that motivational variability (expectancy, attitude, etc.) plays a part.

Other experimental support for the selective-sensitization or vigilance approach comes from a report by Allport and Kramer (1946), who noted that anti-Semitic individuals are more accurate in their identification of photographs of Jews and non-Jews. They concluded that "we are dealing here with an interesting instance of 'social perception.' People who are unprejudiced are less sensitive to the identity of those with whom they deal. . . . The question of racial identity is of small importance to the person free from prejudice" (1946, p. 116). Although we must be cautious in interpreting this study, especially since the prejudice was measured by responses to a questionnaire, it does again suggest that values may differentially sensitize individuals to pay greater attention to certain attributes of a stimulus complex, e.g., to Semitic features or characteristics.

EVALUATION, CRITIQUE, AND EXPLANATION. Eriksen (1963) has raised a question whether the interpretation of Solomon and Howes is adequate to account for the full range of phenomena found in the perceptual-defense and vigilance studies. We have already noted that the long recognition thresholds and the heightened GSRs may result from deliberate response suppression by the subject (the reader is referred to Diggory et al., earlier in this chapter). We shall return to this point later.

The second interpretation of Solomon and Howes attributes the longer recognition thresholds of the taboo words to their relative unfamiliarity (and hence relative unavailability) to the subject. This is tantamount to saying that perception as a response follows a single law of learning, namely, frequency. At best, says Eriksen, this is a gross simplification of the perceptual facts. Actually, it is at serious odds with general learning theory and at variance with the facts of experimental and practice effects of perception reported in Chapters 7 and 9 of this book.

A second criticism by Eriksen refers to the adequacy of the Thorndike-Lorge word count as a reliable index of frequency and familiarity. Eriksen relates that inspection of scatter diagrams of the original Solomon and Howes data reveals that "practically all of the relationship (between frequency and recognition) is due to a difference between words having 0 or very low frequencies and words having high frequencies." There is essentially no relationship between these two variables when we look at the range of frequencies between 10 and 3,000 occasions per million. Moreover, the Thorndike-Lorge count is based on the frequency of occasion in children's books or popular adult magazines.

How representative and current are these books and magazines? Eriksen suggested that the Thorndike-Lorge count seriously underestimates the actual frequency of taboo words. This suggestion has some backing from a pilot study made at his laboratory at the University of Illinois. The frequencies of a large sample of Thorndike-Lorge words and taboo words were correlated with the number of subjects who could define them. The correlation was approximately 0.6 for the neutral words but only 0.03 for the taboo words. If we assume—which seems a logical thing to do—that familiarity is related to meaning and the ability to define words, then we conclude that somewhere in the taboo words this relationship is lacking. The most plausible explanation would be that the count underestimates their frequency. To correct adequately for this error, we should know more about the actual reading habits of the general population. Children probably spend more time reading comic books, for example, and adults read mystery stories where taboo words are more likely to occur.

If the Thorndike-Lorge counts do in fact underestimate the frequency of taboo words, then the practice, following Solomon and Howes, of "equating" for word frequency in the subsequent studies in this field virtually obviates any possibility of finding a positive perceptual-defense effect because the taboo word used would actually have a much greater familiarity and therefore would be more likely to be accepted by the subject. Because of these criticisms Eriksen goes on to relate perceptual vigilance to the effects of positive reinforcement and perceptual defense to the effect of anxiety-provoking or negative reinforcement upon perceptual response.

Thus he systematically relates perceptual defense to the clinical conception of defense mechanisms.[4]

First, there are experiments which show that the frequency is not a sufficient condition to account for the threshold phenomena. Many investigators (Eriksen and Brown, 1956; Postman and Solomon, 1950; Spence, 1957a; 1957b) have found that stimuli which are of approximately equal familiarity elicit different (high or low) recognition thresholds, depending upon whether or not the stimuli have been associated with success or failure or upon the relative values of the stimuli. With this type of data in mind Eriksen goes on to offer a learning (reinforcement) interpretation of these clinical phenomena.

What is the case for linking these experimental findings to general defense mechanisms? First, we must remember that repression theory does not state that all aggressive or sexlike stimuli are automatically repressed by all or even the majority of subjects. There are wide individual differences in what kinds of stimuli are anxiety provoking and in whether a person withdraws from or attacks anxiety-provoking situations. These differences are probably tied to the effects of the individuals' past learning experiences in such situations.

In order to link perceptual-defense phenomena to personality, two conditions must be met. First, it must be established independently that the stimuli are anxiety provoking to the subject and, second, that the subject typically responds to anxiety-provoking stimuli by avoiding them. Actually, as Eriksen points out, there are two broad classes of defense mechanisms, namely, repression, which should be accompanied by avoidance or higher recognition thresholds; and the group consisting of intellectualization, reaction formation, and projection, which should be accompanied by vigilance or lowered recognition thresholds. Here are some relevant experiments: in one study Eriksen (1951a) found that psychiatric patients who exhibited a high degree of disturbance and avoidance in *word association* to words in the emotional categories of aggression, homosexuality, and dependence also showed higher recognition thresholds for the corresponding pictures as opposed to neutral pictures. Further to clarify these results, other studies (Eriksen, 1951b; Lazarus, Eriksen, and Fonda, 1951) found subjects who were able to give freely aggressive and sexual content in Thematic Apperception Test (TAT) stories or sentence completion tests showed heightened sensitivity to hostile and sexual stimuli which were either visual or auditory. So it is not the nature of the stimulus per se which counts but the subject's characteristic mode of responding to it—whether the stimulus is a *sensitizer* or a *represser*. Furthermore, other investigators (Stein, 1953) have indicated that these characteristic modes of responding are reliable and repeatable from one set of stimuli to another.

[4] See Eriksen (1951a; 1951b; 1954).

In summing up his explanation of perceptual defense, Eriksen points out that most of these experiments present the subject with a situation which is more like a guessing game than a perceptual task. The subject has to "guess" or discriminate from inadequate cues. What the subject is likely to call up depends on relative habit strengths of various categories. Thus Eriksen is making a distinction between the *perceptual process* and the *response* to the percept resulting from that process. He attributes the perceptual-defense data to the response variable primarily because of the lack of evidence showing the effect of learning on the perceptual process per se in these phenomena. Moreover, various studies [5] indicate that the frequency effect of Solomon and Howes (which these authors presumably thought influences the perceptual process itself) upon the recognition threshold can be obtained in the absence of any perceptual stimuli. The case is strong to attribute these phenomena to response bias, "which in turn is probably due to conditional avoidance response to the anxiety-provoking stimuli" (Eriksen, 1963, p. 57).

SUBCEPTION AND SUBLIMINAL EVENTS. Lazarus and McCleary (1951) conducted a fascinating study which, like those of Eriksen, attempted to determine how association to perceptive stimuli develops. But their explanation was quite different from Eriksen's. In their study of subception they started with nonsense syllables so as to control as completely as possible for past experience. Five out of ten of these nonsense syllables were conditioned to a GSR by shocking the subject after these syllables had been presented visually. Then the authors tachistoscopically exposed each nonsense syllable at duration levels such that the verbal recognitions were 50 per cent correct. The complete results are presented in Figure 12-2.

The result of greatest interest is the difference between the two MW (mean wrong) categories. In every case the shock syllable gave a greater GSR than the nonshock syllable. The t score of the difference of means (7.45) is highly significant statistically. Lazarus and McCleary interpreted their data in terms of subception, "a process by which some kind of discrimination is made when the *S* is unable to make a correct conscious discrimination."

Much debate has centered on the problem of perceptual defense and subception. Eriksen (1956a) has probably made the strongest criticism. He maintains that the appearance of subception is a statistical artifact, and he asserts that the verbal report and the GSR are each correlated (but less than perfectly) with the stimulus and that the two response systems, the verbal report and the GSR, are themselves correlated (but less than perfectly). The subception phenomenon results because one of the variations (the verbal-report range) is held constant while variables in the other (the GSR) are measured. Eriksen reasons statistically that if two response systems are correlated with the same stimulus and with each other, holding

[5] For example, Goldiamond and Hawkins (1958); M. J. Goldstein (1962).

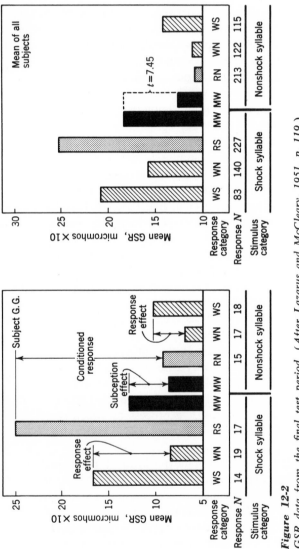

Figure 12-2

GSR data from the final test period. (After Lazarus and McCleary, 1951, p. 119.)

WS = wrong, shock   WN = wrong, no shock
RS = right, shock   MW = mean wrong
RN = right, no shock   WS = wrong, **shock**

one constant will lead to the remaining responses being correlated with the stimulus. (This is usually the case but is not necessarily so. The magnitude of the various correlations would determine whether this event would occur. It is possible that in holding one of the responses constant the correlation between the remaining response and the stimulus will disappear.) It is this correlation which has led to the definition of subception. In rebuttal Lazarus (1956) states that Eriksen's argument deals with statistical reasoning and not with the psychological event taking place. He agrees that two response systems are working and that the restriction of one is in keeping with real-life situations. Thus he points out that while a number of visual discriminations to the color spectrum are possible, our verbal-response categories limit their designations. Moreover, people may be able to discriminate stimuli before they can report them accurately.

Ranken (1956) put the alternative hypotheses of Eriksen and Lazarus to a critical experimental test. After determining thresholds, some of the three-letter nonsense syllables used were conditioned to the GSR. The criterion for conditioning was that the average amplitude of the GSR for the shock syllables had to be three times as great as the average GSR for the nonshock syllables. Then the standard subception experiment was essentially repeated with the syllables presented for varying exposure times, from subliminal to supraliminal. GSR and verbal reports were recorded. As shown in Figure 12-3, the results indicated, first, that there was heightened GSR for the shock syllables. Second, the GSR for shock syllables was much greater than the GSR for nonshock syllables as the duration of exposure was increased. We might say that with increasing duration of exposure the subjects were able to extract more information from the stimulus. Third, it seems that the GSR was related to the actual reporting of shock syllables and not to the probability of shock syllables' occurring (this is seen in Figure 12-4). Thus we see that the correct reporting of shock syllables gave the greatest GSR for all exposure durations.

The debate as to what causes the so-called subception effect has not been settled. Eriksen (1960) points out that there are three possibilities, which are:

    A. Stimulus → perceptual process → verbal response → GSR
    B. Stimulus → GSR → perceptual process
    C. Stimulus → perceptual process → GSR

Eriksen goes on: If *A* were the explanation, then the subception effect could not have been obtained. If *B* were true and GSR were held constant, then we would not find a correlation between stimulus and verbal report. Eriksen did find such a correlation, and thus alternative *C* is the most plausible explanation. Moreover, in many studies conducted and reviewed by Eriksen, a significant partial correlation was obtained between either response and the stimuli, the other response being held constant. In addition, the

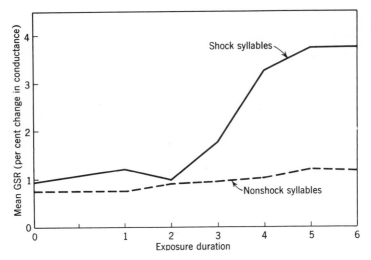

Figure 12-3
Results of a subception experiment. (After Ranken, 1956.) Actual durations were different for each S. Duration 3 was the longest duration giving zero probability of correct verbal report in preliminary testing; duration 6 was the shortest duration giving 1.0 probability of report. Durations 1 and 2 were one-half and three-quarters, respectively, of duration 3.

relative independence of the two response systems was seen in noncorrelated errors between the two concurrent response systems. These distracting stimuli introduce increased error into GSR response while not affecting verbal response, and the number of competing alternative verbal responses

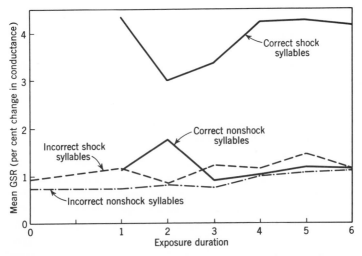

Figure 12-4
Results of subception experiment. (After Ranken, 1956.)

affects the verbal judgment but does not concurrently influence the accuracy of GSR (Eriksen, 1956b). Thus Eriksen concluded that there is no proof that the GSR or any other response reflects more sensitive discrimination than S's verbalization. Rather, the verbal report is limited in conveying S's perceptual experience.

FURTHER CONSIDERATIONS. It does seem from the foregoing that the subject can make some kind of discrimination of stimuli even when he does not report them accurately. There must therefore be some basis for this discrimination. The nature of this basis is suggested by an experiment of Bricker and Chapanis (1953), whose work indicates that subliminal presentation of syllables does convey some information to the subjects. By varying the similarity of the nonsense syllables, they found that on the incorrect trials the subjects guessed the correct syllables in fewer than a chance number of trials. Similarity was varied by altering the letters used in the syllables. Syllables which were more similar to the shock syllables also elicited the GSR more frequently than syllables which were less similar. A comparable result was obtained by Murdock (1954). Also, Eriksen (1956b) found that when verbal response is held constant, a generalization gradient for the GSR as a function of the size of a square (the original conditioned response) is obtained. The GSR is affected by some "configurational" aspect of stimulus complex, and the subject is extracting varying amounts of information from the stimulus situation. Thus we might even expect a stimulus generalization gradient to be present.

In a recent comprehensive and excellent survey Goldiamond and Hawkins (1958) have maintained that this subception effect involves a discrepancy between two responses, an automatic indicator and an accuracy indicator. *We would maintain that these responses have different thresholds for elicitation.* The autonomic indicant (GSR), being of a gross discriminative nature, may operate with extraction of partial information, while the accuracy indicant (correct recognition) requires extraction of total information. The difficulty with this interpretation is that fractional stimuli without the context of the total pattern carry little meaning. (Let us compare the words "birch" and "bitch." The difference between "r" and "t" carries little meaning without the total context.)

A problem similar to subception is that of *subliminal perception,* a phenomenon which has been of public interest recently because of its so-called effect in advertising. In this type of event a message of subliminal nature is communicated to the subject. It is assumed that he "unconsciously" registers the stimulus and acts in accordance with the information contained in the symbol. In the usual experiment two problems are actually involved: how the information is obtained if it is subthreshold and why the subject acts on it. Only the former is pertinent here; the latter is a motivational problem and has received little study.

As an example of this phenomenon, during a motion picture the message

"Buy popcorn" is flashed on the screen intermittently at so-called subliminal light intensities and exposure durations. It is assumed that many individuals receive the message unconsciously and that more popcorn is sold than if the message were not flashed on the screen. In experiments described in popular magazines it has been reported that subliminal advertising has been effective. Consumption of popcorn or some other product has been compared for subliminal and nonsubliminal periods, but these experiments suffer from a number of methodological faults. For example, many factors which can affect popcorn consumption or that of other products—namely, seasonal economic fluctuations, climatic conditions (temperature and humidity, especially), quality of the various motion pictures during the two periods, type of audience attending the pictures, etc.—have not always been controlled.

Goldiamond and Hawkins (1958) have treated this event in the same manner as that of subception, viewing the effect as a discrepancy between semantic and accuracy indicators. Likewise, we would maintain that the subject is extracting partial information but cannot indicate through verbal reporting what event is occurring. It is very important, however, in both the subception and the subliminal-perception experiments that the threshold of each subject be determined and that the threshold be defined as the lowest level at which the subject can correctly recognize the symbol. If the threshold is defined in the usual manner (as the 50 per cent point or average of a number of threshold determinations), then it is obvious that at some time the subject will be extracting total information because the stimulus energy will be suprathreshold. In fact, in some instances of subliminal-advertising attempts members of the audience have indicated that they have received ("consciously") or extracted partially or totally the message.

M. Wiener and Schiller (1960) have maintained that the experiments which have been cited as indicating subliminal processes have not excluded the possibility of the operation of some supraliminal cues. When a complex stimulus is used, it is reasonable to assume that some portion of the stimulus is perceived even when the response is incorrect. In response to the complex stimulus, these authors maintain that it is possible (1) to be correct in verbal or motor responses by supraliminally perceiving the stimulus, (2) to be correct by perceiving a part of the stimulus, (3) to be correct by guessing, (4) to be incorrect but to have perceived a part of the stimulus, and (5) to be incorrect by guessing. The advocates of subliminal perception (specifically those concerned with the subception effect) have assumed that the incorrect responses are due to guessing, but the experiments of Wiener and Schiller indicate that incorrect responses may occur even when the subject perceives some portion of the stimulus. In one experiment a circle presented below absolute threshold was effective in influencing choice behavior only when the subliminally present stimulus was reported as "seen" or as "possibly seen." The possibly seen conditions would in most studies not be identified and thus would constitute subliminal events. There was no effect on choice behavior when subjects reported not seeing the stimulus at all. These results are somewhat similar to those of Ranken, which were discussed above.

In another experiment Wiener and Schiller investigated the response of subjects to words which were semantically and structurally similar to shock words. For example, a shock word was "ship"; a semantically similar word was "boat"; a structurally similar word was "shop." The authors maintained that GSR responses should be greater to the semantically similar words than to structurally similar words if unconscious discrimination occurs; if perception of partial cues is involved, however, then the GSR responses to structurally similar words would be greater than to semantically similar words. The results indicated that when the subjects incorrectly identified the words under subliminal conditions, the GSR to structural words was greater than the GSR to semantic words. There was also a successive decrease in GSR to the shock words as the amount of identification (supraliminal, correct subliminal, incorrect subliminal) decreased. Moreover, Wiener and Schiller reported from this experiment that the incorrect verbal guessing behavior revealed that the subjects appeared to be responding verbally as well as autonomically to perception of portions of the stimuli. Some of these results are essentially the same as those reported by Bricker and Chapanis and discussed above. They also raise the possibility that visual information rather than meaning is extracted without effects of the subliminal type.

Another experiment concerned with peripheral stimuli was reported with similar results. Wiener and Schiller maintain that the results of the three experiments tend to support a "perception-of-partial-cue" hypothesis for so-called subliminal conditions. The partial-cue hypothesis is exactly the same as the "extraction-of-partial-information" hypothesis.

A preliminary experiment by Wohl [6] at Wilkes College suggests that the partial-information-extraction (or partial-cue) approach is most appropriate. In this experiment the threshold of each subject for a number of nonsense syllables at two tachistoscopic duration exposures above threshold and two below threshold was tested. Likewise, a control condition in which nonsense syllables were present (but were completely covered) was used to indicate the guessing level for the subjects. There was an increase from the control condition to two units below, one unit below, one unit above, and two units above threshold both for extraction of partial information (one or two letters of three-letter syllables) and for total extraction of information.

In summary, it appears that the organism is extracting information continuously from the stimulating situation and, likewise, that there is no need

[6] Courtesy of personal communication from John Gaito.

to introduce the notion of unconscious. What we call unconscious is merely the condition wherein the subject is extracting very little information from the stimulus.

The experiments on social perception, perceptual sensitization, vigilance, and defense all seem to suggest that, under conditions where it is not easy for the subject to make a discrimination, such factors as value, set, attitude, and anxiety can influence the nature of the discrimination, emphasizing one or another aspect of the stimulus field. Furthermore, there is the suggestion that there are certain cues in the stimulus complex to which the subject is more sensitive. This sensitivity is developed by such experiential factors as conditioning and familiarity. An experiment of Bitterman and Kniffin (1953), who found that the higher recognition thresholds for taboo words are lowered with practice, further supports this fact. Thus, although the taboo words still tend to have higher recognition thresholds than neutral words, the last presentation of the taboo words in a series of trials has a significantly lower recognition threshold than the first presentation.

In conclusion, I want to stress the importance of determining independently the individuals' typical reactions to anxiety-provoking stimuli, as Eriksen did, if we are to conclude that personality or values influence perception.

Summary

In summary, we would state that the social-perception studies can be fitted into two descriptive classes. The work of the Europeans has given us a technique for investigating the determiners of the judgment of emotional and motivational expression. Their studies suggest that this judgment is based on configurational principles, such as common fate, radius of action, similarity, proximity, and so on. Whether we respond to social aspects of these configurations innately or whether we learn to do so is an open question to be answered experimentally. While the gestaltists have stated that the gestalt laws operate independently of experience, it would seem reasonable to expect that the social relevance of these laws is probably influenced by social learning; most studies tend to support this expectation.

It also seems that the American data on social perception can most parsimoniously be fitted into the third kind of perceptual learning which we discussed at the end of Chapter 9. This we designated as the influence of learning on the development of differential-reaction sets. Thus we think that such factors as value, anxiety, and the like influence our ability to perceive by affecting our discrimination or judgment of already perceived stimuli through making us more or less sensitive to certain attributes of the stimulus complex or by accentuating certain parts of errors when the stimulus is unclear.

Anti-Semitic individuals are therefore more prone to react to Semitic types of configurations. Through learning individuals can respond differently to the potential cues or information carried by unclear or impoverished stimulus complexes, and so on. We are saying that the kind of learning affects the response system. By exploring the field this way, i.e., by realizing that emotions, motivation, or personality factors can only influence the reaction to already perceived things, we shall clear away a lot of the mystery and mysticism which tend to be prevalent in the area of social perception.

13

Sets in
Cognitive Behavior
and Thinking

In a recent review of research and theory about problem solving, Gagne (1959) starts by formulating briefly the sequences involved in the productive solution of a problem. The stages are as follows:

1. The instructions, stated or assumed, and the stimulus situation establish behavioral *sets* and define the *task* or *goal* for the subject.
2. Once the information has been received (the amount transmitted being determined by the noise in the system, which depends partly on how relevant the generated sets already are), the subject invents *concepts* to categorize the information into the most meaningful relationships. These concepts either transfer from previous training or constitute the utilization of concepts already formed.
3. After the concepts have been invented or emitted, the subject determines some course of action. The courses adopted partly reflect the personality and the effects of the past experience of the subject and might consist of conservative or gambling *strategies*. Whether the strategy is relatively conservative or liberal in turn depends partly on the expected payoff function or perceived cost.
4. The various alternatives having been considered, the subject must either choose between them or adopt another strategy if one *decision* has proved to be relatively poor.
5. Finally there is the *verification* of the problem process as a result of feedback from the solution.

Since the first three stages represent the essence of the problem-solving process, the last two being elaborations of the third phase, we shall deal with these three aspects separately in the next three chapters. Because we have already considered the role of organismic sets (attitudes, motives, etc.) on perception and because sets initiate the problem-solving process, we shall begin with the role of set in thinking. We shall define a set as a *perception which is structured toward a single, or few, reactions.* Thus sets operate to predispose *S* toward certain kinds of behavior rather than other kinds; i.e., they reduce the number of response alternatives.

Set in Perception and Concept Invention

Before we proceed to a detailed analysis of the operation of set, let us illustrate the similarities between the ways sets operate in perception and conceptual behavior. In one study Epstein and Rock (1960) performed an experiment in which they tried to separate the influences of frequency, recency, and perceptual set on the ease with which later stimuli were discriminated. Frequency and recency were manipulated by the amount of previous exposure to the stimuli, and recency in terms of the time and other stimuli which had elapsed since the last exposure to the stimuli to be tested. Expectancy or set was determined by instructions to the subjects. The authors found that recency controlled the determination of the subsequent perception. They concluded that the set or perception is misdirected. It should be pointed out, however, that the effect of set is not only induced by instructions but can in fact be aroused by some aspect of the stimulus. This is clearly seen in the classical experiments on set performed by Luchins, which we shall presently examine. Thus the attribution of set to instruction and other effects to stimulus factors as made by Rock and Epstein is not a logically exclusive dichotomy.

In a series of experiments reported by Long and his coworkers (Long, Reid, and Henneman, 1960; Reid, Henneman, and Long, 1960), they found that reducing the number of response alternatives through such techniques as informing the subjects of the alternatives increased the frequency of subsequent correct identifications of stimuli which were moderately ambiguous. A very instructive experiment was constructed by Binder and Feldman (1960), who required subjects to group stimuli into various classes by learning to give class names to those having common cases. After giving the subjects stimulus-predifferentiation training they found that the relative frequency with which a stimulus appeared in this prior training directly influenced the rate at which it was later classified or recognized. This finding held for nonsense, but not for meaningful, figures.

The difference in the findings with respect to nonsense vs. meaningful form is important because it raises the question of the relative effectiveness of short-term vs. long-term set in perceptual discrimination and thinking. We have already seen the influence of long-term personality set on perception in Chapter 12, and we shall now proceed to an analysis of set in thinking, beginning with experimentally induced short-term set and then continuing to its relation to long-term problem-solving set within *S*.

We have stated that the attitude with which the subject commences to classify elements can be induced by experimental instructions. In one experiment, Reed (1946a) studied the influence of set on the learning of concepts. The subject was presented with a pack of 42 cards, on each of which were written four common English words. One word on each card was an instance of one of six concepts, the remaining three words being irrelevant to the concept. There were thus seven instances of each concept, and each was defined by the same nonsense names which defined that concept. All KUN cards contained a word for an animal; all BEP cards, a word for a vegetable; all DAX cards, a word for a color; and so on.

One group of subjects was merely told to learn the nonsense name of each card. To induce experimental set, another group was required to learn the nonsense names and discover their meanings and was also presented with information about the characteristics of a concept. The rate of learning and the retention of these names were better in the set group, which also showed superior comprehension of the meanings of the concepts. Ewert and Lambert (1932) reported similar results. Reed suggested that the greater efficiency of the second group occurs because the positive set makes it more likely that the individuals of this group will keep the goal (learning the concepts) in mind and show more effective problem-solving participation by actively searching for possibilities of hypothesis testing, grouping, and so on.

Since the success of problem solving is largely dependent on how the individual goes about grouping the problem materials, it follows that set should have a powerful influence on how he goes about thinking. When a task is presented to a subject, a set or sets can be produced by the nature of the task (presentation of stimulus materials, etc.), the instructions, the individual's attitudes, his assumptions about the task, or an interaction of these four conditions. Moreover, the set may facilitate or impede efficient problem-solving behavior. The studies dealing with the role of set in thinking have a long history, and we shall start our analysis with a brief review of the highlights of the classical work.

Würzburg School Studies

At the turn of the twentieth century an extensive research program on thinking was initiated at Würzburg University under the general direction of Oswald Kulpe. The experimental paradigm of the Würzburg school is characterized by the classical "thought experiment." In essence it consists of the following: The subject is presented with a stimulus and given instructions to do something with it. After the task has been completed, he is asked to introspect about the events which preceded his completion of the

task. This simple method was extended to produce a mass of data on thinking during the first quarter of the present century. A critique of part of
this work is presented by Titchener (1909), and extensive summaries and
discussions are provided by Woodworth (1938) and Humphrey (1951).
Since the reviews by these psychologists contain excellent treatments and
are readily available classics, we shall present only a flavor of the Würzburg
work for the sake of historical continuity.

Carrying on the introspective method started by the school of structural
psychology under Wundt at Leipzig, the Würzburgers were studying the
association of ideas in thinking. Like Wundt, they advocated a presentational
psychology. Their basic assumption was that knowledge presents itself to
consciousness through ideas, which are presented after the perception has
called up images. This is *content psychology.* But these psychologists soon
were to produce reports which ran against the mainstream of the structuralists which they had followed. They reported that individuals could think
without having images. This, in the climate of Wundt and Titchener!
Their reports led to a long debate, "the imageless-thought" controversy,
which was waged between the Würzburg adherents and Titchener and the
old Cornell group. Titchener, Wundt's famous student, countered that the
Würzburg subjects were reporting thought contents incorrectly; they were
committing "stimulus errors" in introspection. The debate ended in a stalemate. *Nobody could agree on what the contents of thought were.*

On one fact all agreed, however: Ideas of objects do present themselves
to consciousness during thinking. The nature of this presentation was
described by various terms, all having similar denotations. Mayer and
Orth, who in 1901 started the chain reaction with their classificatory study
of mental events, called it the *Bewusstseinslage,* which simply means a state
of consciousness without sensory content. In 1905 Ach, studying introspective reports in the classical reaction-time experiments, referred to it
as a *Bewusstheit,* a vague knowing (*Wissen*). August Messer merely called
the conscious presentations *Gedanken,* or thoughts which somehow lead
to the somewhat unconscious meanings.

Karl Marbe and Bühler reiterated the importance of the state of consciousness. Bühler asserted that the *Bewusstseinslagen* are the turning
points of thought; the meaning is represented in these conscious experiences. Expressing dissatisfaction with the simple association and reaction-
time experiments, he stated that he was interested in studying higher
thought, such as occurred when his subjects were ascertaining the meaning
of Friedrich Nietzsche's aphorism, "I explain to you your virtues from those
of the future." The sensory reception of this sentence presents the mind
with doubts, contemplations, and so on. The essential experience of thought
is a fresh mental category not reducible to images.

So all agreed that thinking consists of a conscious state, but the status
of images was unresolved. Because of these methodological difficulties

experimental psychologists gradually turned away from observing the contents of thought toward studying the *act* of thinking. Here the soil was fertile. The impetus for these researches also came from the Würzburg studies on set.

TASK SET. Watt (1905) gave us one of the first successful experimental studies of the role of set in thinking. He used the method of controlled association. The experimenter presented the subject with a task, and then after a certain time interval, called the *fore period,* the stimulus was presented on a card. Examples of the tasks were: given a genus, name the species; given the species, name the genus; given the whole, name the part; given a part, name the whole, etc. In such controlled associations the subject cannot make a specific preparation beforehand since he does not know what the stimulus word will be. When the stimulus word was presented, the experimenter also measured the reaction time, i.e., the time which elapsed from the presentation of the stimulus to the subject's report. In the period after the presentation of the stimulus word, called the *main period,* the subjects were asked to give introspective reports of their experience following their response.

Two kinds of introspective reports emerged. When the task was unfamiliar and relatively new, the subject made the task clear to himself during the fore period, in a visual, verbal, or kinesthetic way, by defining for himself the relationships, and so on. When the stimulus word was presented, the response followed sometimes automatically, sometimes after a period of waiting and searching, and sometimes after a wrong response had been suppressed. Only if the last-named alternative occurred was the task recalled into consciousness. With familiar or well-practiced tasks, the task set became more efficient and less conscious. When the stimulus word was presented, the response generally followed automatically. The reaction time also decreased.

Watt concluded that the task set (or simply the *Aufgabe,* which is the German word for task) was established in the fore period; its efficiency resulted from its selection in advance, during this period.

May (1917) extended Watt's study by using greater numbers of subjects and stimulus cards and a mechanical device for presenting the task and the cards visually and by varying the length of the fore period at the command of either the subject or the experimenter. When the subject was in control, he exposed the task and the stimulus word whenever he felt he was ready. After practice his fore period became shorter. The experimenter varied the fore period for durations up to 0.5 sec when he was in control. As the fore period became longer, i.e., as the preparation or selection in advance became more complete, the reaction time became shorter. The introspective reports agreed with these objective measures. One subject reported a decrease in the set content with practice; it began with detailed motor adjustments, decreased with practice to "normal" preparation, and finally ended in a state of readiness. May states: "We have here a descending series of processes with the length of the fore period getting shorter as the series descend." These introspective reports were also correlated with the objective measures of the duration of the reaction-time and fore periods.

The experiments thus initiated by Watt at the Würzburg school and followed by May and others produced three criteria for specification of set: (1) the subject's awareness of getting ready and being ready, i.e., his state of preparation; (2) the effects of practice and the nature of the time records; and (3) the correctness of the reactions. In the last two criteria, the more effective the set, the lower the reaction time and the more nearly correct the response.

Ach, a colleague of Watt, also dealt with the nature of the *Aufgabe*. The general conclusion of this work was that the task leads to an *Einstellung* (set) which acts as a determining tendency; i.e., the task leads to reproductive tendencies.

Much later, Selz (1922) rejected this conception of separating the task from the reproductive tendencies which it was supposed to control. Instead, he conceived of a unitary *Aufgabe* which was productive. Humphrey (1951) has stated that this conception of the *integrative* nature of thought was a great theoretical advance over the Würzburg position.

The essential criticism of Selz was that the Würzburg formulation dealt with reproductive thinking. But problem solving does not consist only of reproducing from the past: something new is produced. For Selz, the newness of productive thinking consisted of the application of past experience to new materials. As an example, he pointed to Charles Darwin's use of the principle of Thomas Robert Malthus in his theory of natural selection. Maier (1930) went even further than Selz. He pointed out that Darwin did not merely select from his previous experience but remade his experience. Malthus had predicted ruin from overpopulation, whereas Darwin saw that not all but only the unfit would perish. Productive thinking consists not of the completion of a complex by selecting from past experience but of *the formation of a new whole by reorganizing past experience to meet the demands of the problem*. This is a statement of the gestalt theory of productive thinking, which led to many experiments on set and to which we now turn.

Set in Problem Solving

A DEFINITION OF THINKING. From a consideration of the issues discussed in the preceding section, we conclude that thinking is not synonymous with learning, although the two are closely interwoven in actual behavior. While these two processes are conceivably on the same broad continuum, they can be separated theoretically on the basis of content and act. *Learning* is the acquisition of new content into the organism's repertoire of habits. *Thinking* is the act whereby already acquired content is manipulated to meet new demands on the individual. The stimulation for thinking may come from the environment (environmental demands) or from within the organism (state demands). The act of thinking thus takes place on a broad continuum ranging from the low levels, as in reveries or dreams, to the highest levels, as in scientific creations. A high level of thinking is usually called *reasoning* or *problem solving* because in these situations a great deal of reorganization of the present stimulation and learned content is necessary to emit the required behavioral patterns. The more uncertain the stimulus situation is for the individual, the more creative or productive his thinking must be to grasp its significance and construct a new, meaningful system. The efficiency of thinking is based not only on genetic endowment but on what has been learned from past experience (available concepts). New learning can obviously also include some thinking, but it is the productive and integrative aspect of thinking that gives it its privileged status.

DIRECTION TO THOUGHT. Watt had shown that set can be advantageous in thinking, in that it increases the probability that a particular class of reaction will be made. But if the problem task requires that old stimuli be used in a new way, continuation of the old use can lead to inefficient or unsuccessful problem-solving behavior. Maier's research has shown that strong habits can direct thinking in a specific way and thus inhibit the emittance of alternative reactions which are required for the successful solution of problems. He has also demonstrated that certain kinds of instructions generate other sets which may provide the new directions to thinking which are necessary to solve the problems.

In one set of experiments Maier (1930) attempted to show that the application of the elements of past experience does not lead to successful problem-solving behavior unless some directive set is given in the present task situation. This he did by using his well-known pendulum problem. Each subject was brought into a room with a very low ceiling, 2 m high, which had an immovable heavy bench located next to one of the walls. The room also contained numerous wooden strips of various lengths, a C clamp, two Y clamps, strips of wire, and pieces of chalk. The subject's task was to construct two pendulums, each of which would swing over one of a pair of chalk marks located on the floor. Solution of the problem required the following stages: (1) two plumb lines had to be constructed by attaching wire to each of the Y clamps and fitting a piece of chalk into each clamp; (2) the top parts of these plumb lines were then to be attached to the ends of a strip of wood so as to produce two "potential" pendulums hanging from the ends of a horizontal wooden strip; (3) two other wooden strips were to be joined with the C clamp so as to provide a vertical support for the horizontal strip; and (4) the final solution consisted of wedging the horizontal strip against the ceiling by using the vertical support. This support could be adjusted in length because the strips could overlap in the clamp. Once the clamp was tightened, there would be a firm vertical and horizontal support for the pendulums, which could then move freely when pushed. The whole construction simply amounts to building a firm T support with the pendulums swinging from the ends of the horizontal bar of the T.

In Maier's experiment, the subjects were 84 college students, 62 of whom were divided into four groups as follows: Group 1 was merely given a statement of the problem, to build the pendulum. Group 2 was told to build the pendulum and had also been given preliminary training on the construction of subparts of the total structure (making a plumb line by attaching a string to a Y clamp and inserting a pencil into the clamp; clamping two wooden strips together). Group 3 received the same training as group 2, with the additional comment, "If you combine these ideas which I just gave you in the right manner, you will have the best solution to the problem." Group 4, like group 1, was told to build the pendulum but was also given a hint identical to that given to group 5. Group 5, consisting of the remaining 22 subjects, was treated like group 2, but it was also given a hint that the solution would be very easy if there only were two nails in the ceiling.

The results were that only 1 of the 62 subjects in the first four groups solved the problem, whereas 8 of the 22 in group 5 solved it. What is the central significance of these findings? We note first that the hint alone did not lead to success (group 4), nor did the mere possession of knowledge which could be applied to the problem (groups 2 and 3). What was more effective was the reorganization of relevant knowledge to meet the requirements of the problem. One way of facilitating this desired reorganization was to give the subject a positive set which would direct his thinking to the locus of the problem. Maier called this giving "direction" to reasoning. He distinguished direction from the determining tendencies of the Würzburg group and Selz. *Determining tendencies do not lead to anything new since they are confined to situations having the same sort of quality as the past situations which are relevant. They are therefore a statement of the problem in terms of the past. Direction is a much larger concept which involves seeing new meanings or properties.*

We should repeat, however, that instructions represent only one way of fostering the onset of the desired direction. It is very significant that 14 of the 22 subjects in the direction group still did not achieve the solution. One factor which could limit an individual's problem-solving behavior would be his *functional intelligence,* which we tentatively define as the performance level of an individual's intellectual capacity. (It presumably results from an interaction between assumed genetic endowment and the nature of developmental experience.) Depending on the nature of the specific problems, functional intelligence might, therefore, vary from situation to situation. Relevant to this point is the repetition of Maier's pendulum experiment by Weaver and Madden (1949), who controlled for intelligence. They noted that the subjects exhibited many and varied sequences of responses which appeared to have directed their problem-solving behavior.

The subjects in groups 3 and 5 devised a variety of solutions, some just as good as the vertical type which was Maier's criterion, and these two groups exhibited an equal number of vertical-support solutions. In all, 10 of the 52 subjects, of whom 5 were in group 3 and 4 in group 5, solved the problem. Again, only 1 in the hint or direction group solved the problem. This seems to indicate that past experience can be valuable if it builds up habits of searching, rearranging, and seeking new relationships. Again we notice that direction by itself, with no skill to anchor it, is quite ineffective. The correlation between IQ and success was negligible and insignificant. So if the subjects in groups 3 and 5 who did not solve the problem were inferior intellectually, this was probably not a general inferiority in intelligence but a lack in some specific ability. The subjects given no help accomplished almost nothing. The difference in intellectual ability involved must therefore have something to do with profiting from short-term practice, training, or instruction.

Weaver and Madden also noted that many of the unsuccessful subjects in groups 3 and 5 attempted solutions which led to the construction of unstable structures, but once they started in a particular direction they seemed to be unwilling to change their *modus operandi*.

The conditions favoring the expression of one direction rather than another have been further investigated. In a more recent study, Maier (1945) presents interesting data that throw some light on the factor which differentiates between an individual's shifting and not shifting his direction of attacking a problem. In this experiment the subject was required to make a hat rack by clamping two wooden strips together and wedging this new vertical support between the floor and the ceiling. The handle of the clamp would be the hook on which the hat was to be hung. Maier used three groups of subjects. Group 1 had been led to solve the pendulum-type problem in 10 min and was presented with the hat-rack problem while the pendulum structure was still in sight. Group 2 was given identical training, but the pendulum structure was removed before the hat-rack problem was presented. Group 3 was given no previous training. It was found that 72 per cent of group 1, 48 per cent of group 2, and 24 per cent of group 3 solved the new problem.

If the superiority of groups 1 and 2 can be attributed to profiting from the previous short-term experience, why was there a difference between them? Since members of group 2 had to recall the pendulum structure, it might be more difficult for them to separate the function of the clamp from the previous context in which its function was to hold strips together.

Group 1, however, was not only familiar with building supports but could see the structure in front of them. The perceptual cue which was required to mediate the symbolic response "hook" was more distinctive since it had greater situational support from the environment. After all, the handle of the clamp was sticking out from the support directly in the subject's field of vision. By having the stimulus material concretely in front of him in a specific relationship, the subject had a more definite anchor for his set and for changing his set.

Another interesting experiment showing other ways in which perceptual support makes the required set more available was reported by Saugstad (1957), who repeated Maier's pendulum experiment using a narrow hallway rather than a room. He found that members of the half that did not receive the "direction" were as good as members of the half that did. Saugstad reasons that the ceiling, the use of which was necessary for a successful solution, was made equally available to both groups by the narrow hallway. Thus direction may help to make the requirement more available, but it is the availability which leads to the integration of concepts into a total solution.

While these experimentally manipulated conditions can influence the genesis of the correct problem-solving set, the big problem which remains is why so few people are affected by these conditions. The factor of individual differences looms large; evidently the experimental conditions "take" only if the individual personality is susceptible. This can be seen, for example, from the experiment of Staats (1957), who found that while there is no relation between preproblem verbal responses and solution of the two-string problem, there is a relation between solution and general verbal fluency. Evidently long-term sets are most important.

Thus far we have seen that the cues to be utilized in establishing or changing a particular direction of problem solving can be made more distinctive by the nature of stimulus presentation, the kind of proximate pretraining, and the instructions given to the problem solver. A fourth factor, and probably the most important variable, which predisposes an individual to certain sets is presumably the hierarchical effect of various classes of long-term past experience. Thus Maier had noted that of the subjects who failed the hat-rack problem about 66 per cent were women and about 34 per cent were men. Moreover, Guetzkow (1951) found that although men and women were equally susceptible to falling into one set on both the pendulum problem and the Luchins-type problem discussed below, men were more successful in overcoming the influence of the inhibitory sets. It is reasonable to suppose that there was more positive transfer for men since in our culture this sex generally has greater opportunity to manipulate mechanical devices and numbers. The importance of background experience in building up skill to be used in problem solving has further been demonstrated by Birch (1945). We shall present additional discussions of

Birch and Guetzkow later in this chapter and in Chapter 15, but first we need to look at the other side of the coin.

Negative Effects of Set

While the transfer of relevant experience has a positive effect on problem solving, the transfer of the same experience may be deleterious if the problem demands that the experience be used in a new light. To these negative effects of set we now turn.

FIXATION OF FUNCTION. Maier (1931) studied this phenomenon in a situation in which the subjects were required to change the familiar use of a tool to a new function that was demanded by the nature of the problem. Each subject was brought into a room which had a low ceiling and a heavy bench next to one of its walls. Two light strings were suspended from different locations on the ceiling. The subject had to tie the two strings together at the free ends without moving the bench. Except for a pair of pliers, no other relevant objects were present. Unfortunately for the subject, the distance between the two strings was so great that he could not hold one string and reach out for the other. Standing on the bench would not help either since it was too far from the strings. The only way the subject could solve the problem was to use the pliers as a pendulum bob, tie it on one string, set this constructed pendulum in motion, go over to the other string, wait for the pendulum to come over, and then stop the pendulum, remove the bob, and connect the two strings.

Only 39 per cent of the subjects solved the problem within the 10 min allowed. Those who did not were "accidentally" given a hint by Maier when he casually brushed against one string, setting it in motion. An additional 38 per cent were able to achieve the correct solution within a mean time of 42 sec after the hint was given.

More than 60 per cent of Maier's subjects were unable to use the pliers as a weight for a pendulum bob, presumably since its customary use had been different. It is very easy to fall into mechanical habits when we do not remind ourselves of this tendency. Even when Maier redirected his subjects' thinking, the 38 per cent who followed the hint reported that they were not aware of it. The change of set took place almost automatically. As C. E. Osgood has stated, the redirection of a set takes place spontaneously through some occurrence of distinctive cues which set off the appropriate process mediating the correct solution.

Battersby, Teuber, and Bender (1953), working with normal and brain-damaged Ss, have again shown how the instructions can facilitate the redirection of a set in the string problem. Members of a group who were told to use only the five objects on the table in front of them solved the problem in a median time of 2 min. Those told to use any object in the room, including the ones in front of them, solved it in a median time of 7 min. A third group, told to use any object in the room without any additional instructions about the objects on the table, had a median time of 18 min to solution. While these differences due to instructions were large and significant, differences due to brain damage were quite small. The redirection of set in this situation appears to be strongly affected by the momentary situation or by a short period preceding it. This view is supported by the data of Cofer (1951), who showed that a group of subjects who memorized a list containing "rope," "swing," "pendulum," etc., subsequently produced a greater number of pendulum solutions of the string problem than subjects who memorized words which were irrelevant to the nature of the problem task. Also, Maier (1933) demonstrated that a group of subjects who were given a 20-min lecture on the necessity for shifting set was slightly superior in problem solving which followed immediately than a control group not so instructed.

FUNCTIONAL FIXITY. Duncker (1935; 1945) reported similar phenomena, which he called functional fixity and embeddedness, in his classic monograph on problem solving. The general paradigm of Duncker's problem is as follows. An object is first assigned a particular function in the presence of the subject. Then the subject has to use the same object in another function if he is to solve the problem. Duncker was interested in ascertaining whether the object becomes so "fixed" in the first function that it is difficult for the subject to see a new function for it.

The "weight" problem is a typical example. Subjects in the experimental group are first presented with a weight tied to the bottom of a string. They are then required to construct a pendulum swinging freely alongside a wall so that they may perform "experiments on motion." The way to solve the problem is to use the weight to hammer a nail into the wall and to use a joint which is available as the bob for the pendulum. The pendulum can then be attached to the nail. Only 50 per cent of the experimental subjects solved the problem, while 100 per cent of the control group, who had not previously seen the weight in the pendulum-bob function, were successful. Duncker concluded that the object is fixed or embedded in the old function (we may compare the embeddedness of perceptual objects in Gottschaldt's experiment in Chapter 7). One important factor which therefore hinders the reconstruction of a problem is *constraint,* e.g., it is difficult for an object to become part of a new organization when it has already been assigned a use.

The habitual use of objects and words certainly acts as a constraining force on our thinking in everyday life. Duncker gives a vivid example of this. During a mountain trip in which he ascended on one day and descended on another he pondered the question whether he would ever be at a particular place at exactly the same time on the two successive days. This assumes that he started and ended his journey at exactly the same time on each day. The more he thought about it, the more confused or cloudy the problem became. The locus of the difficulty was that he could not conceive of *meeting* himself. The familiar meaning of meeting constrained his thinking: we do not meet ourselves. When he realized the source of the difficulty, he was able to rephrase the problem as follows: Why not use two persons, one ascending and one descending but both starting off at the same time? Clearly they would have to meet when they passed one another. Now the exact nature of the problem and its solution came clearly into focus. In this case words restrict our sets in the same way objects do, since in the former case we cannot "walk around" the object and survey the situation as readily. *Anything which can thus be done to externalize the source of the difficulty, such as diagrams, should aid in overcoming constraint.*

In his demonstrations of functional fixedness, Duncker devised many additional problems. Three of these, the box, gimlet, and paper-clip problems, were used by Adamson (1952) in a repetition of Duncker's study. In the box problem the subject has to mount three candles at eye level (about 5 ft) for "experiments on vision." This is done by tacking three boxes upside down to a door and using the candle's own wax for mounting. In the gimlet problem three cords have to be suspended from an overhead beam. This is done by tying the cords to two screw hooks and to the gimlet after screwing them into the beam. In the paper-clip problem four small black squares have to be attached to a big white square, which must then be hung on an eyelet screwed into the beam. The problem is solved by using paper clips to attach the small squares to the large square and another paper clip as a hanger to attach the large square to the eyelet.

These three problems were presented in the order discussed to the subjects. The control group was simply given the problems. In the case of the experimental group, however, the *critical object*—box, gimlet, or paper clip—was first presented in some other, usually familiar, function. For example, the boxes were first presented as containers holding the tacks, and so on. In the box problem 24 out of 28 in the control group solved it, whereas only 12 out of 29 in the experimental group did so. This difference is statistically significant. The mean times to solution in the gimlet and paper-clip problems showed significant differences between the groups, although the number in each group that solved it was similar. These experiments, using a greater number of subjects, verified Duncker's finding that functional fixedness has a detrimental effect on problem solving.

Adamson and Taylor (1954) explored further the conditions leading to functional fixedness, adding the variable of time between the first use of the object and the second use required by the problem. Ten groups of subjects were used over two conditions of the first task and five conditions of the time variable. All subjects were required to construct an electric circuit by following a diagram. The subjects in groups M1, M2, M3, M4, and M5 utilized a microswitch to complete the circuit, whereas those in groups R1, R2, R3, R4, and R5 used a small relay. All subjects were then presented with Maier's two-string problem. The five subgroups in each of the main groups differed with respect to whether the problem was presented after time intervals of 1 min, ½ hr, 1 hr, 1 day, or 1 week. Of the objects available only the microswitch and the relay were heavy enough to be used as the pendulum bobs.

The results showed that 69 per cent of the subjects preferred the object which had not previously been assigned a different function; i.e., subjects in the M groups used the relay, while subjects in the R groups used the microswitch for the pendulum bobs. The time variable was not important. The effect of a task-induced set was demonstrated. The results were explained by invoking the construct of retroactive inhibition.

Birch and Rabinowitz (1951) had performed a somewhat different version of the previous experiment. The two experimental groups, consisting of naïve subjects with respect to electrical training, were treated like groups M and R above (no time variable was used). The control group, consisting of engineering students with a wider range of electrical knowledge, was not given the first task. The results were that 17 out of 19 subjects in the experimental groups used as the pendulum bob the object which had not previously been assigned a given function. On the other hand, 50 per cent of the control group used the microswitch for the pendulum bob, and the other 50 per cent used the relay. This experiment not only supports Duncker's conclusion but also suggests that a wider range of functional experience with specific objects facilitates the flexibility of sets which is necessary for solving many kinds of problems. The engineer had "relevant general broad nonspecific notions" which are necessary for productive thinking. In the nonengineer there was the perception of specific limited function. This leads us to a consideration of the important difference between adopting a set and overcoming ineffective sets. A discussion of this difference is continued in the next section.

Mechanization in Problem Solving

Luchins (1942) performed the most extensive series of studies to determine the conditions leading to the adoption of, and recovery from, a set. The basic pattern for the set of problems used is shown in Table 13-1. Subjects are usually tested in groups. They are told that they must measure a certain quantity of water by using empty jars which have certain fixed capacities in quarts. Then problem 1 is explained as an example: fill the 20-qt jar and pour off 3 qt into the 3-qt jar three times $(29 - 3 - 3 - 3 = 20)$. These numerical manipulations are written on the blackboard. The formula for the procedure may be written as $A - 3B$. Then the subjects are given 2½ min to solve problem 2 by writing it on paper. Again the procedure, $B - A - 2C$, is written on the blackboard and explained: fill the 127-qt jar, pour off 21 qt once and 3 qt twice $(127 - 21 - 3 - 3 = 100)$.

Table 13-1

The Einstellung Problem. (After Luchins, Psychol. Monogr., 1942, 54, pp. 1–95.)

Problem	Jars			Total, qt
1	29	3	–	20
2	21	127	3	100
3	14	163	25	99
4	18	43	10	5
5	9	42	6	21
6	20	59	4	31
7	23	49	3	20
8	15	39	3	18
9	28	76	3	25
10	18	48	4	22
11	14	36	8	6

After this the subjects are permitted to work on the remaining problems without further interruption from the experimenter. The problems are presented on the blackboard one at a time, and the subject is given up to $2\frac{1}{2}$ min to solve each problem. Numbers 2 to 6 are called the *Einstellung* (the German word for set) or E problems, since they are devised to induce a mental set. They can be solved only by the $B - A - 2C$ method. Problems 7 and 8 are called the *criticals* since they can be solved by either the set solution (indirect method) or the more direct methods of $A - C$ or $A + C$. Those who use the set method indicate that they have developed the set which was experimentally induced. Problem 9 is called the *extinction problem* because it can be solved not by the set method but by the direct method of $A - C$. Some individuals become so highly mechanized by the set that they fail to solve problem 9 within $2\frac{1}{2}$ min. Performance on problem 9, therefore, represents a measure of the tendency to recover from the set. The extent of recovery is further measured by performance on a second set of criticals (C_3, C_4), which can again be solved by either method.

In general, Luchins concluded that the *Einstellung* effect was produced to about the same degree in all age, educational, and intelligence groups. Yet a small proportion of individuals did not become set. Discussions with the subjects after the experimental sessions suggested that the primary factors operating were the tacit assumptions that the individual made with respect to the requirements of the task. Thus many individuals assumed that they had to start with the big jar first, use all three jars, and use the method of subtraction exclusively. These verbal reports seemed to have some objective support from the behavior of subjects in situations in which the basic experimental design was modified. For example, when one of the critical problems was 34, 85, 17, get 17, some subjects wrote $85 - 34 -$

17 − 17 = 17! Others wrote 34 − 17 = 17! In another variation Luchins said, "Don't be blind," just before problem 7 was attempted. This had the effect of lowering the frequency of *Einstellung* solutions.

Since individuals in the general population seem to be equally susceptible to adopting a set and since certain task and organismic variables appear to lower the *Einstellung* effect, the first question to be answered concerns the conditions affecting the production of a set. The second concerns the factors affecting recovery from a set. For example, Luchins concluded that public school children who are taught arithmetic by drill methods show little recovery from set compared with college students and adults. Analyses of certain experiments threw some light on the factors involved in these two phenomena.

Factors Influencing Susceptibility to Set

CONDITIONS OF TRAINING AND THE NATURE OF THE TASK. Luchins reported that requiring the subjects to work faster increases the *Einstellung* effect. In comparable groups this speed factor increased the effect from 60 to 100 per cent. Similarly, H. H. Kendler et al. (1952) found that spacing successive problem trials leads to more direct solutions than massing successive problems. These findings were corroborated by Rokeach (1950), who varied the period of delay between the time the subject first saw the problem and the time when he was permitted to begin writing his solution. The group which spent only 10 sec in looking over each problem exhibited greater susceptibility to set than groups viewing each problem for 30 or 60 sec. The former had 78 per cent of *E* solutions, while the last two groups had only 58 per cent of indirect solutions.

Luchins also showed that difficulty or increased effort heightens susceptibility to set. In this variation subjects were presented with paper-and-pencil maze tests. In the first few mazes the goal was reached by a zigzag path, while on the critical mazes it could also be reached by a straight path. An extinction maze was presented as well. Two experimental groups were used. Group 1 first traced a series of mazes by looking at the mazes' mirror images. This task was followed by a series in which the tracings were done with a direct view of the mazes. Group 2 accomplished their tasks in the reverse order.

On the first series, the mirror-training group, which had to expend more effort since the task was more difficult, showed more numerous zigzag solutions on the critical mazes than the direct-tracing group. During the second series of tracings both groups produced few zigzag solutions. Presumably the first tracing series had greatly reduced susceptibility to this particular set.

These two classes of experiments on speed, spacing, and effort suggest that any condition which serves to emphasize the particular method rather than the demands of the problem tends to maximize the effect of that particular set. Luchins even showed that concretizing the task, i.e., having subjects work with actual jars and water in front of a tap, led to little reduction of the set. Furthermore, Luchins and Luchins (1950) discovered that stressing the need for economy by changing the water to milk still did not lead to a significant reduction of set solutions. These findings were corroborated by Tresselt and Leeds (1953), who found that whether the problem was solved by verbal means or by actual performance made little difference in the frequency of *Einstellung* solutions; nor did the order effect, i.e., whether verbal or actual performance came first. The only difference was that actual performance led to a great improvement in the time taken to complete the task.

Anything which serves to lessen the importance of the method per se should consequently lead to a minimization of the effect of a set. Luchins found that if the *E* method had been used on the first two or three problems, then the introduction of critical problems did not reduce the effect. But if from the beginning the *E* problems were interspersed with problems which could only be solved by a direct method, then the effect of *Einstellung* was greatly reduced. Moreover, Jersild's work (1927) on the establishment of higher-order sets points out an additional advantage of multiple sets. In this experiment the subjects were required to shift rapidly back and forth between two or more kinds of task sets, such as subtracting 3s and giving opposites. The college-student subjects actually preferred this alternation and worked more rapidly on alternate sets when the task and stimuli were dissimilar. A variation on the last experiment was presented by Schroder and Rotter (1952), who gave the subjects an opportunity to *learn* to shift rather than instructing them to shift. The subjects had to classify cards on the basis of designs or color. When the basis of the classification was changed frequently, they learned to shift more quickly. The number of "carry-over" responses from the last classificatory criterion was a function of the expectancies which the subject built up during the training. Finally, Youtz (1948) has shown that it becomes progressively harder for a subject to change his hypothesis as he achieves more success with a particular method of attack.

SPECIFICITY OF SUSCEPTIBILITY TO SET. The evidence reported in the preceding section has led certain investigators to consider whether there is any general organismic factor of "rigidity" which would differentiate individuals with respect to susceptibility to adopting any particular set. The available evidence does not offer good support for such an hypothesis (Cattell and Tiner, 1949; Cattell and Winder, 1952; Oliver and Ferguson, 1951). This means that the individuals who adopt a fixed set in one situation are not necessarily the ones who adopt a fixed set in a different situation, although the correlation is higher when the types of sets involved are more similar (Cowen, Wiener, and Hess, 1953). Luchins (1942) had found that a group of high school students with a high aptitude for mathematics and science showed much less of the *Einstellung* effect. This is reminiscent of Birch's and Rabinowitz's finding that engineering students were more flexible in their use of microswitches and relays in the two-string problem. All of this suggests that the wider the range of an individual's experience and competence within specific task areas, the less likely it is that he will succumb to a restricting set in those areas. Since set is usually induced by the nature of a specific situation, the susceptibility to that set can be reduced by the extent of the individual's facility in manipulating the elements contained in the specific situation. Fisher (1949; 1950), following a review, has made a plea that we stop looking for all kinds of correlations but study instead the range and complexity of rigidity phenomena.

Recovery from Set

The extent of recovery from set appears to depend on a more general organismic factor, although present data have been able to distinguish only between extremes. Luchins (1951) reported that individuals who show more concreteness of thought, as measured by the similarities subtest in intelligence test batteries, show less recovery from set as evidenced by a greater proportion of failures on the extinction problem.

Adamson and Taylor (1954), in a study previously discussed, reported a significant relationship between the strength of functional fixedness in individuals and their inability to overcome set as measured by failure on the extinction problem. McNemar (1954) found that individuals with high reasoning ability, i.e., individuals who were in the upper fifteenth percentile on four subtests of Guilford's test battery of reasoning, exhibited a greater tendency to overcome set, although they were as susceptible to its onset as individuals with low reasoning ability.

The data of Guetzkow (1951) shows, however, that the differentiation between susceptibility to set and the ability to break it when necessary is more complex than is implied in the foregoing statements. First, he did confirm previous findings that there is a difference between these two variables; i.e., while most people are susceptible to set, there are those who can overcome it. Furthermore, there is no general susceptibility factor or recovery factor. The two factors tend to be specific to certain areas related to experience, as we mentioned earlier.

But Guetzkow went one step further and suggested that there is not such a clear-cut distinction between susceptibility to set and recovery from set. He selected two pairs of extreme groups on the basis of performance on the *Einstellung* test and the Maier two-string problem. The highly susceptible group consisted of those who gave *E* solutions on the *Einstellung* test and stereotyped solutions to the two-string problem, while the group of low susceptibility did not. The latter were superior to the highly susceptible group on tests of the Gottschaldt figures and gestalt-type reasoning tests but not on the ACE (American Council on Education) intelligence test. The high-recovery group consisted of those who solved the extinction problem and gave the pendulum solution on the two-string problem while the low-recovery group did not. The former were also superior in their performance on the Gottschaldt test and on a test of finding concealed animals in a drawing. Thus while there is no general correlation between susceptibility to set and recovery from it, some relationship seems to underlie extreme manifestations of these phenomena, at least in the tests used by Guetzkow.

We can understand this seeming paradox if we keep in mind that it is probably quite sensible to continue to use the set during the criticals since it has become a habit which saves time. Thus the establishment of a set does not necessarily distinguish the thinking abilities of individuals. Those who are susceptible to the set and who give very stereotyped "solutions" on the two-string problem, however, are not only using a habit but have become "slaves" to habit. Hence they would also show low recovery from set. Similarly those who break the set in the criticals would undoubtedly recover easily from set and also would be more likely to show "original" solutions on the two-string problem. What makes the highly stereotyped different from the highly flexible is not yet known. Indeed, it is very doubtful that there is a general personality trait although a few "pathological" persons might be generally constricted; at least, this seems to be the case in certain kinds of schizophrenia and in obsessive-compulsive neurotics. But for the general population it is probably more nearly true that stereotyped thinking is specific to certain kinds of tasks, usually those in which the subject does not feel very confident or secure.

Some support for what I have written in this chapter comes from an experiment by Van De Geer (1957, pp. 89–116), who has thrown some light on the nature and specificity of stereotyped thinking. In a well-conceived, well-controlled factorial study in which he systematically investigated the effects of six variables and the possible interaction between them, he obtained the following significant findings.

1. The set effect is strengthened when the set is an instrumental process, i.e., when there are factors motivating S to stick to the *Einstellung* solution. In Van De Geer's experiment this strengthening was accomplished by preceding the *Einstellung* problem with two unsolvable problems. The group which had this experience showed a significantly greater number of E solutions than a control group which did not have the unsolvable problems. The effect of these problems presumably produced some motivating state, such as a fear of failure. When the solution by the E method in the *Einstellung* problems reduced this fear (or anxiety) drive, its effect was strengthened. Other, more long-term experimental effects could be pro-

duced, for example, by a fear of failure induced by feeling relatively incompetent in the problem area required by the task.

2. In keeping with previous findings, the girls being tested, even without special experimental motivating conditions, showed more of the *Einstellung* effect than the boys. Two or three different conditions showed this sex difference. For example, while the number of set problems did generally seem to be an important variable, it was even a stronger producer of the strength of set in the females than in the males. One additional point of interest, however, throws some light on the specificity of this sex difference. While the girls required more time to solve the first extinction problem, no difference in solution time was found in the second extinction problem. Van De Geer concluded that this showed that while the girls may have trouble in surmounting set, once this has been achieved they do not persist in using the *Einstellung* solution. He reasoned that the difficulty in surmounting set cannot be attributed to difference in ability but presumably to difference in motivating conditions (internal) for the two sexes. This induction is supported by the fact that the difference in susceptibility to and recovery from set were not related to intelligence.

Van De Geer's conclusion that the *Einstellung* effect (especially the process involved in surmounting it) is probably related to motivating conditions which are threatening opens up very interesting research possibilities. First of all, it links the effect of set on thinking to the influence of set on perception, which we discussed in Chapter 12. The hypothesis-information theory of Bruner and Postman [1] is relevant here. For example, they too stated that the effect of an hypothesis is stronger if it is part of instrumental activity. The attempt that we made in Chapter 12 to link certain general perceptual (response) effects to personality variables also is relevant. It would be very instructive to continue this work on thinking by performing such experiments as determining whether we can use stimuli or problem traits which are inherently more threatening to males (as opposed to arithmetic, which is more threatening in general to females) and then find out whether boys in this case show a stronger *Einstellung* effect. This field has great research potential.

Summary

As a transition from Chapter 12, the present chapter began with a report of Reed's experiment in which it was found that a positive set to discover the meaning of the nonsense syllables facilitates the attainment of concepts in the modified memory method. This was followed by a detailed analysis of the influence of set, defined as a perception which is structured within narrow bounds that facilitate a certain specific type of activity or thinking.

It was pointed out that the great impetus for the experimental work on mental set could be traced to the work of the Würzburg school,

[1] See, for example, Bruner (1951); Postman (1951).

which began at the beginning of the twentieth century under the direction of Kulpe. Adopting the presentational psychology of the Wundtian structuralists, these psychologists began by investigating the nature of association involved in thinking. Their method was concerned mainly with the introspective analysis of consciousness. One of the greatest outcomes of these investigations was the conclusion that thinking can occur without calling up images for presenting knowledge to consciousness. This was a negation of the structuralist position and led to the imageless-thought controversy, which ended in a stalemate. While no agreement was reached about the contents of thought, all concluded that thinking is usually accompanied by a "state of consciousness."

A more positive contribution of the Würzburg school was Watt's demonstration that a preliminary adoption of tasks facilitates reaction to stimulus words which are presented later. Watt postulated that the acceptance by the subject of the various tasks, as defined by the experimenter, leads to the development of task sets (*Aufgaben*) which are characterized by reproductive tendencies. Selz, going even further, criticized the Würzburgers for separating the task and its reproductive tendencies. In its place, he postulated that thought consists of a unitary task which is productive. The production consists of the completion of past experiences.

Although Selz made an important advance when he thus emphasized the integrative nature of thought, he was criticized by the gestalt psychologists, who maintained that productive thinking consists of the reorganization of past experience to meet the requirements of the present problem situation. This theoretical advance led further to the distinction between the positive and negative effects of set as they influence the direction of thought, particularly as shown in the research of Maier, Duncker, and Luchins. Finally, some evidence was reported to suggest that susceptibility to set is universal, although individuals who are particularly trained in a specific area might be more resistant to adopting a narrow set in that area. But it seems more probable that individuals can be differentiated with respect to their tendency to recover from a restrictive set. The work of Guetzkow and Van De Geer, for example, suggests that this difference might be related to motivating conditions which are threatening and thus to specific personality variables.

The major advance which was made in the movement which began with the Würzburg school and ended with the gestalt research was that the investigation of thinking moved away from analyzing the contents of thought to studying the act of thought as the process of thinking. This was experimentally more desirable because of the greater objectivity which became possible.

14

Concept
Formation
and Language

A critical analysis of the principles of cognitive behavior indicates that concept formation is the process which bridges the gap between perception, learning, and thinking. An adequate treatment of cognition must thus describe how these three processes are interrelated, and this will be attempted in this chapter.

In the first twelve chapters we analyzed the evidence which supports the view that perceptual phenomena can be described on various levels of an ordinal hierarchy. This can be called the *organizational-levels* approach. The view taken was that perception is the primary process involved in man's adjustment to his environment. Perception is first concerned with man's reception and meaningful interpretation of information received through his senses. It was found that the reaction to some of these informational patterns is primarily unlearned (e.g., whiteness perception) while the response to certain more complex patterns is learned (e.g., patterns of identity).

When we say that perception is involved with man's adjustment to the world, we are acknowledging its functional role. Functionalistic interpretations of perception have also been given by other psychologists, as discussed in Chapter 12. Just as perception is concerned with the reception and interpretation of information, so is thinking concerned with the manipulation of this information in order to adjust to the world and to solve problems. One of the best aids to effective thinking is the formation of concepts through learning, which involves the operation of generalizing a similar property or properties over stimulus dimensions and abstracting this property to form a class or category. The main function that such conceptualization serves is to reduce the number of alternative responses we make to information received and thereby to facilitate the manipulation involved in thinking and problem solving.

It will be remembered that the more complex aspects of the perceptual process already involve the formation of simple concepts. In the perception of these phenomena learning plays an important role. Thus Fields (1932) showed that rats have great difficulty in learning to respond to the concept of form (e.g., triangularity), and the author (1954) found that rats can learn the identity of forms only after much training. Just as we find this level of complexity and difficulty in perception, we also find it in the process of concept formation. As a matter of fact, Osgood (1953, p. 283) has suggested that certain responses, such as the perceptual constancies, already involve concept formation. If we accept this statement, we see that the perception of identity, the relational aspects of the constancies, and the meaning of form represent levels of conceptualization. We shall learn further that the ease with which concepts are formed can also be ordered on a hierarchy, depending on the stimulus characteristics and relationships, the species of the organism, age, experience, and so on. We turn now to a detailed examination of this process of concept formation.

Process of Forming Concepts

One of the important dimensions of good thinking relates to how well we can group elements which go together on the basis of some logical or other relationship. When we do this, we say that we are using concepts in our thinking. When, for example, the child can use the name "doggy" to designate a stimulus configuration containing fur and four legs, we commonly agree that he has learned the concept "dog." But this commonsense definition does not tell us whether the child has actually learned to *generalize* the essential attributes of dog correctly—i.e., by *abstracting* the common characteristics and limiting the generalization by accurate *discrimination*— or whether he has merely learned a simple discriminative label. Thus we know that when a young child learns to say the word "dog," he often over-generalizes it to include all four-legged animals. This usage is overgeneralization; the concept has not become sufficiently differentiated. It appears that the use of language for identification purposes develops in the child from the general to the specific. On the other hand, the concepts used by children are generally limited to relatively concrete characteristics. As a matter of fact, this tendency is used as a criterion for measuring intelligence in various tests. Thus if a child says that oranges and bananas are similar because they both have skins, this is considered a less abstract (i.e., more concrete) and thus a less intelligent answer than the answer that they are similar because both are fruits. If we stop to consider the possible range of difficulty of concept formation, we shall see that it extends from simple concepts, in which the information containing the common attributes is carried in the stimulus characteristics (e.g., form), to highly abstract and difficult concepts, in which the information is hidden and depends on some logical definition (e.g., the concepts of fascism and democracy). By "hidden" we mean that the concept attributes are not contained in the physical stimulus complex; i.e., the concept is intangible.

The question which naturally suggests itself is how we are able to form these concepts, i.e., what the common attributes or characteristics are on the basis of which we form effective concepts.

Characteristics Abstracted in Concept Formation

Experiments which have attempted to answer this question have been performed within the framework of one of four theoretical approaches, as described by Osgood. There are those who believe that the concept is formed on the basis of certain *identical elements* possessed by the objects of the concept. Thus we might respond to the concept of the color "red" and thus group all red objects together, irrespective of their shapes, uses, and so on. Or we might define the concept "house" as that class which contains the identical elements—doors, windows, rooms, floors, ceilings, and so on—and ignore the differences in color, shape, and architectural design.

A second group of psychologists believes that a concept is defined by some common *relationship* or configuration. Thus the concept "circle" is applied to all round objects like plate, moon, ball, and dime despite the other differences which exist. All contain the gestalt property of roundness. Then there are those who have defined a concept not on the basis of stimulus characteristics but on that of some common *function* served by the instances of the concept. Thus, trains, ships, automobiles, buses, streetcars, and aircraft belong to the concept "vehicle." This functional designation of a concept can be extended even to concepts which are based on logical similarities. The concept "democracy" includes those political systems in which freedom of the individual is of primary importance, while fascism refers to those systems in which the authority of the government or the state is of first importance.

It should be obvious that these three approaches are not mutually exclusive. Some concepts could be formed on the basis of identical elements, others by involving some relationship, and still others according to some function. Osgood has probably given us the most general common characteristic found in concept formation. He states that perhaps "the only essential common characteristic is that a group of discrete situations be associated through learning with the *same mediating or symbolic reaction*. Beets, pole beans, and spinach would certainly be classed as 'vegetables,' yet there are neither any identical elements nor any common perceptual relations" (Osgood, 1953, p. 666). Osgood's designation, which thus emphasizes the cortical basis of concept formation, would subsume the first three approaches listed and also include the cases involving the utilization of hidden information in such concepts as prejudice, liberal, calculus, and so on. But while such a general designation of the common characteristic of concept formation is more inclusive, we must still look for the various specific factors leading to this common symbolic reaction. Let us thus go ahead and see how adequate the various alternative theoretical approaches are in explaining the common characteristics of concept formation.

IDENTICAL ELEMENTS. The classic study using this approach was performed by Hull (1920), who reasoned that concepts are formed in everyday life by abstracting common elements. As an illustration, he discussed how he thought that a child learned the concept of dog. A child might first find himself in a situation, respond to it in a certain way, and hear the word "dog." Later he is in a different situation and again hears the word "dog." This time he is not anticipating dog and consequently reacts differently. Eventually, after many unpredictable situations in which the word is heard, the child learns to abstract the common elements of the dog in these situations. He has then learned the meaning of "dog," or the concept "dog."

Following this reasoning, Hull performed an experiment in which 144 Chinese characters were drawn on cards. The cards were divided into 12 packs, each containing 12 cards, and each pack consisted of one instance of each of the 12 concepts which Hull used. Each card was exposed to the subject for 5 sec by means of a modification of the Wirth memory apparatus. After each card had been presented, the experimenter uttered a nonsense syllable which was associated with that character. The subject was merely told to learn the label, i.e., the nonsense syllable connected with each card. He was not told, or given a set, to abstract the common elements forming the concept since Hull had assumed that concepts are formed on a more or less accidental basis in real life.

After the subject had gone through the first pack in this manner, he was requested to state what the label of each character was. If he could not do so, the experimenter would prompt him or tell him what the label was. This procedure was continued from pack 2 to pack 12. The first 6 packs were considered the learning series, and the last 6 packs the test series. The test series was graded in order of difficulty. The three measures of concept acquisition used were (1) the ability to state the label of the concept when the learning series was repeated, (2) the number of promptings required during the learning and test series, and (3) a drawing of each concept or identical elements of each character.

From his results Hull concluded that the development of concepts followed the course of typical discrimination-learning situations. Typical learning curves were obtained. Thus a greater number of labels were named as the learning and test series progressed, and fewer promptings were required. Moreover, *there appeared to be no advantages in learning a concept by gradually proceeding from a simple instance to more complex instances* rather than vice versa.

It is doubtful, however, whether Hull actually studied the process of concept formation. This is evident in the fact that the subjects had difficulty in drawing the concepts despite the fact that a learning curve had been achieved. It seems rather that Hull was studying the development or learning of labeling, as Osgood has pointed out. Thus the subject learned the name which went with some of the identical elements in each concept. He achieved some measure of abstracting common elements and attaching a label to them. Smoke (1932) thinks that this was rather a study of abstracting. But the actual abstraction or generalization of the essential relationships which defined the concept was not studied by Hull or learned by his subjects. Such "genuine" concepts are usually more complex and probably involve higher-order learning. In this case we might expect learning of these concepts to be facilitated if the subject went from simpler to more complex instances rather than vice versa. This, of course, Hull did not find. But more research is needed in this area. Let us then go ahead and examine the studies based on the assumption that concepts involve the abstraction and generalization of common relationships.

COMMON RELATIONSHIPS. Smoke criticized Hull's experiment by pointing out that, in everyday life, concepts are rarely characterized by distinguishing identical elements or class marks. Rather, says Smoke, concepts are defined by the common perceptual relationships which are used. Thus, to study the formation of concepts as they occur in more usual situations, he performed the following experiments. Examples of 10 concepts were drawn in the form of geometrical designs on pieces of cardboard, each of which was given a nonsense-syllable label. Figures illustrating each concept varied in color, size, shape, width of line, and so on, but they always contained a common fundamental relationship. Thus, DAX was defined as a circle and two dots, one dot being within and the other without the boundary of the circle; MIB, as a triangle and a line extending at right angles from its shortest line; POG, as a blue rectangle enclosing a blue circle that touches only the long side of the rectangle; and so on. Examples of a positive and a negative instance of MIB are shown in Figure 14-1.

From the examples of the definitions given and the drawing presented in the figure, it can be seen that a relationship capable of being defined and verbalized exists between the instances of each concept despite the fact that it would be extremely difficult, if not impossible, to specify any identical elements. It is the gestalt or configurational pattern which defines the concept.

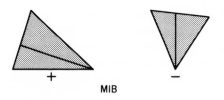

Figure 14-1
Example of a correct and an incorrect instance of MIB. (*From the materials used in the concept-formation experiment of Smoke, 1932.*)

In Smoke's experiment the cards containing the figures were mechanically exposed to the subject. For each concept the subject was told that he would see a number of drawings, each of which would be called, for example, a DAX. Then the 16 instances illustrating that concept were exposed serially. In the main experiment the subject could substitute another figure by pressing a contact key and could raise his hand when he thought he knew what, for example, DAX was. This sequence was repeated for the 10 concepts. Twenty subjects were used.

Three criteria for mastery of the concept were employed: (1) verbal definition; (2) drawing; and (3) choosing examples of the correct instance from a series of figures containing "correct" and "incorrect" designs. Smoke found that the subjects could generally meet the last two criteria without necessarily meeting the first. *Thus a subject can form and use a concept without verbalization.* The experiment also demonstrated that concepts based on the common features of material more complex than that used by Hull can be formed even when no identical elements exist. Therefore, the formation of concepts does not necessarily follow the gradual acquisition course of ordinary discrimination. The insight into the common perceptual relationship may come quite suddenly. Another psychologist who emphasizes the role of perceptual relationships in concept attainment is Heidbreder. We now begin an examination of her work.

FUNCTIONAL ROLE. The role of common functions was propounded by Heidbreder (1946a; 1946b; 1947; 1948), who also emphasized the importance of perceptual and situational supports in the formation of concepts. She used a method which was similar to Hull's and materials which were similar to Smoke's, in that the concepts were defined by some common relationship. Nine concepts were used in one experiment, three of concrete objects, three of spatial forms, and three of abstract numbers. Sixteen series of drawings were presented to each subject. Each series consisted of nine drawings, each of which contained a different instance of the nine concepts. Each drawing was presented on a memory drum and was followed by a nonsense label. There were nine labels, one for each concept. After the first series the subject was requested to anticipate the label of each drawing before the label was presented. Two criteria of learning were used: (1) the number of the series in which the first correct anticipation of the nonsense label was made and (2) the number of the series after which the subject consistently gave the correct nonsense label to all instances of the concept. The results of the second criterion are presented in Table 14-1.

Table 14-1

The Mean of the Number of Series on Which the Subjects Consistently Gave the Correct Label for Each of the Concepts.
(*After Heidbreder, 1946a, p. 192.*)

Concrete Objects			Spatial Forms			Abstract Numbers		
Face	(RELK)	3.35	◯ (FARD)	4.46		2	(LING)	6.14
Building	(LETH)	3.48	✗ (PRAN)	5.05		6	(MANK)	8.76
Tree	(MULP)	3.94	◖ (STOD)	5.19		5	(DILT)	10.22

From these results Heidbreder concluded that the concepts of concrete objects are attained most readily, with spatial objects next and abstract numbers last. Why should this be so? According to Heidbreder (1945), the perception of concrete objects is the dominant mode of cognitive reaction, related to the phylogenetic priority of the locomotive and manipulative capacities of the organism. The perception of spatial objects, however, is phylogenetically more primitive and is not so dominant in human beings. Abstracting numbers, on the other hand, like the use of other highly abstract symbols, is even more uncommon and requires more than "mere" perception.

Heidbreder summarizes her view by stating that the rate of concept attainment is facilitated by the degree of *situational support* provided by the instances of each concept. Thus the concepts of concrete objects were attained readily because such objects were immediately given by the drawing. Consequently the subject had to do no more than group all the faces together, all the buildings (houses, etc.) together, and all the trees together. But with the spatial objects a higher level of abstraction was required. Thus one circle consisted of a clock and another of a wreath, a church had a cross inside it, and so on. In the concrete objects the subject merely grouped similar objects together; in the spatial form he had first to ignore the differences in the functional meaning of the objects and abstract the common circular form. Moreover, we note that it was easier to group the familiar forms (circle) than the less familiar forms (labeled PRAN and STOD). Heidbreder, however, dismissed the importance of familiarity. Lastly, we notice that the number concept involved the highest degree of abstraction because it received the least amount of situational support; i.e., in these cases the defining characteristic was not found in the objects per se but required some abstract process like counting.

While we would agree with Heidbreder that the situational support is an important determiner of concept attainment, we wonder about the generality of her explanation in terms of the dominant cognitive reaction. There are many variables which must be considered. In the first place, her materials favored the concrete objects. This fact was supported in the last paragraph when we noted that the concrete-object instances contained only drawings of the concrete object, whereas the spatial forms, for example, contained other objects or elements in addition to the forms (e.g., the cross in the circle). Thus the level of abstraction required was not controlled.

A similar criticism was made by Dattman and Israel (1951), who believed that Heidbreder's order was influenced by the fact that the concrete-form instances were perceptually more effective than instances of the other two concepts. When they controlled for this by making equivalent the directness with which each instance expressed the concept (e.g., the presence of features which were irrelevant to that concept), the order was not obtained. Heidbreder (1952) has replied that Dattman and Israel misinterpreted her views as evidenced by their equating the terms *conceptual capacities* and *perceptual equivalences* with her terms *conceptual processes* and *situational support*. Furthermore, she claimed that they did not test her hypothesis since they did not provide "restricted situational support" for the spatial concepts vs. the concrete objects. Part of the difficulty in understanding the controversy here might be that Heidbreder has not given a clear operational definition of situational support. It seems to the present writer that greater situational support was provided by her concrete objects because of the functional relevance and adaptiveness of these objects for the everyday life of average people. It would seem very profitable to test my assumption by using experience and age as a variable. Her experiments were performed with college students. We might find that in young, relatively inexperienced children the perceptual reaction to color and regular spatial forms (good gestalts) might be more dominant. This is in keeping with what we might expect from the facts of hierarchical organization of perception, discussed in Chapter 2.

So it seems that the factor of past experience was not controlled in Heidbreder's study. Moreover, she used female college students. It is quite likely that people using numbers quite frequently (mathematicians, accountants, and so on) might have responded more readily to the number concepts, a supposition which leads to the third point. The functional meaning of the spatial forms was clearly less apparent to these subjects than the functional meaning of building and tree, the concrete objects. This we can infer from the kinds of experience we have in our culture.

These criticisms are not meant to dismiss Heidbreder's important findings and conclusions. We agree with her that situational support is an important determiner of concept attainment. In fact, in other studies (Baum, 1954; D. A. Grant, 1951) which were well controlled Heidbreder's order was confirmed. Attempts to extend learning theory to explain these findings are offered by Baum. We cannot say, however, that reaction to concrete objects is always the more dominant perceptual reaction in human beings. The dominance of perceptual reactions depends, among other factors, on the nature of the stimulus, the age of the individual, and his relevant past experience. Experiments concerned with these aspects will be discussed below.

COMMON MEDIATION PROCESS. Osgood, an example of a psychologist extending learning theory, as mentioned above, theorizes that the formation of concepts in everyday life and in the experiments of Heidbreder and others is based on a common mediation process. When we think of such countries as Japan, England, Spain, and Russia, we can hardly say that they contain any common elements, perceptual relations, or functional equivalence, and yet we group them into the concept "countries." As Osgood states, "It would seem that the only *essential* condition for concept formation is the learning of a common mediating response (which is the meaning of the concept) for a group of objects or situations" (1953, p. 668). He asserts that identical elements and common perceptual relations merely facilitate the establishment of such mediations. This theoretical direction is certainly more general than the other positions adopted. We would add that the common functional uses also facilitate the development of such mediations and that we should be searching for other possible ways of facilitating the development of these mediators which underlie the meaning of concepts.

The common mediation process is applied to Heidbreder's finding in the following way. Osgood's explanation of Heidbreder's data emphasizes two factors: (1) the comparative *availability* of the correct mediation processes and (2) the comparative degree of *interference* among potential mediators. Thus the concrete objects and the familiar spatial form would have mediation processes which were more available. One way of checking this conclusion would be to show a picture to a group of subjects and tell them to state which label first occurred to them. Osgood reports that such informal checking usually elicited concrete names first. An experiment of the author, reported in the next section, supports this finding. Unfamiliar forms would have zero availability. But why were the number concepts attained last? Probably this occurred because other mediators were interfering with the number mediators. This explanation is highly plausible since many of the objects which were grouped in the number category consisted of such high-availability concepts as glasses, sponges, and other concrete objects, which would undoubtedly create a lot of interference. Baum, previously cited, also interpreted his data in terms of interference and intrusion errors.

Of course, many questions remain to be answered. What determines the relative availability of mediators? Is the availability influenced by such variables as the age and experience of the subject? Answers to these and other questions will be attempted in the section "Conditions Affecting

Concept Formation," but more should first be said about Osgood's discussion of mediators.

In an attempt to establish the generalizable character of the mediation hypothesis to explain the ease of concept attainment, Osgood analyzed the studies of Reed (1946a; 1946b; 1946c) dealing with the learning and retention of concepts. Reed defined a concept as any word or idea that stands for any one of a group of things. His subjects were presented with a list of cards, each card containing four English words (e.g., coffee, pilot, clay, carrot), one of which was an instance of a given concept, like BEP. The nonsense syllable defining each concept was written on the back of each card and spoken by the experimenter after the card had been seen by the subjects. All BEP cards contained the word of one vegetable, all DAX cards the word of one color, and so on. The subjects had to learn the correct nonsense syllable that went with each card, like the concept which was common to each DAX card, and so on.

Osgood's analysis of what the subjects were required to do is stated in terms of the mediation hypothesis, a diagrammatic illustration of which is duplicated in Figure 14-2. The essential stages in the learning process, as diagramed in the figure, can be summarized in the following way. First, the subject has to discriminate the correct word in each list. Then the correct mediation responses r_m, e.g., thinking of beet as a vegetable, must be called up. This conceptualizing process requires very little additional effort since it was presumably learned prior to the experimental situation. The mediated response, e.g., thinking of vegetable, becomes the stimulus S_m to be associated with the correct nonsense syllable, e.g., BEP, as an overt response. How do the results of Reed fit this model?

The measure of learning used by Reed was the number of promptings required to learn the correct nonsense syllable for each card. The following results which support the mediation hypothesis were obtained by Reed. (1) Subjects who were given a set to look for general concepts—i.e.,

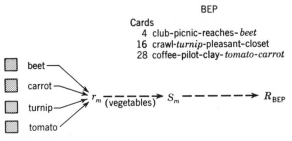

Figure 14-2
Sample materials in Reed's experiment on concept formation and a mediational model suggested as the learning paradigm involved. (After Osgood, 1953, p. 669.) The italicized word is the appropriate one for the specific category.

instructed that each nonsense syllable stood for a definite class of things—required fewer promptings than those who were merely instructed to learn the correct nonsense syllables for each card. The set presumably facilitated calling up the mediational response in the former group. (2) When the number of cards in the list was increased, only a slight increase in effort was required to learn the correct concept. This is consistent with the mediational hypothesis. Once the correct mediational response had been associated with the correct overt response (e.g., BEP for vegetable), additional vegetables would require little learning since the subject had learned the vegetable names prior to the experimental session. Whatever additional effort was required would be due to selecting the correct word from the list. Once this was identified, no new learning was required since the class "vegetable" had already been learned to be associated with BEP, and so on. (3) "Finally, the mediation hypothesis leads to the prediction that there would be no differences in degree of retention as the number of cards for each concept is increased. This is borne out neatly in Reed's data: the number of promptings per concept during relearning was .38 for the 24-card list, .91 for the 42-card list, and only .36 for the 60-card list, none of these differences being significant" (Osgood, 1953, pp. 670–671).

Enough has been said to support the view that the mediational process, usually of a linguistic nature, is the most general approach of those offered to account for concept formation. Of course, we still do not know exactly how the mediational process develops. This is essentially a learning problem, and the best we can say at present is that the construct of mediational process is used as an intervening variable.

Many years ago S. C. Fisher, working within the framework of the structural psychology of Wundt and Titchener, attempted to define the nature of the development of *ideas* (presumably similar to Osgood's mediation response) representing concepts by using the introspective method. Employing a technique similar to Smoke's, she presented her five subjects, all prominent psychologists of the introspection school, with four series of drawings, one series being completed before the next was presented, and so on. Each series contained 10 drawings and had a nonsense name attached to it. There were similar features in all of the 40 drawings, but the 10 of a particular series had a defining characteristic which was the concept. Under each card of each series the nonsense name was printed, the names being ZALOF, DERAL, TEFOG, and KAREG. The instructions were: "You are to be shown a series of ten drawings of figures which represent a group or species. The group name will be shown with every drawing; it is Zalof (or Deral, etc.). These drawings do not represent real objects; they are to be regarded merely as objects. Do not attempt to associate them with familiar objects, but confine your definition to what is shown. If such associations occur spontaneously, however, do not inhibit them. Each drawing will be followed immediately by another. After all have been exposed, you will be given the task of defining the group name Zalof (or Deral, etc.). You will be asked to furnish detailed introspective accounts not only of your experiences during the examination of the series but also of the mental processes involved in defining the group name" (Fisher, 1916).

At a stated interval, usually a week after the original presentation, the subject was asked to define each of the four nonsense names together with detailed introspective reports. He was then permitted to inspect the drawings again and was asked to continue his introspections and change or modify his definitions, as he wished. This was repeated until no new features were discovered.

The most significant finding of Fisher's experiment was that the concept developed gradually. At the beginning of the process the imagery was predominantly of the visual type, which was followed by a verbal type, and the process gradually became mechanized until all imagery disappeared in recall. So the concept eventually came "to stand by itself," with no sensory or imaginal content present, or at least no sensory or imaginal content which could be verbally expressed.

While these subjective reports might tell us something about the gradual learning process involved in concept formation, it is difficult to state how much reliability we can place on subjective reports. Whether in fact we can develop objective measurement of the mediational process is an open question although some attempts have been made to answer it. If the process is used merely as an intervening variable, we need only specify the antecedent conditions (independent or stimulus variables) which affect the overt response of the concept class (the dependent variable). Let us then go ahead and examine the conditions which determine the availability of concepts and the ease with which concepts are learned.

Conditions Affecting Concept Formation

It is apparent from what has been written in the preceding sections that psychologists, such as Osgood, have become dissatisfied with the traditional theories used to explain the nature of concept formation. The classical stimulus-response theories of learning and the theories based on perceptual principles are inadequate because they have neglected to consider organismic variables. Similarly, the information theory developed by the communication engineers, which treats information transmission in terms of input to and output from a channel, has been an interesting framework but is too mechanistic when applied to the complex and variable human organism. These theories must be modified to handle the complex nature of the mediational process within the individual.

We have stated earlier that it is extremely difficult to study the nature of the mediational process directly, but we can study the effects of certain antecedent conditions on the ease of concept formation. We can infer that the observed changes in the overt behavior involved in manipulating concepts are a result of the ways the antecedent conditions affect the mediational process. In thus attempting to organize the factors influencing concept formation, we see that they can conveniently be classified into *stimulus conditions* and *organismic conditions.*

NATURE OF THE STIMULUS MATERIAL. We have already discussed the limitations of Heidbreder's view that if cognitive reactions are arranged in an hierarchy, the order of dominance is usually concrete, spatial, and number concepts. This generalization is limited by, at least, the nature of stimulus material and the age and experience of the individual. Dattman and Israel have also pointed out that Heidbreder's results may have resulted from the inequalities in the perceptual effectiveness (situational support) provided by the instances in her material. Consequently, in their experiment they provided instances which were equivalent in directedness and effectiveness of the features to be conceptualized. For example, the "disadvantage" of the circle concept in Heidbreder's experiment, in which it had to be abstracted by ignoring the nature of the objects involved, was controlled. The directedness of all the other spatial, concrete, and number concepts was controlled also, but in other respects Heidbreder's study was essentially replicated. From their results these authors argued that "when Heidbreder's materials were altered so as to supply equivalent perceptual instances uniformly over the three categories, the order among the categories disappeared" (Dattman and Israel, 1951). They concluded that they had confirmed the principle that the relative ease with which concepts are attained is directly dependent upon the degree of perceptual effectiveness with which the instances serve to present the features to be conceptualized. We have already described Heidbreder's answer.

This principle has been verified in two experiments by D. A. Grant and his associates. In the first experiment, Grant, Jones, and Tallanis (1949) presented each of their 96 college subjects with a pack of 64 cards. Each card contained a drawing which simultaneously provided an instance of a color concept, a spatial-form concept, and a number concept. The subjects had to sort the cards into four labeled compartments without further instructions except that each sorting of a card would be called "right" or "wrong" by the experimenter. The four labeled compartments were a single red triangle, two green stars, three yellow crosses, and four blue circles.

At first the experimenter arbitrarily called the cards "right" if they were sorted according to *color;* but after 10 consecutive correct sortings according to this principle he shifted without warning to *form,* and then after a few trials to *number,* and then once more around the list of concepts. Of course, sometimes the subject would start with number, in which case the experimenter would shift in order to the other two concepts, and so on. It took the subjects only 3 or 4 trials, on the average, to discover the first rule but 14 trials to discover the first unexpected shift. On the second time around they discovered the first shift in 13 trials, on the third round in 9 trials, and so on, until they finally discovered it in less than 8 trials.

On the basis of which concept was mastered first and the ease with which a subject shifted from one subject to another, the authors presented the following results. Sorting on the basis of the color concept was more difficult than sorting on the basis of form, which in turn was more difficult than sorting on the basis of number. The last two concepts were in the reverse order to that found by Heidbreder. Why the difference? Grant pointed out that it was probably attributable to the special features of the instances of the number concepts in the Wisconsin Card Sorting Test, which was used as the pack of cards in this experiment. The number concepts were arranged as follows in this test: "*One* consisted of a single figure always centered, *two* consisted of two figures along the principal diagonal of the card, *three* figures always formed an equilateral triangle, and *four* figures always formed a square" (D. A. Grant, 1951). Thus the subjects could have been sorting according to the configurational principle rather than number.

To control for the last-mentioned variable, Grant and Curran (1953) repeated the previous experiment, except that they increased the purity of the number concept by removing the constant configurational aspect. The results showed that sorting by number was especially difficult at the beginning of the process. These results are more nearly in line with Heidbreder's findings. The authors also found that sorting by color was more difficult than by form and number, which were of approximately equal difficulty.

An experiment which neatly demonstrates how concept attainment is facilitated by the extent to which the informational aspects of the concept are directly contained in the stimulus dimensions was performed by Welch and Long (1940). Being concerned with the hierarchical arrangement of concepts, they studied the acquisition of concepts at various levels of abstraction. The subjects consisted of 103 children between the ages of forty-two and eighty-three months. Using the prompting method, the children were first taught that a certain triangle was called MEF, another triangle TOV, a certain rectangle YOP, another rectangle ZIL, and so on. This kind of associative learning, which requires abstraction, was mastered quite readily by the children.

The experimenters then proceeded to test a first and a second level of abstraction. A sample of the test materials used together with the nonsense labels (concept names) is shown in Figure 14-3. The children were told that all triangles belonged to the class VIC, and all rectangles to the class DAX. They were able to learn these class names, VIC and DAX, at the first level of abstraction, fairly well: 66 per cent reached the criterion for the triangles, while 67 per cent reached it for the rectangles. Finally, the children who passed the first level were taught that all triangles and rectangles, i.e., all forms called either VIC or DAX, were to be called XIP. Only 29 per cent of the children were able to meet the criterion of learning this more difficult concept at the second level of abstraction.

The investigators concluded that "it is easier for a child to learn to identify three objects than to learn to identify a hierarchical structure of two objects and their class." Moreover, mastering a second hierarchical structure of four objects and three class concepts proved to be a still more difficult task.

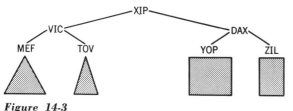

Figure 14-3
Sample of materials in a study of concepts involving various levels of abstraction. (After Welch and Long, 1940.)

To test further how well they had learned the meanings of the concepts and their class names, the experimenters then investigated the children's ability to follow commands involving these names. They were readily able to put all the objects in the correct piles when no level of abstraction was required. Then they were commanded to put all the VICs together and all the DAXs together (first level of abstraction), and later all the XIPs in the middle of the table (second level of abstraction).

They made many errors when obeying commands at the first level of abstraction, but obeying commands at the second level turned out to be easier than expected. This suggests that although more abstract concepts are more difficult to learn, their attainment can be facilitated by a learning procedure which involves the gradual progression into higher levels of abstraction. This leads nicely into the consideration of age and experiential variables, which we shall now consider.

AGE AND EXPERIENCE. The experiments discussed in the last section which were performed by Dattman and Israel, Grant et al., and Welch and Long indicate that Heidbreder's idea of establishing a dominance hierarchy of concepts is a sound one. The order that she attained is not a constant one, however, but depends on such factors as configurational principles and structure contained by the stimulus material and the age and relevant experience of the individual.

Heidbreder's finding that the order of dominance is concrete object, spatial form, and number holds pretty well for the adult experienced human being. It has been verified by Heidbreder, Bensley, and Ivy (1948) and by Wenzel and Flurry (1948). Moreover, Hines (1951), using a method similar to that of Reed, previously discussed, found that the learning of highly abstract concepts like discipline and religion requires twice as much practice as the learning of concrete concepts, like tree.

It would seem that the privileged status of concrete concepts can be attributed to the fact that their functions are more readily apprehended from the nature of the information transmitted by their instances. If this is so, then it follows that they will be more readily available for use in solving problems. The history of science and knowledge in general is full of examples which support this principle. Concepts like vitamins, germs, and atoms are assimilated more readily than concepts involving the use of electronic fields and mathematical relationships. Moreover, it has always been easier to blame a "bad" person for his delinquent behavior and to say that he chose to do wrong than it has been to understand his behavior in terms of experiential influences and other personality influences, such as "unconscious" motivation. Educators could make greater use of this principle when teaching the difficult formalistic concepts of science and philosophy. They have attempted to facilitate the mastery of numerical concepts, the structure of chemical compounds, and the like by translating them into graphic and spatial forms or by constructing visual models. But more can be done by translating the formalistic content of mathematics into statements which are related to the functional experience of the child. This he understands more easily, and after he has mastered these relationships, it will be easier to proceed progressively to the more formalistic relationships which involve higher and higher levels of abstraction. We shall have much more to say about this in our later chapters on problem-solving activity.

That the familiar functional use of objects exerts a primary influence on how they are conceptualized has been demonstrated in other experiments. In a repetition of some of the original studies of Duncker (1945) on problem solving, Adamson (1952), using a greater number of subjects and more specific conditions, confirmed Duncker's conclusion that "problem solving may in some instances be delayed through the *functional* fixedness of solution objects." [1] This means that if an object has previously been used in a function different from that demanded by the present problem, the subject is often inhibited in discovering the new function. Adamson and Taylor (1954) have also pointed out that the fixedness of an object probably results from its association with a particular function. It, therefore, becomes more difficult to use this object in a new function. Anything which weakens the association between an object and a specific function consequently tends to weaken the functional fixedness of that object. The way this might be done will be considered in the later chapters. Here we should emphasize that the functions which an individual can understand depend on his age and previous experience. There also is a dominant tendency to respond most readily to concrete functions. This principle

[1] Italics mine.

should clearly be applied to the differential selection of teaching materials and methods which should be used at different age levels.

An experiment which demonstrates that the dominance hierarchy of concept availability is determined by the interaction between the nature of the stimulus and the relevant past experience was performed by the author (Forgus and Fowler, 1957). Reasoning that the subject's past experience led to the dominance of the concepts of concrete things in Heidbreder's experiment, we set out to control for this variable. The card-sorting technique was used, and 240 college students, 120 males and 120 females, served as subjects. In the first experiment, in which 20 subjects of each sex were involved, a pack of 27 cards was used. Each card contained simultaneously an example of a concrete thing, a spatial form, and a color. There were three classes of concrete things (faces, trees, buildings), three classes of spatial forms (triangles, rectangles, ellipses), and three classes of colors (red, green, blue). Since one instance of each of the three concepts was presented simultaneously on each card, there were nine instances of each concept in the pack of 27 cards. The subject was merely told to sort the cards into three piles. The technique used was similar to the one employed by Grant in 1951 and Heidbreder in 1949. If the subject started to sort on the basis of color, he was permitted to continue this way until the entire pack was sorted. If during the first sorting he switched to either form or concrete concepts, he was told that this was wrong and was required to correct his error. Similarly, if the first sorting sequence was done on the basis of either form or concrete concepts, he had to stay with this criterion until the entire pack was sorted.

After he had successfully sorted the pack the first time, he was asked to sort it a second time by using another principle. Then he was required to sort it still a third time. Since we were interested in establishing the order of dominance in the availability of the three concepts, we assigned to each of the concepts a rank order of 1, 2, or 3, depending on the class criterion that the subject used for each sorting.

It will be noticed that the instances of the concepts used in the first experiment were all drawings of objects which were familiar to the college subjects (triangles, trees, etc.). In the five other experiments performed, each using 40 different subjects, the variable of experience was systematically changed. In other respects these experiments were essentially replications of the first experiment. The plan of the six experiments is shown in Table 14-2.

From the table it can be seen that we were able to study the influence of experience on the order of dominance of various types of concepts. When the instances of concrete things were to be nonexperiential (unfamiliar), for example, we used drawings of amoeba, hydra, and bryozoan. For unfamiliar spatial forms we used various nonsense geometrical forms, and so on. On the basis of the statistical analysis of the three sortings in each

Table 14-2

*Plan of the Six Experiments Testing the Dominance Hierarchy of Concepts.
E Means That the Instances Were Familiar; N, That They Were Unfamiliar.
(Forgus and Fowler, 1957.)*

Concept	Experiment					
	1	2	3	4	5	6
Concrete	E	N	N	E	N	E
Spatial	E	N	N	N	E	E
Color	E	N	E	E	E	N

of the six experiments, we drew the following conclusions: (1) Concepts
which are based on familiar experience are attained most readily. (2)
When experience is not favored, i.e., when nonexperiential instances are
used, spatial-form concepts are dominant, with color concepts next and
concrete things last. The second finding depends on sex, for women tend to
prefer thinglike concepts in general. The meaning of Heidbreder's results
becomes clearer. The concepts of concrete things are dominant because we
have probably had more experience with their functions. Somehow, in our
culture at least, women tend to generalize this experience to other concrete
things. This could result from the fact that women have less experience
with abstract things. They are generally engaged in types of work (as house-
wives, office clerks, etc.) which are less abstract than those engaged in by
men (as scientists, engineers, etc.).

Two generalities suggest themselves from the results of the last study:
(1) When experience is not present, concepts are most readily attained
when the stimulus structure is limited in information but high in redundancy. This is true of spatial forms which are regular and symmetrical and
of color which gives a lot of redundant information (we recall the primacy
of stimulus factors in color constancy). It is not true of "things" which are
nonregular and complex and require much learning for accurate discrimination. We have already discussed the limitation of this principle as far as
women in our culture are concerned. (2) When concept attainment is
based on familiar examples, the most functionally relevant objects (concrete
things) are most readily attained. The interaction between the nature of
the stimulus and the relevance of the individual in determining the dominance hierarchy of concepts (their relative availability, for example) is
expressed in these two generalizations.

INTELLIGENCE. Since functional intelligence is somewhat influenced by
what the individual has profited from in past experience, we might expect
to find some relationship between intelligence and conceptual ability.
Because concept formation involves abstraction, the ability to form con-

cepts would partly depend on the individual's ability to generalize. But individuals do not generalize in identical ways. Many of the investigators whom we cited—e.g., Hull, Smoke, Fisher, and Heidbreder—have pointed out that there are wide individual differences in how human beings go about forming concepts.

We might think that this difference is a reflection of differences in intelligence, but that there is one factor which can be called ability to conceptualize is doubtful. It seems rather that one individual can generalize better in one situation while others do better in another context. W. E. Vinacke has stated that children's performance on concept tests correlates only moderately with intelligence and vocabulary, indicating that "conceptualization is at least not identical with either general intelligence or vocabulary" and confirming the existence of a separate ability to conceptualize.

This ability to conceptualize, however, does contribute to general intelligence. Smoke reported a rank difference correlation of 0.52 between intelligence and ability to generalize. Ewert and Lambert (1932) reported a higher correlation between 0.86 and 0.93. Thus it seems reasonable to state that those who show the highest conceptual ability also score high on intelligence tests. In Chapter 15 we shall deal with the difference between young and older children in conceptual problem solving and also with the informational aspect of concept manipulation.

LANGUAGE EXPRESSION AND AGE. As a child develops in age, so does his mental ability. He becomes capable of solving more difficult problems, of understanding higher levels of abstraction. We have seen that Welch and Long found that it was very difficult for children between the ages of $3\frac{1}{2}$ and seven years to develop concepts requiring a second level of abstraction. It is easier to explain the meaning of dog to these young children than it is to explain the meaning of an abstract term, such as democracy. Since a child often expresses his thoughts in words, we are able to obtain an index of the development of his conceptual ability by studying his language expression at various ages. The scientist who has investigated this area more extensively than anyone else is the eminent Swiss psychologist Piaget (1928a; 1928b; 1930; 1932; 1950; 1952).[2]

An indication of Piaget's work can be obtained if we look at his analysis of the child's understanding of physical causality. In one illustration the experimenter blew puffs of air into the child's face by expanding and compressing cupped hands. When the experimenter asked where the air was coming from, the child replied, "Through the window." When asked whether the window was open, the child replied, "No, shut." "And yet the air could come through? . . ." "Yes." "How?" These four-year-olds do not identify air with the room or space around them but with the wind outside, and therefore it must be blown into the room. The eight-year-old identifies

[2] See also Flavell (1963).

wind with *concrete* objects. The wind blows or moves trees, papers, and so on.

In discussing the development of intelligence, Piaget (1950) points out that the seven- or eight-year-old is not capable of utilizing fairly abstract concepts like volume but responds to one aspect of this relationship, either the height or the width. This concreteness of thinking is also expressed in the concreteness of language. "Wind" cannot be detached from the concrete objects with which it is associated; it is in the trees and other objects which it moves. W. Stern (1924) has referred to the same behavior as *transductive inference*, by which he means that the child draws illogical deductions (from the adult point of view) from his experience. Werner (1940) has reached similar conclusions by noting that the child's thought and language are concrete and diffuse (holophrastic)—i.e., while the causes of things are linked to concrete objects, the child has not yet learned to separate identities; hence the diffuseness. In the child's phenomenal world objects and events are joined together illogically. Werner calls this *syncretic* thought.

Piaget has drawn his observations together and also concluded that the child's thinking is *global*. During early childhood (around four years of age) the world and the self are one: the self has not become differentiated as such. When the self does become a distinct entity (around eight years of age), the world is still not completely objective; it is conscious and full of intentions. This is borne out by the animistic nature of the child's language: "The wind caused the tree to blow," "The stone caused me to fall," as if they had animal intentions. Part of the child's internal experience adheres to the external world. The child believes that thoughts are in words themselves. Thus his language is a fairly direct expression of his inner thoughts. This conclusion seems highly plausible, despite the phenomenological nature of the data, when we examine the mass of observations and conversations of Piaget with children. It is only after much experience and a gradual development of the process of high abstraction that the child develops an objectivity toward the world. At this stage the self is clearly demarcated, objects and events in the world are separated, and language becomes more abstract, more specific, and less animistic, although the self and thought are regarded with a high degree of subjectivity.

Some psychologists might doubt the reliability of the age norms which Piaget presents. Some might expect the child to learn the syncretic aspects before the age of eight. Since there are, of course, wide individual differences, the establishment of age norms awaits verification from further studies; but the order of the stages of the development of thought and language seems logical. Vinacke (1951) has added that the development of concepts in the child goes from the *inductive* to the *deductive* stage. During the inductive stage, which lasts up to eight years of age, the child develops generalizations about his environment as a result of familiarity with it. The deductive stage which follows is characterized by greater abstraction whereby the child is able to employ already formed generalizations to deal appropriately with new objects and events or with familiar objects in new ways. Piaget has called this last phase, which is very apparent in the twelve- to fifteen-year-old, the stage of *formal operations* (which follows the earlier stage of concrete operations). During this stage of "higher" thinking, the child's thought is relatively free of concrete objects in the real world, and he is capable of reversing, recentering, and decentering relationships in his thought and thus of constructing new relationships. Vinacke has appropriately suggested that school curricula and teacher attitudes be guided by the particular needs of the children, which may be determined by whether the child is in the inductive or the deductive stage.

Language as a Medium of Concept Expression

Any discussion of concept formation must necessarily parallel a discussion of language, since words form the labels for concepts. Because this is so, we shall borrow heavily in this chapter from the work of Roger Brown (1958), who describes the process of the formation of a concept and the application of a linguistic label to that concept as "The Original Word Game." In this game Brown has schematized and simplified the process of language and concept learning to a minimum. His description of the game is an idealized situation in which two persons, the *tutor,* who knows the language, and the *player,* who is learning the language, participate in the formation and testing of a concept. "The tutor names things in accordance with the semantic custom of his community. The player forms hypotheses about the categorical nature of the things named. He tests his hypotheses by trying to name new things correctly. The tutor compares the player's utterances with his own anticipations of such utterances and in this way checks the accuracy of fit between his own categories and those of the player. He improves the fit by correction."

Let us imagine a situation in which you are standing on a busy street corner with an Eskimo friend, attempting to teach him English. You are the tutor; he is the player. As the tutor, you are attempting to teach him the different categories of motor vehicles which are passing by. You say "car" and point to one. He says "car" and points to a truck. You say, "No, truck," and so on into the afternoon. Soon your friend's concepts match your concepts rather accurately. He is able to name every motor vehicle which passes with the same word which you would use to describe it. You have successfully taught him to perceive objects in the motor-vehicle realm in the same fashion as you, to group them together into the same classes as you, and to apply the same labels as you to these objects, *on this particular level of abstraction.*

Obviously, any object may be classed with other objects, depending upon the level of abstraction chosen and the particular set of concepts chosen within that level. For example, a single automobile may be described in a variety of ways, depending upon the level of abstraction chosen and the particular way in which we wish to slice that level of abstraction. It may be variously termed a Ford, a convertible, a means of transportation, a blue object, a mechanical contrivance, Mr. Jones's car with serial number 170448227, a car of 1962 vintage, a mass of electrons, etc. There are almost an infinite number of ways to describe the car, to class it with other objects, to abstract certain qualities relevant for the topic under discussion. This state of affairs becomes more troublesome when you try to differentiate further the concept "car" by attempting to teach your friend to discriminate between brands of cars.

You point at a passing Ford convertible and, in your role of tutor, utter the proper combination of sounds, "Ford." The player nods, waits for another convertible to pass, and says, "Ford." He has responded to the wrong collection of attributes. You had in mind a certain set of criterial attributes which are relevant and essential for defining the concept of a Ford. He noted a particularly outstanding noncriterial attribute and responded by placing all cars having that attribute in the class "Ford," which, from your point of view, is incorrect.

For any concept there are criterial, defining attributes which are shared in common by members of that concept class and which distinguish them from nonmembers of that class. There are also, usually, noncriterial attributes to the members of that class. Sometimes these noncriterial attributes for a particular concept are criterial for another concept. For example, the noncriterial concept to which the Eskimo responded above is criterial for the formation of the class "convertibles." If, in pointing to the first car, you had said "convertible," your friend would have been correct in applying this concept to the second instance, but you chose to slice reality in a different way.

For the concept "Ford" the attribute "cloth-top" is noncriterial and "noisy" in current terminology (Bruner, Goodnow, and Austin, 1956). It is noisy because it is present in some members of the concept class, absent in other members, and both present and absent in nonmembers of the concept. Certain noncriterial attributes are "quiet," since they are present in all members of the class and in all nonmembers too. "Wheels," for example, is a quiet, noncriterial attribute for this particular concept-formation problem.

Obviously, the situation is not so simple as it may appear at first glance. For example, what is the criterial, defining attribute separating dogs from cats? It is probably an impossible task to define a single criterial attribute which you use to separate the two groups of animals. On the other hand, you can probably define many attributes which are more or less criterial for the distinction in question. The defining differences between dogs and cats probably form a subtle criterial gestalt or pattern which is difficult to analyze in terms of the relative contribution of each of its component parts. (See our previous discussion of common mediation.)

LINGUISTIC RELATIVITY AND LINGUISTIC DETERMINISM. If we study a foreign language, we probably have occasion to notice that different languages parcel out the same reality in slightly different ways. Certain concepts in foreign languages, we say, are "untranslatable." Words like *Zeitgeist, savoir-faire,* and *simpatico* lose some of their meaning when translated into English. Their characteristic flavor somehow disappears. It is a gross distortion of meaning to translate *savoir-faire* as "know-how," which seems to be describing a hardheaded American inventor-engineer-businessman rather than an urbane, poised French diplomat. What has become of all that meaning? Obviously the French word has been mistranslated. As an alternative to translating it with a single English word, we may find ourselves resorting to a phrase or, indeed, to an entire paragraph and still not quite feeling that the meaning has been entirely captured and remained undistorted. Obviously, the French have a word which describes a concept which is unavailable in English. Indeed, the word has all but entirely crept into the English language intact and unchanged with respect to meaning, as have many foreign words and phrases which bring with them a new container for meaning for which they serve as the label.

It is rare among Indo-European languages that perfect translation is not achieved for concrete nouns. Words such as "horse," "tree," etc., usually have perfect one-to-one equivalents. More abstract concepts, even very common ones, however, do not retain this perfect correspondence. For example, the verb "to be" in English corresponds to two verbs in Spanish: *estar* and *ser.* The Spaniard uses *estar* to denote a temporary state of being, while *ser* denotes a permanent state of being. For example, while it is a compliment to tell a Spanish woman that she *es* (a form of *ser*) beautiful, it is decidedly not a compliment to use the other verb form in the same sentence, since it implies that her beauty is due to cosmetics and that when she washes her face that particular state of beauty will be gone. Now, it is obvious, if only in the fact that explaining the meanings of *ser* and *estar* took several sentences rather than two single words, that they carry more meaning (i.e., more information is conveyed) than any single English word which would be used to translate them. Examples of this kind may be multiplied indefinitely.

To convince ourselves of this lack of correspondence between related languages on abstract terms we need only thumb through a language dictionary. The words which require the most space to define, presumably those lacking good correspondence, are quite abstract concepts, words such as "through," "by," "with," "is," "take," etc., which can stand for a variety of different relationships and together form to us, in English, a coherent concept, although one which is difficult, even in English, to define. Let us try defining "with." Even if we restrict the word to its most commonly used meanings, we shall find that a multiplicity of relationships are expressed with the one word. Obviously this may become a problem for a student of English who speaks another native tongue. In German, for example, depending upon its context, the word "with" may be translated as *mit, nebst, bei, über, durch, von, vor,* etc. The Germans simply do not have a word corresponding to our concept "with" and therefore lack that particular concept. On the other hand, if we attempt to translate one of the German words, *bei,* for example, into English, we find that there is an equally large collection of words from which we must select according to the context. *Bei* means about, amidst, amongst, at, with, in possession of, by, upon, at the house of, during, for, in company with, near, to, on, under penalty of, in connection with, along with, considering, in spite of, in the presence of, etc. And let us keep in mind that we are discussing linguistically related languages! We may imagine the extent of noncorrespondence between English and Chinese, for example.

A linguist, Benjamin Lee Whorf (1956), who worked primarily with North American Indian languages, was much impressed by the amount of noncorrespondence between English and these languages. Together with Edward Sapir, he formulated an hypothesis of linguistic relativity and linguistic determinism, generally called the Whorf hypothesis, which states that reality can be viewed in an infinite number of ways and that a language constitutes one particular way to view the world. Yet, Whorf goes a step further in espousing the principle of linguistic determinism. According to him, language determines thought. A language perpetuates the view of the world held by its speakers because it forces concept formation into a particular framework, dictated by the labels available to the language learner.

To take a most familiar example on a very concrete level, the Eskimo has three different words for "snow." In the first place, the fact that the Eskimo has more numerous words for snow than we have indicates that snow is more important to Eskimo culture than to ours and that consequently there is a need to differentiate the concept more fully than we do. Secondarily, Whorf would hold that the possession of these three labels enables the Eskimo to perceive subtler differences between types of snow than we do. To an Eskimo the three types of snow are as distinct, according to Whorf, as, for example, snow and sleet are to us. The Eskimo sees his world differently than we do, and the possession of a greater number of categories dealing with snow makes it easier for him to classify snowy events. If we switch roles with our Eskimo friend in playing "The Original Word Game," it may take us some time to discover the criterial attributes separating the three different concepts for snow. Nonetheless, it is possible for us to do so and for us to translate the three words into English, using a phrase of the general form: "snow which . . . ."

Here is another familiar example of linguistic relativity. The language of the Lakuti has a single word for "blue" and "green." Here is a case in which English is better differentiated. Further, let us consider the central, most easily classified colors for us and for the Lakuti. Perhaps a nice royal blue will fall right in the center of our blue category and an emerald green will be most easily codable as green. Blue green, on the other hand, is peripheral to both our concepts, but when the Lakuti classify colors, they have no difficulty in placing blue green, for it falls right in the middle of their concept.

The Whorf hypothesis is by no means uncritically accepted by contemporary linguists and psycholinguists. It is presented here in order to acquaint the student with one of the principal questions toward which a science of cognition must address itself: to what extent does language influence perception and thinking? For an interesting and productive attempt to quantify the meaning of words, the reader should see the technique known as the semantic differential, developed by Osgood and his associates (Osgood, Suci, and Tannenbaum, 1957).

Conceptualizing in Pathological Cases

BRAIN DAMAGE. Since it is plausible to suppose that the mediational process functions in the brain, it can be expected that the availability of concepts to the individual is also affected by the condition of his brain. This hypothesis has been supported during the last 30 years by the study of patients with brain pathology and abnormal personalities.

Some of the earliest studies in this area were reported by K. Goldstein and Gelb (1918; 1924), who investigated the intellectual impairment of German soldiers who had suffered brain damage during World War I. Among other things, they presented these soldiers with a collection of varicolored yarns (the Holmgren woolens) and asked them to sort these yarns according to certain classes. Although the soldiers could group a few yarns which closely resembled a test color, they appeared to be unable to generalize widely or to shift from one type of classification to another. The authors concluded that these brain-damaged patients exhibited a concrete level of performance in their conceptual ability.

Goldstein further hypothesized that individuals can function intellectually at two distinct levels, concrete and abstract. Individuals with brain injury, especially in the frontal lobes, suffer impairment of the abstract ability, he asserted. Goldstein and Scheerer (1941) present many case studies which demonstrate the concrete attitude of mental patients who seem to be unable to manipulate objects in the abstract as members of a class. For example, "A patient can count numbers on his fingers and by various roundabout methods; in this fashion he can even obtain the results which look like subtraction and addition, but he is entirely unable to state whether 7 or 4 is more, and he has no concept of the value of numbers whatsoever" (*ibid.,* p. 7). Individuals who have engaged in therapy or research with aphasics [3] can report many similar instances.

On the basis of their observations the authors constructed the Goldstein-Scheerer object sorting test. The subject is presented with objects with which he should have had much experience; e.g., the male form of the test contains such objects as hammer, knife, fork, cigar, pipe, matches, and so on, while the female form includes domestic objects, feminine apparel, and the like. The subject is told to classify them in many ways: first, to group them with an object he has selected; then to group them with an object the experimenter has selected; next to group all the objects which he thinks belong together; and, finally, to group them in another way. Actually the objects can be classified on the basis of function (knives, forks, etc.) or of various stimulus properties, such as color, material, substance, and so on. The normal subject finds it easy to classify according to function and readily shifts to stimulus-based classifications. The patient with frontal-lobe pathology cannot do this.

We have mentioned the work of Gelb and Goldstein here mainly to point to the fact that there are investigators interested in the relationship between brain function and the quality of thinking. It is beyond the scope of this book to discuss the controversy concerning the function of the frontal lobes of the cerebral cortex.

The nature of brain function has also been extended to psychotics. Thus certain psychoanalytic and field-oriented theorists (Birenbaum and Zeigarnik, 1935; Storch, 1924; Werner, 1946; White, 1926) have hypothesized that schizophrenic thinking shows regression to more infantile levels of adjustment. They differ in the theoretical explanations of this regression, the psychoanalysts emphasizing the modes of libidinal satisfaction in the child and the field theorists postulating that cognitive systems of schizophrenics and the child are less differentiated. It is doubtful, however, whether we can equate the thinking of psychopathological individuals and children. We say this for three reasons: (1) Although organics, schizophrenics, and children exhibit types of concrete attitudes, the latter two groups are more flexible and flexible in different ways. (2) The behavior of schizophrenics and children is qualitatively different. (3) The schizophrenic might not be able to cooperate during the testing because of his personality disorder. We remind the reader of our discussion of set and rigidity in Chapter 13.

NORMALS, ORGANICS, AND SCHIZOPHRENICS. The study which threw much light on this problem was reported by Hanfmann and Kasanin (1942). First, Hanfmann and Kasanin (1937) had developed a test of abstract ability which was an extension of a technique initiated by Ach and of

[3] Persons who have difficulty with understanding spoken language because of brain damage.

methods used by two Russians, Sakharof and Vigotsky.[4] The test consists of 22 wooden blocks of various colors, heights, shapes, and top-surface areas, which the subject has to classify into four groups. The subject is told that there are four kinds of blocks, each class being represented by a different nonsense name written at the bottom of each block. The blocks are presented in a jumbled arrangement. The experimenter then turns one block around, puts it in one corner, and suggests that the subject begin by putting all similar blocks in that corner and continue to sort the rest of the blocks into the three other corners.

The correct classification ignores both color and shape and is based on the form combinations of height and top-surface area. The large tall objects are LAGS; the large flat ones, BIKS; the small tall ones, MURS; and the small flat ones, CEVS. After the sorting has been completed, the experimenter turns over the wrongly placed blocks and requests that the subject discover for himself what the basis of the classification is.

There are wide differences between normals and abnormals on this test. The former actively try out various verbally expressed hypotheses and are more successful in attaining the experimenter's criteria for classification. The abnormals may group identical colors together, identical shapes together (all red, all circles, all squares, etc.), and so on, but they cannot combine two dimensions into a concept (small flat vs. small tall, etc.) or shift readily from one classification to another.

But while normals differ from abnormals, what specifically is the nature of this difference, and are there differences among the abnormals as well? Hanfmann and Kasanin present observations which indicate that the distinct dichotomy of Goldstein into abstract and concrete levels is an oversimplification. They report wide *individual differences* among normals and psychotics in levels of abstract thinking. The following generalizations are based on a study of 62 schizophrenics, 24 patients with organic brain disease, and 95 normal controls, both of college and noncollege level: (1) Only the college-educated normal group, on the whole, performed consistently at a high conceptual level. (2) The mean performance of the noncollege normal group was at an intermediate conceptual level; i.e., there were many mistakes in the abstract classifications. (3) The mean performance of the college-educated schizophrenics was lower than that of their normal controls but higher than that of the noncollege normal group. (4) The noncollege schizophrenic group performed at a lower level of conceptual ability than the noncollege normal group. (5) The organic patients consistently performed at the most primitive level of thought, even more so than the noncollege schizophrenics.

The picture is indeed complicated. The best that can be said at present is that the organization of brain function in both the functional psychotic and the brain-damaged patient is disturbed, with direct organic damage

[4] See, for example, Vigotsky (1934).

being more serious. But much more research is needed to develop a more specific theory.

Summary

We began by postulating that successful thinking depends largely on the individual's ability to group or reorganize problem material into a more meaningful relationship. Concept formation, therefore, becomes the important basis for problem solving since it provides the categories which the individual will have available for grouping the elements presented in a problem statement. Following Osgood, it was suggested that the formation of concepts involves development of a mediational process. Later, when stimuli are presented, various mediation responses arise which call up specific concepts.

Since the dominance hierarchy of available concepts for any individual depends on the interaction between the nature of the stimulus and his past experience, it is variable. The relative availability of various concepts is therefore determined by the type and complexity of the stimulus materials and the age, experience, intelligence, and language ability of the individual. The role of language in concept expression was discussed. Finally, we noted that there is usually some impairment of the conceptual thinking of individuals who have suffered organic brain damage or schizophrenic illness. An important distinction presented by Goldstein, but disputed by others, is that of the concrete and the abstract abilities. In brain damage or schizophrenic cases there appears to be some defect in the abstract ability but little disturbance of the concrete ability.

15

Problem
Solving

While discussing the stages involved in problem solving at the beginning of Chapter 13, we mentioned that concept invention is an important part of the thought process. We have already discussed the nature of set and concept formation. Sets and concepts which carry over from past experience sometimes enable an individual to solve a problem, but often the problem is difficult enough so that he has to invent new concepts or at least use old concepts in a novel way. These new concepts are nothing more than hypotheses which are generated as sets to organize the problem information into classes which are more meaningful; i.e., they suggest possible ways of obtaining solutions. While these concepts are being invented, the subject begins to develop strategies for attempting solutions to the problem. In this chapter we want to consider some of the work which deals with concept invention and the nature of problem-solving strategies.

Concept Invention

In 1955 Hovland and Kendler, ending a report on a symposium held on problem solving at New York University, wrote that they detected "a resolution on the part of nearly everyone to see to it that a conference held ten years from now on the same topic will make our present knowledge seem very meager and completely out of date." Well, we have arrived at that "ten years from now," and I am afraid that the optimism expressed in their prognosis has probably not been vindicated. The lack of conceptualization needed to formulate the nature of thinking which those authors noted then is still with us today. Nevertheless, there have been some valiant attempts to attack this area experimentally, although unifying theory is still lacking. Instead of merely reporting on the different findings in this section, I have chosen to discuss the work of Hovland, H. H. Kendler, and Harlow on concept invention because there appears to me to be an underlying theme represented by these studies. Perhaps if we try to understand what this theme is and do more concentrated research on our hunches, we shall move forward in at least one area.

These three investigators have concerned themselves with the influences of such variables as *stimulus presentation, perceptual assimilation,* and *age* on the ease with which concepts and sets are established. We shall begin with the work of Hovland.

Assimilation of Information Through Positive and Negative Instances

Carl Hovland (Hovland, 1952; Hovland and Weiss, 1953) has concerned himself primarily with the problem of trying to distinguish operationally between the two systems involved in the communication channel, namely, the information contained in the stimulus (input) and the information received from the organism (output). In trying to place his conception in the general context of information theory, it would be worth recalling George Miller's model, which we discussed in Chapter 8. What we try to measure is the amount of information transmitted T. Since the channel consists of information contained in the stimulus S and in the organism O, the amount of information transmitted depends on the correspondence between information generated by S and that received by O. The greater the agreement between S and O, the greater the amount of information transmitted.

When we apply this model to concept invention, it is clear that T is determined by at least two interacting systems. One system is represented by how effectively the stimulus presentation generates information to the organism, and the second system by how well the organism can assimilate the information which is generated. Formulating the problem in this way adds conceptual power to our analysis of the process, because it not only enables us to borrow the advantages that informational analysis gives us in the investigation of form perception but also reminds us that the problem of concept invention is part of the larger problem of the thought process. As we shall see when we enter the area of strategies in problem solving, the interaction between the conditions of stimulation and the nature of the organism seems to represent the core of what needs to be analyzed.

In the case of the informational analysis of form we pointed out that two questions needed answering. First, we had to find ways of measuring the amount of information transmitted; and, second, we had to proceed to a determination of how that information was transmitted. Two similar problems exist in the analysis of concept invention. First, we have to measure, logically or by some other means, how much information is generated by the stimulus presentation; and, second, we have to determine why certain kinds of information are easier to assimilate than others.

One of the ways this problem has been attacked in the case of concept invention has been to find out whether positive instances of a concept transmit more assimilable information than do negative ones.

Hovland begins his analysis by referring to the fact that Smoke (1932; 1933) had concluded from his experimental data that negative instances, as contrasted with positive instances, do little to facilitate the learning of concepts. He reasons, however, that we cannot decide from the unstructured situation used by Smoke whether the advantage of positive instances over negative instances was caused by the amount of information transmitted by the stimulus or by the relative ease with which the organism could assimilate the information.

In trying to separate these two parameters of information generation and assimilation, Hovland (1952), in a work previously cited, developed a model which we now exemplify. Let us suppose that the stimulus material is generated from four dimensions (e.g., form, color, size, and number) and that each dimension has four values. In such a case there would be a virtually impossible number of combinations of instances which could be generated. If the subject had to consider, or at least realize, all the combinations which were possible if all dimensions and all values within each dimension were relevant, he would have a mammoth if not impossible task because of our limited ability (channel capacity) to process information. Thus the task has to be limited.

In trying to describe how Hovland limits or structures the task so that the two variables (information transmission and assimilation) can be measured, let us take a simpler example which he gave. A concept is transmitted through successive presentations of stimulus cards. The subject is told that there are three possible stimulus dimensions, namely, form, color, and size, and that there will be three values of each. In such a situation Hovland limits the amount of information generated in the following way. The subject is further told that the concept will consist of a combination of *one value of each of two dimensions* (e.g., black square). It will therefore take a minimum of 2 positive instances and 10 negative instances to define the correct combination; i.e., 2 positive instances transmit as much information as 10 negative ones. Thus, if there is perfect transmission of information, the subject should discover the correct concept with 2 positive or 10 negative instances. If, for example, the first positive instance contains a small black square and the second a large black square, the subject could deduce that the concept is black square (of any size). But it will require

10 negative instances to define the correct concept. In the example above the following 10 concepts will be wrong: small black triangle, small white circle, small yellow square, large white triangle, large black circle, large yellow square, medium yellow triangle, medium black circle, small white square, and medium white square. These 10 will eliminate all the other negative instances, most of them eliminating 3 combinations at a time.

So we see in fact that while there are 27 combinations in all [3 dimensions ($_3C_1$) and 9 values ($_3C_1)^2$], of which 3 are positive and 24 negative, the subject can solve the problem with only 2 positive or 10 negative instances. Thus, in this kind of experiment, if we want to determine whether it is the transmission of information or the assimilation of information which is involved, we have to keep one of these variables constant. In the example given above we have to give 10 negative instances to transmit the same amount of information as 2 positive instances to keep this variable constant. Only then can we determine whether positive instances facilitate the assimilation of information.

In the report by Hovland and Weiss (1953) previously cited, three experiments testing the application of this model are presented. The first experiment compares the relative ease with which information transmitted by positive and negative instances is assimilated. The technique is similar to that in the example just presented, and the amount of information coming from positive and negative instances is held constant. The essence of the experimental design and a summary of the results are presented in Table 15-1.

Table 15-1

Percentage of Ss Attaining Correct Concept with All Positive vs. All Negative Instances: Successive Presentation.
(After Hovland and Weiss, 1953, p. 177.)

Stimulus Series						% Ss Attaining Concept		
Total No. of Dimensions	Total No. of Values	No. of Dimensions Relevant	No. of Values Correct	No. of Pos. Instances Required	No. of Neg. Instances Required	All Pos. Instances	All Neg. Instances	P
3	3	2	1	2	10	100 (N-24)	16.7 (N-24)	0.001
3	2	2	1	2	5	100 (N-24)	16.7 (N-24)	0.001
4	2	2	1	2	5	(a) 95.8 (N-24)	4.2 (N-24)	0.001
						(b) 94.7 (N-95)	13.7 (N-95)	0.001

Thus it seems that even when the amount of information generated is held constant, positive instances facilitate the assimilation of information to a highly effective degree, negative instances being quite ineffective. It might be objected, however, that since there were so many more items to remember in the case of the negative instances and since the instances were presented successively, the difference could be accounted for as the difficulty in remembering all the negative instances. Consequently, although experiment 2 was a modification of the first experiment, this time all the instances were presented simultaneously. The experimental paradigm and essential results are presented in Table 15-2.

Table 15-2

Percentage of Ss Attaining Correct Concept with All Positive and All Negative Instances: Simultaneous Presentation.
(After Hovland and Weiss, 1953, p. 178.)

Stimulus Series						% Ss Attaining Concept		
Total No. of Dimensions	Total No. of Values	No. of Dimensions Relevant	No. of Values Correct	No. of Pos. Instances Required	No. of Neg. Instances Required	All Pos. Instances	All Neg. Instances	$P \times 2$
3	3	2	1	2	10	100	50.0	0.02
3	2	2	1	2	5	100	83.3	0.12
4	2	2	1	2	5	100	66.7	0.10

Again we see that the positive instances are consistently superior. Under simultaneous conditions, however, the information transmitted by negative instances is much more effective than that transmitted in successive presentation. Thus, retention, or the factor of contiguity,[1] does make a significant difference.

Finally, Hovland and Weiss tested the difference between positive and negative instances when the total number of instances required to transmit the same amount of information was identical for both the positive and the negative instances. This technique could be worked out by using the naturalistic set of flower designs reported by Hovland (1953). These flower designs could be varied in four dimensions (blossom shape, number of leaves, shape of leaf, and color), and each dimension had four values. This experiment compared all positive, all negative, and also mixed positive and negative instances. The summary of the experimental results is presented in Table 15-3 (three trials with three different, equivalent lists were given). All the differences between positive and negative instances were significant. By the time the third trial was reached, the difference

[1] See Underwood (1952).

Table 15-3

Concept Attainment of First, Second, and Third Presentations of All Positive, All Negative, and Mixed Positive and Negative Instances: Series N-24. (After Hovland and Weiss, 1953, p. 180.)

Stimulus Series					Cumulative % of Ss Attaining Concept		
Total No. of Dimensions	Total No. of Values	No. of Dimensions Relevant	No. of Values Correct	Presentation	All Pos.	Mixed Pos. & Neg.	All Neg.
3	4	2	3	1	79.2	54.2	20.8
				2	95.8	70.8	41.7
				3	100.0	79.1	54.2
				1	91.7	37.5	12.5
4	4	2	3	2	95.8	45.8	33.3
				3	95.8	58.3	50.0

between the positive and the mixed instances was significant while that between the latter and the negative instances was not.

Hovland and Weiss theorized that the facilitation of information assimilation produced by positive instances (as against negative instances) results from such features as the following: (1) The positive instances are perceptually more effective (this is possibly similar to Heidbreder's perceptual support). (2) When the organism sees the positive instances, he can more readily generate organizing hypotheses for finding the unifying principle.

In subsequent studies Hovland and his associates further explained some of the variables facilitating concept invention or attainment. For example, Cahill and Hovland (1960) found that simultaneous presentation of instances is superior to successive presentation. More numerous errors in perceptual inference are made in successive presentation because the subject has to remember the preceding information. Moreover, the number of errors is greater when the number of instances intervening between presentation and final concept identification is increased; i.e., a typical type of forgetting curve is obtained. Hunt and Hovland (1960) found further that conjunctive and relational concepts are more readily discovered than disjunctive ones.[2]

The factors, such as fewer dimensions, simultaneity, and conjunctivity,

---

[2] Later in this chapter, in the section "Purpose of Strategies," where we discuss Bruner's work on thinking, these terms are defined.

which Hovland and his associates found to facilitate concept attainment are related to the position of Underwood (1952), in which he attempted to develop an orientation for research in thinking. Other factors, in addition to memory, which is discussed by Underwood, are as follows: (1) Perceptual presentation (e.g., a picture) is superior to symbolic presentation (e.g., a word standing for the picture presentation) (this is again related to perceptual support). (2) Similarity among stimuli facilitates concept invention. (3) Response bias (e.g., set) can either facilitate or hinder concept attainment.

In his theoretical paper Underwood attempts to unify these factors under the principle of contiguity. In essence, his hypothesis is that for new relationships to be attained the relevant responses to stimuli must occur contiguously. The factors discussed in this section describe the conditions which facilitate the contiguous occurrence of these relevant responses. It would be fruitful to see how much new information would be generated by this directional research principle. It is to be expected that other principles will be formulated.

Reversal and Nonreversal Shifts

Since the assimilation of information is almost certainly affected by the mediational ability of the individual, we should examine the nature of mediation more deeply. Let us recall Osgood's analysis of mediation in concept formation, which we discussed in Chapter 13. It is in fact doubtful that the kinds of problem solving found in human beings could have developed without the concurrent development of cortical mediation.

Kendler and his associates [3] have been engaged in a research project analyzing the nature of mediation in problem solving. They have used the reversal-nonreversal shift technique which is diagramed in Figure 15-1. In these experiments the subjects (children) first have to learn to discriminate stimuli (cups) that have patterns which vary simultaneously in two dimensions (in this case, size and brightness). If they choose the correct cup, they are rewarded with a marble. In the first discrimination size is relevant, whereas brightness is irrelevant.

In typical experiments [4] using such stimuli the performances of four-year-old and seven-year-old children are compared. After the children have learned the first discrimination to some acceptable degree, they are presented with one of the two second discriminations. Since the large square was positive, a second discrimination in which the small square is positive is called a reversal shift. Conversely a second discrimination in

---

[3] See, for example, H. H. Kendler and T. S. Kendler (1962) for a review of this work.

[4] See H. H. Kendler and T. S. Kendler (1962); T. S. Kendler, H. H. Kendler, and Wells (1960).

First
discrimination

Second
discrimination

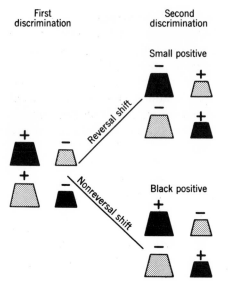

Small positive

Black positive

Figure 15-1
Examples of a reversal and a non-reversal shift. (After H. H. Kendler and T. S. Kendler, 1962, p. 5.)

which black is positive is called a nonreversal shift since brightness was irrelevant in the first discrimination.

In all experiments conducted by the Kendlers they have found that the older children learn the reversal shift significantly faster than the younger children do, but the latter learn the nonreversal shift more quickly. They invoke a mediational hypothesis to account for these results. The assumed way that the mediational process operates is diagramed in Figure 15-2.

The crucial part of this sequence is the r-size–S-size intervention which mediates the correct response. Since the older children readily make the reversal shift, it is inferred that this mediational process is at work for them. In the younger children, however, it seems that they simply respond to either large or small without relating the two into the concept "size." Hence they have greater difficulty in shifting from large to small.

The transition from large to black in the nonreversal shift is accounted for by noting that in the first discrimination black is rewarded (incidentally) 50 per cent of the time. Thus the straightforward application of reinforcement theory accounts for this effect. But why are the older children slower at making this transition? The reason is that they have responded, and are still responding, to another dimension, the size relationship. Only after they break this set (which is not present in most of the younger children) do they make the transition.

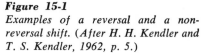

Figure 15-2
A mediational S-R analysis of a reversal shift. (After H. H. Kendler and T. S. Kendler, 1962, p. 6.)

In another experiment (H. H. Kendler and T. S. Kendler, 1961) this mediational explanation was tested further by forcing all children to verbalize their discrimination during the first learning situation. The situation is diagramed in Figure 15-3. Three groups of subjects were used. One, a

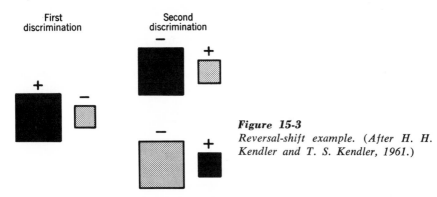

Figure 15-3
Reversal-shift example. (After H. H. Kendler and T. S. Kendler, 1961.)

control group, had no verbalization instructions. A second group, the relevant group, was told to say that large square was correct. The third group, nonrelevant, was told that black square was correct. The results comparing the four-year-olds and the seven-year-olds are presented in Figure 15-4.

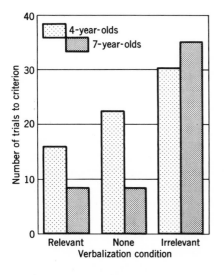

Figure 15-4
Effect of verbalization of the acquisition of a reversal shift for four- and seven-year-old children. (After H. H. Kendler and T. S. Kendler, 1961, p. 1620.)

First, we note that the relevant groups in both ages were superior to the nonrelevant groups because the relevant verbal mediation was presumably induced in the relevant groups. The differences were statistically significant, but the difference between the four-year-old and seven-year-old relevant groups was not statistically significant. Perhaps the common verbal instructions obviated any natural intellectual difference between the two age groups. It is interesting to note, however, that there was no difference between the relevant and no-verbalization groups in the seven-year-olds. Presumably these older children already used verbal mediating responses without instruction from the outside being necessary. Finally, the irrelevant verbal mediator seemed to confuse the older children more often than the younger children.

The difference reported between older children and younger children in mediation suggests that this process develops at a later age and is probably related to learning and evolutionary development. Kendler and Kendler list the phylogenetic differences in reversal-shift learning which support this deduction.

Learning Sets

The difference between reversal- and nonreversal-shift learning and its relationship to the phylogenetic, ontogenetic, and experiential level probably constitute part of the larger problem of set. That is to say, the ease with which an individual can solve a problem depends on how available the relevant set is for categorizing (mediating) responses. In the problems just reviewed, language is an effective mediator, but other symbolic mediators undoubtedly develop through experience. The classic work of Harlow (1949) presents an excellent paradigm for investigating the genesis of such sets experimentally.

In these studies, which were begun with monkeys, the Wisconsin General Test Apparatus (WGTA) was used. The WGTA consists of an enclosure in which the monkey is sealed, a stimulus tray with two objects on it being located in front of him. The experimenter watches the monkey through a one-way-vision screen. If the monkey chooses the "correct" object, he is rewarded.

The first task required of the monkey is to learn to discriminate the difference between the object quality of two forms. The percentage of correct responses is plotted for a great number of such problems. On each successive problem, two different objects are used, and one is arbitrarily designated as correct. The left-right positions are, of course, randomized. After the discrimination problems had been learned, Harlow investigated discrimination-reversal problems; i.e., after each learning set was established, the other object was suddenly designated as correct. The percentages of correct responses for discrimination problems and discrimination-reversal problems are presented in Figure 15-5.

Two results should be emphasized. First, in the case of the original discrimination problems the percentage of correct responses in trial 2 was only about 50 per cent for problems 1 to 14 but steadily increased to about 90 per cent for problems 99 to 112. This illustrates the development of the learning set; i.e., the animal was learning how to learn or how to

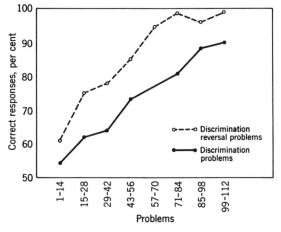

Figure 15-5
Discrimination-reversal and discrimination learning-set curves based on trial 2 responses. (After Harlow, 1949, p. 58.)

approach the problem. The learning set can be considered the mediating response of how to approach the problem; e.g., "chooses one of the objects." It can thus be seen that the curve for learning sets differs from the slow trial-and-error learning curves of most rote situations.

The second result of interest is the fact that the percentage of correct responses for the discrimination-reversal problems was consistently higher. Harlow accounts for this by stating that analysis of the data shows that in original learning certain factors seem to produce errors. We can thus conclude that as the sets are learned, something happens to inhibit these error-producing factors. This is a novel idea since learning is usually thought of as the building up of habit strength rather than the inhibiting of certain response tendencies. In a more recent paper Harlow analyzes error factor more fully (1959).

This notion of the inhibition of error-producing factors seems to the present writer to be similar to Gibson's notion of stimulus differentiation (as opposed to enrichment) in perceptual learning. But in both cases it appears to me that we do not find this inhibition or differentiation until some acquisition or enrichment has first occurred.

Similar data were collected for three- to five-year-old children. An example of discrimination-reversal learning by nine children is presented in Figure 15-6. A comparison of the data on monkeys and children and the analyses of error-producing factors indicate that similar set-developing mechanisms are present in both species, with children clearly superior to monkeys on the reversal discrimination. (This difference is similar to older children's superiority on reversal shifts.) The permanence and stability of learning sets are shown in Figure 15-7. It is clear that the monkey can shift

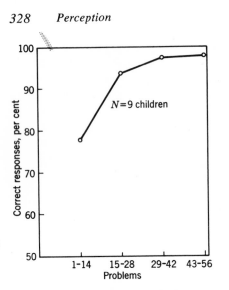

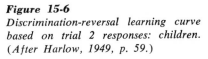

Figure 15-6
Discrimination-reversal learning curve based on trial 2 responses: children. (After Harlow, 1949, p. 59.)

from object quality to positional discriminaion with ease and that this flexibility is facilitated by the number of previous set problems.

Finally we note that once the sets have been established, they are not easily destroyed. We notice that brain damage impairs the ability to learn the sets but that educated (second-series) hemidecorticated animals are superior to uneducated (first-series) unoperated monkeys. To quote Harlow, "Such data suggest that half a brain is better than one if you compare the individuals having appropriate learning sets with the individuals lack-

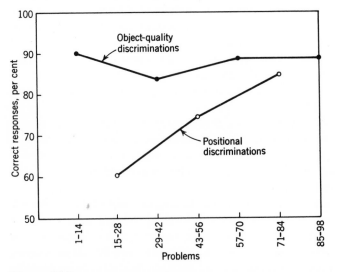

Figure 15-7
Learning-set curves for problem series with alternating object-quality and positional discriminations, based on total trial responses. (After Harlow, 1949, p. 62.)

ing them" (1949, p. 63). The implication of this finding and suggestion is tremendous for the education of socially and ethnically underprivileged people.

Problem-solving Strategies

From what we have said about set and concepts, we should be in a better position to appreciate the nature of problem solving. First, we might say operationally that *S* is faced with a problem when the amount of information transmitted is less than the potential information in the stimulus. Under such conditions the correct response for adaptive behavior is not immediately available. We might say further that the difficulty of the problem is related to the relative ease with which *S* can call up the relevant response or responses to reach the goal that is the solution of the problem.

The first stage in this process of calling up available responses is the genesis of sets or hypotheses to categorize the stimuli. This is done for two reasons: (1) It reduces the total number of alternatives. (2) It makes the remaining alternatives more meaningful (this is similar to what we called concentrated points of information when we discussed perception).

Thus information theory again provides a useful tool for conceptualizing problem-solving behavior. In extracting information from the problem situation the subject also makes decisions about the future. A useful definition of a problem-solving strategy, given by Van De Geer, states that "a sequence of decisions in view of the attainment of ultimate validation, of information may be called a strategy. . . . most of our thinking proceeds by such strategies" (1957, p. 195).

A very significant study which attempted to uncover the conditions affecting the choice of various problem-solving strategies was reported by Bruner et al. (1956), who began with the assumption that virtually all cognitive activity involves and is dependent on the process of categorizing. A category, which is defined as a range of discriminably different events that are treated "as if" equivalent, depends on man's capacity to infer from sign to significate. A *sign* is a stimulus which has cue value, and a *significate* is a goal or an end. Thus we can say that categorizing behavior intervenes between the presentation of signs and the attainment of problem solutions.

The authors contend that while the term *categorizing* is conventionally reserved for various forms of conceptual behavior, any behavior involving the placement of objects or events on the basis of selected (criteria) cues may be conceived as categorizing. Hence categorizing is involved in concept formation, perception, and general problem solving. In fact, the authors hold that category learning is the principal means by which members of culture are socialized, and they generalize the conclusions drawn from their research to any phenomenon in which an organism is faced with the task of identifying and placing events into classes on the basis of using certain criterial cues and ignoring others. Furthermore, these categories do not exist in the world but are invented by the subject.

Since the invention of categories is considered the prototype of all problem solving and cognitive learning, the authors have investigated the strategies by which people come to discover what cues can appropriately be used for inferring the category membership of objects and events. In this way they feel that they have studied paradigms of the kinds of behavior called problem solving or thinking in everyday life.

At the beginning of this section we stated that a strategy could be considered a sequence of decisions with respect to attaining some end. Bruner et al. point out that each decision and test could be regarded as providing potential information by limiting the number of attributes or attribute values that can be considered predictive.

Purpose of Strategies

There are reasons in addition to information gathering why these sequences of decisions or strategies are invented. The authors (Bruner et al.) see three functions served by these strategies: (1) *maximizing the information* gained from each decision and test of an instance; (2) keeping the *cognitive strain* involved in the task within manageable or appropriate limits, especially within the limits imposed by the individual's cognitive capacity; and (3) regulating the *risk* of failing to attain the concept within a specifiable time or energy limit and regulating any other forms of risk consequent to making a decision and testing it.

With respect to *maximizing information* gained from each decision or test, it should be noted that different kinds of concepts transmit differential amounts of information. The easiest concepts to attain are *conjunctive,* a term which is defined by the *"conjoint presence of several attribute values, so that only when all such values are present may an object be considered as an exemplar of the category."* The concepts used in connection with the discussion of Hovland's work are conjunctive concepts. The most difficult information to assimilate is that transmitted from negative instances and from concepts which are *disjunctive*. Disjunctive concepts are stated in an either-or manner. Thus an individual might belong to a class admissible to vote in a particular community if he lived there, or owned property there, or had a business there, and so on. This is the most difficult concept to master since it seems to violate the expectation that for each effect there be but one cause. In the course of attempting to solve problems in the attainment of disjunctive concepts, subjects tend to fall back on primitive additive or conjunctive assumptions.

With respect to *cognitive strain*, the authors note that it is increased by the following conditions: (1) increasing the number of attributes and values to be sought in pursuit of the correct cues, (2) using abstract rather than concrete materials, (3) arranging instances in a random rather than an orderly form, and (4) accelerating the pace.

Risk conditions may be varied by different payoff matrices, i.e., by varying the set of consequences, such as the cost of the risk or the value of the correct decision. They are also varied by asking such questions as the following: "How does one categorize if one is a sentry as compared with a searcher after accuracy?" "What is the effect of changing the probability of obtaining instances for test of a particularly useful kind?"

Kinds of Strategies

By using such stimulus material as thematic cards, geometric design (varying in combinations of color, size, border, etc.), facial types, and aircraft designs and depending on the condition of information, cognitive strain, and risk, Bruner et al. obtained in their experiments the four kinds of strategies described below. In all these strategies the subject has to find his own positive instance. Thus they are called *selection strategies*.

1. *Simultaneous scanning.* In this strategy S uses each instance encountered as an occasion for deducing which hypotheses (of many) are tenable and which have been eliminated. Simultaneous scanning is very exacting for memory and deduction since S mentally tests the instance against a number of hypotheses. While the purpose of this strategy is to increase the amount of extracted information, it tends to produce high cognitive strain and also involves risk.

2. *Successive scanning.* Here S tests a single hypothesis at a time and continues to test hypotheses until he finds the correct one. To be successful the scanner has to limit his chances to those instances that provide a direct test of his hypothesis. While this strategy has low cognitive strain and low risk, it tends to extract less information from each instance than simultaneous scanning.

3. *Conservative focusing.* S finds a positive instance to use as a focus, then makes a sequence of changes, each of which alters only one attribute value of the first focus card, and tests to see whether the change yields a positive or a negative instance. It is interesting to compare this strategy with the preceding one. In successive scanning S starts with an hypothesis about what the concept is and goes on testing one hypothesis at a time until he finds the correct solution. In conservative focusing he starts with a positive instance and then eliminates one attribute at a time until he arrives at the combination of attributes which is correct. It would seem that the former is more of an inductive process while the latter is more of a deductive process. It would be interesting to relate the differential uses of conservative focusing and successive scanning to intellectual activity and organizational ability. In any case, both strategies provide less information than simultaneous scanning, and both are low on cogitive strain and risk.

4. *Focus gambling.* S uses a positive instance as a focus and then changes more than one attribute value at a time. A risk is involved here: he might succeed in fewer choices than in conservative focusing, but then, again, he might require many more. This strategy could also be high in cognitive strain. Bruner et al. found that conservative focusing is generally favored by intelligent subjects, but when conditions become more pressing in terms of time or number of trials, it risks complete failure, and subjects usually shift to focus gambling, which is more strenuous cognitively but increases the probability of attainment.

Further Data on Conditions Affecting Selection Strategies

Bruner et al. report interesting exploratory experiments on some of the factors influencing the selecting of one of the four strategies reported in the previous section. These factors are naturally related to the three conditions served by strategies, namely, information, cognitive strain, and risk regulation.

INCREASING COGNITIVE STRAIN. In one such experiment 12 Harvard undergraduate students were used as subjects. Each subject was presented with a large board that contained an orderly array of 81 sequences which varied in form, color, number, and border. The subject was presented with three problems; i.e., three concepts had to be attained. In the first two problems the board was always in sight, but for the third problem the board was not in front of the subject, thus increasing cognitive strain.

Most of the subjects selected two kinds of strategies: modified forms of conservative focusing and successive scanning. One important function served by the strategy of modified conservative focusing was the confirmation of redundancy. For example, if the first focus card (which was called "correct") was "two *red* squares with one border," the subject would then go on, for example, to "two *green* squares with one border." This would clearly, by inference, eliminate color as a criterial attribute, but the subject would not be satisfied with such indirect information and would go on to more direct confirmation by next selecting "two black squares with one border." This choice is clearly redundant but apparently is part of a generally verified principle guiding the process of concept attainment, i.e., the *need for direct test.* This kind of double checking is resorted to particularly when the problem situation becomes very difficult.

The most interesting finding is related to what happened when the task shifted from solving the problem with the board in sight to solving it "in the head." A brief capsule of the salient results follows. Five of the subjects who had used modified focusing showed the same level of effectiveness when the problem had to be solved from memory, while the sixth resorted to the redundant process of the direct test. The memory of the seventh subject failed him; he forgot the values of the form cards and ended up in complete confusion. Of the five subjects who chose scanning, four were quite confused by the in-the-head problem, and the fifth resorted to a focusing strategy.

Some quantitative findings are also of interest. While the focusers required only a median of 5 choices to solve the third problem, the scanners required 13. Similarly the scanners made a median of 6 redundant choices, and the focusers only one. Finally, the 13 choices of the scanners represented an increase of 10 over those required to solve the second problem. The focusers did not require any increase.

Clearly, the focusing strategy is superior, especially when cognitive strain is increased. While Bruner, Goodnow, and Austin state that the more intelligent subjects generally prefer focusing strategies, it would be interesting to look further into other factors, such as the history of the individual, which might throw some light on why subjects typically choose the strategies that they do.

Other pilot experiments are reported which suggest some conditions of cognitive strain and risk regulation which affect the nature of the strategy chosen and its relative effectiveness. Since it would require too much space to review these experiments here, all we can do is point out some of the tentative findings.

Two generalizations can be made about cognitive strain: (1) If the stimulus array is presented so as to emphasize the systematic way in which attribute values vary (e.g., presentation on the board or in ordered rather than random fashion), a focusing or modified focusing strategy is used. This is the best strategy in such cases because the subject is making use of the information provided by the systematic nature of the presentation. (2) If the stimulus material contains "familiar" identities, such as adult figures in thematic cards, the subject uses a scanning strategy. This appears reasonable since he brings certain expectancies about familiar identities to the task (e.g., mothers give things to children). These expectancies from the past are used as a basis for generating hypotheses which are tested across all the instances in a scanning fashion. This often leads to behavior which is similar to the *Einstellung* effect and which Bruner, Goodnow, and Austin call *persistence forecasting*.

RISK REGULATION. Two separate questions must be kept in mind with respect to risk regulation: (1) How much does the subject value the various outcomes of a particular decision? (2) What is the subject's estimate of the probability with which the valued outcome will occur? The authors liken the first question to the situation faced by a scientist. If he has unlimited time in which to pursue his research, he is likely to use a conservative focusing strategy; but if the nature of his situation dictates that he can perform only one final experiment, the risk is large and he is faced with an ambivalent choice. If he considers himself part of the larger team of the ongoing scientific community, he will probably choose the safe or sound solution, e.g., extirpate one area of the cortex and learn whether it is necessary or not for one kind of behavior. If, however, he wants to make a "killing," he is perhaps more concerned about his "name" in science, and he may therefore extirpate five areas. In such a case, if the particular behavior in question were still intact, he would receive the fame he is looking for. If not, his experiment has provided equivocal information. The alternatives are these. If extirpating one area destroyed the particular aspect of behavior, much information would be provided. If the behavior were still intact, very little would be added. In the second, gambling strategy the converse is true. Destruction of the particular behavior would produce equivocal information, whereas the presence of intact behavior after the extirpation of many areas would provide much useful information. We would learn that these five areas are unimportant for that particular behavior. Whether an individual chooses the safe or the more dramatic strategy can be known only by understanding the psychological value of either outcome to him, i.e., by knowing something informative about his motives. Again we see the importance of considering personality variables in the study of thought processes. This is a young field in which the experimental work is still formative and quite tentative.

The second question about risk regulation can be analyzed more affirmatively. Let us suppose the subject is working toward some valued outcome (for example, one alternative of two possible outcomes). The higher he estimates the probability of the favored outcome to be, the more likely is it that he will use a gambling strategy. Thus Bruner et al. found that of 24 subjects who encountered all positive instances in an experiment, the number who changed more than one attribute increased from 10 on the first choice to 21 on the fourth choice. Conversely, of 24 subjects who encountered all negative instances, the number who changed more than one attribute decreased from 13 on the first choice to only 2 on the fourth choice. Similarly, for the first group, the average number of changed attributes increased from 1.54 on the first choice to 2.67 on the fourth choice. The corresponding values for the second group were 1.75 and 1.08, respectively.

We may summarize the prediction of the choice of strategy as conditioned by risk regulation by stating that the prediction can be made by calculating the *expected utility* of the decision. This calculation follows the rules of decision theory. First, following Marschak (1950), we assign values between 0 and 1, depending on how favorable the outcome is for the subject. Second, we assign a probability value to each outcome, depending on the estimation of its occurrence. We then find the product of these values for each outcome and sum the products to find the expected utility.

Let us take an example which is worked out in Table 15-4. In the last experiment mentioned, the following situation could be obtained. The subject might estimate that the probability of obtaining a positive instance is 0.75, and that of obtaining a negative instance 0.25. Hence we can calculate the expected utilities for the two alternatives by changing either one attribute or more than one attribute. We note that in the case of changing

Table 15-4

Calculating Expected Utilities.

	Anticipated Events		
Decision Alternative	*Pos. Instance*	*Neg. Instance*	*Expected Utility of Decision*
Changes One Attribute	$0.5 \times 0.75 = 0.375$	$0.5 \times 0.25 = 0.125$	0.5
Changes More Than One Attribute	1×0.75	0×0.25	0.75
Estimated Probability	0.75	0.00	

one attribute the value or desirability of the positive and negative instances is the same (0.5); but in the case of changing more than one attribute the value of the positive instance is 1 and that of the negative is 0, since the former presents much more information. Hence in this example we predict that the subject will change more than one attribute at a time.

A Working Framework for Problem-solving Strategies

We end this chapter by returning to the statements with which we opened it. An individual is faced with a problem when the correct response demanded by the stimulating situation is not immediately available. The relative unavailability of the correct response is determined by the interaction between stimulus presentation and organismic state. Thus the subject's first task is to extract the relevant potential information from the stimulus. The ease with which this can be done depends on the following factors:

1. The nature of the stimulus presentation. For example, positive instances usually generate more information than negative instances. This conclusion is related to the principle of contiguity.
2. The sequential relationship of task presentation. For example, reversal-shift learning is more difficult than nonreversal-shift learning. Also, learning sets facilitate subsequent problem solving.
3. The ease with which the subject can assimilate transmitted information. This ability depends on such factors as the presence of relevant sets which the subject can generate to categorize stimuli and the facility of changing these sets as necessary, cognitive strain, and risk regulation. Thus the work of Bruner, Goodnow, and Austin on the factors influencing the

selection of problem-solving strategies and the theoretical guideposts which stem from a combination of information theory and decision theory can be used as a research starting point for conceptualizing the problem-solving process.

Summary

This chapter began with a brief description of the stages and purposes of problem solving. We then proceeded to a discussion of how effectively information is transmitted and assimilated from such varying stimulus conditions as positive and negative instances in concept attainment (the work of Hovland). Next we looked at sequential effects in problem solving in the work of such people as H. H. Kendler on reversal-shift learning and Harlow on learning sets. We ended with a discussion of some problem-solving strategies which come from the work of Bruner, Goodnow, and Austin. A theoretical starting point, based on information theory and decision theory, was described as a framework for further research in the field of problem solving.

16

Productive and
Creative Thinking

One of the first questions which probably comes to mind when we consider the nature of creative thinking is whether this process differs from productive problem solving only in degree or more drastically in kind. While this is a difficult question to answer, it might help to put the situation in an enlightened perspective if we could produce some heuristic, classificatory scheme for different kinds of problem solving.

A Working Classification of Thinking Systems

It seems to me that we can classify problem-solving systems in three categories, based on the extent to which models from past experience are successful and the extent to which almost entirely "new" models have to be invented. Systems more closely tied to experience would be like those involved in traditional troubleshooting, while those dependent on inventions of new models would be like those encountered in scientific and artistic creations. This, of course, raises a question about the extent to which creative thinking is learned or can be taught. We shall return to this subject later. In any case, this suggested classification of thought systems would consist of the following: (1) closed systems, (2) partially open systems, and (3) open systems.

CLOSED SYSTEMS. The formal techniques of measurement developed by the information theorists are most obviously applicable to the closed systems of thought. I have in mind the kind of problem situation in which the relevant knowledge or sets are already present in the repertoire of the individual, the task consisting essentially of generating the appropriate sets to categorize the potential information contained in the stimulus. In this way all the potential information is transmitted, and error or noise is zero or minimal. Noise or error is present when the organism generates incorrect sets. Thus, the process involved in this kind of system is similar to the inhibition of error or irrelevant sets which we discussed in Chapter 15 while presenting Harlow's error-factor theory of learning sets.

The most obvious example of a closed system is troubleshooting, in which the troubleshooter has to discover why a particular mechanism has broken down. Let us take the situation of an automobile mechanic who is trying to diagnose why an automobile will not run. This is a closed system since the experienced mechanic has all the relevant knowledge about what makes a car go. Thus he proceeds by considering the electrical, fuel, and transmission subsets in the total power set of the automobile. By asking the right kinds of questions and making the appropriate tests, he can eliminate many inappropriate inspections by each crucial test. Eventually he will, let us say, narrow the trouble down to the fuel system, then locate it in that subset, perhaps in the fuel pump, and correct the difficulty.

The process of thinking within a closed system can be structured experimentally by using the following kind of model. Let us play a game on the grid diagramed in Figure 16-1. We have a grid with 32 squares, and I say to the subject that I am thinking of one particular square and if he can guess which it is in no more than five questions, he will win the prize. Let us say that the square I am thinking of is the one with the dot marked on it. If the subject proceeds according to a system similar to information theory, he will realize that

$$H = \log_2 32 = 5 \text{ bits}$$

In order to transmit all 5 bits of information, each question must eliminate half of the squares remaining. As we pointed out in Chapter 8, this can be accomplished by using the technique of successive halving of the alternatives.

An experiment using a modified "20-questions" game was performed by Bendig (1953) to study the extent to which the subjects can extract the maximum possible information from each question. Three successive

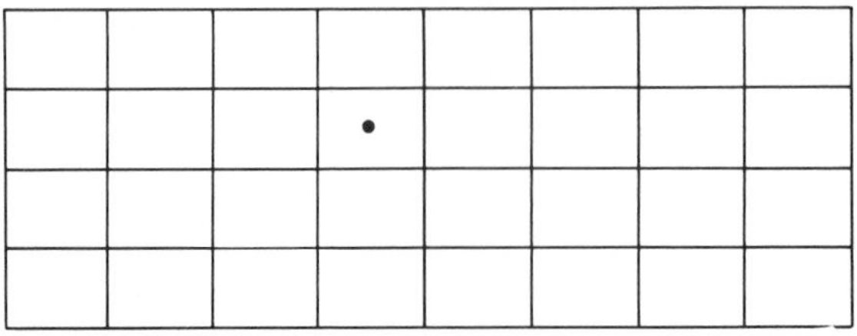

Figure 16-1
A grid for a closed-system problem game.

games were participated in by 127 subjects. The task was to guess the animal topics from a list of 16 after each of four questions. The interesting finding was that Ss used 86 per cent of the information generated by three of the questions but only 21 per cent of the information provided by the fourth question. Thus, if we recall our previous formula that $T = H - E$, we note that transmission is not perfect and that there is noise or error even in this relatively simple, closed system of communication. It is not known why three of the questions transmit about four times as much information as the fourth. Definitive research on this question would be very instructive.

A second finding was noted: namely, that no consistent increase in the transmission of information attributable to learning was found over the three games. Since the experimental design confounded learning and topic effects and since the effects of learning would depend on the initial familiarity of Ss with the task elements, it would be difficult to generalize this second finding.

Future research in problem solving within closed systems should isolate the effects of an interaction between information transmission, information facilitation, nature of the task, experience of the Ss, and different kinds of training or learning.

PARTIALLY OPEN SYSTEMS. A good example of what I mean by partially open systems is provided by the coin problems employed by Simmel (1953) to investigate thinking. Three problems were used: the 8-coin problem, the 9-coin problem, and the 25-coin problem. In the 8-coin problem the subject was told that there were 8 coins and that 1 coin was lighter than the other 7. By using a balance, S had to determine in no more than two weighings which was the coin of a different weight. The problem was almost identical for the 9-coin problem: 1 coin was lighter than the other 8. In the 25-coin problem S had to determine in no more than three weighings which coin was lighter than the other 24.

The nature of the experimental sequence was as follows. In the first experiment all subjects worked on the 8-coin problem. In a second experiment, consisting of a new group of 27 subjects, 18 subjects were first given the 8-coin problem, then the 9-coin problem, and finally the 25-coin problem; whereas the other 19 subjects were first given the 9-coin problem, then the 8-coin problem, and finally the 25-coin problem. We notice that the 25-coin problem, which in pilot testing had proved to be extremely difficult, was always given last. Before presenting a discussion of Simmel's results, let us state what the solutions of these problems are:

1. *The 8-coin problem.* In the first weighing, place 3 coins on either side of the balance. If they balance, the odd coin is one of the other 2. In the second weighing, place 1 of each of the other 2 coins on either side of the balance. Whichever scale goes up contains the lighter coin. If in the first weighing the coins do not balance, then the lighter coin will be one

of the 3 coins which are on the side of the balance which goes up. For the second weighing, take any 2 of these coins and place 1 each on either side of the balance. The side that goes up contains the lighter coin. If they balance, then the third coin left of the 3 is the lighter coin.

2. *The 9-coin problem.* In the first weighing, place 3 coins on one side of the balance and 3 on the other side. If they balance, then the odd coin consists of 1 of the other 3. In that case the second weighing would consist of the second sequence outlined for the 8-coin problem. If they do not balance, the lighter side contains the lighter coin; the second weighing would again consist of the second sequence in the 8-coin problem, but these 3 coins would be used from the lighter side of the balance.

3. *The 25-coin problem.* Divide the 25 coins into three groups of 8, 8, and 9. In the first weighing, place 8 coins on each side of the balance. If they balance, then the lighter coin is in the other 9. In this case we use two more weighings, as in the 9-coin problem, to find the lighter coin. If they do not balance, then we use the two weighings, as outlined in the 8-coin problem, to find the lighter coin, but from among the 8 coins located on the lighter side of the balance.

In the experiment by Simmel, she concluded that two factors probably determined the problem-solving process. The first was the factor of symmetry. Thus, practically all the subjects who were first exposed to the 8-coin problem started off by placing 4 coins on either side of the balance. The factor of symmetry seemed, however, to interact with the factor of totality. Thus, since 9 coins total an odd number, a symmetrical dimension would not use up all the coins. In this case only 27 out of 37 subjects started with one of the four symmetrical weighings (1 vs. 1, 2 vs. 2, 3 vs. 3, 4 vs. 4).

Besides the interaction between symmetry and totality, i.e., the fact that symmetry was more likely to be used in the case of even numbers, a factor of experience was noted. Thus, subjects who worked the 8-coin problem after the 9-coin problem showed a significant tendency to overcome the totality factor. That is, more of them used the 3 vs. 3 weighing on the first weighing. Similarly, in the case of the 9-coin problem, only 2 inexperienced subjects tried 3 vs. 3 on the first weighing, whereas 8 tried the correct combination on the first weighing after experience with the 8-coin problem.

What we seem to have here is something similar to Harlow's learning sets discussed in Chapter 15: the individuals were "learning how to learn or learning how to approach a problem." Thus, even though the total number of coins was different, the subjects were learning how to break the total down into subgroups which, from past experience, were readily analyzable and thus "pregnant with meaning of informational content." Similar transfer effects were noted from experience with 8- and 9-coin problems to the 25-coin problem.

Because all the usable information is not readily available in the coins but since the total number can be broken down into subgroups which immediately transmit all the available information, we have designated this kind of problem a partially open or partially closed system. If we had an entirely closed system, 8 coins, for example, would transmit 3 bits of information. But *S* is allowed only two weighings. Thus he must solve the problem by extracting the 2 "pregnant" bits of information. This he can do only by the kind of categorizing noted in presenting the solution to this problem.

It would be very illuminating to work with other families of coin combinations (extending the present families of 8, 9, and 25) to tease out further the kind of factors facilitating transfer in the genesis and development of these kinds of problem-solving sets. We should uncover some useful principles which could actually be employed in teaching individuals the art of problem solving just as we now teach them other kinds of skills.

THE OPEN SYSTEM. The open system is illustrated in the following problem. The ages of a man and his wife total 98 years. He is twice as old as she was when he was as old as she now is. How old is the man now, and how old is his wife?

We call this an open system since the subject cannot immediately apply a model or a principle which has worked in the past. Unlike the closed system, the order is not present in the stimulus presentation. The subject has to do something to the stimulus presentation (*reorganize* it) to establish an order which he can then manipulate with a past model, a tool to arrive at the solution. Similarly, a family of problem-solving sets, as in the case of the partially open system, is also less available. Most of the difficulty is caused by the second sentence, in which the ratio of noise to transmission is too high; i.e., the noise is drowning out the transmission of usable information.

In order to solve this problem the subject must first be able to generate sets into the problem situation to categorize into statements which transmit more information than the original statements. Probably the most effective set in this case would be to generate appropriate algebraic equations which would order the information. The first equation, given by the first sentence, is simple enough. If we let *X* equal the age of the man now and *Y* equal the age of the wife now, then

$$X + Y = 98$$

Now, if we can only generate a second equation, we shall be on our way to a solution, but establishing this equation is more difficult. We can begin as follows. The second statement says that "he is twice as old as she was." Thus

$$X = 2(Y - ?)$$

At this point the subject usually has trouble because the rest of the statement, "when he was as old as she now is," is low in transmission and high in noise or equivocation (we recall that $T = H - E$). In these types of problems, in which the stage of low transmission is reached, it is appropriate to say that the subject has reached a *gap,* the crossing of which is difficult. It seems to me that the way to facilitate the crossing or closing of such gaps is to give youngsters a variety of symbolic experiences to develop different strategies which could be utilized when such problems are encountered in the future. For example, we may suggest to the subject that the equivocal statement, "He is twice as old as she was when he was as old as she now is," be replaced by the statement, "He is twice as old as she was Z years ago." Now we can complete the second equation by stating that

$$X = 2(Y - Z)$$

Having clarified some of the confusion, we can go back and ask what Z is. From the second statement we know that Z years ago, X was Y (when he, X, was as old as she, Y, now is). If Z years ago X was Y, then

$$X = Y + Z$$

or

$$Z = X - Y$$

which we can substitute in the second equation above. Therefore

$$X = 2[Y - (X - Y)]$$

Now, assuming that the student has learned how to "solve" simple equations, the problem is reduced to a closed system, and the rest of the process is fairly mechanical. Thus

$$X = 2Y - 2X + 2Y$$
$$3X = 4Y$$
$$X = \tfrac{4}{3}Y$$

Now substitute Y for X in equation 1:

$$X + Y = 98$$
$$\tfrac{4}{3}Y + Y = 98$$
$$\tfrac{7}{3}Y = 98$$
$$Y = 98 \times \tfrac{3}{7}$$
$$Y = 42$$

and

$$X = 56 \text{ (by subtraction)}$$

The problem is solved.

As a check, we can go back to any of the equations we have written along the way and see when their demands are satisfied by substituting the values 42 for Y and 56 for X. These check out.

The example given above illustrates how a gap can be filled by capturing the essential relationship which constitutes the information in the message.

What seem to be needed in the study of creative problem solving are (1) determining the kinds of strategies that individuals can use to transform the statements of problems to reduce their equivocal information and thereby increase the amount of transmitted information; and (2) ascertaining what kinds of training and learning experience facilitate the ability to generate such transformation. A beginning in this dimension was made by Max Wertheimer, the founder of gestalt psychology, in his book on productive thinking (1945).

Max Wertheimer and the Gestalt Treatment of Productive Thinking

The following discussion is based on Wertheimer's conceptualization of productive thinking. His main contention is that traditional education has concerned itself principally with drilling the student to memorize mechanical formulas without stressing the importance of understanding the nature of the relationships underlying them. The narrow transfer resulting from such habituation inhibits the process of productive thinking in the open system.

Wertheimer attributes this tradition of what he calls *blind drill* to the associative trial-and-error learning theory originated by Edward L. Thorndike. An example of this kind of teaching is the way children have been taught to divide by fractions. For example, many of us recall that when we were first introduced to this kind of problem in school, the teacher would proceed somewhat as follows:

$$10 \div \tfrac{1}{2} = 10 \times \tfrac{2}{1} = 20$$

We were told simply to change the division to multiplication and to invert the fraction. This is tantamout to giving the student a mechanical "gimmick" to memorize, without a serious attempt to get him to understand or reason why this device works.

A more sensible method, calculated to engender in the child the habit of approaching problems with the attitude of uncovering relationships that can be manipulated, would be to illustrate graphically what division is. Let us take the example given above. We can arrange the 10 units in something like the following manner:

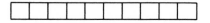

The child counts the 10 units. We now ask him to divide the figure by units. He still counts 10 units. If he divides by 2 (i.e., takes 2 units at a time), he gets 5 (pairs). Now if he divides by ½, he proceeds as follows:

The shorter lines represent the operation of taking the total of 10 and breaking it down to half units (i.e., when dividing by 2, we take larger sections of the total, but when we divide by $\frac{1}{2}$, we take proportionally smaller sections at a time). Now the child can count the new total number of sections and see that they equal 20. Experience with these kinds of operations develops insight into the true meaning of mathematical manipulation in all its richness. The child should now be able to transfer to other problems of dividing fractions. Take the following case:

$$\tfrac{3}{4} \div \tfrac{1}{2}$$

Let us start with the unit and first divide it into halves:

and then into quarters:

From this model the child can see that $\frac{3}{4}$ is the same as $\frac{1}{2}$ taken $1\frac{1}{2}$ times. Thus he can understand why $\frac{3}{4} \div \frac{1}{2} = \frac{3}{4} \times \frac{2}{1} = \frac{3}{2}$, or $1\frac{1}{2}$.

Having mastered the basic set of operations and understanding that the inversion of the fraction representing the division merely puts the subunits by which we are dividing in the numerator, the child comes to understand the complementary relationship of division and multiplication. Thus he can transfer to more complicated problems, such as $\frac{5}{8} \div \frac{3}{4}$ or $3\frac{7}{8} \div \frac{3}{16}$, and so on.

INSIGHTFUL SOLUTIONS OF GEOMETRIC PROBLEMS. One of the most vivid illustrations of Wertheimer's contentions is represented by what he calls the *structural method* of teaching such subjects as geometry. The following demonstration, while not identical with Wertheimer's procedure, is based on the material in one chapter of his book and is representative of techniques we have used with success in our attempts to teach children in Grade 5 and later grades to understand the structural relationships of plane geometry.

We start with a practical problem. Let us suppose we have the task of laying square tiles on the floor of a room and want to know how many tiles are required. The dimensions of the room are, let us say, 12×15, and the dimensions of each tile are 1×1. How many tiles do we need? Let us start by laying 1 row of tiles. Clearly, we require 15 tiles to fill 1 row. How many such rows will there be? There will be 12, since the width of the room is 12. So the child can count the total number and arrive at 180 tiles. He can also multiply 15×12 and arrive at 180. Thus he has verified that the area of a rectangle (or square) is $L \times W$ (length times width).

Now we proceed to another figure, a right-angled triangle. There is immediate transfer. The child begins by laying a row of tiles and finds, to his dismay, that the last tile runs over the figure. At first he is somewhat disturbed and thinks we have changed the rules of the game or "cheated." But we encourage him to discover whether there is any relationship between the rectangle and the triangle. With perseverance he learns that he can dissect the rectangle through one of its diagonals and produce two triangles. Thus the area of the triangle is half the area of the rectangle. The area of the triangle is $\frac{1}{2}(L \times W)$, or $\frac{1}{2}(B \times H)$, if we substitute base for length and height for width. Thus the textbook formula of the area of a triangle, namely $\frac{1}{2}B \times H$, becomes clear. We can also transfer from a right-angled triangle to one without right angles by pointing out that the latter can be made part of two rectangles which, when put together, give us Figure 16-2. The bigger rectangle consists of two sides

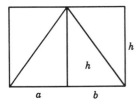

Figure 16-2
The relationship between the dimensions of a triangle and the rectangle which contains it.

equal to the base $(a + b)$ and height (h) of the triangle. Thus again the area of this triangle is equal to $\frac{1}{2}[(a + b) \times H]$. The relationships are illustrated in Figure 16-2.

Finally we move on to a parallelogram of the following variety:

We direct the student to discover whether he can so reorganize the parallelogram as to reduce it to the two basic figures (square and triangle) with which he is now familiar and the areas of which he knows how to compute. Again, with encouragement, he will see that he can cut off a triangle on the left of the parallelogram and insert it on the right. This is shown in Figure 16-3. Thus the area of the parallelogram is $b \times h$.

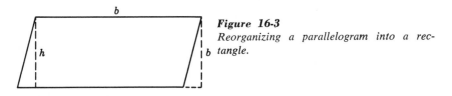

Figure 16-3
Reorganizing a parallelogram into a rectangle.

What we have done is to give a structural meaning (i.e., in terms of basic relationships which are visible and understandable) to the textbook formal operation of dropping perpendiculars and proving something about the congruence of the triangles. Quite frequently the student does not really know why we are proving the congruence of triangles. The whole process seems highly artificial to him. By "cutting off" one triangle and "putting it back in," the notion of simplifying and yet holding areas constant becomes clear. Thus when the student proceeds to the formal operation of geometry, he understands why he is doing what he does.

In fact, we have found transfer to all kinds of figures after children were taught by the structural method, much greater transfer than is evident in those taught initially by exposure to the formal, traditional method which is not so meaningful to the student. Thus our children can transfer to such figures as those represented in Figure 16-4. With such straight-lined figures,

Figure 16-4
Figure for testing transfer from learning by the structural method.

even those which look "weird" and are never seen in textbooks, the child undertakes to reconstruct the figures into basic squares, rectangles, and triangles.

The insights of Wertheimer were remarkable, especially when we consider that he made his assertions long before information theory became an important conceptual tool in psychology for analyzing perception, language, and thinking. What he was in fact antedating is the contemporary concern with factors which facilitate the accessibility of relevant problem-solving sets or models. To translate into terms of information theory, the subject's reorganizing of the stimulus material produces a structure which transmits more information and, by so doing, correspondingly decreases noise or equivocation.

While we cannot measure the increase in transmitted information produced by such reorganization as readily as Hovland did in his concept-attainment experiments and while it is difficult to separate the aspect of information transmission from information assimilation, the innovations of Wertheimer have advanced our understanding of productive thinking and pushed us closer to realizing its relationship to creative invention. In fact, the rest of his book contains rich examples of how his analysis could be applied to understanding the creative thought process of such great thinkers as Galileo, Gauss, and Einstein. Furthermore, these insights have been assimilated into the "educational revolution" evident in the United States during the past decade. I am referring to the concern modern educators have with establishing in young children competence in discovering *patterns* in such disciplines as the so-called new mathematics. Bruner (1961) has extended this kind of analysis and teaching method to many other disciplines. A couple of examples, one from the analysis of Gauss's reasoning process and the other following from Bruner's suggestions on how to teach such subjects as social studies, will illustrate this point.

GAUSS AND THE ESTABLISHMENT OF PATTERNS. All of us who have studied some algebra are familiar with the formula for the sum of the first *N* natural integers. The usual textbook formula for this quantity is expressed as

$$\frac{N(N+1)}{2}$$

where *N* represents the last integer in the series. What we may not know is that the famous German mathematician Karl Friedrich Gauss discovered this formulation when he was a young student in the equivalent of our grade school. The story goes something as follows. The teacher of the class in which Gauss was a pupil was giving the students practice (as Wertheimer would say, drill) in finding the sum of series of numbers such as the following:

$$1 + 2 + 3 + 4 + 5 + 6 + 7 + 8 + 9 + 10 \cdots N$$

He was astounded by the fact that the numbers were no sooner presented than young Gauss would flash the correct answer. He asked Gauss the nature of the mysterious process by which he so quickly arrived at the answer. Did he have a "photographic" mind or some other particular talent? The answer was, "No!" Young Gauss was simply able to uncover the underlying structural relationship, the pattern by which these numbers were, or could be, organized.

Gauss noticed that since each successive number proceeding from the left increased by 1 and since each successive number proceeding from the right decreased by 1, the sum of each pair must be a constant. This insight is diagramed in Figure 16-5. In this example the constant is equal to 11

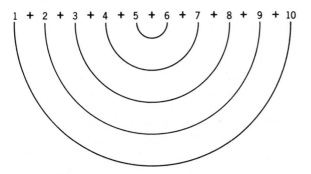

Figure 16-5
The formulation of Gauss for the sum of the first natural integers.

$(10 + 1, 9 + 2, 5 + 6,$ etc.$)$, and since each constant represents the sum of a pair, there are 5 ($\frac{1}{2}$ of 10) pairs. Thus the sum is $11 \times 5 = 55$. The general expression is represented by $(N + 1) \times N/2$, which shows the structural relationships more clearly than $[N(N + 1)]/2$.

In fact, if the individual truly grasps the nature of the relatedness, he does not even have to memorize a formula because he can immediately look for the pattern when another series is presented. Thus in the example

$$1 + 2 + 3 + 4 + 5 + 6 + 7 + 8 + 9$$

the constant is 10, and the constant has to be multiplied by $4\frac{1}{2}$, since we have an odd number in the series. The sum of 45 can also be computed by noting the 4 pairs of 10 plus the off number 5 in the middle of the sequence.

Not only is the retention of a formula unnecessary, but mechanical application of it without genuine comprehension of the structural relationships it relates is disastrous. Let us illustrate by looking at the following problem:

$$3 + 6 + 9 + 12 + 15 + 18$$

If we were to apply blindly to formula, we would get 19×9 $(N + 1 \times N/2)$, or 171, which is, of course, ridiculous. The true answer is $21 \times 3 = 63$, because the constant is 21 and there are 3 pairs. So, in the formula, N really stands for the number of digits, and $N + 1$ for the sum of the constant. In many cases the constant cannot be obtained by using $N + 1$.

If we thus teach youngsters to look for these structural patterns or train ourselves to look for them, we can go a long way to facilitate the growth of productive thinking. For example, in an extension of the Gaussian approach, we shall easily be able to generalize to any combination of numbers having some common relationship and by simple modification transfer to operations besides addition, such as multiplication and the use of fractions.

INCREASING INFORMATION TRANSMISSION THROUGH PATTERNING OR CHUNKING. Not only have Wertheimer's insights been incorporated into new methods of instruction and learning, but they have also been extended by contemporary psychologists. For example, George Miller (1956a; 1956b), reiterating the fact that our capacity to process information is limited, has applied the principles of categorization or patterning to both problem solving and memory. He reasons that not only are elements in and of themselves rather meaningless but also that they are hard to remember. Therefore, we can facilitate memory, problem solving, and transfer by organizing elements in large (and therefore fewer) meaningful wholes or patterns, which he calls *chunks,* as opposed to bits, which are a measure of the element. The way one organizes bits into chunks would presumably follow processes similar to what Wertheimer calls looking for structural or inner relatedness.

I mentioned earlier in this chapter that it is difficult to measure the increase in transmitted information in structural patterns as compared with unorganized elements, but Miller provides a clue in this direction. Let us suppose there are 16 elements in a message. The amount of information would be equal to 4 bits. What is more, only 8 elements or 2 bits might be transmitted, 2 bits being lost in the process of communication. If we organized the elements into chunks, 4 elements to a chunk, we would have 4 larger units or chunks and all would probably be transmitted. Hence, by chunking or patterning on the basis of structural relatedness, we have increased our transmission from 50 to 100 per cent, or at least by decreasing the number of alternatives we have facilitated information assimilation. What is more, the principles (only four of them) underlying the chunking permit us to deduce and thus generate all the original elements. Presently I shall refer to an experiment we performed in which the fact that chunking increases the efficiency of problem solving, transfer, and memory is demonstrated.

In the previously mentioned book on the process of education which is his conceptualization of a conference of many leading educators, Bruner, extending the work on structural analysis of Wertheimer and Piaget, points out that this kind of teaching method can be used to promote productive thinking in a variety of disciplines. He is guided by his belief that any subject worth teaching can be taught to a child at any age (presumably after the child has developed some conceptual ability, which usually requires a mental age of thirty months), provided that the teacher has enough imagination to translate the formal principles of the subject into language or models that the child can relate to his intuitive thought, which, in turn, is based on his functional experience.

Let us apply this approach to the teaching of some aspect of social studies. Sometime during grade school most students are introduced to the history of the geographic expansion of the United States as the settlers moved westward across the Appalachian Mountains. Usually the textbooks are written in a very matter-of-fact style, simply narrating what happened. Would it not be far more beneficial to the development of the child's thought process, and more interesting to boot, if we taught this topic as a "thought exercise" in figuring out the principle of economic geography? For example, we could start by drawing an outline of the United States and listing the populated areas of the Eastern states prior to the great westward expansion. Then we could explain to the children why people tend to live in certain areas: the presence of natural harbors, waterways, natural resources, etc. Following this, we would state that many settlers wanted to move west, either to escape from the overpopulated areas or to seek religious and other freedoms. We would then draw the mountain ranges, valleys, lakes, and natural resources and ask them to "guess" where cities eventually sprang up in America.

Through this reasoning process the child would learn to think about social studies, not merely to memorize elements. Any variation from expected principles, e.g., the rise of Las Vegas, must then be accounted for on other bases. But by organizing this part of social studies around meaningful principles or into meaningful patterns much of the entropy of the economic geography of the United States would be reduced, and meaningful chunks of information would be transmitted.

Similar improvements in teaching and learning can be effected by looking for the structures in such diversified subjects as the natural sciences, other branches of the social sciences, and even such disciplines of the humanities as grammar and literature. In fact, it is my belief that we are missing an opportunity with respect to the promotion of social integration and psychological health by neglecting any formal concern with these areas until the individual reaches college. If psychology is a science and if the natural determinants of human behavior and adjustments have their foundations in childhood, then we should guide the child to uncover these patterns and incorporate "psychologically relevant sets" into his attitudes while his personality is being formed and not wait until repression has worked too well or the origins of habits are rather dim in consciousness. I can think of a number of interesting psychological "principles" which could very profitably be learned and assimilated by children in grade school. The beneficial transfer effects of such learning to the later solution of social problems should be very effective. In any case, this important area seems to me to be crying out for research.

Ability to Learn Productive Thinking

Until this point in the chapter we have strongly asserted that productive thinking can be learned and significantly influenced by teaching and training. Many people have challenged this view, and the viewpoint that high intelligence and creativity are talents with which individuals are endowed at birth is not lacking among the public in general. In fact, a colleague of Max Wertheimer, Wolfgang Köhler, apparently held to an essentially nativistic position about problem solving. This view is adopted, among other sources, in his interpretation of his famous work (Köhler, 1924) on the thought process of apes. Representative of these observations is the behavior of a chimpanzee when confronted with the classical "stick" problem. In a typical situation the chimpanzee is hungry and is in a cage with steel bars. Located at some distance from the cage are incentives, such as bananas, but these goal objects are so far from the perimeter of the cage that the chimpanzee cannot reach them merely by reaching for them with his arms. In the general area, within easy reach of the animal, is a variety of sticks. Some chimpanzees apparently do not perceive the significance of the sticks, but the "bright" ones do. They use the sticks as an extension of the arm's length to "work the bananas in." Particularly brilliant chimpanzees insert a long narrow stick into a hole in a shorter, wider stick, thus making a rake. With this tool they can more efficiently "rake in" bananas.

Köhler could not find any reason to believe that past experience differentiated the behavior of the unsuccessful and the productive chimpanzees, and he asserted therefore that the "insight" exhibited by the productive thinkers resulted from the organization of their brains, which presumably was genetically determined. Birch (1945), however, in a study which did utilize training as a variable, found that "insightful" solutions were more prevalent in animals that had had experience with manipulating sticks as compared with those that had not had such experience. What are the implications of this kind of research for the understanding of creative discovery in human beings? It should be of great concern to us to do the kind of research which would determine to what extent creative human beings are born and to what extent they are made.

AN EXPERIMENT ON THE FACILITATIVE EFFECTS OF CHUNKING OR PATTERNING. While discussing Miller's work earlier in this chapter, we referred to how information transmission or assimilation can be facilitated by chunking. Actually one of the earliest psychologists to attack this problem was another member of the gestalt school, George Katona (1940), who concluded from his studies that the solution of card-trick problems and memory of the procedure were facilitated if the subject organized the relationship between the elements of the trick. Since Katona had been criticized for lack of objectivity and adequate controls, Hilgard et al. (1953) extended his work on card-trick problems, using an improved experimental design. These authors did not find that the memory of the group which learned the tricks by organization was superior to that of the group which learned by rote memorization.

It occurred to me that part of the reason for the difference between Katona's and Hilgard's results can be attributed to the fact that the principles or relationships in the card tricks are rather obscure and not clear-cut. Consequently we (Forgus and Schwartz, 1957) attempted to measure the effects of chunking or patterning, using a clearly defined structural principle for each chunk and extending the dependent variables to include transfer in addition to learning and retention. A representation of the stimulus material used in this experiment is shown in Figure 16-6.

Three groups of college students, all female, were used in this study.

Figure 16-6
An identical reproduction of the symbols and their English-letter equivalents which was given to the observer group during the preliminary learning period and the transfer period. (After Forgus and Schwartz, 1957, p. 136.)

Members of group O, the observer group, were presented with the 26 symbols of the "new" alphabet and their English equivalents and were also taught the principle by which the new symbols were generated. Members of group P, the participant group, were presented with the identical material and were told that a principle underlay the construction but were instructed to discover it for themselves. Members of group M, the memorization group, were presented with the 26 symbols and their English-letter equivalents but in a rearranged sequence so that they would not readily see that there was an organizational principle. The members of each group were required to learn the entire list of 26 symbols until they could reproduce them and their English equivalents in two successive errorless reproductions. As further insurance that they knew the meaning of the symbols, they had to translate a passage written in this code into English. All subjects were able to do this perfectly within 15 min after meeting the first criterion of learning.

One week later all subjects were brought back for the tests of retention and transfer. First, the subjects were asked to translate a second passage written in the code they had learned the first week. Second, they were given a test of simple transfer. They were presented with 5 representative symbols based on a new code and told that they could figure out the new system underlying their genesis. If they did this successfully, they could translate another passage written in this second code. The code involved only a slight variation from the first one. Instead of putting 4 letters into each chunk, this time we put 5 letters in each chunk. Hence there were 5 groups and Z was a lone member of the sixth group. Finally, a transfer test involving considerable new organization was given. Again the alphabet was divided into 7 groups, 4 letters in the first 6 groups and 2 in the seventh. Each letter was represented by two numbers, the first indicating the group it was in and the second representing the particular number in that group. Thus, A was 11, B was 12, E was 21, and H was 24; X was 64, Y was 71, and Z was 72. Again the subject was given 5 representative symbols and the English-letter equivalents and told that she would be able to translate a third passage if she could figure out how all 26 symbols could be generated.

On all three criteria, *memory, transfer,* and *transfer with considerable reorganization,* groups O and P were vastly superior to group M. There was no significant difference between groups O and P, although the latter was slightly superior on all criteria. In fact, the two groups that learned by principle even learned the original list in significantly fewer trials. On the two transfer tests, the first two groups translated more than three times as many correct letters as did the memorization group. On the retention test they translated four times as many correct letters, and group P had a perfect score.

If we look at the code symbols in Figure 16-6 again, we can see what was happening. Group M had to remember 26 separate items, or between 4 and 5 bits of information. Groups O and P had to remember only 7 chunks based on a principle, or the equivalent of only 3 bits of information. What is more, they could generate all the 26 symbols from the 7 principles. Thus we found that in the retention test group P transmitted 100 per cent, group O almost 100 per cent, and group M only about 70 per cent. Moreover, the clear superiority of the two "principle and organizing" groups on the second, difficult transfer test has significance for productive thinking and creative thinking. The greater the variety of experience the developing individual has with learning to discover principles, the greater the range of associations available to him, and the greater the number of associative ties between the various sets and models he can generate, the more creative will he be.

A Final and Brief Word on Exploration of the Creative Personality

The last two sentences imply that creative thought is, at least partly, developed through relevant learning experiences by discovery that builds up sets which can have high associative strength. In this final section I want to deal with one kind of experimental paradigm verifying the plausibility of this conclusion and then end with a statement about the variety of associated areas easily accessible or arousable in the creative personality.

EXPERIMENTAL INVESTIGATION OF ASSOCIATIVE BASIS OF CREATIVITY. In a recent publication, Mednick (1963) presents an interesting and, shall we say, creative attack on measuring the range and strength of associations in creative individuals. He begins with the assertion that the range and strength of associatives to various symbols, such as words, differ for the creative and the relatively noncreative individuals. This difference is graphically illustrated in Figure 16-7.

Basically, what Mednick is saying is this: If we ask an individual to give

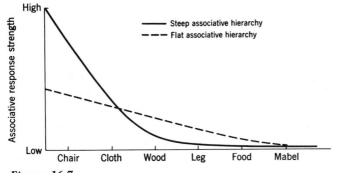

Figure 16-7
Associative hierarchies to the word "table." (After S. A. Mednick, 1963, p. 586.)

associations to the word "table," we can get, at the extremes, two kinds of outcomes. The individual who is low in creativity has a high associative strength for a few, and almost none for other, words. Thus he has a steep associative hierarchy. The highly creative individual, on the other hand, has medium levels of associative strength for a number of words which he can generate. Hence he has a flat associative hierarchy and can call up many associative responses (through mediation). There is a greater probability that the correct set or model (to be used in organizing the pattern) will be found in the individual with a wider range of associatives than in one with a narrow range. Hence he should be more productive in problem solving, which to people like Wertheimer and others (Newell, Shaw, and Simon, 1963), forms the basis of creative thinking.

Mednick has put his theoretical conceptualization to experimental analysis by constructing a test of creativity which he called the Remote Associates Test (RAT) and finding out whether people with differing degrees of demonstrable creativity can be discriminated by performance on this test. In the RAT the subject is given a list of three words, such as those presented in Figure 16-8, and asked to call up a fourth word which has something in common with the other three.

Examples			
1.	rat	blue	collage
2.	railroad	girl	class
3.	wheel	electric	high
4.	out	dog	cat

Figure 16-8
Examples from the RAT. (After S. A. Mednick, 1963, pp. 590–591.) Answers to examples 1 to 4, respectively, could be cheese, working, chair, and house.

Mednick reports that the test has high reliability and some interesting findings of concurrent validity. For example, there was a correlation of 0.70 ($p < 0.01$) between performance on the RAT and the rating of creativity in architecture of a group of architectural students by their mentors, who had worked with them for more than 2 years. Furthermore, at the University of Michigan performance on the RAT was a much better indicator of research creativity in graduate students in psychology than the Miller Analogies Test, which is widely used as one of the admission criteria. Here research creativity was defined as the invention of new research methods, the pulling together of disparate theory or research areas, or both. Finally, it was found that the RAT scores were negatively correlated with grades. High RAT performers received better grades from teachers rated as liberal and open-minded, however, whereas low RAT performers received high grades from teachers rated as authoritarian and dogmatic.

The interests and attitudes of those with the high RAT scores and rated high on creativity are also significant. Their views are more atypical and "liberal" than those with low RAT scores. They show greater interest in art, psychologist, physician, mathematician, and author-journalist on the

Strong Vocational Interest Blank and low on farmer and math-physical science high school teacher.

Mednick ends by pointing to other variables that should be experimentally manipulated. They include the following:

1. High creativity (associativeness) should be more readily generated under massed than under distributed work sessions. Others have suggested that creative ideas would be fostered if we gave students more numerous "take-home" tests and let them have more time for associations to occur.
2. Creative warm-up sessions.
3. Experience in combating stereotyping of associative responses or functional fixedness.

EXPLORATORY COMMENTS ON THE PERSONALITY OF CREATIVE INDIVIDUALS. Thus far in this chapter we have been dealing almost exclusively with the effects of certain variables, such as the ability to analyze into structural relationships and the range of associatedness, on creative and productive thinking. The kinds of data presented, which are typical of what has come to be called experimental psychology, have been obtained by using the analysis-of-variance design. This design seeks to determine the extent to which certain independent variables influence the phenomenon (in this case, thinking) or the dependent variable under consideration. But as we pointed out in Chapter 12, "Social Perception, Motives, and Personality," the exclusive use of the analysis-of-variance design often discards much valuable potential information. For example, in discussing the work of Eriksen, we saw how the analysis-of-variance approach to perceptual defense was inadequate. Instead, as Eriksen found, some individuals are consistent attackers of anxiety-provoking (for them) stimuli while others are consistent defenders. It also seems plausible that all individuals will not react to some variables, such as those listed by Mednick, in the same ways; nor is it necessarily to be expected that those who exhibit high ability for structural analysis in one area will exhibit similar levels of ability for structural analysis in unrelated areas.

Ever since Guilford [1] conceptualized problem solving and creative ability as combinations of different factors of intellect, some psychologists have used the technique of factor analysis to determine whether there are certain patterns of basic factors or types which characterize creative thinking. Debate over the structure of intellect goes back many years. One point of view, represented by Karl Spearman, the famous British psychologist, is that there are a general factor G for overall intelligence and then a number of specific factors S, each of which is partially correlated with G. Guilford's view is that there are three basic factors (each of which contains subsets) which interact in various combinations to produce different kinds of creative acts. Guilford refers in his 1963 article to a study supervised by

[1] See, for example, Guilford (1956; 1963).

Merrifield. one of his colleagues, which supports his view that the variables underlying creativity can be analyzed in terms of the factors designated in his theory about the structure of intellect. Moreover, Getzels and Jackson (1962) have empirical evidence that young people who were judged creative in terms of novel reactions to stimuli could not be differentiated purely on the basis of intelligence above a certain minimum; that is, an IQ of 120 was all that was required for creativity to be evidenced, but in addition some other measures of creativity were necessary. What some of these other measures might be have been investigated by other psychologists. We shall report here the studies of R. B. Cattell (1963) to give some flavor of this work and then list the work of some other investigators in the field.

Cattell states that he began developing his ideas about the personality underlying creativity while reading the biographical material of creative artists and scientists. His intuitions were, by and large, verified in a more experimentally oriented study utilizing his 16 Personality Factor test. He found that the personality profiles of 140 eminent researchers in physics, biology, and psychology differed significantly on several of the factors from the range of the control group for the general adult male population. Five of the factors deviated at a statistical significance level of $p = 0.01$. The eminent scientific researcher is more schizothyme, more intelligent, more dominant, and more inhibited. Furthermore, he tends to be more emotionally sensitive, more self-sufficient, more Bohemian, and more radical but less emotionally stable.

It is left to the reader to form his own composite image of the pattern of traits depicted above. One statement will be made, however: it is not difficult to see why a highly intelligent, emotionally sensitive, fairly radical, dominant, independent, and schizothymic individual (one with much internal use of intellect or cerebration) would be creative. In interpreting the introverted or moderately inhibited aspect of creative individuals, Cattell refers further to the statement of Golovin in the same symposium. The latter had stated that the use of too many channels for input (as in the talkative individual) reduces the number of channels available for scanning (searching for new ideas).

Other investigators have verified the tendency toward radicalism (sometimes designated as a motive to be creative) on the part of creative individuals. Thus Golann (1963) and Barron (1963b) have both found that individuals who were classified as creative on an independent test of creativity preferred pictures and stimuli which were more ambiguous and preferred to render designs that were more complex rather than symmetrical; i.e., they seemed to deviate to some extent from the principle of *Prägnanz* or redundancy to one of seeking more complex patterns of stimuli.

In all these exploratory investigations it seems that the process of creative thinking is concerned with effective surprise.[2] Cattell states that the kind of personality profile for creative people in the arts is probably much the same as that for creative people in the sciences. This seems quite reasonable as far as underlying motives are concerned, but it also seems quite probable that the effectiveness with which individuals can deal with different kinds of surprises will differ in widely different areas of knowledge. In fact, even insofar as personality and biography are concerned, Roe (1953) found that while physical and biological scientists developed an early social independence, the social scientists had more of an overprotective interaction with their parents. Thus the mere fact of different amounts of time spent by these two groups in social and nonsocial environments should make them differentially sensitive to extracting cues or information from these different kinds of stimuli while engaged in creative thinking endeavors. What we need, of course, is a continuing development of the psychology of individual differences with respect to creativity. One way of approaching this would be not only to look at the past histories of people, as Cattell and Roe have done, but also to try deliberately to produce more creative individuals through direct intervention in the educational system. We end this chapter with a brief report of one psychologist's noble attempts to accomplish this goal.

DEVELOPING CREATIVE THINKING THROUGH SCHOOL EXPERIENCE. Paul Torrance (1962a; 1962b) at the University of Minnesota has spent a number of years studying the development of creative thinking in children and trying to facilitate its growth through school experiences. I think it would be constructive to list some of his ideas and some of his data. They provide a good framework for future productive research in this hard-to-get-at area. Here are some of his guiding principles.

1. Increasing sensitivity to environmental stimuli. With reference to Cattell's belief that the personality pattern characterizing creative thinking is common to creative artists and scientists, it is interesting to note Torrance's feeling that creative individuals are differentially sensitive to stimuli which furnish the raw materials for the particular kind of creativity involved. As illustrations of his point of view, he cites his own findings that a certain kind of individual, such as a creative psychologist or social scientist, can be creative about interpersonal relationships by being sensitive to human feelings, emotions, motives, and ways of thinking despite his insensitivity to chemical phenomena. On the other side of the coin, M. I. Stein (1956) found that creative chemists are, of course, highly sensitive to chemical phenomena but show strong insensitivity to interpersonal relationships, a tendency which goes back to childhood, when they already preferred to play with animals and mechanical objects rather than other people.

Torrance goes on to contend, however, that we should be developing more numerous pedagogical techniques to make young children more sensitive to a

[2] See Bruner (1963).

greater variety of stimuli—or we should really say *stimulus cues,* which are the purveyors of information. Again he refers to a demonstration by Littwin, which is reported in a book by Russell (1956). The study concerned itself with assessing the relative effects of three methods (of teacher stimulation) on the development of imaginative writing in three matched groups of seventh- and eighth-grade students. The training or stimulating period lasted 10 weeks. One group practiced writing vivid descriptions of pictures which they had studied. Group 2 studied literary models containing systems of sound, color, and movement. The third group practiced describing all the possible sensory images— auditory, visual, olfactory, and gustatory—that they could experience while examining an object or situation. It was found that the third group showed the most significant increase in composition tests on the basis of grading for imagination and content.

Relevant to the finding that experience with variety and novel stimulation (direct or imaginal) facilitates creative development is the report of Getzels and Jackson (1958) that there was no difference in scholastic achievement between a group of children whose IQs fell below the 80th percentile but who were highly creative (upper 20 per cent), as judged by their tests, and a group whose IQs were in the upper 20 per cent but whose creativity scores were below 80 per cent. The teachers, however, preferred the high IQs over the highly creative. This preference is reminiscent of Mednick's work. It might very well be that teachers who cannot match the creativity of these highly creative children are threatened by them. In any case, this whole area of the effect of teachers' attitudes and personalities (and, for that matter, those of parents) on the development of creative thinking is fascinating and very important, and fairly crying out for more research.

2. In the promotion of attitudes to test new stimulus situations, manipulatory experience plays a significant role. In one of Torrance's research projects, first, second, and third graders were asked to think of ways in which they could change certain toys (which were visually present) to make them more interesting. While they figured out these tasks, they were observed by a team that rated them with respect to manipulation on a three-point scale: high, medium, and low. For all of the grades it was found that the high-manipulation group was superior to the medium group, which in turn was superior to the low-manipulation group, in terms of the number of modifications suggested. Of even greater importance and interest was the fact that the low-manipulation third graders were inferior to medium- and high-manipulation first graders on these creativity scores.

These examples give enough of an idea, I think, of the kind of research that can and is being done in this area. Other suggestions made by Torrance include the following:

3. Teach how to test systematically each new idea. As reasonable as this sounds, it is often not done by teachers and parents. Instead, they frequently give the child the answers or are impatient of novel ideas or courses of action on his part. So become tolerant of new ideas.

4. Try to avoid forming an *Einstellung.*

5. Develop a creative classroom atmosphere.

6. Teach skills for avoiding peer sanctions. Torrance states that personality

research indicates that the highly creative student invariably alienates his peers. While this is partly to be expected and should be accepted as reality, he can nevertheless be taught to maintain originality without being hostile or aggressive to the less creative or to regard them as "stupid." That is, while he must learn that people generally will dislike others not because of the others but because of their own feelings of inadequacy, they can nevertheless learn to be kind to others and to have a healthy social interest.

7. Encourage the acquisition of knowledge in a variety of fields.

8. Encourage and evaluate self-initiated learning.

9. Give information about the creative process. What is more important is that Torrance's research indicates that training, in addition to information about the variables influencing creativity, had stronger facilitative effects on creativity scores. The training was on such effective principles as the following: putting objects to other uses, adapting, modifying (e.g., changing color, motion, sound, odor, form, etc.), magnification, minification, substitution, rearranging, reversing or changing positions, combining, and so on.

Probably the most important point to stress here, as in the work of Wertheimer, is the need to develop teachers who can provide these necessary kinds of stimulation for the growing child.

Summary

This chapter began with a classification of the problem-solving process into closed, partially open, and open systems, and the characteristics of each were illustrated.

Next we discussed more fully the nature of thinking within the open system, which is labeled *productive thinking*. The view of Wertheimer on how productive thinking can be taught through training to analyze problems into their structural relatedness was analyzed and extended to scientific inventions and the nature of chunking of information in such diverse subjects as mathematics, language, and social studies.

Finally, we discussed some exploratory studies on the personalities of creative individuals and the determination of remote associations in these people. We ended with a description of some pioneering attempts to increase the child's sensitivity to a wider range of stimuli through creative school experiences.

This book has dealt with the processing and utilization of information by the organism. We began with the nature of built-in programming ability and proceeded up an hierarchy to more complex programming which is modified by experience and learning. It is my hope that we have highlighted some of the important conceptualizations in current cognitive work and that the reader has been aided in developing an appreciation for this very important and broad area of human behavior; this for his own knowledge and also so that he may carry on with new research and useful conceptualizations. Above all, it is my desire that all of us be impressed with the tremendous flexibility and modifiability of man's ability to deal with information. Through imaginative and devoted teaching, the creative abilities of our children are unlimited. This should be of great concern to us all.

Bibliography

Abe, K. An investigation of the law of memory trace deviation. I—Reproduction method and its verification. *Jap. J. Psychol.,* 1951, **21,** 33–46.

Adams, O. S., Fitts, P. M., Rappaport, M., and Weinstein, M. Relations among some measures of pattern discriminability. *J. Exp. Psychol.,* 1954, **48,** 81–85.

Adamson, R. E. Functional fixedness as related to problem solving: A repetition of three experiments. *J. Exp. Psychol.,* 1952, **44,** 288–291.

Adamson, R. E., and Taylor, D. W. Functional fixedness as related to elapsed time and set. *J. Exp. Psychol.,* 1954, **47,** 122–126.

Allport, F. *Theories of perception and the concept of structure.* New York: Wiley, 1955.

Allport, G. W., and Kramer, B. M. Some roots of prejudice. *J. Psychol.,* 1946, **22,** 9–39.

Alpern, M. Meta contrast. *J. Opt. Soc. Amer.,* 1953, **43,** 648–657.

Ames, A. *Some demonstrations concerned with the origin and nature of our sensations: A lab manual.* Hanover, N.H.: Dartmouth Eye Inst., 1946.

Ansbacher, H. Perception of number as affected by the monetary value of the objects. *Arch. Psychol., N.Y.,* 1937, No. 215.

Aronfreed, J. M., Messick, S. A., and Diggory, J. C. Reexamining emotionality and perceptual defense. *J. Pers.,* 1953, **21,** 517–528.

Asch, S. E., and Witkin, H. A. Studies in space orientation. I. Perception of the upright with displaced visual fields. *J. Exp. Psychol.,* 1948a, **38,** 325–337.

Asch, S. E., and Witkin, H. A. Studies in space orientation. II. Perception of the upright with displaced visual fields and with body tilted. *J. Exp. Psychol.,* 1948b, **38,** 455.

Atkinson, R. C., and Ammons, R. B. Experiential factors in visual form perception: Latency as a function of repetition. *J. Exp. Psychol.,* 1952, **43,** 173–178.

Attneave, F. Some informational aspects of visual perception. *Psychol. Rev.,* 1954a, **61,** 183–193.

Attneave, F. The verbal description of shapes. *Staff Res. Mem. Skill Components Res. Lab.,* AFBTRC, Lackland Air Force Base, April 21, 1954b.

Attneave, F. Symmetry, information, and memory for patterns. *Amer. J. Psychol.,* 1955, **68,** 209–222.

Attneave, F. Physical determinants of the judged complexity of shapes. *J. Exp. Psychol.,* 1957, **53,** 221–227.

Attneave, F. Perception and related areas. In S. Koch (Ed.), *Psychology: A study of a science.* Vol. 4. New York: McGraw-Hill, 1962.

361

Attneave, F., and Arnoult, M. D. The quantitative study of shape and pattern perception. *Psychol. Bull.,* 1956, **53,** 452–471.

Bales, J. F., and Follansbee, G. L. The after-effect of the perception of curved lines. *J. Exp. Psychol.,* 1935, **18,** 499–503.

Bappert, J. Neue Untersuchungen zum Problem des Verhältnisses von Akkommodation und Konvergenz zur Wahrnehmung der Tiefe. *Z. Psychol.,* 1923, **90,** 167–203.

Barnes, T. C. The terror of loneliness. Paper presented at APA meetings, New York, 1959.

Barron, F. *Creativity and mental health.* Princeton, N.J.: Van Nostrand, 1963a.

Barron, F. The disposition toward originality. In C. W. Taylor and F. Barron (Eds.), *Scientific creativity.* New York: Wiley, 1963b.

Bartlett, F. C. An experimental study of some problems of perceiving and imagining. *Brit. J. Psychol.,* 1916, **8,** 222–266.

Bartlett, F. C. *Remembering.* London: Cambridge, 1932.

Bartley, S. H. The psychology of vision. In S. S. Stevens (Ed.), *Handbook of experimental psychology.* New York: Wiley, 1951.

Battersby, W. S., Teuber, H. L., and Bender, M. B. *J. Psychol.,* 1953, **35,** 329–351.

Baum, M. H. Simple concept learning as a function of intralist generalization. *J. Exp. Psychol.,* 1954, **47,** 89–94.

Beck, J. Texture-gradients and judgments of slant and recession. *Amer. J. Psychol.,* 1960, **73,** 411–416.

Beck, J., and Gibson, J. J. The relation of apparent shape to apparent slant in the perception of objects. *J. Exp. Psychol.,* 1955, **50,** 125–133.

Bender, M. B., and Teuber, H. L. *Arch. Neurol. Psychiat.,* 1946, **55,** 627.

Bendig, A. W. Twenty questions: An information analysis. *J. Exp. Psychol.,* 1953, **46,** 345–348.

Berlyne, D. E. Attention to change. *Brit. J. Psychol.,* 1951, **42,** 269–278.

Berlyne, D. E. Attention to change, conditional inhibition (sIr) and stimulus satiation. *Brit. J. Psychol.,* 1957a, **48,** 138–140.

Berlyne, D. E. Uncertainty and conflict: A point of contact between information-theory and behavior-theory concepts. *Psychol. Rev.,* 1957b, **64,** 329–339.

Berlyne, D. E. The influence of complexity and change in visual figures on orienting responses. *J. Exp. Psychol.,* 1958, **55,** 289–296.

Bevan, W. Perceptual learning: An overview. *J. Gen. Psychol.,* 1961, **64,** 69–99.

Bevan, W. Subliminal stimulation: A pervasive problem for psychology. *Psychol. Bull.,* 1964, **61,** 81–99.

Bexton, W. H., Heron, W., and Scott, T. H. Effects of decreased variation in the sensory environment. *Canad. J. Psychol.,* 1954, **8,** 70–76.

Binder, A., and Feldman, S. E. The effects of experimentively controlled experience upon recognition responses. *Psychol. Monogr.,* 1960, **74,** No. 9.

Birch, H. G. The relation of previous experience to insightful problem-solving. *J. Comp. Psychol.,* 1945, **38,** 367–383.

Birch, H. G., and Bitterman, M. E. Reinforcement and learning: The process of sensory integration. *Psychol. Rev.,* 1949, **56,** 292–308.

Birch, H. G., and Rabinowitz, H. S. The negative effect of previous experience on productive thinking. *J. Exp. Psychol.,* 1951, **41,** 121–125.

Birenbaum, G., and Zeigarnik, B. A. Dynamic analysis of thought disturbances. *Sov. Neuropath. Psychiat. Psychohyg.,* 1935, **4,** No. 6.

Bitterman, M. E., and Kniffin, C. W. Manifest anxiety and "perceptual defense." *J. Abnorm. Soc. Psychol.,* 1953, **48,** 248–252.

Bitterman, M. E., Krauskopf, J., and Hochberg, J. E. Threshold for visual form: A diffusion model. *Amer. J. Psychol.,* 1954, **67,** 205–219.

Blakely, W. *The discrimination of short empty temporal intervals.* Unpublished doctoral dissertation, Univer. of Illinois, 1933.

Blank, H. R. Psychiatric problems associated with congenital blindness due to retrolental fibroplasia. *New Outlook Blind,* 1959, **53,** 237–244.

Bleuler, M., and Bleuler, R. Rorschach's inkblot test and racial psychology: Peculiarities of Moroccans. *Charact. & Pers.,* 1933, **4,** 97–114.

Bobbitt, J. M. An experimental study of the phenomenon of closure as a threshold function. *J. Exp. Psychol.,* 1942, **30,** 273–294.

Boring, E. G. *Sensation and perception in the history of experimental psychology.* New York: Appleton-Century-Crofts, 1942.

Boring, E. G. The moon illusion. *Amer. J. Phys.,* 1943, **11,** 55–60.

Boring, E. G. *A history of experimental psychology.* New York: Appleton-Century-Crofts, 1950.

Bourdon, B. *La perception visuelle de l'espace.* Paris: Schleicher, 1902.

Boyle, D. G. A contribution to the study of phenomenal causation. *Quart. J. Exp. Psychol.,* 1960, **12,** 171–179.

Braly, K. W. The influence of past experience in visual perception. *J. Exp. Psychol.,* 1933, **16,** 613–643.

Breese, B. B. On inhibition. *Psychol. Monogr.,* 1899, **3,** No. 1 (Whole No. 11).

Bricker, P. D., and Chapanis, H. Do incorrectly perceived stimuli convey some information? *Psychol. Rev.,* 1953, **60,** 181–188.

Bridgen, R. F. A tachistoscopic study of the differentiation of perception. *Psychol. Monogr.,* 1933, **44** (1), 153–166.

Brown, G. G. Perception of depth with disoriented vision. *Brit. J. Psychol.,* 1928, **19,** 117.

Brown, J. F. The visual perception of velocity. *Psychol. Forsch.,* 1931a, **14,** 199–232.

Brown, J. F. On time perception in visual movement fields. *Psychol. Forsch.,* 1931b, **14,** 233–248.

Brown, J. F., and Voth, A. C. The path of seen movement as a function of the vector field. *Amer. J. Psychol.,* 1937, **49,** 543–563.

Brown, J. L., Duhns, Margaret P., and Adler, H. Relation of threshold criterion to the functional receptors of the eye. *J. Opt. Soc. Amer.,* 1957, **47,** 198–204.

Brown, J. L., Phares, L., and Fletcher, Dorothy E. Spectral energy for the resolution of acuity. *J. Opt. Soc. Amer.,* 1960, **50,** 950–960.

Brown, R. *Words and things.* New York: Free Press, 1958.

Bruner, J. S. Personality and perception. In R. R. Blake and G. V. Ramsay (Eds.), *Perception: An approach to personality.* New York: Ronald, 1951.

Bruner, J. S. On perceptual readiness. *Psychol. Rev.*, 1957, **64**, 123–152.

Bruner, J. S. *The process of education.* Cambridge, Mass.: Harvard, 1961.

Bruner, J. S. The conditions of creativity. In *Contemporary approaches to creativity.* New York: Atherton, 1963.

Bruner, J. S., and Goodman, C. C. Value and need as organizing factors in perception. *J. Abnorm. Soc. Psychol.*, 1947, **42**, 33–44.

Bruner, J. S., Goodnow, J. J., and Austin, G. A. *A study of thinking.* New York: Wiley, 1956.

Bruner, J. S., and Postman, L. An approach to social perception. In W. Dennis (Ed.), *Current trends in social psychology.* Pittsburgh: Univer. of Pittsburgh Press, 1948.

Bruner, J. S., and Rodrigues, J. S. Some determinants of apparent size. *J. Abnorm. Soc. Psychol.*, 1953, **48**, 17–24.

Bruner, J. S., and Tagiuri, R. The perception of people. In G. Lindzey (Ed.), *Handbook of social psychology.* Reading, Mass.: Addison-Wesley, 1954.

Brunswik, E. Zur Entwicklung der Albedowahrnehmung. *Z. Psychol.*, 1929, **109**, 40–115.

Brunswik, E. Thing constancy as measured by correlation coefficients. *Psychol. Rev.*, 1940, **47**, 69–78.

Brunswik, E. Distal focusing of perception: Size constancy in a representative sample of situations. *Psychol. Monogr.*, 1944, No. 254.

Brunswik, E. Historical and thematic relations of psychology to other sciences. *Sci. Mon.*, 1956, **83**, 151–161.

Brunswik, E. (Ed.), et al. Untersuchungen über Wahrnehmung Gegenstände. *Arch. Ges. Psychol.*, 1933, **88**, 377–628.

Burkamp, W. Versuche über das Farbenwiedererkennen der Fische. *Z. Sinnesphysiol.*, 1923, **55**, 133–170.

Burzlaff, W. Methodologische Beiträge zum Problem der Farbenkonstanz. *Z. Psychol.*, 1931, **119**, 177–235.

Butter, R. A., and Harlow, H. F. Discrimination learning and learning sets to visual exploration incentives. *J. Gen. Psychol.*, 1957, **57**, 257–264.

Cahill, H. E., and Hovland, C. I. The role of memory in the acquisition of concept. *J. Exp. Psychol.*, 1960, **59**, 137–144.

Campbell, D. T., Lewis, N. A., and Hunt, W. A. Context effects with judgment language that is absolute, extensive, and extra-experimentally anchored. *J. Exp. Psychol.*, 1958, **55**, 220–228.

Campbell, I. G. Factors which work toward unity or coherence in visual design. *J. Exp. Psychol.*, 1941, **28**, 145–162.

Carlson, J. B., and Duncan, C. P. A study of autonomous change in the memory trace by the method of recognition. *Amer. J. Psychol.*, 1955, **68**, 280–284.

Carlson, V. R. Overestimation in size constancy judgments. *Amer. J. Psychol.*, 1960, **73**, 199–213.

Carr, H. A. *An introduction to space perception.* New York: Longmans, 1935.

Carter, L. F., and Schooler, K. Value need and other factors in perception. *Psychol. Rev.*, 1949, **56**, 200–207.

Casperson, R. C. The visual discrimination of geometric forms. *J. Exp. Psychol.*, 1950, **40**, 668–681.

Cattell, R. B. The personality and motivation of the researcher from measurement of contemporaries and from biography. In C. W. Taylor and F. Barron (Eds.), *Scientific creativity*. New York: Wiley, 1963.

Cattell, R. B., and Tiner, L. G. The varieties of structural rigidity. *J. Pers.*, 1949, **17**, 321–341.

Cattell, R. B., and Winder, A. E. Structural rigidity in relation to learning theory and clinical psychology. *Psychol. Rev.*, 1952, **59**, 23–39.

Chalmers, E. L., Jr. Monocular and binocular cues in the perception of size and distance. *Amer. J. Psychol.*, 1952, **55**, 415–423.

Chapanis, A. How we see: A summary of basic principles. In *Human factors in undersea warfare*. Washington, D.C.: National Res. Council, 1949. Pp. 3–60.

Chapanis, A., and McCleary, R. A. Interposition as a cue for the perception of relative distance. *J. Gen. Psychol.*, 1953, **48**, 113–132.

Christian, P., and Weizäcker, V. V. On the vision of figured movement of luminous points. *Z. Sinnesphysiol.*, 1943, **70**, 30–51.

Clark, W. C., Smith, A. H., and Rabe, A. Retinal gradients of outline distortion and binocular disparity as stimulus for slant. *Canad. J. Psychol.*, 1956, **10**, 77–81.

Cocquyt, P. *Shell Aviation News*, 1952, No. 178.

Cofer, C. N. Verbal behavior in relation to reasoning and values. In H. Guetzkow (Ed.), *Groups, leadership and men*. Pittsburgh: Carnegie Press, 1951.

Cohen, H. B. The effect of contralateral visual stimulation on visibility with stabilized retinal images. *Canad. J. Psychol.*, 1961, **15**, 212–219.

Cohen, W. Spatial and textural characteristics of the Ganzfeld. *Amer. J. Psychol.*, 1957, **70**, 403–410.

Cohen, W. Color perception in the chromatic Ganzfeld. *Amer. J. Psychol.*, 1958a, **71**, 390–394.

Cohen, W. Apparent movement of simple figures in the Ganzfeld. *Percept. Mot. Skills*, 1958b, **8**, 32.

Cook, P. H. The application of the Rorschach test to a Samoan group. *Rorschach Res. Exch.*, 1942, **6**, 51–60.

Cowen, E. L., Wiener, M., and Hess, J. Generalization of problem-solving rigidity. *J. Consult. Psychol.*, 1953, **17**, 100–103.

Craik, K. J. W., and Vernon, M. D. Perception during dark adaptation. *Brit. J. Psychol.*, 1942, **32**, 206–230.

Cruikshank, R. M. The development of visual size constancy in early infancy. *J. Genet. Psychol.*, 1941, **58**, 327–351.

Dattman, P., and Israel, H. The order of dominance among conceptual capacities: An experimental test of Heidbreder hypothesis. *J. Psychol.*, 1951, **31**, 147–160.

Davies, A. E. An analysis of elementary psychic process. *Psychol. Rev.*, 1905, **12**, 166–206.

Day, R. H. Application of the statistical theory to form perception. *Psychol. Rev.*, 1956, **63**, 139–148.

Deese, J. Some problems in the theory of vigilance. *Psychol. Rev.*, 1955, **62**, 359–368.

Delayfresnaye, J. E. (Ed.) *Brain mechanisms and consciousness.* Oxford: Blackwell, 1954.

Dember, W. N. *The psychology of perception.* New York: Holt, 1960.

Dember, W. N., and Earl, R. W. Analysis of exploratory, manipulatory, and curiosity behavior. *Psychol. Rev.,* 1957, **64,** 91–96.

Dennis, W. Cultural and developmental factors in perception. In R. R. Blake and G. V. Ramsay (Eds.), *Perception: An approach to personality.* New York: Ronald, 1951. Pp. 148–169.

De Wolfe, R. K. S., and Duncan, C. P. Time estimation as a function of level of behavior of successive tasks. *J. Exp. Psychol.,* 1959, **58,** 153–158.

Diamond, A. L. Foveal simultaneous brightness contrast as a function of inducing-and-test-field luminances. *J. Exp. Psychol.,* 1953, **45,** 304–314.

Diamond, A. L. A theory of depression and enhancement in the brightness response. *Psychol. Rev.,* 1960, **67,** 168–199.

Dickinson, C. A. Experience and visual perception. *Amer. J. Psychol.,* 1926, **37,** 330–344.

Diggory, J. C. Personal communication regarding experiment on perceptual defense, 1956.

Djang, S. The role of past experience in the visual perception of masked forms. *J. Exp. Psychol.,* 1937, **20,** 29–59.

Doane, B. K., Mahut, H., Heron, W., and Scott, T. H. Changes in perceptual function after isolation. *Canad. J. Psychol.,* 1959, **13,** 210–219.

Douglas, A. G. A tachistoscopic study of the order of emergence in the process of perception. *Psychol. Monogr.,* 1947, **61,** No. 6.

Drury, M. B. Progressive changes in non-foveal perception of line patterns. *Amer. J. Psychol.,* 1933, **45,** 628–646.

Dukes, W. F. A study of early size-constancy by representative design. *Amer. Psychologist,* 1950, **5,** 460.

Dukes, W. F. Ecological representativeness in studying perceptual size-constancy in childhood. *Amer. J. Psychol.,* 1951, **64,** 87–93.

Duncan, C. P. Recent research on human problem-solving. *Psychol. Bull.,* 1959, **56,** 397–429.

Duncker, K. Über induzierte Bewegung: Ein Beitrag zur Theorie optisch wahrgenommener Bewegung. *Psychol. Forsch.,* 1929, **12,** 180–259.

Duncker, K. *Zur Psychologie des produktiven Denken.* Berlin: Springer, 1935.

Duncker, K. The influence of past experience upon perceptual properties. *Amer. J. Psychol.,* 1939, **52,** 225–265.

Duncker, K. On problem-solving. (Tr. L. S. Lees) *Psychol. Monogr.,* 1945, **58,** No. 270.

Dusek, E. R., Teichner, W. H., and Kobrick, J. L. The effects of angular relationships between the observer and the base surround on relative depth-discrimination. *Amer. J. Psychol.,* 1955, **68,** 438–443.

Ehrenfels, C. Weber von. Gestaltqualitäten. *Vtljschr. Wiss. Phil.,* 1890, **14,** 249–292.

Eissler, K. See Brunswik, E. (Ed.), et al., 1933.

Ellis, W. D. *A source book of gestalt psychology.* New York: Humanities Press, 1950.

Epstein, W. Experimental investigations of the genesis of visual space perception. *Psychol. Bull.*, 1964, **61**, 115–128.

Epstein, W., and Rock, I. Perceptual set as an artifact of recency. *Amer. J. Psychol.*, 1960, **73**, 214–228.

Eriksen, C. W. Perceptual defense as a function of unacceptable needs. *J. Abnorm. Soc. Psychol.*, 1951a, **46**, 557–564.

Eriksen, C. W. Some implications for TAT interpretation arising from need and perception experiments. *J. Pers.*, 1951b, **19**, 283–288.

Eriksen, C. W. Psychological defenses and ego strength in the recall of completed and incompleted tasks. *J. Abnorm. Soc. Psychol.*, 1954, **49**, 45–50.

Eriksen, C. W. Subception: Fact or artifact? *Psychol. Rev.*, 1956a, **63**, 74–80.

Eriksen, C. W. An experimental analysis of subception. *Amer. J. Psychol.*, 1956b, **69**, 625–634.

Eriksen, C. W. Discrimination and learning without awareness: A methodological survey and evaluation. *Psychol. Rev.*, 1960, **67**, 279–300.

Eriksen, C. W. Perception and personality. In J. M. Wepman and R. W. Heine (Eds.), *Concepts of personality*. Chicago: Aldine, 1963. Pp. 31–62.

Eriksen, C. W., and Brown, C. T. An experimental and theoretical analysis of perceptual defense. *J. Abnorm. Soc. Psychol.*, 1956, **52**, 224–230.

Evans, R. M. *An introduction to color*. New York: Wiley, 1948.

Ewert, P. H. A study of the effect of inverted retinal stimulation upon spatially coordinated behavior. *Genet. Psychol. Monogr.*, 1930, **7**, 177.

Ewert, P. H., and Lambert, J. F. The effect of verbal instructions upon the formation of a concept. *J. Gen. Psychol.*, 1932, **6**, 400–413.

Fantz, R. L. The origin of form perception. *Sci. Amer.*, 1961a, **204**, 66–72.

Fantz, R. L. A method for studying depth perception in infants under six months of age. *Psychol. Rec.*, 1961b, **11**, 27–32.

Fehrer, Elizabeth V. An investigation of the learning of visually perceived forms. *Amer. J. Psychol.*, 1935, **47**, 187–221.

Fernberger, S. W. New phenomena of apparent visual movement. *Amer. J. Psychol.*, 1934, **46**, 309.

Fieandt, K. von. Über Sehen von Tiefengebilden bei wechselnder Beleuchtungsrichtung. *Psychol. Abstr.*, 1939, **13**, 4524.

Fieandt, K. von, and Gibson, J. J. The sensitivity of the eye to two kinds of continuous transformation of a shadow pattern. *J. Exp. Psychol.*, 1959, **57**, 344–347.

Fiedler, F. E. The psychological-distance dimension in interpersonal relation. *J. Pers.*, 1953, **22**, 142–150.

Fields, P. E. Studies in concept formation. I. The development of the concept of triangularity by the white rat. *Comp. Psychol. Monogr.*, 1932, **9**, 1–70.

Filer, R. J., and Miles, D. W. The effect of motivating conditions on the estimation of time. *J. Exp. Psychol.*, 1949, **39**, 327–331.

Fisher, S. An overview of trends in research dealing with personality rigidity. *J. Pers.*, 1949, **17**, 342–351.

Fisher, S. Patterns of personality rigidity and some of their determinants. *Psychol. Monogr.*, 1950, **64**, Whole No. 307.

Fisher, S. C. The process of generalizing abstraction and its product, the general concept. *Psychol. Monogr.*, 1916, No. 90.

Fitts, P. M., et al. Stimulus correlates of visual pattern recognition: A probability approach. *J. Exp. Psychol.,* 1956, **51,** 1–11.

Flavell, J. H. *The developmental psychology of Jean Piaget.* Princeton, N.J.: Van Nostrand, 1963.

Forgus, R. H. The effect of early perceptual learning on the behavior organization of adult rats. *J. Comp. Physiol. Psychol.,* 1954, **47,** 331–336.

Forgus, R. H. Early visual and motor experience as determiners of complex maze learning ability under rich and reduced stimulation. *J. Comp. Physiol. Psychol.,* 1955a, **48,** 215–220.

Forgus, R. H. Influence of early experience on maze-learning with and without visual cues. *Canad. J. Psychol.,* 1955b, **9,** 231–238.

Forgus, R. H. Advantages of early over late perceptual experience in improving form discrimination. *Canad. J. Psychol.,* 1956, **10,** 147–155.

Forgus, R. H. Perceived shape and perceived tilt as affected by rotation of the visual surround. Unpublished study, 1957.

Forgus, R. H. The effect of different kinds of form pre-exposure on form discrimination learning. *J. Comp. Physiol. Psychol.,* 1958a, **51,** 75–78.

Forgus, R. H. The interaction between form pre-exposure and test requirements in determining discrimination learning. *J. Comp. Physiol. Psychol.,* 1958b, **51,** 588–591.

Forgus, R. H., and Fowler, H. The order of dominance in concept attainment as affected by experience. *J. Psychol.,* 1957, **44,** 105–108.

Forgus, R. H., and Schwartz, R. J. Efficient retention and transfer as affected by learning method. *J. Psychol.,* 1957, **43,** 135–139.

Forgus, R. H., and Strobel, D. The importance of instructions in the perception of phi vs. lateral motion in the "Brown-Voth effect." Unpublished paper, 1964.

Foster, W. S. The effect of practice upon visualizing and upon the reproduction of visual impressions. *J. Educ. Psychol.,* 1911, **2,** 11–22.

Fraisse, P. *The psychology of time.* New York: Harper & Row, 1963.

Francés, R. *Le développement perceptif.* Paris: Presses Univer. France, 1962.

Freeman, G. L. An experimental study of the perception of objects. *J. Exp. Psychol.,* 1929, **12,** 241–258.

French, J. D. The reticular formation. *Sci. Amer.,* 1957, **196,** 54–60.

Fuchs, W. Untersuchung über Sehen der Hemianopiker und Hemiamblyopiker. I. Verlagerungerscheinungen. *Z. Psychol.,* 1920, **84,** 67.

Fujiwara, K., and Obonai, T. The qualitative analysis of figural after-effects. II. Effects of inspection time and the intensity of light stimulus upon the amount of figural after-effects. *Jap. J. Psychol.,* 1953, **24,** 114–120.

Fuster, J. M. Effects of stimulation of brain stem on tachistoscopic perception. *Science,* 1958, **127,** 150.

Gagne, R. M. *An analysis of two problem-solving activities.* AFPTRC-TR-54-77, Lackland Air Force Base, 1954.

Gagne, R. M. Problem-solving. *Annu. Rev. Psychol.,* 1959, **10,** 147–172.

Gaito, J. An informational approach to problem solving and thinking behavior. *Dissertation Abstr.,* 1959a, **20,** 388.

Gaito, J. Visual discrimination of straight and curved lines. *Amer. J. Psychol.,* 1959b, **72,** 236–242.

Gaito, J. A biochemical approach to learning and memory. *Psychol. Rev.,* 1961, **68,** 288–292.

Gaito, J. Stages of perception, unconscious processes, and information extraction. *J. Gen. Psychol.,* 1964, **70,** 183–197.

Galanter, E. Contemporary psychophysics. In R. Brown, E. Galanter, E. H. Hess, and G. Mandler, *New directions in psychology.* New York: Holt, 1962.

Gardner, R. A. A note on theory and methodology in the study of figural after-effects. *Psychol. Rev.,* 1960, **67,** 272–276.

Garner, W. R., and Hake, H. W. The amount of information in absolute judgments. *Psychol. Rev.,* 1951, **58,** 446–459.

Gelb, A. Die 'Farbenkonstanz' der Sehdinge. *Handb. Norm. Path. Physiol.,* 1929, **12**(I), 594–678.

Geldard, F. A. *The human senses.* New York: Wiley, 1953.

Geldard, F. A. *Fundamentals of psychology.* New York: Wiley, 1962.

Gellerman, L. W. Chance order of alternating stimuli in visual discrimination experiments. *J. Genet. Psychol.,* 1933, **42,** 207–208.

George, F. H. Errors of visual recognition. *J. Exp. Psychol.,* 1952, **43,** 202–206.

Gerathewohl, S. J. Comparative studies on animals and human subjects in the gravity-free state. *J. Aviat. Med.,* 1954, **25,** 412–419.

Gerathewohl, S. J. Personal experiences during short periods of weightlessness reported by 16 subjects. *Astronaut. Acta,* 1956, **2,** 203–217.

Gerathewohl, S. J. Weightlessness. *Air Univer. Quart. Rev.,* 1958, **10,** 121–141.

Gerathewohl, S. J., Strughold, H., and Stablings, H. D. Sensorimotor performance during weightlessness. *J. Aviat. Med.,* 1957, **28,** 7–12.

Gesell, A. The developmental aspect of child vision. *Science,* 1949, **109,** 442.

Getzels, J. W., and Jackson, P. W. The meaning of "giftedness"—an examination of an expanding concept. *Phi Delta Kappan,* 1958, 75–77.

Getzels, J. W., and Jackson, P. W. *Creativity and intelligence: Explorations with gifted children.* New York: Wiley, 1962.

Ghent, L. Recognition by children of realistic figures presented in various orientations. *Canad. J. Psychol.,* 1960, **14,** 249–256.

Ghent, L., and Bernstein, L. Influence of the orientation of geometric forms on their recognition by children. *Percept. Mot. Skills,* 1961, **12,** 95–101.

Gibson, Eleanor J. Improvement in perceptual judgment as a function of controlled practice or training. *Psychol. Bull.,* 1953, **50,** 401–431.

Gibson, Eleanor J. The effect of prior training with a scale of distance on absolute and relative judgments over ground. *J. Exp. Psychol.,* 1955, **50,** 97–105.

Gibson, Eleanor J. Perceptual learning. *Annu. Rev. Psychol.,* 1963, **14,** 29–56.

Gibson, Eleanor J., Tighe, T. J., and Walk, R. D. Behavior of light- and dark-reared rats on a visual cliff. *Science,* 1957, **126,** 80–81.

Gibson, Eleanor J., and Walk, R. D. The effect of prolonged exposure to visually presented patterns on learning to discriminate them. *J. Comp. Physiol. Psychol.,* 1956, **49,** 239–242.

Gibson, Eleanor J., and Walk, R. D. The "visual cliff." *Sci. Amer.,* 1960, **202** (4), 64–71.

Gibson, J. J. Adaptation, after-effect, and contrast in the perception of curved lines. *J. Exp. Psychol.*, 1933, **16**, 1–31.

Gibson, J. J. Adaptation, after-effect, and contrast in the perception of tilted lines. II. Simultaneous contrast and the areal restriction of the after-effect. *J. Exp. Psychol.*, 1937a, **20**, 553–569.

Gibson, J. J. Adaptation with negative after-effect. *Psychol. Rev.*, 1937b, **44**, 222–244.

Gibson, J. J. *The perception of the visual world.* Boston: Houghton Mifflin, 1950.

Gibson, J. J. What is a form? *Psychol. Rev.*, 1951, **58**, 403–412.

Gibson, J. J. The relation between visual and postural determinants of the phenomenal vertical. *Psychol. Rev.*, 1952, **59**, 370–375.

Gibson, J. J. The visual perception of objective motion and subjective movement. *Psychol. Rev.*, 1954, **61**, 304–314.

Gibson, J. J. Optical motions and transformations as stimuli for visual perception. *Psychol. Rev.*, 1957, **64**, 288–295.

Gibson, J. J. Perception as a function of stimulation, in S. Koch (Ed.), *Psychology: A study of science.* Vol. I. Sensory, perceptual, and physiological formulations. New York: McGraw-Hill, 1958.

Gibson, J. J. The information contained in light. *Acta Psychol.*, 1960a, **17**, 23–30.

Gibson, J. J. The concept of stimulus in psychology. *Amer. Psychologist*, 1960b, **15**, 694–703.

Gibson, J. J. The useful dimensions of sensitivity. *Amer. Psychologist*, 1963, **18**, 1–15.

Gibson, J. J., and Gibson, Eleanor J. Perceptual learning: Differentiation or enrichment? *Psychol. Rev.*, 1955, **62**, 32–41.

Gibson, J. J., and Gibson, Eleanor J. Perceptual learning: Differentiation or enrichment? *Americana*, 1956, **2**, 83–94.

Gibson, J. J., and Gibson, Eleanor J. Continuous perspective transformations and the perception of rigid motion. *J. Exp. Psychol.*, 1957, **54**, 129–138.

Gibson, J. J., and Glaser, N. M. In J. J. Gibson (Ed.), *Motion picture testing and research. AAF Aviat. Psychol. Program Res. Rep.*, 1947, Chap. IX.

Gibson, J. J., and Mowrer, O. H. Determinants of the perceived vertical and horizontal. *Psychol. Rev.*, 1938, **45**, 300.

Gibson, J. J., Olum, P., and Rosenblatt, F. Parallax and perspective during aircraft landings. *Amer. J. Psychol.*, 1955, **68**, 372–385.

Gibson, J. J., and Radner, M. Adaptation, after-effect, and contrast in the perception of tilted lines. I. Quantitative studies. *J. Exp. Psychol.*, 1937, **20**, 453–467.

Gibson, J. J., Smith, O. W., Steinschneider, A., and Johnson, C. W. The relative accuracy of visual perception of motion during fixation and pursuit. *Amer. J. Psychol.*, 1957, **70**, 64–68.

Gibson, K. S., and Tyndall, E. P. T. The visibility of radiant energy. *Sci. Pop. U.S. Bur. Stand.*, 1923, **19**, No. 475.

Gilinsky, A. S. Perceived size and distance in visual space. *Psychol. Rev.*, 1951, **58**, 460–482.

Gilinsky, A. S. The effect of attitude on the perception of size. *Amer. J. Psychol.*, 1955, **68**, 173–192.

Gilliland, A. R. The effect of practice with and without knowledge of results in grading handwriting. *J. Educ. Psychol.*, 1925, **16**, 532–536.

Golann, S. E. Psychological study of creativity. *Psychol. Bull.*, 1963, **60**, 548–565.

Goldiamond, I., and Hawkins, W. F. Vexierversuch: The log relationship between word frequency and recognition obtained in the absence of stimulus words. *J. Exp. Psychol.*, 1958, **56**, 457–463.

Goldstein, K., and Gelb, A. Zur Psychologie des optischen Wahrnehmunger und Erkennungs-vorgänge. *Z. Ges. Neurol. Psychiat.*, 1918, **41**, 1.

Goldstein, K., and Gelb, A. Über Farbenamnesie. *Psychol. Forsch.*, 1924, **6**, 127–199.

Goldstein, K., and Scheerer, M. Abstract and concrete behavior: An experimental study with special tests. *Psychol. Monogr.*, 1941, No. 239.

Goldstein, M. J. A test of response probability theory of perceptual defense. *J. Exp. Psychol.*, 1962, **63**, 23–28.

Gollin, E. Developmental studies of visual recognition of incomplete objects. *Percept. Mot. Skills*, 1960, **11**, 289–298.

Gottschaldt, K. Über den Einfluss der Erfahrung auf die Wahrnehmung von Figuren. I. Über den Einfluss gehäufter Einprägung von Figuren auf ihre Sicherheit in umfassen der Konfigurationen. *Psychol. Forsch.*, 1926, **8**, 261–317.

Gottschaldt, K. Über den Einfluss der Erfahrung auf die Wahrnehmung von Figuren. *Psychol. Forsch.*, 1929, **12**, 1–87.

Graham, C. H., Brown, R. H., and Mote, F. A., Jr. The relation of size of stimulus and intensity in the human eye. I. Intensity thresholds for white light. *J. Exp. Psychol.*, 1939, **24**, 555–573.

Graham, C. H., and Margaria, R. Area and the intensity-time relation in the peripheral retina. *Amer. J. Physiol.*, 1935, **113**, 299–305.

Grant, D. A. Perceptual versus analytical responses to the number concepts of a Weigl-type card sorting test. *J. Exp. Psychol.*, 1951, **41**, 23–39.

Grant, D. A., and Curran, J. F. Relative difficulty of number, form, and color concepts of a Weigl-type problem using unsystematic number cards. *J. Exp. Psychol.*, 1953, **43**, 408–413.

Grant, D. A., Jones, O. R., and Tallanis, B. Relative difficulty of number, form, and color concepts of a Weigl-type problem. *J. Exp. Psychol.*, 1949, **39**, 552–557.

Grant, V. W. Accommodation and convergence in visual space perception. *J. Exp. Psychol.*, 1942, **31**, 89–104.

Gregory, R. L., and Wallace, J. G. Recovery from early blindness. *Exp. Psychol. Sci. Monogr.*, 1963, No. 2.

Gruber, H. E. The relation of perceived size to perceived distance. *Amer. J. Psychol.*, 1954, **67**, 411–426.

Gruber, H. E. The size-distance paradox: A reply to Gilinsky. *Amer. J. Psychol.*, 1956, **69**, 469–476.

Gruber, H. E., Fink, C. D., and Damm, V. Effects of experience on perception of causality. *J. Exp. Psychol.*, 1957, **53**, 89–93.

Gruber, H. E., Tenell, G., and Wertheimer, M. *Contemporary approaches to creative thinking.* New York: Atherton, 1963.

Guetzkow, H. An analysis of the operation of set in problem-solving behavior. *J. Gen. Psychol.,* 1951, **45**, 219–233.

Guilford, J. P. (Ed.) Printed classification tests. *AAF Aviat. Psychol. Program Res. Rep.,* 1947, No. 5.

Guilford, J. P. The structure of intellect. *Psychol. Bull.,* 1956, **55**, 267–293.

Guilford, J. P. Intellectual resources and their values as seen by scientists. In C. W. Taylor and F. Barron (Eds.), *Scientific creativity.* New York: Wiley, 1963.

Gulick, W. L. The effect of prior stimulation upon contour perception of moving stimuli. *Psychol. Rec.,* 1959, **9**, 143–152.

Hake, H. W. *Contributions of psychology to the study of pattern vision.* USAF WADC-TR-57-621, October, 1957.

Hake, H. W., and Garner, W. R. The effect of presenting various numbers of discrete steps on scale reading accuracy. *J. Exp. Psychol.,* 1951, **42**, 358–366.

Hambacher, W. O. An experimental investigation of whiteness constancy with suggestions for an explanatory approach. *Dissertation Abstr.,* 1956, **16**, 1924.

Hammer, E. R. Temporal factors in figural after-effects. *Amer. J. Psychol.,* 1949, **62**, 337–354.

Hanawalt, E. M. Memory trace for figures in recall and recognition. *Arch. Psychol., N.Y.,* 1937, No. 216.

Hanawalt, N. G. The effect of practice upon the perception of simple designs masked by more complex designs. *J. Exp. Psychol.,* 1942, **31**, 134–148.

Hanfmann, E., and Kasanin, J. A method for the study of concept formation. *J. Psychol.,* 1937, **3**, 521–540.

Hanfmann, E., and Kasanin, J. Conceptual thinking in schizophrenia. *Nerv. Ment. Dis. Monogr. Ser.,* 1942, No. 67.

Harlow, H. F. The formation of learning sets. *Psychol. Rev.,* 1949, **56**, 51–65.

Harlow, H. F. Learning set and error factor theory. In S. Koch (Ed.), *Psychology: A study of a science.* Vol. II. New York: McGraw-Hill, 1959. Pp. 492–537.

Hartline, H. K. The nerve messages in the fibers of the visual pathway. *J. Opt. Soc. Amer.,* 1940, **30**, 239–247.

Harton, J. J. The influence of the difficulty of activity on the estimation of time. *J. Exp. Psychol.,* 1938, **23**, 270–287.

Hastorf, A. H. See Ittelson, W. H., and Kilpatrick, F. P., 1951; 1953.

Hastorf, A. H., and Way, L. Apparent size with and without distance cues. *J. Gen. Psychol.,* 1952, **47**, 181–188.

Hebb, D. O. The innate organization of visual activity. I. Perception of figures by rats reared in total darkness. *J. Genet. Psychol.,* 1937a, **51**, 101–126.

Hebb, D. O. The innate organization of visual activity. II. Transfer of response in the discrimination of brightness and size by rats reared in total darkness. *J. Comp. Psychol.,* 1937b, **24**, 277–299.

Hebb, D. O. *The organization of behavior.* New York: Wiley, 1949.

Hebb, D. O. The American revolution. *Amer. Psychologist,* 1960, **15,** 735–745.

Hebb, D. O. The semi-autonomous process: Its nature and nurture. *Amer. Psychologist,* 1963, **18,** 16–27.

Hebb, D. O., and Foord, E. N. Errors of visual recognition and the nature of the trace. *J. Exp. Psychol.,* 1945, **35,** 335–348.

Hecht, S., and Schlaer, S. An adaptometer for measuring human dark adaptation. *J. Opt. Soc. Amer.,* 1938, **28,** 269–275.

Hecht, S., Schlaer, S., and Pirenne, M. H. Energy, quanta, and vision. *J. Gen. Physiol.,* 1942, **25,** 819–840.

Hecht, S., and Williams, R. E. The visibility of monochromatic radiation and the absorption spectrum of visual purple. *J. Gen. Physiol.,* 1922, **5,** 1–34.

Heidbreder, E. Toward a dynamic psychology of cognition. *Psychol. Rev.,* 1945, **52,** 1–22.

Heidbreder, E. The attainment of concepts. I. Terminology and methodology. *J. Gen. Psychol.,* 1946a, **35,** 173–189.

Heidbreder, E. The attainment of concepts. II. The problem. *J. Gen. Psychol.,* 1946b, **35,** 191–223.

Heidbreder, E. The attainment of concepts. III. The process. *J. Psychol.,* 1947, **24,** 93–138.

Heidbreder, E. The attainment of concepts. VI. Exploratory experiments on conceptualization at perceptual levels. *J. Psychol.,* 1948, **26,** 193–216.

Heidbreder, E. Experiments by Dattman and Israel on the attainment of concepts. *J. Psychol.,* 1952, **34,** 115–136.

Heidbreder, E., Bensley, M. L., and Ivy, M. The attainment of concepts. IV. Regularities and levels. *J. Psychol.,* 1948, **25,** 299–329.

Heider, F. *The psychology of interpersonal relations.* New York: Wiley, 1958.

Heider, F., and Simmel, M. L. An experimental study of apparent behavior. *Amer. J. Psychol.,* 1944, **57,** 243–249.

Heinemann, E. S. Simultaneous brightness induction as a function of inducing-and-test-field brightness. *J. Exp. Psychol.,* 1955, **50,** 89–96.

Helmholtz, H. *Treatise on physiological optics.* Tr. from 3d ed. (Ed. J. P. C. Southall) Opt. Soc. Amer., 1924.

Helson, H. Fundamental problems in color vision: The principle governing changes in hue, saturation, and lightness of non-selective samples in chromatic illumination. *J. Exp. Psychol.,* 1938, **23,** 439–476.

Helson, H. Adaptation level as a basis for a quantitative theory of frames of reference. *Psychol. Rev.,* 1948, **55,** 297–313.

Helson, H. Adaptation level theory. In S. Koch (Ed.), *Psychology: A study of a science.* Vol. I. New York: McGraw-Hill, 1959. Pp. 565–617.

Helson, H. *Adaptation level theory.* New York: Harper & Row, 1964.

Helson, H., and Fehrer, E. V. The role of form in perception. *Amer. J. Psychol.,* 1932, **44,** 79–102.

Hempstead, L. The perception of visual form. *Amer. J. Psychol.,* 1900, **12,** 185.

Henneman, R. H. A photometric study of the perception of object color. *Arch. Psychol., N.Y.,* 1935, No. 179, 444.

Henry, J. Rorschach technique in primitive cultures. *Amer. J. Orthopsychiat.,* 1941, **11,** 230–234.

Hermans, T. G. The perception of size in binocular, monocular, and pin-hole vision. *J. Exp. Psychol.,* 1940, **27,** 203–207.

Heron, W. The pathology of boredom. *Sci. Amer.,* 1957, **196,** 52–56.

Heron, W., Doane, B. K., and Scott, T. H. Visual disturbances after prolonged perceptual isolation. *Canad. J. Psychol.,* 1956, **10,** 13–18.

Hess, E. H. Development of the chick's responses to light and shade cues of depth. *J. Comp. Physiol. Psychol.,* 1950, **43,** 112–122.

Hess, E. H. Imprinting: An effect of early experience, imprinting determines later social behavior in animals. *Science,* 1959, **130,** 133–141.

Hilgard, E. R. *Theories of learning.* New York: Appleton-Century-Crofts, 1956.

Hilgard, E. R., Edgren, R. D., and Whipple, J. E. Rote memorization, understanding, and transfer: An extension of Katona's card-trick experiments. *J. Exp. Psychol.,* 1953, **46,** 288–292.

Hillebrand, F. Das Verhältnis von Accommodation und Konvergenz zur Tiefenlokalization. *F. Z. Vergl. Physiol.,* 1894, **7,** 98.

Hindle, Helen. Time estimates as a function of distance traveled and relative clarity of a goal. *J. Pers.,* 1951, **19,** 483–501.

Hines, R. *The formation and retention of concepts as a function of their abstractness.* Hays, Kans.: Fort Hays Kansas State Coll., 1951.

Hochberg, J. E. The psychophysics of pictorial perception. *Audio-Vis. Communic. Rev.,* 1962, **10,** 22–54.

Hochberg, J. E. *Perception.* Englewood Cliffs, N.J.: Prentice-Hall, 1964.

Hochberg, J. E., and Beck, J. Apparent spatial arrangement and perceived brightness. *J. Exp. Psychol.,* 1954, **47,** 263–266.

Hochberg, J. E., and Brooks, V. The psychophysics of form: Reversible-perspective drawings of spatial objects. *Amer. J. Psvchol.,* 1960, **73,** 337–354.

Hochberg, J. E., Gleitman. H., and MacBride, P. D. Visual thresholds as a function of simplicity of form. *Amer. J. Psychol.,* 1948, **60,** 341–342.

Hochberg, J. E., and Hardy, D. Brightness and proximity factors in grouping. *Percept. Mot. Skills,* 1960, **10,** 22.

Hochberg, J. E., and McAlister, E. A quantitative approach to figural "goodness." *J. Exp. Psychol.,* 1953, **46,** 361–364.

Hochberg, J. E., and Silverstein, A. A quantitative index of stimulus similarity: Proximity vs. differences in brightness. *Amer. J. Psychol.,* 1956, **69,** 456–458.

Hochberg, J. E., Triebel, W., and Seaman, G. Color adaptation under conditions of homogeneous visual stimulation (Ganzfeld). *J. Exp. Psychol.,* 1951, **41,** 153–159.

Holway, A. H., et al. Factors influencing the magnitude of range errors in free space and telescopic vision. Boston: Harvard Business Sch., Div. Res., 1945.

Holway, A. H., and Boring, E. G. Determinants of apparent visual size with distance variant. *Amer. J. Psychol.,* 1941, **54,** 21–37.

Horowitz, M. W., and Kappauf, W. E. *Aerial target range estimation.* SRD Report No. 5301, 1945, Publ. Bd. No. 15812, U.S. Dep. Commerce, 1946.

Hovland, C. I. A communication analysis of concept learning. *Psychol. Rev.,* 1952, **59,** 461–472.

Hovland, C. I. A set of flower designs for concept-formation experiments. *Amer. J. Psychol.,* 1953, **66,** 140–142.

Hovland, C. I., and Kendler, H. H. The New York University conference on human problem solving. *Amer. Psychologist,* 1955, **10,** 64–68.

Hovland, C. I., and Weiss, W. Transmission of information concerning concepts through positive and negative instances. *J. Exp. Psychol.,* 1953, **45,** 175–182.

Howard, H. J. A test for the judgment of distance. *Amer. J. Ophthal.,* 1919, **2,** 656–675.

Hsia, Y. Whiteness constancy as a function of difference in illumination. *Arch. Psychol., N.Y.,* 1943, No. 284.

Hull, C. L. Quantitative aspects of the evolution of concepts. *Psychol. Monogr.,* 1920, No. 123.

Humphrey, G. *Thinking: An introduction to its experimental psychology.* London: Methuen, 1951.

Hunt, E. B., and Hovland, C. I. Order of consideration of different types of concept. *J. Exp. Psychol.,* 1960, **59,** 220–225.

Hurvich, L. M., and Jameson, Dorothea. Spectral sensitivity of the fovea. I. Neutral adaptation. *J. Opt. Soc. Amer.,* 1955, **43,** 485–494.

Hyman, R., and Hake, H. W. *Form recognition as a function of the number of forms which can be presented for recognition.* USAF WADC-TR-54-164, May, 1954.

Ikeda, H., and Obonai, J. The quantitative analysis of figural after-effects. II. On "self-satiation." *Jap. J. Psychol.,* 1953, **24,** 179–192.

Ikeda, H., and Obonai, J. The studies of figural after-effects: The contrast-confluence illusion of concentric circles and the figural after-effect. *Jap. Psychol. Res.,* 1955a, **2,** 17–23.

Ikeda, H., and Obonai, J. Figural after-effect, retroactive effect and simultaneous illusion. *Jap. J. Psychol.,* 1955b, **26,** 235–246.

Irwin, F. W. Stated expectations as functions of probability and desirability of outcomes. *J. Pers.,* 1953, **21,** 329–335.

Ittelson, W. H., and Kilpatrick, F. P. Experiments in perception. *Sci. Amer.,* 1951, **185**(2), 50–55.

Ittelson, W. H., and Kilpatrick, F. P. Equivalent configurations and the monocular and binocular distorted rooms. In F. P. Kilpatrick (Ed.), *Human behavior from the transactional point of view.* Office Naval Res., Contract No. 4961(a). Hanover, N.H.: Inst. Ass. Res., 1952.

Ittelson, W. H., and Kilpatrick, F. P. The size-distance invariance hypothesis. *Psychol. Rev.,* 1953, **60,** 223–231.

Ives, W. C., and Schilling, C. W. *Object identification with the Hecht-Schlaer adaptometer.* Night Vision Board, U.S. Submarine Base, New London, Conn., S24-1 (102) WCI fgl/aam., Dec. 26, 1941.

James, W. *The principles of psychology.* New York: Dover, 1950.

Jenkin, N., and Hyman, R. Attitude and distance-estimation as variables in size-matching. *Amer. J. Psychol.,* 1959, **72,** 68–76.

Jersild, A. T. Mental set and shift. *Arch. Psychol., N.Y.,* 1927, No. 89.

Johannson, G. *Configurations in event perception.* Uppsala: Almquist and Wiksell, 1950.

Judd, C. H. Practice and its effects on the perception of illusions. *Psychol. Rev.,* 1902, **9,** 27–39.

Kardos, L. Eine experimentelle Untersuchung über die Grundlagen des Farbensehens (Thing and shadow: an experimental investigation on the basis of color vision). *Z. Psychol.*, 1934, **23**, x + 189.

Katona, G. Zur Analyse der Helligkeitskonstanz. *Psychol. Forsch.*, 1929, **12**, 94–126.

Katona, G. *Organizing and memorizing.* New York: Columbia, 1940.

Katz, D. Die Erscheinungsweisen der Farben. *Z. Psychol.*, 1911, No. 7.

Katz, D. (Ed.) *Der Aufbau der Farbenwelt.* Leipzig: Barth, 1930. Tr. R. B. MacLeod and W. Fox. *The world of color.* London: Routledge, 1935.

Kaufman, L., and Rock, I. The moon illusion. *Sci. Amer.*, 1962, **207**, 120–132.

Kendler, H. H., et al. The influence of massed and distributed practice on the development of mental sets. *J. Exp. Psychol.*, 1952, **43**, 21–25.

Kendler, H. H., and Kendler, T. S. Effect of verbalization on reversal shifts in children. *Science*, 1961, **134**, 1619–1620.

Kendler, H. H., and Kendler, T. S. Vertical and horizontal processes in problem solving. *Psychol. Rev.*, 1962, **69**, 1–16.

Kendler, T. S., Kendler, H. H., and Wells, D. Reversal and non-reversal shifts in nursery school children. *J. Comp. Physiol. Psychol.*, 1960, **53**, 83–88.

Kilpatrick, F. P. (Ed.) *Human behavior from the transactional point of view.* Office Naval Res., Contract No. 4961(a). Hanover, N.H.: Inst. Ass. Res., 1952.

Kilpatrick, F. P. *Explorations in transactional psychology.* New York: New York Univ. Press, 1961.

Kilpatrick, F. P., and Ittelson, W. H. The size-distance invariance hypothesis. *Psychol. Rev.*, 1953, **60**, 223–231.

Klemmer, E. T., and Frick, F. C. Assimilation of information from dot and matrix patterns. *J. Exp. Psychol.*, 1953, **45**, 15–19.

Klimpfinger, S. See Brunswik, E. (Ed.), et al., 1933.

Koffka, K. *The principles of gestalt psychology.* New York: Harcourt, Brace & World, 1935.

Kohler, I. *Über Aufbau und Wandlungen der Wahrnehmungswelt: Insbesondere über "bedingte" Empfindungen.* Vienna: Rudolph M. Rohrer, 1951.

Kohler, I. Experiments with prolonged optical distortions. *Acta Psychol.*, 1955, **11**, 176–178.

Köhler, W. Optische Untersuchungen am Schimpansen und am Hahnshühn. *Abh. Königliche Preuss. Akad. Wiss.*, 1915, Phys-Math. Kl., No. 3.

Köhler, W. *The mentality of apes.* London: Routledge, 1924.

Köhler, W. *Gestalt psychology.* New York: Liveright, 1929.

Köhler, W., and Emery, D. A. Figural after-effects in the third dimension of visual space. *Amer. J. Psychol.*, 1947, **60**, 159–201.

Köhler, W., and Fishback, J. The destruction of the Müller-Lyer illusion in repeated trials. *J. Exp. Psychol.*, 1950, **40**, 267–281, 398–410.

Köhler, W., and Wallach, H. Figural after-effects: An investigation of visual processes. *Proc. Amer. Phil. Soc.*, 1944, **88**, 269–357.

König, A., and Brodun, E. Experimentelle Untersuchungen über die psychophysiche Fundamentalformen in Bezug auf den Gesichtsinn. *Königliche Akad. Wiss. Berlin Sitzber.*, 1888, 917–931. (After Woodworth and Schlosberg, 1954, p. 229.)

Kopferman, H. Psychologische Untersuchungen über die Wirkung zweidimensionaler Darstellungen körperlicher Gebilde. *Psychol. Forsch.*, 1930, **13**, 293–364.

Korte, A. Kinematoskopische Untersuchungen. *Z. Psychol.*, 1915, **72**, 193–296.

Krantz, D. L., and Campbell, D. T. Separating perceptual and linguistic effects of context shifts upon absolute judgments. *J. Exp. Psychol.*, 1961, **62**, 35–42.

Krauskopf, J., Duryea, R. A., and Bitterman, M. E. Threshold for visual form: Further experiments. *Amer. J. Psychol.*, 1954, **67**, 427–440.

Krauskopf, J., and Riggs, L. A. Interocular transfer in the disappearance of stabilized images. *Amer. J. Psychol.*, 1959, **72**, 248–252.

Kubzansky, P. E. Methodological and conceptual problems in the study of sensory deprivation. Paper presented at APA meetings, Washington, D.C., 1958.

Lacey, J. I., and Dallenbach, K. M. Acquisition by children of the cause-effect relationship. *Amer. J. Psychol.*, 1939, **52**, 103–110.

Lambercier, M. La constance des grandeurs en comparaisons sériales. *Arch. Psychol., Genève*, 1946, **31**, 79–282.

Lambert, W. W., Solomon, R. L., and Watson, P. D. Reinforcement and extinction as factors in size estimation. *J. Exp. Psychol.*, 1949, **39**, 641–647.

Landauer, T. K. Two hypotheses on physiological basis of memory. *Psychol. Rev.*, 1964, **71**, 167–179.

Langdon, J. The perception of changing shape. *Quart. J. Exp. Psychol.*, 1951, **3**, 157–165.

Langdon, J. Further studies in the perception of changing shape. *Quart. J. Exp. Psychol.*, 1953, **5**, 89–107.

Langdon, J. The role of spatial stimuli in the perception of shape. Part I. *Quart. J. Exp. Psychol.*, 1955a, **7**, 19–27.

Langdon, J. The role of spatial stimuli in the perception of shape. Part II. *Quart. J. Exp. Psychol.*, 1955b, **7**, 28–36.

Langdon, J. The perception of three-dimensional solids. *Quart. J. Exp. Psychol.*, 1955c, **7**, 133–146.

Lashley, K. S. The mechanism of vision. XV. Preliminary studies on the rat's capacity for detail vision. *J. Gen. Psychol.*, 1938, **18**, 123–193.

Lashley, K. S., Chow, K. L., and Semmes, J. An examination of the electrical field theory of cerebral integration. *Psychol. Rev.*, 1951, **58**, 123–136.

Lauenstein, L. Über räumliche Wirkung von Licht und Schatten. *Psychol. Forsch.*, 1938, **22**, 267–319.

Lawrence, D. H. Acquired distinctiveness of cues. I. Transfer between discrimination on the basis of familiarity with the stimulus. *J. Exp. Psychol.*, 1949, **39**, 770–784.

Lawrence, D. H. Acquired distinctiveness of cues. II. Selective association in a constant stimulus situation. *J. Exp. Psychol.*, 1950, **40**, 175–188.

Lawrence, D. H. Generalization gradients and transfer of a discrimination along a continuum. *J. Comp. Physiol. Psychol.*, 1952, **45**, 511–516.

Lazarus, R. S. Subception: Fact or artifact? A reply to Eriksen. *Psychol. Rev.*, 1956, **63**, 343–347.

Lazarus, R. S., Eriksen, C. W., and Fonda, C. P. Personality dynamics in auditory perceptual recognition. *J. Pers.,* 1951, **19,** 471–482.

Lazarus, R. S., and McCleary, R. A. Autonomic discrimination without awareness: A study of subception. *Psychol. Rev.,* 1951, **58,** 113–122.

Leeper, R. A study of a neglected portion of the field of learning: The development of sensory organization. *J. Genet. Psychol.,* 1935, **46,** 42–75.

Leibowitz, H. Relation between the Brunswik and Thouless ratios and functional relations in experimental investigations of perceived shape, size, and brightness. *Percept. Mot. Skills,* 1956, **6,** 65–68.

Leibowitz, H. Personal communication, 1961.

Leibowitz, H., and Bourne, L. E., Jr. Time and intensity as determiners of perceived shape. *J. Exp. Psychol.,* 1956, **51,** 277–281.

Leibowitz, H., Bussey, T., and McGuire, P. Shape and size constancy in photographic reproductions. *J. Opt. Soc. Amer.,* 1957, **47,** 658–661.

Leibowitz, H., and Chinetti, P. Effect of reduced exposure duration on brightness constancy. *J. Exp. Psychol.,* 1957, **54,** 49–53.

Leibowitz, H., Chinetti, P., and Sidowski, J. Exposure duration as a variable in perceptual constancy. *Science,* 1956, **123,** 668–669.

Leibowitz, H., Mitchell, E., and Angrist, N. Exposure duration in the perception of shape. *Science,* 1954, **120,** 400.

Leibowitz, H., Mote, F. A., and Thurlow, W. R. Simultaneous contrast as a function of separation between test and inducing fields. *J. Exp. Psychol.,* 1953, **46,** 453–456.

Leibowitz, H., Myers, Nancy A., and Chinetti, P. The role of simultaneous contrast in brightness constancy. *J. Exp. Psychol.,* 1955, **50,** 15–18.

Leibowitz, H., Myers, Nancy A., and Grant, D. A. Frequency of seeing and radial localization of single and multiple visual stimuli. *J. Exp. Psychol.,* 1955, **50.** 369–373.

Leibowitz, H., Waskow, I., Loeffler, N., and Glaser, F. Intelligence level as a variable in the perception of shape. *Quart. J. Exp. Psychol.,* 1959, **11,** 108–112.

Lettvin, J. Y., Maturana, H. R., McCulloch, W. S., and Pitts, W. H. What the frog's eye tells the frog's brain. *Proc. Inst. Radio Engr.,* 1959, **47,** 1940–1951.

Lilly, J. C. Mental effects of reduction of ordinary levels of physical stimuli on intact, healthy persons. *Psychiat. Res.,* 1956, **5,** 1–9.

Lindsley, D. B. Emotion. In S. S. Stevens (Ed.), *Handbook of experimental psychology.* New York: Wiley, 1951. Pp. 473–516.

Locke, N. M. A comparative study of size constancy. *J. Genet. Psychol.,* 1937, **51,** 255–265.

Loehlin, J. C. The influence of different activities on the apparent length of time. *Psychol. Monogr.,* 1959, **73,** No. 474.

Long, E. R., Reid, L. S., and Henneman, R. H. An experimental analysis of set: The role of sense-modality. *Amer. J. Psychol.,* 1960, **73,** 563–567.

Lorenz, K. Z. Der Kunysan in der Umwelt des Vogels: Der Artgenosse als aus lösendes Moment Sozial-u. Verhaltensweisen. *J. Ornithol., Leipzig,* 1935, **83,** 137–213.

Lorenz, K. Z. The evolution of behavior. *Sci. Amer.,* 1958, **199,** 67–83.

Lowenstein, W. R. Biological transducers. *Sci. Amer.,* 1960, **203,** 98–104.

Luchins, A. S. Mechanization in problem solving. *Psychol. Monogr.,* 1942, **54,** No. 6, 1–95.

Luchins, A. S. The Einstellung test of rigidity: Its relation to concreteness of thinking. *J. Consult. Psychol.,* 1951, **15,** 303–310.

Luchins, A. S. The autokinetic effect and gradations of illumination of the visual field. *J. Gen. Psychol.,* 1954, **50,** 29–37.

Luchins, A. S., and Luchins, E. H. New experimental attempts at preventing mechanization in problem solving. *J. Gen. Psychol.,* 1950, **42,** 279–297.

Luneberg, R. Metric methods in binocular visual perception. In *Studies and Essays Presented to R. Courant.* New York: Interscience, 1948. Pp. 215–240.

McGinnies, E. Emotionality and perceptual defense. *Psychol. Rev.,* 1949, **56,** 244–251.

MacLeod, R. B. An experimental investigation of brightness constancy. *Arch. Psychol., N.Y.,* 1932, No. 135.

MacLeod, R. B. Brightness-constancy in unrecognized shadows. *J. Psychol.,* 1940, **27,** 1–22.

MacLeod, R. B. The effects of "artificial penumbrae" on the brightness of included areas. In *Miscellanea psychogica, Albert Michotte.* Paris: Librairie Philosophique, 1947.

McNemar, O. W. *Word association, methods of deduction and induction, and reactions to set in good and poor reasoners.* Rep. No. 2 (Contract N. 225-02). Stanford, Calif.: Stanford Univer., 1954.

Maier, N. R. F. Reasoning in humans. I. On direction. *J. Comp. Psychol.,* 1930, **12,** 115–143.

Maier, N. R. F. Reasoning in humans. II. The solution of a problem and its appearance in consciousness. *J. Comp. Psychol.,* 1931, **12,** 181–194.

Maier, N. R. F. An aspect of human reasoning. *Brit. J. Psychol.,* 1933, **24,** 144–155.

Maier, N. R. F. Reasoning in humans. III. The mechanisms of equivalent stimuli and of reasoning. *J. Exp. Psychol.,* 1945, **35,** 349–360.

Malinowski, B. Psychoanalysis and anthropology. *Psyche, London,* 1923–24a, **4,** 293–333.

Malinowski, B. The psychology of sex and the foundations of kinship in primitive societies. *Psyche, London,* 1923–24b, **4,** 98–129.

Malmo, R. B. Activation: A neuropsychological dimension. *Psychol. Rev.,* 1959, **66,** 367–386.

Maltzman, I. Thinking: From a behaviorist's point of view. *Psychol. Rev.,* 1955, **62,** 275–286.

Mann, C. W. Visual factors in the perception of verticality. *J. Exp. Psychol.,* 1952, **44,** 460–464.

Mann, C. W., et al. The perception of the vertical. I. Visual and non-labyrinthine cues. *J. Exp. Psychol.,* 1949, **39,** 538–547.

Mann, C. W., and Boring, R. O. The role of instruction in experimental space perception. *J. Exp. Psychol.,* 1953, **45,** 44–48.

Marschak, J. Rational behavior, uncertain prospects and measurable utility. *Econometrika,* 1950, **18,** 111–141.

Marshall, A. J., and Day, R. H. The resolution of grating test objects during the course of dark adaptation. *Austral. J. Psychol.,* 1951, **3,** 1–21.

Marshall, W. A., and Talbot, S. A. Recent evidence for neural mechanisms in vision leading to a general theory of sensory acuity. In H. Klüver (Ed.), *Visual mechanisms.* Lancaster, Pa.: Jacques Cattell, 1942. Pp. 117–164.

May, M. A. The mechanism of controlled association. *Arch. Psychol., N.Y.,* 1917, No. 39.

Meade, R. D. Time estimates as affected by motivational level, goal distances, and rate of progress. *J. Exp. Psychol.,* 1959, **58,** 275–279.

Mednick, S. A. The associative basis of the creative process. In M. T. Mednick and S. A. Mednick (Eds.), *Research in personality,* New York: Holt, 1963. Pp. 583–596.

Mednick, M. T., and Mednick, S. A. (Eds.), *Research in personality.* New York: Holt, 1963.

Mercury Project Summary. (Including results of fourth manned orbital flight.) Washington, D.C.: NASA, 1963.

Metzger, W. *Psychol. Forsch.,* 1926, **8,** 114 (Quoted by M. D. Vernon, 1954.)

Metzger, W. *Gesetze des Sehens.* Frankfurt: Waldemar Kramer, 1953.

Michotte, A. *La perception de la causalité.* Louvain Institu Supérieur de philosophie: 1946.

Michotte, A. Lecture given at Oxford Univer., 1950a. (Quoted by M. D. Vernon, 1954.)

Michotte, A. À propos de la permanence phénoménale: Faits et théories. *Acta Psychol.,* 1950b, **7,** 298–322. (Quoted by M. D. Vernon, 1954.)

Michotte, A. The emotions regarded as functional connections. In M. L. Reymert (Ed.), *The international symposium on feelings and emotions.* New York: McGraw-Hill, 1950c. Pp. 50–93.

Miles, W. R. Light sensitivity and form perception in dark adaptation. *J. Opt. Soc. Amer.,* 1953, **43,** 560–566.

Miller, G. A. What is information measurement? *Amer. Psychologist,* 1953, **8,** 3–11.

Miller, G. A. The magical number, seven, plus or minus two: Some limits on our capacity for processing information. *Psychol. Rev.,* 1956a, **63,** 81–97.

Miller, G. A. Information and memory. *Sci. Amer.,* 1956b, **195,** 42–46.

Miller, G. A. *Psychology: The science of mental life.* New York: Harper & Row, 1962.

Miller, G. A., Galanter, E., and Pribram, K. *Plans and the structure of behavior.* New York: Holt, 1960.

Moed, G. Satiation-theory and the Müller-Lyer illusion. *Amer. J. Psychol.,* 1959, **72,** 609–611.

Mooney, C. E. A factorial study of closure. *Canad. J. Psychol.,* 1954, **8,** 51–60.

Morgan, C. T. Some structural factors in perception. In R. R. Blake and G. V. Ramsey (Eds.), *Perception: An approach to personality.* New York: Ronald, 1951.

Morgan, C. T., and Stellar, E. *Physiological psychology.* New York: McGraw-Hill, 1950.

Moruzzi, G., and Magoun, H. W. Brain stem reticular formation and activation of the EEG. *EEG Clin. Neurophysiol.,* 1949, **1,** 455–473.

Mulholland, T. Motion perceived while viewing rotating stimulus-objects. *Amer. J. Psychol.*, 1956, **69**, 96–99.

Murdock, B. B., Jr. Perceptual defense and threshold measurements. *J. Pers.*, 1954, **22**, 565–571.

Murphy, G. *An historical introduction to modern psychology*. New York: Harcourt, Brace & World, 1949.

Neff, W. S. A critical investigation of the visual apprehension of movement. *Amer. J. Psychol.*, 1936, **48**, 1–42.

Neuhaus, W. Experimentelle Untersuchung der Scheinbewegung. *Arch. Ges. Psychol.*, 1930, **75**, 315–458.

Newell, A., Shaw, J. C., and Simon, H. A. Elements of a theory of human problem solving. *Psychol. Rev.*, 1958, **65**, 208–212.

Newell, A., Shaw, J. C., and Simon, H. A. The process of creative thinking. In *Contemporary approaches to creative thinking*. New York: Atherton, 1963. Pp. 63–119.

Newhall, S. M., Nickerson, D., and Judd, D. Final report of the OSA subcommittee on the spacing of the Munsell colors. *J. Opt. Soc. Amer.*, 1943, **33**, 385–418.

Obonai, T., and Suto, Y. Studies of figural after-effects by the inspection of short time. *Jap. J. Psychol.*, 1952, **22**, 248. (Abstract)

Obonai, T., and Suzumura, K. Contribution to the study of psychophysiological induction (4) . . . The characteristic of successive induction during periods immediately following retinal stimulation. *Jap. Psychol. Res.*, 1954, **1**, 45–54.

Ogle, K. N. *Researches in binocular vision*. Philadelphia: Saunders, 1950.

Oliver, J. A., and Ferguson, G. A. A factorial study of tests of rigidity. *Canad. J. Psychol.*, 1951, **5**, 49–59.

Olum, V. Developmental differences in the perception of causality. *Amer. J. Psychol.*, 1956, **69**, 417–423.

Oseas, L., and Underwood, B. J. Studies of distributed practice. V. Learning and retention of concepts. *J. Exp. Psychol.*, 1952, **43**, 143–148.

Osgood, C. E. *Method and theory in experimental psychology*. Fair Lawn, N.J.: Oxford, 1953.

Osgood, C. E., and Heyer, A. W., Jr. A new interpretation of figural after-effects. *Psychol. Rev.*, 1952, **59**, 98–118.

Osgood, C. E., Suci, G. J., and Tannenbaum, P. H. *The measurement of meaning*. Urbana, Ill.: Univer. of Ill. Press, 1957.

Østerberg, G. Topography of the layer of rods and cones in the human retina. *Acta Ophthal., Kbh. Suppl.*, 1935, **61**, 1–102.

Oyama, T. Experimental studies of figural after-effects. (1) Temporal factors. *Jap. J. Psychol.*, 1953, **23**, 239–245.

Oyama, T. Temporal and spatial factors in figural after-effects. *Jap. Psychol. Res.*, 1956, **3**, 25–36.

Parnes, S. J., and Harding, H. F. (Eds.), *A source book of creative thinking*. New York: Scribner, 1962.

Pastore, N. Need as a determinant of perception. *J. Psychol.*, 1949, **28**, 457–475.

Penfield, W. Some observations on the functional organization of the human brain. *Proc. Amer. Phil. Soc.,* 1954, **98,** 293–297.

Penrose, L., and Penrose, R. Impossible objects: A special type of visual illusion. *Brit. J. Psychol.,* 1958, **49,** 31–33.

Perkins, F. T. Symmetry in visual recall. *Amer. J. Psychol.,* 1932, **44,** 473–490.

Piaget, J. Psycho-pédagogie et mentalité enfantine. *J. Psychol. Norm. Path.,* 1928a, **25,** 31–60.

Piaget, J. *Judgment and reasoning in the child.* New York: Harcourt, Brace & World, 1928b.

Piaget, J. *The child's conception of physical causality.* London: Routledge, 1930.

Piaget, J. *The moral judgment of the child.* London: Routledge, 1932.

Piaget, J. *La construction du Réel chez l'enfant.* Neuchâtel: Delachaux et Niestlé, 1937.

Piaget, J. *The psychology of intelligence.* New York: Harcourt, Brace & World, 1950.

Piaget, J. Contribution à la théorie générale des structures. *Proc. 13th Int. Congr. Psychol.,* 1951, 197–198.

Piaget, J. *The origins of intelligence in children.* New York: International Univers. Press, 1952.

Piaget, J., and Inhelder, B. *La représentation de l'espace chez l'enfant.* Paris: Presses Univer. France, 1948.

Piaget, J., and Inhelder, B. *La genèse de l'idée de hasard chez l'enfant.* Paris: Presses Univer. France, 1951.

Piaget, J., and Lambercier, M. Recherches sur le développement des perceptions. II. La comparaison visuelle des hauteurs à distances variables dans le plan fronto-parallèle. *Arch. Psychol., Genève,* 1943a, **29,** 173–254.

Piaget, J., and Lambercier, M. Recherches sur le développement des perceptions. III. Le problème de la comparaison visuelle en profondeur (constance de la grandeur) et l'erreur systématique de l'étalon. *Arch. Psychol. Genève,* 1943b, **29,** 255–308.

Piaget, J., and Lambercier, M. Perceptual transpositions and logical transference in depth comparisons. *Arch. Psychol., Genève,* 1946, **31,** 325.

Piaget, J., Lambercier, M., Boesch, E., and Albertine B. V. Introduction à l'étude des perceptions chez l'enfant et analyse d'une illusion relative à la perception visuelle de cercles concentriques (Delboeuf). *Arch. Psychol., Genève,* 1942, **29** (113), 111.

Pierce, Jan. Determinants of threshold for forms. *Psychol. Bull.,* 1963, **60,** 391–407.

Pirenne, M. H. *Vision and the Eye.* London, Chapman & Hall, 1948.

Postman, L. Toward a general theory of perception. In J. H. Rohrer and M. Sherif (Eds.), *Social psychology at the crossroads.* New York: Harper & Row, 1951.

Postman, L. Perception, motivation, and behavior. *J. Pers.,* 1953a, **22,** 17–31.

Postman, L. On the problem of perceptual defense. *Psychol. Rev.,* 1953b, **60,** 298–306.

Postman, L., Bruner, J. S., and McGinnies, E. Personal values as selective factors in perception. *J. Abnorm. Soc. Psychol.,* 1948, **43,** 142–154.

Postman, L., and Crutchfield, R. S. The interaction of need, set, and stimulus structure in a cognitive task. *Amer. J. Psychol.,* 1952, **65**, 196–217.

Postman, L., and Solomon, R. L. Perceptual sensitivity to completed and incompleted tasks. *J. Pers.,* 1950, **18**, 347–357.

Powesland, P. F. The effect of practice upon the perception of causality. *Canad. J. Psychol.,* 1959, **13**, 155–168.

Pratt, C. C. See his review of *Le développement perceptif* by Robert Francés in *Contemp. Psychol.,* 1963, **2**, 38–39.

Pribram, K. Reinforcement revisited: A structural view. *Nebraska Sympos. Mot.,* 1963.

Pritchard, R. M. A collimator stabilizing system. *Quart. J. Exp. Psychol.,* 1960.

Pritchard, R. M., Heron, W., and Hebb, D. O. Visual perception approached by the method of stabilized images. *Canad. J. Psychol.,* 1960, **14**, 67–77.

Quasebarth, K. Zeitschätzung und Zeitauffassung optisch und akustisch ausgefüllter Intervalle. *Arch. Ges. Psychol.,* 1924, **49**, 379–432.

Quastler, H. (Ed.) *Information theory in psychology: Problems and methods.* New York: Free Press, 1955.

Radner, M., and Gibson, J. J. Orientation in visual perception: The perception of tip character in form. *Psychol. Monogr.,* 1935, **46**, (210), 48–65.

Ranken, H. B. Personal communication and paper read at East. Psychol. Ass., Atlantic City, 1956.

Rappaport, M. The role of redundancy in the discrimination of visual forms. *J. Exp. Psychol.,* 1957, **53**, 3–10.

Ratliff, F. The role of physiological nystagmus in monocular acuity. *J. Exp. Psychol.,* 1952, **43**, 163–172.

Ratoosh, P. On interposition as a cue for the perception of distance. *Proc. Natl Acad. Sci.,* 1949, **35**, 257–259, 462.

Ray, W. S. Complex tasks for human problem solving research. *Psychol. Bull.,* 1955, **52**, 134–149.

Razran, G. H. S. Studies in configural conditioning. IV. Gestalt organization and configural conditioning. *J. Psychol.,* 1939, **7**, 3–16.

Reed, H. B. Factors influencing the learning and retention of concepts. I. The influence of set. *J. Exp. Psychol.,* 1946a, **36**, 71–87.

Reed, H. B. Factors influencing the learning and retention of concepts. II. The influence of length of series. III. The origin of concepts. *J. Exp. Psychol.,* 1946b, **36**, 166–179.

Reed, H. B. Factors influencing the learning and retention of concepts. IV. The influence of the complexity of the stimuli. *J. Exp. Psychol.,* 1946c, **36**, 252–261.

Reed, H. B. Factors influencing the learning and retention of concepts. V. The influence of form of presentation. *J. Exp. Psychol.,* 1950, **40**, 504–511.

Reid, L. S., Henneman, R. H., and Long, E. R. An experimental analysis of set: The effect of categorical restriction. *Amer. J. Psychol.,* 1960, **73**, 568–572.

Riesen, A. H. The development of visual perception in man and chimpanzee. *Science,* 1947, **106**, 107–108.

Riesen, A. H. Arrested vision. *Science,* 1950, **183**, 16–19.

Riesen, A. H. Plasticity of behavior: Psychological aspects. In H. F. Harlow and E. N. Woolsey (Eds.), *Biological and biochemical bases of behavior.* Madison, Wis.: Univer. of Wis. Press, 1958. Pp. 425–450.

Riesen, A. H. Stimulation as a requirement for growth and function in behavioral development. In D. W. Fiske and S. R. Maddi (Eds.), *Functions of varied experience.* Homewood, Ill.: Dorsey Press, 1961. Pp. 57–80.

Riesen, A. H., et al. Interocular transfer of habits learned monocularly in visually naive and visually experienced cats. *J. Comp. Physiol. Psychol.,* 1953, **46,** 166–172.

Riggs, Lorrin A., Cornsweet, Janet C., and Lewis, W. G. Effects of light on electrical excitation of the human eye. *Psychol. Monogr.,* 1957, **71,** No. 434.

Riggs, Lorrin A., Ratliff, F., Cornsweet, Janet C., and Cornsweet, T. N. The disappearance of steadily fixated visual test objects. *J. Opt. Soc. Amer.,* 1953, **43,** 495–501.

Rock, I., and Engelstein, Phima. A study of memory for visual form. *Amer. J. Psychol.,* 1958, **72,** 221–229.

Rock, I., and Fleck, F. S. A reexamination of the effect of monetary reward and punishment on figure-ground perception. *J. Exp. Psychol.,* 1950, **40,** 766–776.

Rock, I., and Kaufman, L. The moon illusion. II. *Science,* 1962, **136,** 1023–1031.

Rock, I., and Kremen, I. A re-examination of Rubin's figural aftereffect. *J. Exp. Psychol.,* 1957, **53,** 23–30.

Roe, Anne. A psychological study of eminent psychologists and anthropologists and a comparison with biological and physical scientists. *Psychol. Monogr.,* 1953, **67,** No. 352.

Roff, M. A factorial study of tests in the perceptual area. *Psychometric Monogr.,* 1952, No. 8.

Rokeach, M. The effect of perception time upon rigidity and concreteness of thinking. *J. Exp. Psychol.,* 1950, **40,** 206–216.

Rubin, E. *Visuelle wahrgenommene Figuren.* Copenhagen: Gyldendalske, 1921.

Ruff, G. E., and Levy, E. Psychiatric research in space medicine. *Amer. J. Psychiat.,* 1959, **115,** 793–797.

Rush, G. P. Visual grouping in relation to age. *Arch. Psychol., N.Y.,* 1937, **31,** 217.

Russell, D. H. *Children's Thinking.* Boston: Ginn, 1956.

Samuels, Ina. Reticular mechanisms and behavior. *Psychol. Bull.,* 1959, **56,** 1–25.

Sandström, C. I. *Orientation in the present space.* Uppsala: Almquist & Wiksell, 1951.

Saugstad, P. An analysis of Maier's pendulum problem. *J. Exp. Psychol.,* 1957, **54,** 168–179.

Schachtel, A. H., Henry, J., and Henry, Z. Rorschach analysis of Pilaga Indian children. *Amer. J. Orthopsychiat.,* 1942, **12,** 679–712.

Schafer, R., and Murphy, G. The role of autism in a visual figure-ground relationship. *J. Exp. Psychol.,* 1943, **32,** 335–343.

Scheffler, P. Wie sehen wir Bewegung. *Pyramide,* 1951, **10,** 181–184.

Schiller, P. von. Stroboskopische Alternativversuche. *Psychol. Forsch.,* 1933, **17,** 180–214.

Schlosberg, H. Stereoscopic depth from single pictures. *Amer. J. Psychol.,* 1941, **54,** 601–605.

Schlosberg, H. A note on depth perception, size constancy, and related topics. *Psychol. Rev.,* 1950, **57,** 314–317.

Schriever, W. Experimentelle Studien über stereoskopische Sehen. *Z. Psychol.,* 1925, **96,** 113–170.

Schroder, H. M., and Rotter, J. B. Rigidity as learned behavior. *J. Exp. Psychol.,* 1952, **44,** 141–150.

Scott, D. M., Machen, G. S., and Baker, C. H. *Perceptual problems in estimating range and bearing from PPI overlays.* Toronto Defence Res. Medical Lab., 1955, vii, 23 (Rep. No. 163-1).

Seligman, D. G. The vision of the native of British Guinea. In A. C. Maddon (Ed.), *Report of the Cambridge anthropological expedition to Torres Straits.* Vol. II. London: Cambridge, 1901.

Selz, O. *Zur Psychologie des productiven Denkens und des Irrtums.* Bonn: Cohen, 1922.

Senden, M. von. *Raum und Gestalt Auffassung bei operierten blindgeborenen vor und nach der Operation.* Leipzig: Barth, 1932.

Senden, M. von. *Space and Sight.* (Tr. P. Heath) New York: Free Press, 1960.

Seward, J. P. The effect of practice on the visual perception of form. *Arch. Psychol., N.Y.,* 1931, **20,** No. 130.

Shannon, C. E., and Weaver, W. *The mathematical theory of communication.* Urbana, Ill.: Univer. of Ill. Press, 1949.

Sheehan, D. Discovery of the autonomic nervous system. *Arch. Neurol. Psychiat.,* 1936, **35,** 1081–1115.

Sheehan, M. R. A study of individual consistency in phenomenal constancy. *Arch. Psychol., N.Y.,* 1938, No. 222 (Whole No. 438).

Sherif, M. A study of some social factors in perception. *Arch. Psychol., N.Y.,* 1935, **187,** 60.

Siegel, A. I. Deprivation of visual form definition in the ring dove. I. Discriminatory learning. *J. Comp. Physiol. Psychol.,* 1953, **46,** 115–119.

Simmel, M. L. The coin problem: A study in thinking. *Amer. J. Psychol.,* 1953, **56,** 229–241.

Smith, O. W., and Smith, P. C. Interaction of the effects of cues involved in judgments of curvature. *Amer. J. Psychol.,* 1957, **70,** 361–375.

Smoke, K. L. An objective study of concept formation. *Psychol. Monogr.,* 1932, **42,** No. 191.

Smoke, K. L. Negative instances in concept learning. *J. Exp. Psychol.,* 1933, **16,** 583–588.

Snyder, F. H., and Pronko, N. H. *Vision with spatial inversion.* Wichita, Kans.: McCormich-Armstrong Co., 1952.

Sokolov, E. W. In M. A. B. Brazier (Ed.), *The central nervous system and behavior: Transactions of the third conference.* New York: Josiah Macy, Jr. Found., 1960.

Solomon, R. L., and Howes, D. Word frequency, personal values, and visual duration thresholds. *Psychol. Rev.,* 1951, **58,** 256–270.

Solomon, R. L., and Postman, L. Frequency of usage as a determinant of recognition threshold for words. *J. Exp. Psychol.,* 1952, **43,** 195–202.

Spence, D. P. Success, failure and recognition threshold. *J. Pers.*, 1957a, **25**, 712–720.

Spence, D. P. A new look in vigilance and defense. *J. Abnorm. Soc. Psychol.*, 1957b, **54**, 103–108.

Staats, A. W. Verbal and instrumental response hierarchies and their relationship to problem-solving. *Amer. J. Psychol.*, 1957, **70**, 442–446.

Stavrianos, B. K. The relation of shape perception to explicit judgments of inclination. *Arch. Psychol., N.Y.*, 1945, No. 296 (Whole No. 487).

Stein, K. B. Perceptual defense and perceptual sensitization under neutral and involved conditions. *J. Pers.*, 1953, **21**, 467–478.

Stein, M. I. A transactional approach to creativity. In C. W. Taylor (Ed.), *The 1955 University of Utah research conference on the identification of creative scientific talent*. Salt Lake City: Univer. of Utah Press, 1956.

Steiner, I. D. Human interaction and interpersonal perception. *Sociometry*, 1959a, **22**, 230–235.

Steiner, I. D. *Interpersonal orientation and assumed similarity between opposites: U.S. Public Health Service Grant M1774*. Univer. of Ill., Dep. of Psychol., Group Effectiveness Res. Lab., 1959b. Pp. 1–11.

Stephens, J. M. The influence of different stimuli upon preceding bonds: An examination of the law of effect. *Teachers Coll. Contr. Educ.*, 1931, 493.

Stephens, J. M. The perception of small differences as affected by self-interest. *Amer. J. Psychol.*, 1936, **58**, 480–484.

Stern, C., and Stern, W. *Die Kindersprache*. Leipzig: Barth, 1927.

Stern, W. *Person und Sache System der philosophischen Weltanschauung. III. Wertphilosophie.* Leipzig: Barth, 1924.

Stevens, S. S. On the psychophysical law. *Psychol. Rev.*, 1957, **64**, 153–181.

Stevens, S. S., and Galanter, E. H. Ratio scales and category scales for a dozen perceptual continua. *J. Exp. Psychol.*, 1957, **54**, 377–409.

Stewart, E. C. The Gelb effect. *J. Exp. Psychol.*, 1959, **57**, 235–242.

Storch, A. Erlebnisanalyse und Sprachwissenschaft. *Z. Psychol.*, 1924, **94**, 146–152.

Stott, L. H. The discrimination of short tonal durations. Unpublished doctoral dissertation. Univer. of Ill. Library, 1933.

Stratton, G. M. Vision without inversion of the retinal image. *Psychol. Rev.*, 1897, **4**, 341–360, 463–481.

Sturt, M. *The psychology of time.* New York: Harcourt, Brace & World, 1925.

Sweet, A. L. Temporal discrimination by the human eye. *Amer. J. Psychol.*, 1953, **66**, 185–198.

Sylvester, J. Apparent movement and the Brown-Voth experiment. *Quart. J. Exp. Psychol.*, 1960, **12**, 231–236.

Tanner, W. P., Jr., and Swets, J. A. A decision-making theory of visual detection. *Psychol. Rev.*, 1954, **61**, 401–409.

Taylor, C. W., and Barron, F. (Eds.) *Scientific creativity.* New York: Wiley, 1963.

Taylor, J. G. *The behavioral basis of perception.* New Haven, Conn.: Yale, 1962.

Tees, R. C. The role of field effects in visual perception. *Undergrad. Res. Proj. Psychol., McGill Univer.*, 1961, **3**, 87–96.

Ternus, J. The problem of phenomenal identity. *Psychol. Forsch.*, 1926, **7**, 81.

Thouless, R. H. Phenomenal regression to the real object. I. *Brit. J. Psychol.*, 1931a, **21**, 339–359.

Thouless, R. H. Phenomenal regression to the real object. II. *Brit. J. Psychol.*, 1931b, **22**, 1–30.

Thouless, R. H. Individual differences in phenomenal regression. *Brit. J. Psychol.*, 1932, **22**, 216–241.

Thurstone, L. L. *Primary mental abilities.* Chicago: Univer. of Chicago Press, 1944.

Tinbergen, N. *The study of instinct.* Fair Lawn, N.J.: Oxford, 1952.

Titchener, E. B. *Lectures on the experimental psychology of the thought-process.* New York: Macmillan, 1909.

Toch, H. H. The perceptual elaboration of stroboscopic presentations. *Amer. J. Psychol.*, 1956, **69**, 345–358.

Torrance, E. P. Developing creative thinking through school experiences. In S. J. Parnes and H. F. Harding (Eds.), *A source book of creative thinking.* New York: Scribner, 1962a.

Torrance, E. P. *Finding creative talent.* Englewood Cliffs, N.J.: Prentice-Hall, 1962b.

Tresselt, M. E., and Leeds, D. S. The effect of concretizing the mental set experiment. *J. Gen. Psychol.*, 1953, **49**, 87–95.

Underwood, B. J. An orientation for research on thinking. *Psychol. Rev.*, 1952, **59**, 209–220.

Van De Geer, J. P. *A psychological study of problem solving.* Netherlands: Haarlem De Touts, 1957.

Vernon, J. A., and Hoffman, J. Effect of sensory deprivation on learning rate in human beings. *Science*, 1956, **123**, 1074–1075.

Vernon, J. A., and McGill, T. E. The effect of sensory deprivation upon rote learning. *Amer. J. Psychol.*, 1957, **70**, 637–639.

Vernon, J. A., McGill, T. E., and Schiffman, H. Visual hallucinations during perceptual isolation. *Canad. J. Psychol.*, 1958, **12**, 31–34.

Vernon, M. D. The perception of inclined lines. *Brit. J. Psychol.*, 1934, **25**, 186–196.

Vernon, M. D. *Visual perception.* London: Cambridge, 1937.

Vernon, M. D. *A further study of visual perception.* London: Cambridge, 1952, 1954.

Vigotsky, L. S. Thought in schizophrenia. *Arch. Neurol. Psychiat.*, 1934, **31**, 1063–1075.

Vinacke, W. E. The investigation of concept formation. *Psychol. Bull.*, 1951, **48**, 1–31.

Volkmann, J. Scales of judgment and their implications for social psychology. In J. H. Rohrer and M. Sherif (Eds.), *Social psychology at the crossroads.* New York: Harper & Row, 1951. Pp. 273–298.

Vroom, Victor H. Effect of design on estimation of size of coins. *Canad. J. Psychol.*, 1957, **11**, 89–92.

Wald, George. Eye and camera. *Sci. Amer.*, 1950, **183** (2), 32–41.

Walker, E. L., and Veroff, J. Changes in the memory-trace for perceived forms with successive reproduction. *Amer. J. Psychol.*, 1956, **69**, 395–402.

Wallace, M., and Rabin, A. I. Temporal experience. *Psychol. Bull.*, 1960, **57**, 213–236.

Wallach, H. Brightness constancy and the nature of achromatic colors. *J. Exp. Psychol.,* 1948, **38,** 310–324.

Wallach, H., and Galloway, A. The constancy of colored objects in colored illumination. *J. Exp. Psychol.,* 1946, **366,** 119–126.

Wallach, H., and McKenna, V. V. On size-perception in the absence of cues for distance. *Amer. J. Psychol.,* 1960, **73,** 458–460.

Wallach, H., and O'Connell, D. N. The kinetic depth effect. *J. Exp. Psychol.,* 1953, **45,** 205–217.

Wapner, S., Werner, H., and Chandler, K. A. Experiments on sensory-tonic field theory of perception. II. Effects of body rotation on the visual perception of verticality. *J. Exp. Psychol.,* 1951, **42,** 351–357.

Watt, H. J. Experimentelle Beiträge zu einer Theorie des Denkens. *Arch. Ges. Psychol.,* 1905, **4,** 289–436.

Weaver, H. E., and Madden, E. H. "Direction" in problem-solving. *J. Psychol.,* 1949, **27,** 331–345.

Weber, C. O., and Bicknall, N. The size-constancy phenomenon in stereoscopic space. *Amer. J. Psychol.,* 1935, **47,** 436–448.

Welch, L., and Long, L. The higher structural phases of concept formation of children. *J. Psychol.,* 1940, **9,** 59–95.

Welton, K. The concentrated points of information in a circular scale. Lake Forest Coll. honors thesis, 1963.

Wenzel, B. M., and Flurry, C. The sequential order of concept attainment. *J. Exp. Psychol.,* 1948, **38,** 547–557.

Werner, H. Studies in contour. I. Qualitative analysis. *Amer. J. Psychol.,* 1935, **47,** 40–64.

Werner, H. *Comparative psychology of mental development.* New York: Harper & Row, 1940.

Werner, H. Abnormal and sub-normal rigidity. *J. Abnorm. Soc. Psychol.,* 1946, **41,** 15–24.

Werner, H., and Wapner, S. Sensory-tonic field theory of perception. *J. Pers.,* 1949, **18,** 88–107.

Werner, H., and Wapner, S. Toward a general theory of perception. *Psychol. Rev.,* 1952, **59,** 324–338.

Werner, H., and Wapner, S. Studies in physiognomic perception. I. Effect of configurational dynamics and meaning-induced sets on the position of the apparent median plane, *J. Psychol.,* 1954, **38,** 51–65.

Werner, H., and Wapner, S. The Innsbruck studies on distorted visual field in relation to the organismic theory of perception. *Psychol. Rev.,* 1955, **62,** 130–138.

Werner, H., Wapner, S., and Chandler, K. A. Experiments on sensory-tonic field theory of perception. I. Effect of supported and unsupported tilt of the body on the visual perception of verticality. *J. Exp. Psychol.,* 1951, **42,** 346–350.

Wertheimer, M. Experimentelle Studien über das Sehen von Bewegung. *Z. Psychol.,* 1912, **61,** 161.

Wertheimer, M. Untersuchen zu Lehre von der Gestalt. I. *Psychol. Forsch.,* 1922, **1,** 47–58; II. 1923, **4,** 301–350.

Wertheimer, M. *Productive thinking.* New York: Harper & Row, 1945.

Wever, E. G. Figure and ground in the visual perception of form. *Amer. J. Psychol.*, 1927, **38**, 194–226.

Wexler, D., Mendelson, J., Leiderman, P. H., and Solomon, P. Sensory deprivation. *Arch. Neurol. Psychiat.*, 1958, **79**, 225–233.

White, W. A. The language of schizophrenia. *Arch. Neurol. Psychiat.*, 1926, **16**, 395–413.

Whorf, B. L. *Language, thought, and reality.* Cambridge, Mass.: Technology Press, 1956.

Wiener, M., and Schiller, P. von. Subliminal perception or perception of partial cues. *J. Abnorm. Soc. Psychol.*, 1960, **61**, 124–137.

Wiener, N. *Cybernetics.* New York: Wiley, 1948.

Witkin, H. A. Perception of the upright when the direction of the force acting on the body is changed. *J. Exp. Psychol.*, 1950a, **40**, 93–106.

Witkin, H. A. Individual differences in the ease of perception of embedded figures. *J. Pers.*, 1950b, **19**, 1–16.

Witkin, H. A., and Asch, S. E. Studies in space orientation. III. Perception of the upright in the absence of a visual field. *J. Exp. Psychol.*, 1948a, **38**, 603–614.

Witkin, H. A., and Asch, S. E. Studies in space orientation. IV. Further experiments on perception of the upright with displaced visual fields. *J. Exp. Psychol.*, 1948b, **38**, 762–782.

Woodrow, H. Behavior with respect to short temporal stimulus forms. *J. Exp. Psychol.*, 1928, **11**, 174.

Woodrow, H. The reproduction of temporal intervals. *J. Exp. Psychol.*, 1930, **13**, 473–499.

Woodworth, R. S. *Experimental psychology.* New York: Holt, 1938.

Woodworth, R. S. Reenforcement of perception. *Amer. J. Psychol.*, 1947, **60**, 119–124.

Woodworth, R. S., and Schlosberg, H. *Experimental psychology.* New York: Holt, 1954.

Wulf, F. Über die Veränderung von Vorstellungen (Gedächtnis und Gestalt). *Psychol. Forsch.*, 1922, **1**, 333–373.

Wundt, W. *Outline of psychology.* (Tr. C. H. Judd) Leipzig: Engelmann, 1907.

Youtz, R. P. The relation between number of confirmations of one hypothesis and the speed of accepting a new and incompatible hypothesis. *Amer. Psychologist*, 1948, **3**, 248–249.

Zeigler, H. P., and Leibowitz, H. Apparent visual size as a function of distance for children and adults. *Amer. J. Psychol.*, 1957, **70**, 106–109.

Zigler, M. J., and Barrett, R. J. A further contribution to the tactual perception of form. *J. Exp. Psychol.*, 1927, **10**, 184–192.

Zigler, M. J., Cook, B., Miller, D., and Wemple, L. The perception of form in peripheral vision. *Amer. J. Psychol.*, 1930, **42**, 246–259.

Zigler, M. J., and Northrup, K. M. The tactual perception of form. *Amer. J. Psychol.*, 1926, **37**, 391–397.

Zuckerman, C. B., and Rock, I. A reappraisal of the role of past experience and innate organizing processes in visual perception. *Psychol. Bull.*, 1957, **54**, 269–296.

Index

Koffka's gray ring (After Koffka, 1935.)
See discussion in text, p. 68.